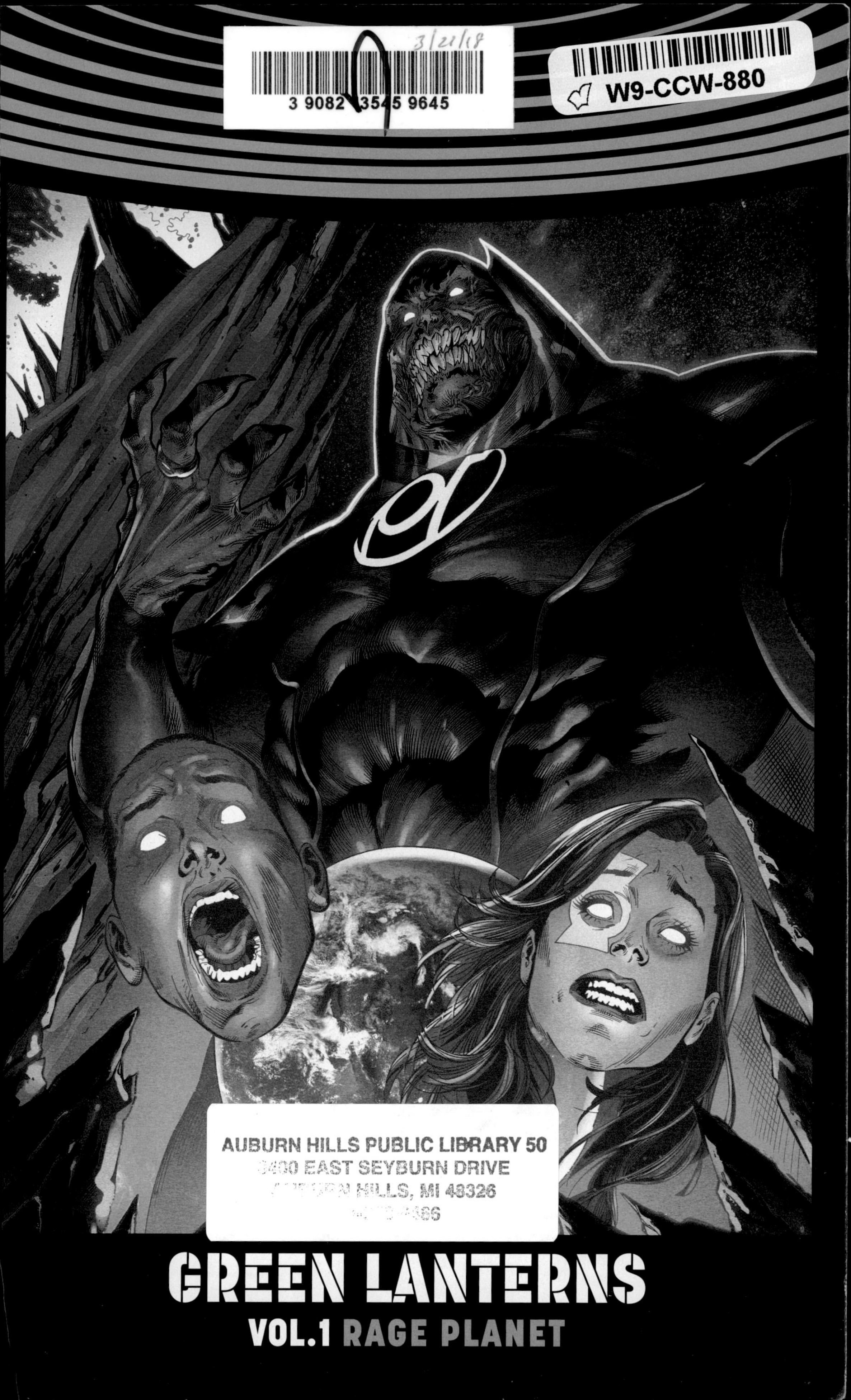

GREEN LANTERNS

VOL.1 RAGE PLANET

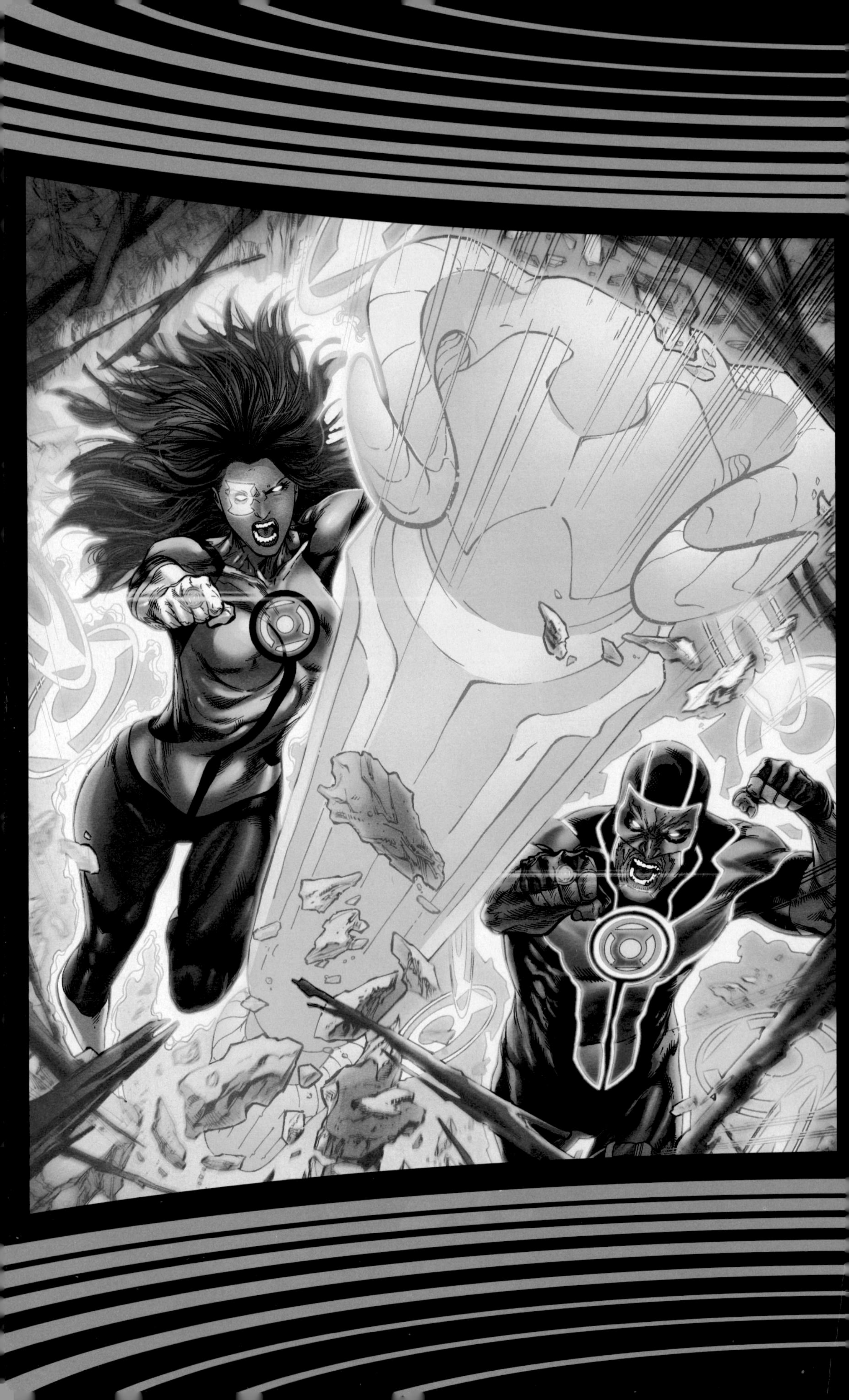

GREEN LANTERNS

VOL.1 RAGE PLANET

SAM HUMPHRIES
GEOFF JOHNS
writers

ETHAN VAN SCIVER * **ED BENES** * **ROBSON ROCHA**
JAY LEISTEN * **TOM DERENICK** * **WILL CONRAD** * **JACK HERBERT**
NEIL EDWARDS * **TOM PALMER** * **KEITH CHAMPAGNE**
ROB HUNTER * **MARK IRWIN** * **VICENTE CIFUENTES**
MARC DEERING * **EDUARDO PANSICA** * **JULIO FERREIRA**
artists

JASON WRIGHT * **BLOND** * **HI-FI**
colorists

TRAVIS LANHAM
DAVE SHARPE
letterers

ETHAN VAN SCIVER and JASON WRIGHT
collection cover artists

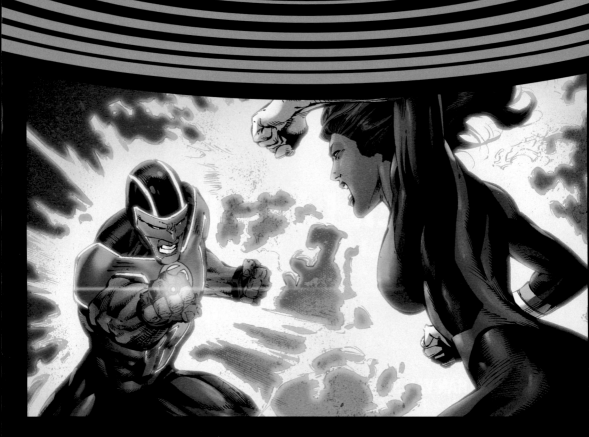

MIKE COTTON Editor - Original Series • **ANDREW MARINO** Assistant Editor - Original Series • **JEB WOODARD** Group Editor - Collected Editions
PAUL SANTOS Editor - Collected Edition • **STEVE COOK** Design Director - Books • **LOUIS PRANDI** Publication Design

BOB HARRAS Senior VP - Editor-in-Chief, DC Comics

DIANE NELSON President • **DAN DiDIO** Publisher • **JIM LEE** Publisher • **GEOFF JOHNS** President & Chief Creative Officer
AMIT DESAI Executive VP - Business & Marketing Strategy, Direct to Consumer & Global Franchise Management
SAM ADES Senior VP - Direct to Consumer • **BOBBIE CHASE** VP - Talent Development • **MARK CHIARELLO** Senior VP - Art, Design & Collected Editions
JOHN CUNNINGHAM Senior VP - Sales & Trade Marketing • **ANNE DePIES** Senior VP - Business Strategy, Finance & Administration
DON FALLETTI VP - Manufacturing Operations • **LAWRENCE GANEM** VP - Editorial Administration & Talent Relations
ALISON GILL Senior VP - Manufacturing & Operations • **HANK KANALZ** Senior VP - Editorial Strategy & Administration
JAY KOGAN VP - Legal Affairs • **THOMAS LOFTUS** VP - Business Affairs • **JACK MAHAN** VP - Business Affairs
NICK J. NAPOLITANO VP - Manufacturing Administration • **EDDIE SCANNELL** VP - Consumer Marketing
COURTNEY SIMMONS Senior VP - Publicity & Communications • **JIM (SKI) SOKOLOWSKI** VP - Comic Book Specialty Sales & Trade Marketing
NANCY SPEARS VP - Mass, Book, Digital Sales & Trade Marketing

GREEN LANTERNS VOLUME 1: RAGE PLANET

DC Comics, 2900 West Alameda Ave., Burbank, CA 91505
Printed by LSC Communications, Salem, VA, USA. 12/23/16. First Printing.
ISBN: 978-1-4012-6775-9

Library of Congress Cataloging-in-Publication Data is available.

PEFC Certified
Printed on paper from sustainably managed forests, controlled sources
PEFC/29-31-337
www.pefc.org

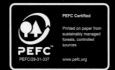

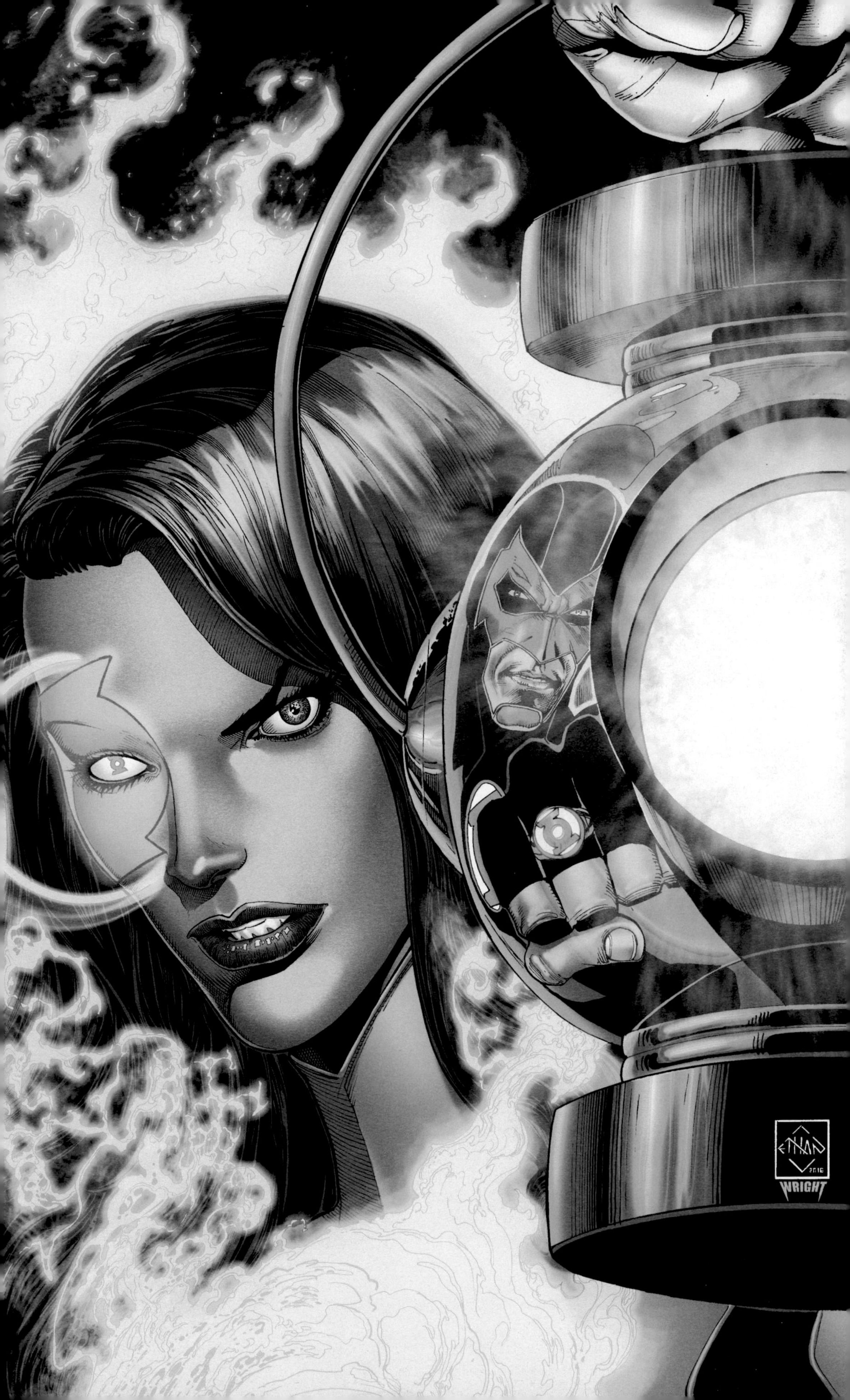
WRIGHT

GREEN LANTERNS: REBIRTH

GEOFF JOHNS and SAM HUMPHRIES writers * ETHAN VAN SCIVER and ED BENES artists * JASON WRIGHT colorist
ETHAN VAN SCIVER and JASON WRIGHT cover artists

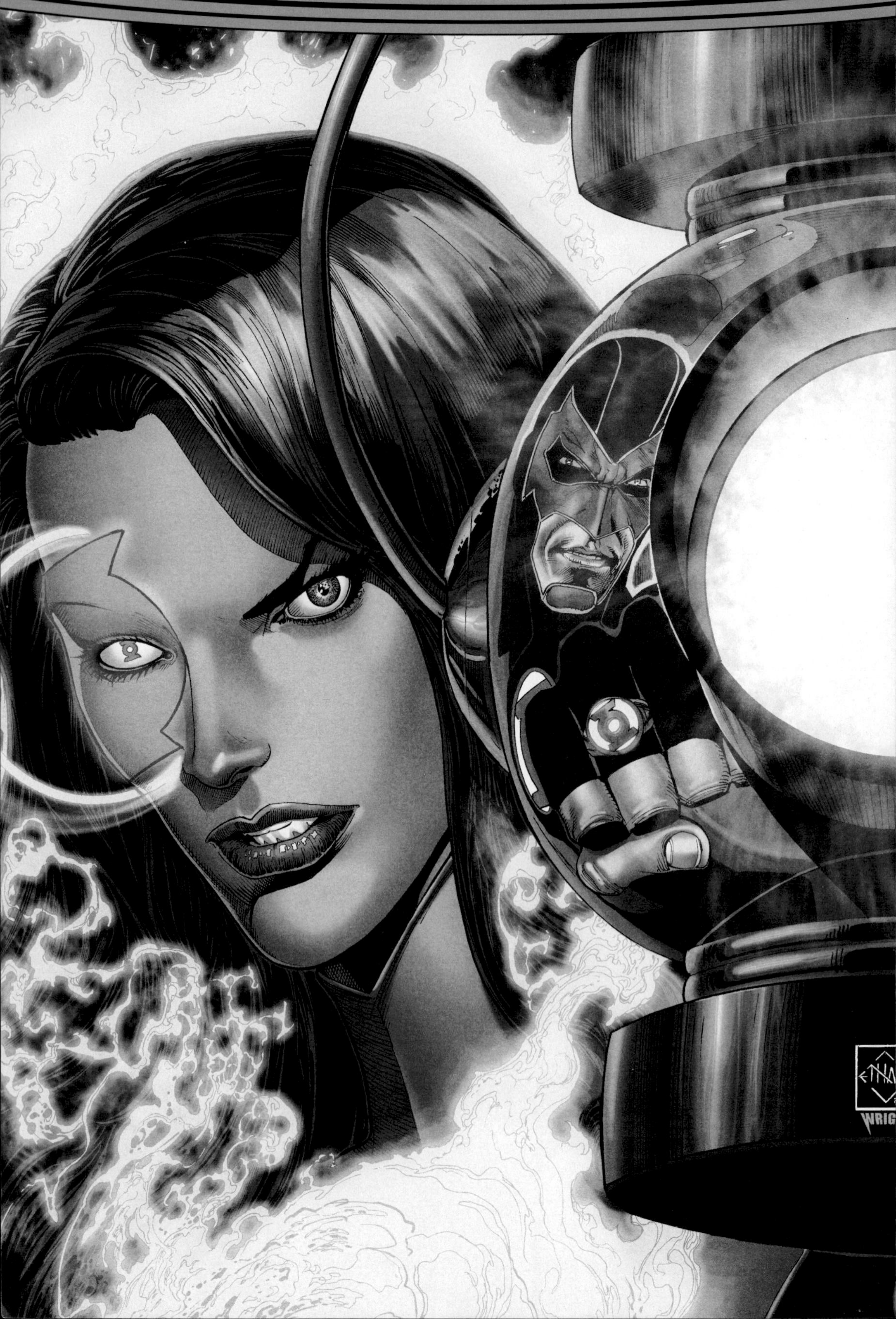

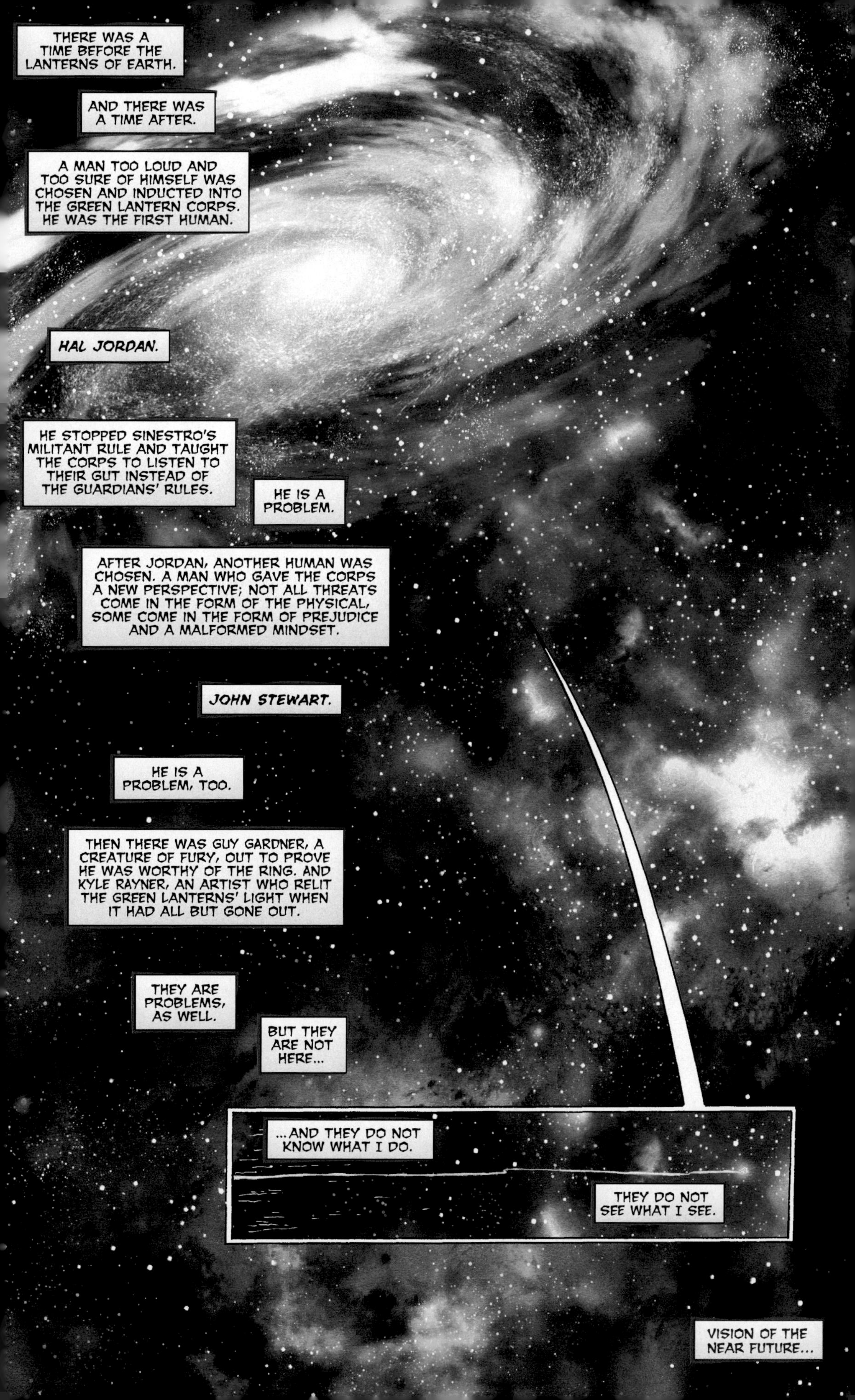
THERE WAS A TIME BEFORE THE LANTERNS OF EARTH.
AND THERE WAS A TIME AFTER.
A MAN TOO LOUD AND TOO SURE OF HIMSELF WAS CHOSEN AND INDUCTED INTO THE GREEN LANTERN CORPS. HE WAS THE FIRST HUMAN.
HAL JORDAN.
HE STOPPED SINESTRO'S MILITANT RULE AND TAUGHT THE CORPS TO LISTEN TO THEIR GUT INSTEAD OF THE GUARDIANS' RULES.
HE IS A PROBLEM.
AFTER JORDAN, ANOTHER HUMAN WAS CHOSEN. A MAN WHO GAVE THE CORPS A NEW PERSPECTIVE; NOT ALL THREATS COME IN THE FORM OF THE PHYSICAL, SOME COME IN THE FORM OF PREJUDICE AND A MALFORMED MINDSET.
JOHN STEWART.
HE IS A PROBLEM, TOO.
THEN THERE WAS GUY GARDNER, A CREATURE OF FURY, OUT TO PROVE HE WAS WORTHY OF THE RING. AND KYLE RAYNER, AN ARTIST WHO RELIT THE GREEN LANTERNS' LIGHT WHEN IT HAD ALL BUT GONE OUT.
THEY ARE PROBLEMS, AS WELL.
BUT THEY ARE NOT HERE...
...AND THEY DO NOT KNOW WHAT I DO.
THEY DO NOT SEE WHAT I SEE.
VISION OF THE NEAR FUTURE...

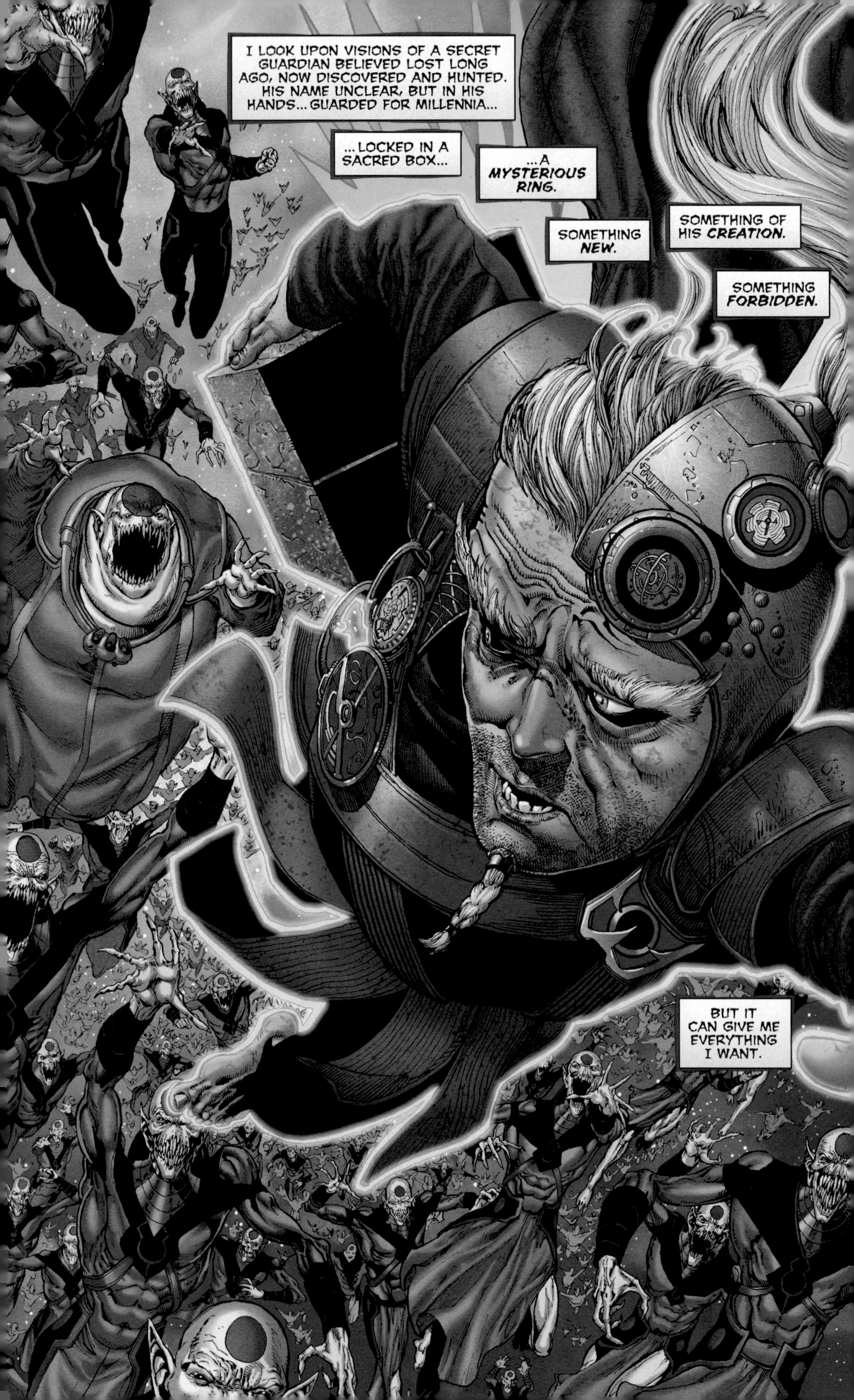
I LOOK UPON VISIONS OF A SECRET GUARDIAN BELIEVED LOST LONG AGO, NOW DISCOVERED AND HUNTED. HIS NAME UNCLEAR, BUT IN HIS HANDS... GUARDED FOR MILLENNIA...
...LOCKED IN A SACRED BOX...
...A MYSTERIOUS RING.
SOMETHING NEW.
SOMETHING OF HIS CREATION.
SOMETHING FORBIDDEN.
BUT IT CAN GIVE ME EVERYTHING I WANT.

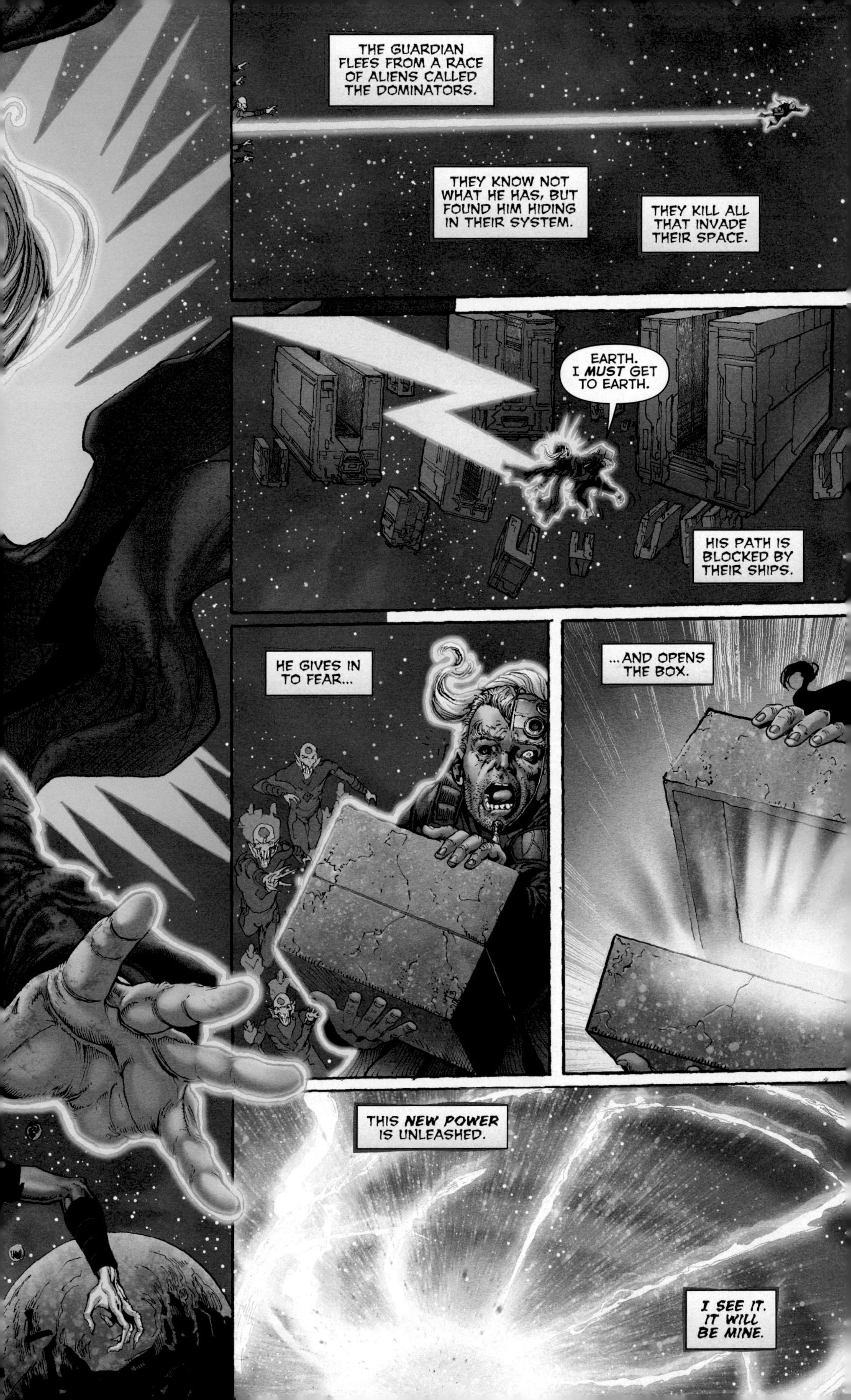
THE GUARDIAN FLEES FROM A RACE OF ALIENS CALLED THE DOMINATORS.
THEY KNOW NOT WHAT HE HAS, BUT FOUND HIM HIDING IN THEIR SYSTEM.
THEY KILL ALL THAT INVADE THEIR SPACE.
EARTH. I *MUST* GET TO EARTH.
HIS PATH IS BLOCKED BY THEIR SHIPS.
HE GIVES IN TO FEAR...
...AND OPENS THE BOX.
THIS *NEW POWER* IS UNLEASHED.
I SEE IT. IT WILL BE MINE.

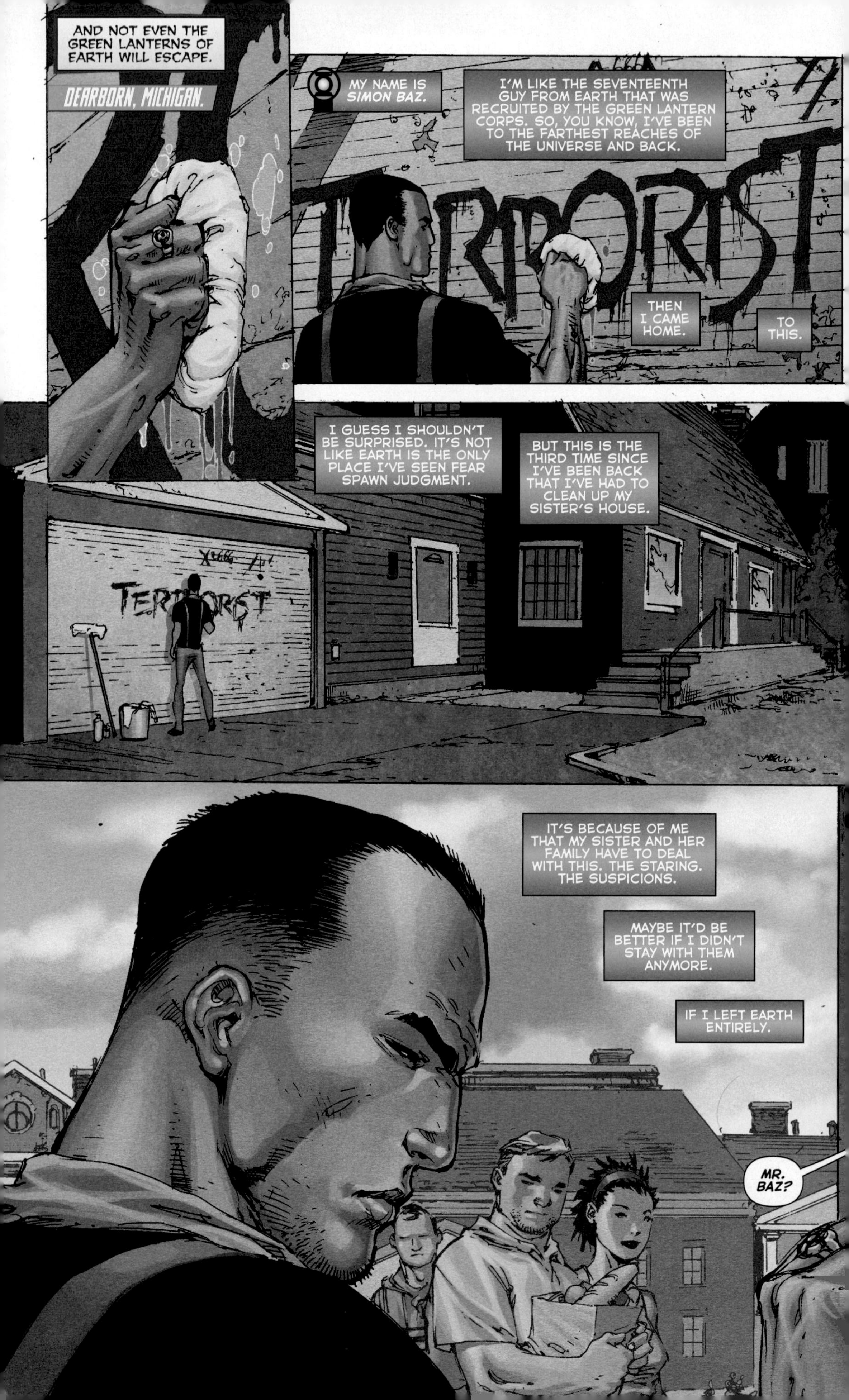
AND NOT EVEN THE GREEN LANTERNS OF EARTH WILL ESCAPE.
DEARBORN, MICHIGAN.
MY NAME IS SIMON BAZ.
I'M LIKE THE SEVENTEENTH GUY FROM EARTH THAT WAS RECRUITED BY THE GREEN LANTERN CORPS. SO, YOU KNOW, I'VE BEEN TO THE FARTHEST REACHES OF THE UNIVERSE AND BACK.
TERRORIST
THEN I CAME HOME.
TO THIS.
I GUESS I SHOULDN'T BE SURPRISED. IT'S NOT LIKE EARTH IS THE ONLY PLACE I'VE SEEN FEAR SPAWN JUDGMENT.
BUT THIS IS THE THIRD TIME SINCE I'VE BEEN BACK THAT I'VE HAD TO CLEAN UP MY SISTER'S HOUSE.
IT'S BECAUSE OF ME THAT MY SISTER AND HER FAMILY HAVE TO DEAL WITH THIS. THE STARING. THE SUSPICIONS.
MAYBE IT'D BE BETTER IF I DIDN'T STAY WITH THEM ANYMORE.
IF I LEFT EARTH ENTIRELY.
MR. BAZ?

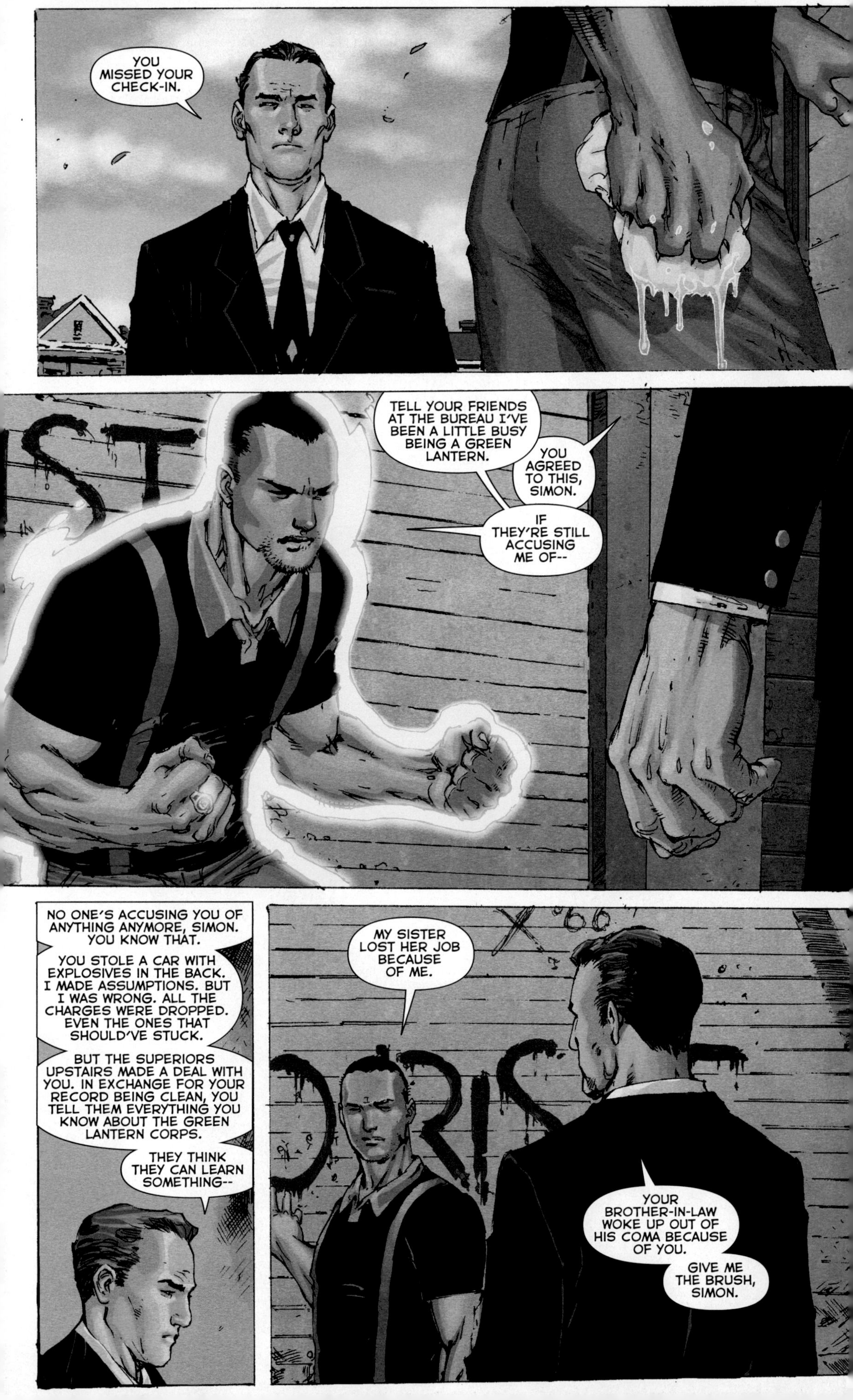
YOU MISSED YOUR CHECK-IN.
TELL YOUR FRIENDS AT THE BUREAU I'VE BEEN A LITTLE BUSY BEING A GREEN LANTERN.
YOU AGREED TO THIS, SIMON.
IF THEY'RE STILL ACCUSING ME OF--
NO ONE'S ACCUSING YOU OF ANYTHING ANYMORE, SIMON. YOU KNOW THAT.
YOU STOLE A CAR WITH EXPLOSIVES IN THE BACK. I MADE ASSUMPTIONS. BUT I WAS WRONG. ALL THE CHARGES WERE DROPPED. EVEN THE ONES THAT SHOULD'VE STUCK.
BUT THE SUPERIORS UPSTAIRS MADE A DEAL WITH YOU. IN EXCHANGE FOR YOUR RECORD BEING CLEAN, YOU TELL THEM EVERYTHING YOU KNOW ABOUT THE GREEN LANTERN CORPS.
THEY THINK THEY CAN LEARN SOMETHING--
MY SISTER LOST HER JOB BECAUSE OF ME.
YOUR BROTHER-IN-LAW WOKE UP OUT OF HIS COMA BECAUSE OF YOU.
GIVE ME THE BRUSH, SIMON.

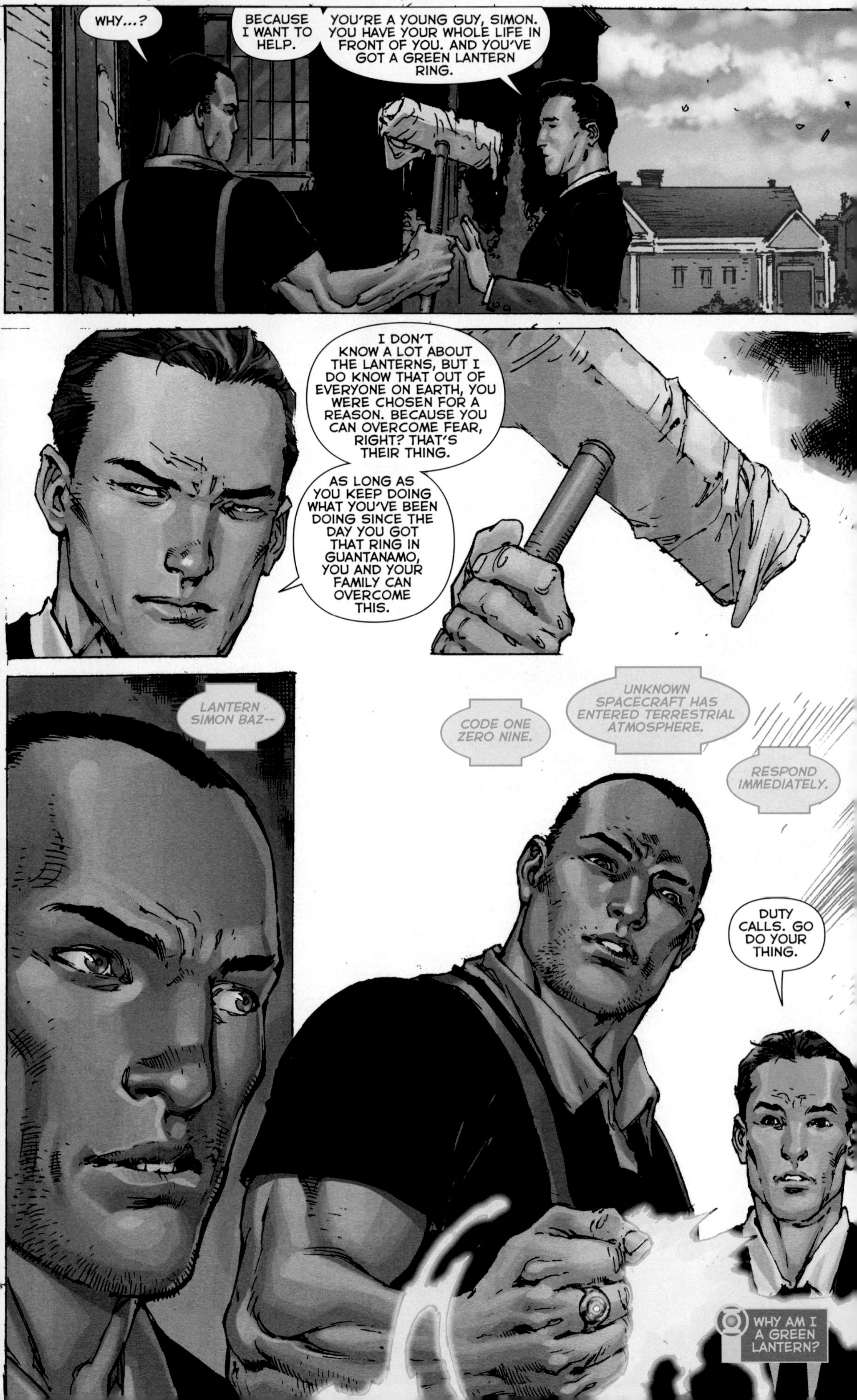
WHY...?
BECAUSE I WANT TO HELP.
YOU'RE A YOUNG GUY, SIMON. YOU HAVE YOUR WHOLE LIFE IN FRONT OF YOU. AND YOU'VE GOT A GREEN LANTERN RING.
I DON'T KNOW A LOT ABOUT THE LANTERNS, BUT I DO KNOW THAT OUT OF EVERYONE ON EARTH, YOU WERE CHOSEN FOR A REASON. BECAUSE YOU CAN OVERCOME FEAR, RIGHT? THAT'S THEIR THING.
AS LONG AS YOU KEEP DOING WHAT YOU'VE BEEN DOING SINCE THE DAY YOU GOT THAT RING IN GUANTANAMO, YOU AND YOUR FAMILY CAN OVERCOME THIS.
LANTERN SIMON BAZ--
CODE ONE ZERO NINE.
UNKNOWN SPACECRAFT HAS ENTERED TERRESTRIAL ATMOSPHERE.
RESPOND IMMEDIATELY.
DUTY CALLS. GO DO YOUR THING.
WHY AM I A GREEN LANTERN?

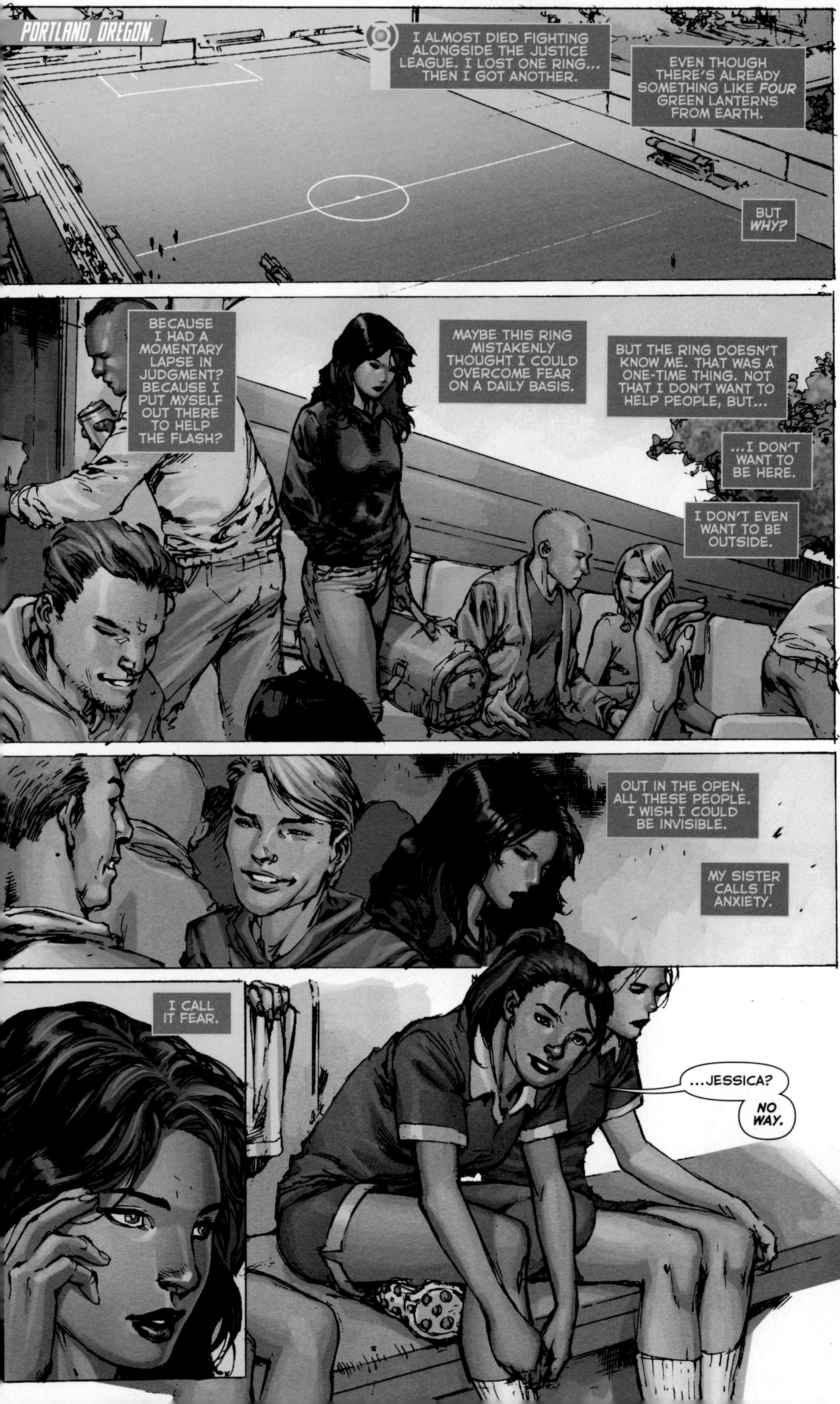
PORTLAND, OREGON.
I ALMOST DIED FIGHTING ALONGSIDE THE JUSTICE LEAGUE. I LOST ONE RING... THEN I GOT ANOTHER.
EVEN THOUGH THERE'S ALREADY SOMETHING LIKE FOUR GREEN LANTERNS FROM EARTH.
BUT WHY?
BECAUSE I HAD A MOMENTARY LAPSE IN JUDGMENT? BECAUSE I PUT MYSELF OUT THERE TO HELP THE FLASH?
MAYBE THIS RING MISTAKENLY THOUGHT I COULD OVERCOME FEAR ON A DAILY BASIS.
BUT THE RING DOESN'T KNOW ME. THAT WAS A ONE-TIME THING. NOT THAT I DON'T WANT TO HELP PEOPLE, BUT...
...I DON'T WANT TO BE HERE.
I DON'T EVEN WANT TO BE OUTSIDE.
OUT IN THE OPEN. ALL THESE PEOPLE. I WISH I COULD BE INVISIBLE.
MY SISTER CALLS IT ANXIETY.
I CALL IT FEAR.
...JESSICA?
NO WAY.

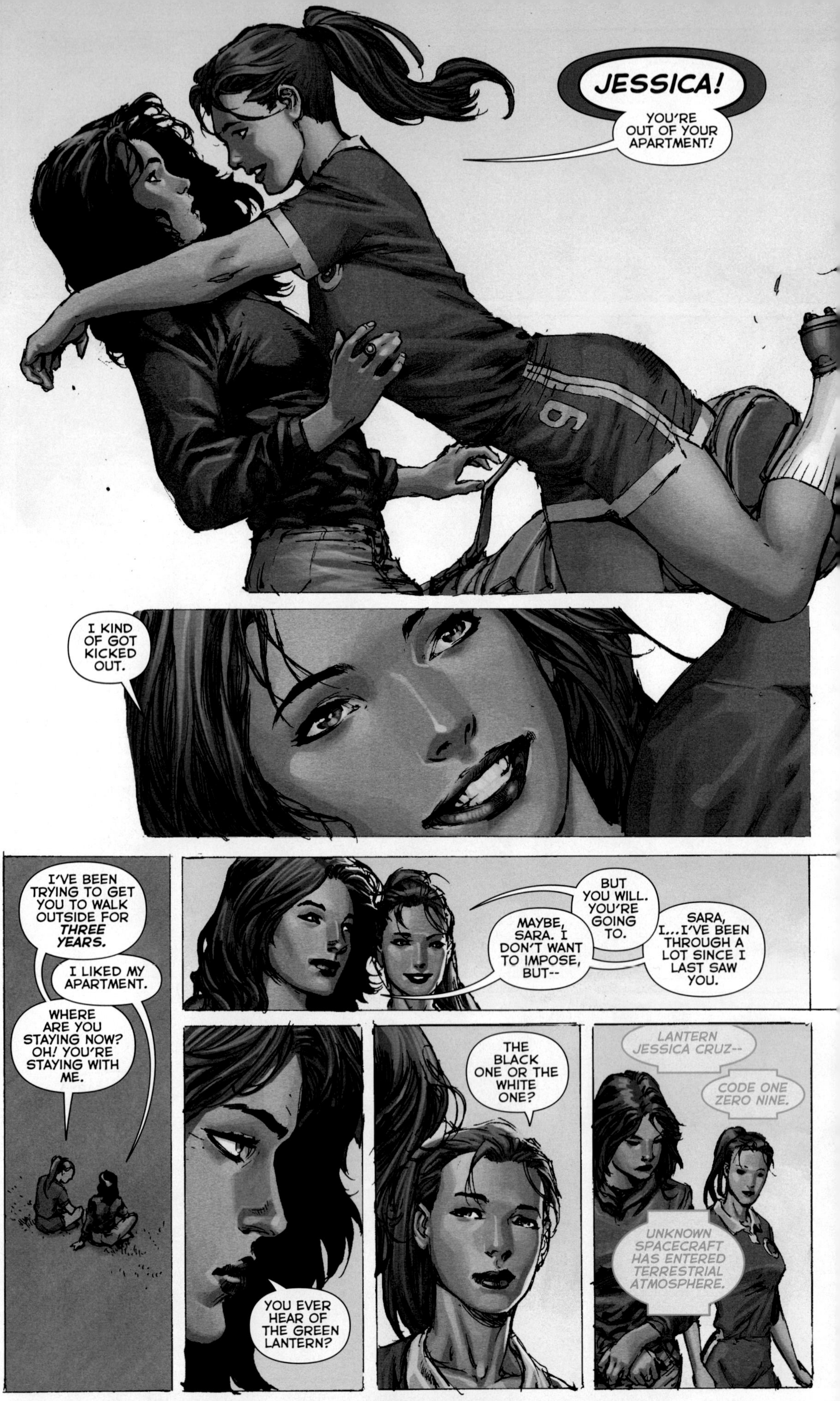
JESSICA!
YOU'RE OUT OF YOUR APARTMENT!
I KIND OF GOT KICKED OUT.
I'VE BEEN TRYING TO GET YOU TO WALK OUTSIDE FOR THREE YEARS.
I LIKED MY APARTMENT.
WHERE ARE YOU STAYING NOW? OH! YOU'RE STAYING WITH ME.
MAYBE, SARA. I DON'T WANT TO IMPOSE, BUT--
BUT YOU WILL. YOU'RE GOING TO.
SARA, I...I'VE BEEN THROUGH A LOT SINCE I LAST SAW YOU.
YOU EVER HEAR OF THE GREEN LANTERN?
THE BLACK ONE OR THE WHITE ONE?
LANTERN JESSICA CRUZ--
CODE ONE ZERO NINE.
UNKNOWN SPACECRAFT HAS ENTERED TERRESTRIAL ATMOSPHERE.

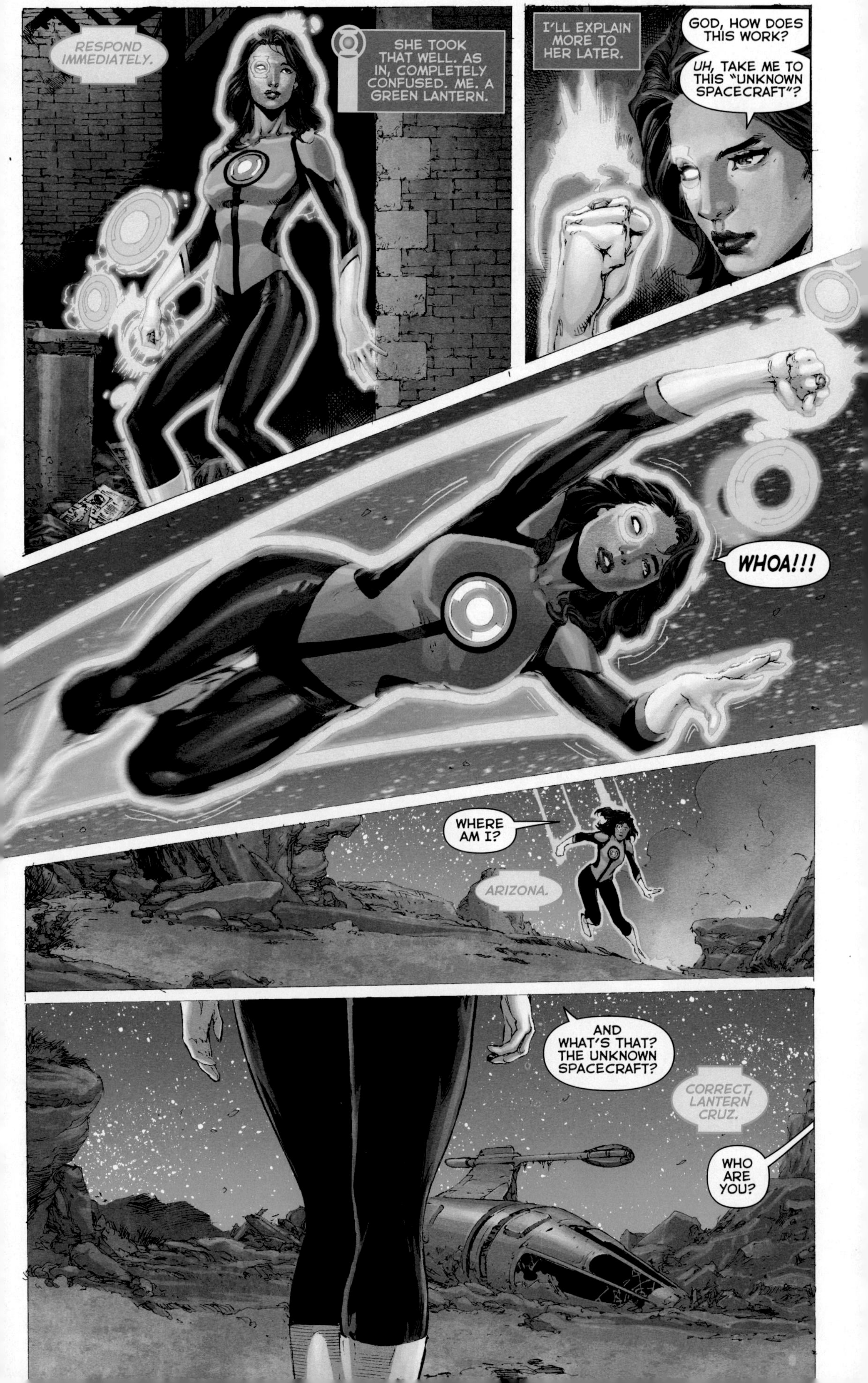
RESPOND IMMEDIATELY.
SHE TOOK THAT WELL. AS IN, COMPLETELY CONFUSED. ME. A GREEN LANTERN.
I'LL EXPLAIN MORE TO HER LATER.
GOD, HOW DOES THIS WORK?
UH, TAKE ME TO THIS "UNKNOWN SPACECRAFT"?
WHOA!!!
WHERE AM I?
ARIZONA.
AND WHAT'S THAT? THE UNKNOWN SPACECRAFT?
CORRECT, LANTERN CRUZ.
WHO ARE YOU?

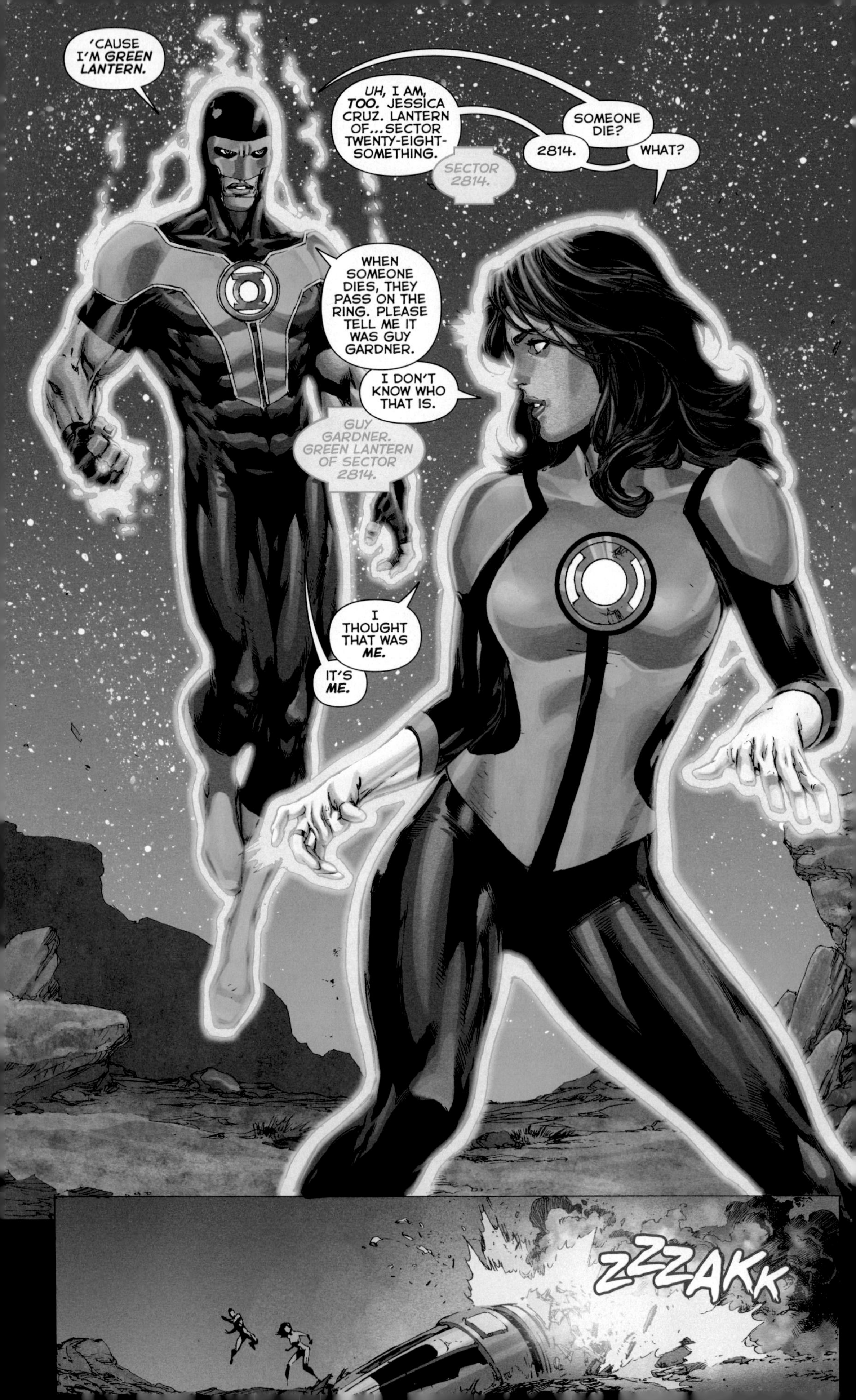

'CAUSE I'M GREEN LANTERN.
UH, I AM, TOO. JESSICA CRUZ. LANTERN OF...SECTOR TWENTY-EIGHT-SOMETHING.
SECTOR 2814.
2814.
SOMEONE DIE?
WHAT?
WHEN SOMEONE DIES, THEY PASS ON THE RING. PLEASE TELL ME IT WAS GUY GARDNER.
I DON'T KNOW WHO THAT IS.
GUY GARDNER. GREEN LANTERN OF SECTOR 2814.
I THOUGHT THAT WAS ME.
IT'S ME.
ZZZAKK

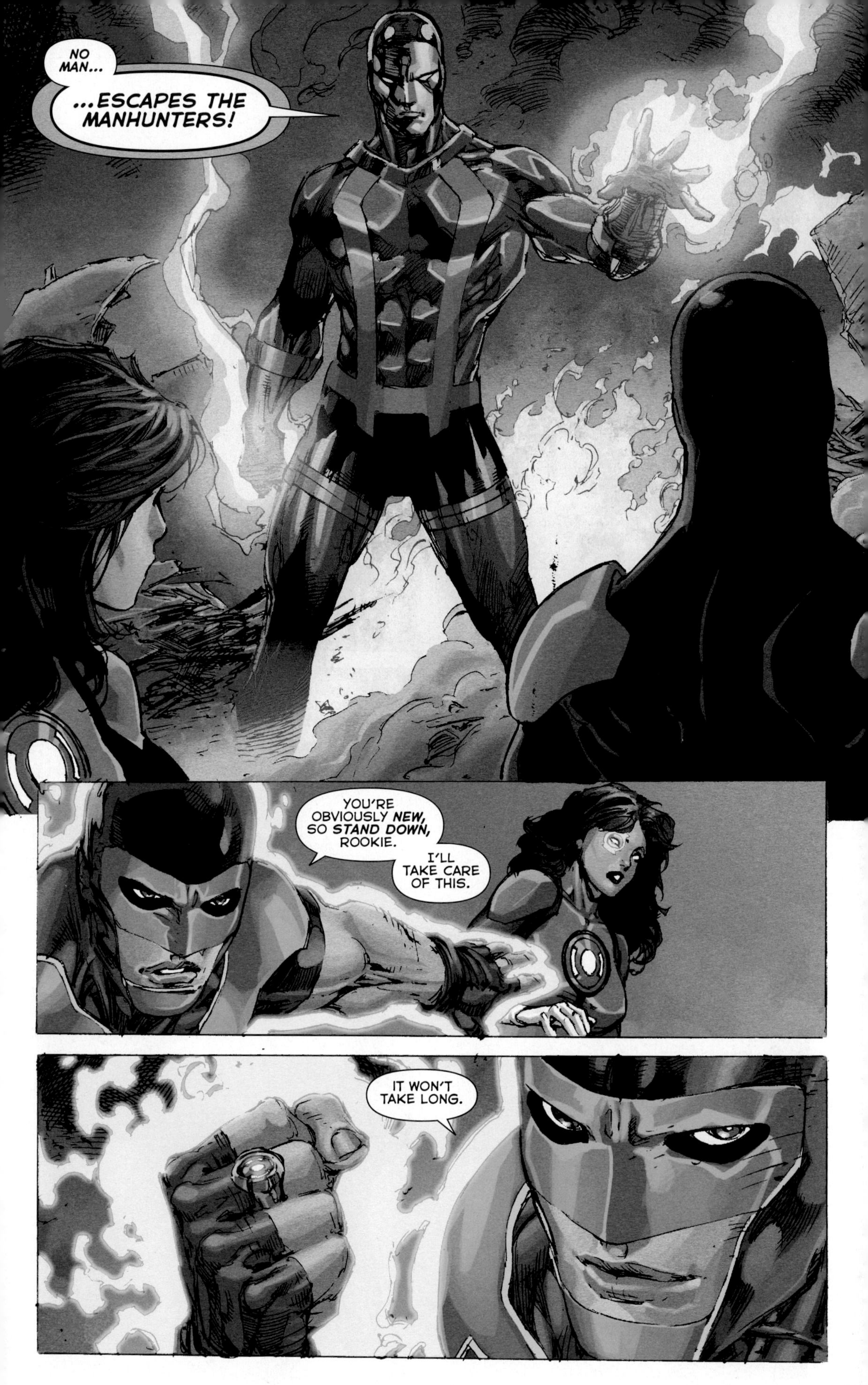
NO MAN...
...ESCAPES THE MANHUNTERS!
YOU'RE OBVIOUSLY NEW, SO STAND DOWN, ROOKIE.
I'LL TAKE CARE OF THIS.
IT WON'T TAKE LONG.

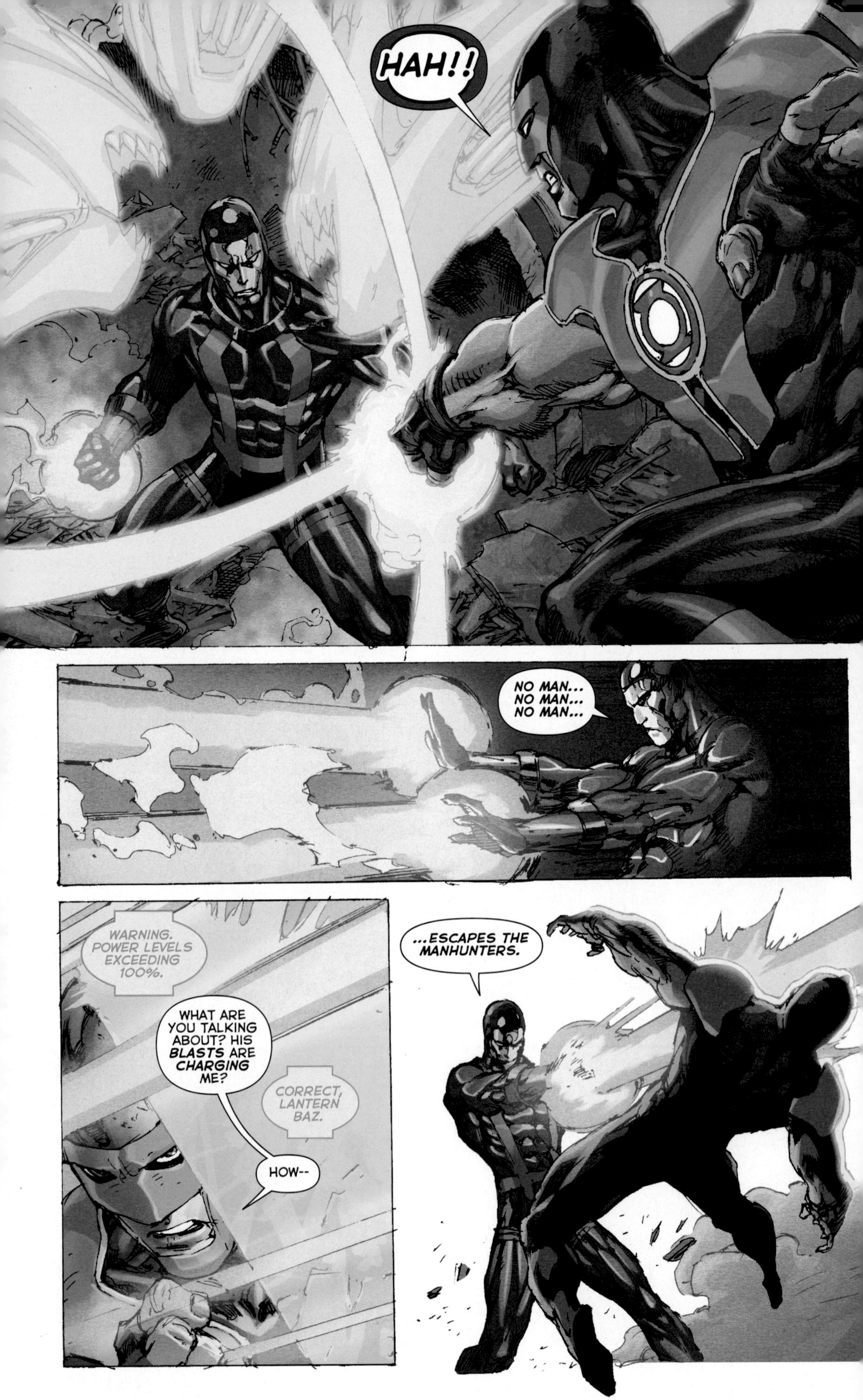
HAH!!
NO MAN... NO MAN... NO MAN...
WARNING. POWER LEVELS EXCEEDING 100%.
WHAT ARE YOU TALKING ABOUT? HIS BLASTS ARE CHARGING ME?
CORRECT, LANTERN BAZ.
HOW--
...ESCAPES THE MANHUNTERS.

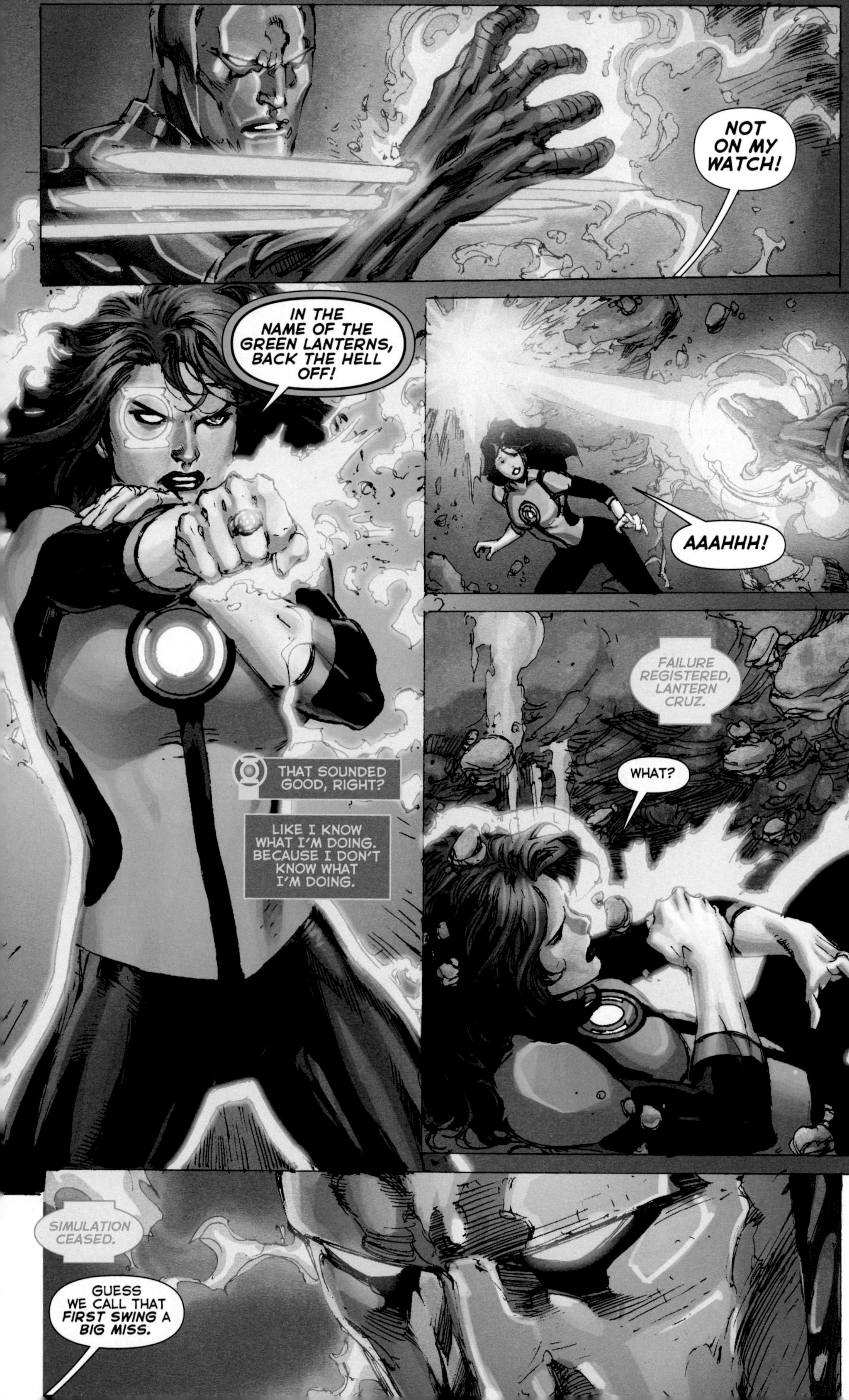
NOT ON MY WATCH!
IN THE NAME OF THE GREEN LANTERNS, BACK THE HELL OFF!
THAT SOUNDED GOOD, RIGHT?
LIKE I KNOW WHAT I'M DOING. BECAUSE I DON'T KNOW WHAT I'M DOING.
AAAHHH!
FAILURE REGISTERED, LANTERN CRUZ.
WHAT?
SIMULATION CEASED.
GUESS WE CALL THAT FIRST SWING A BIG MISS.

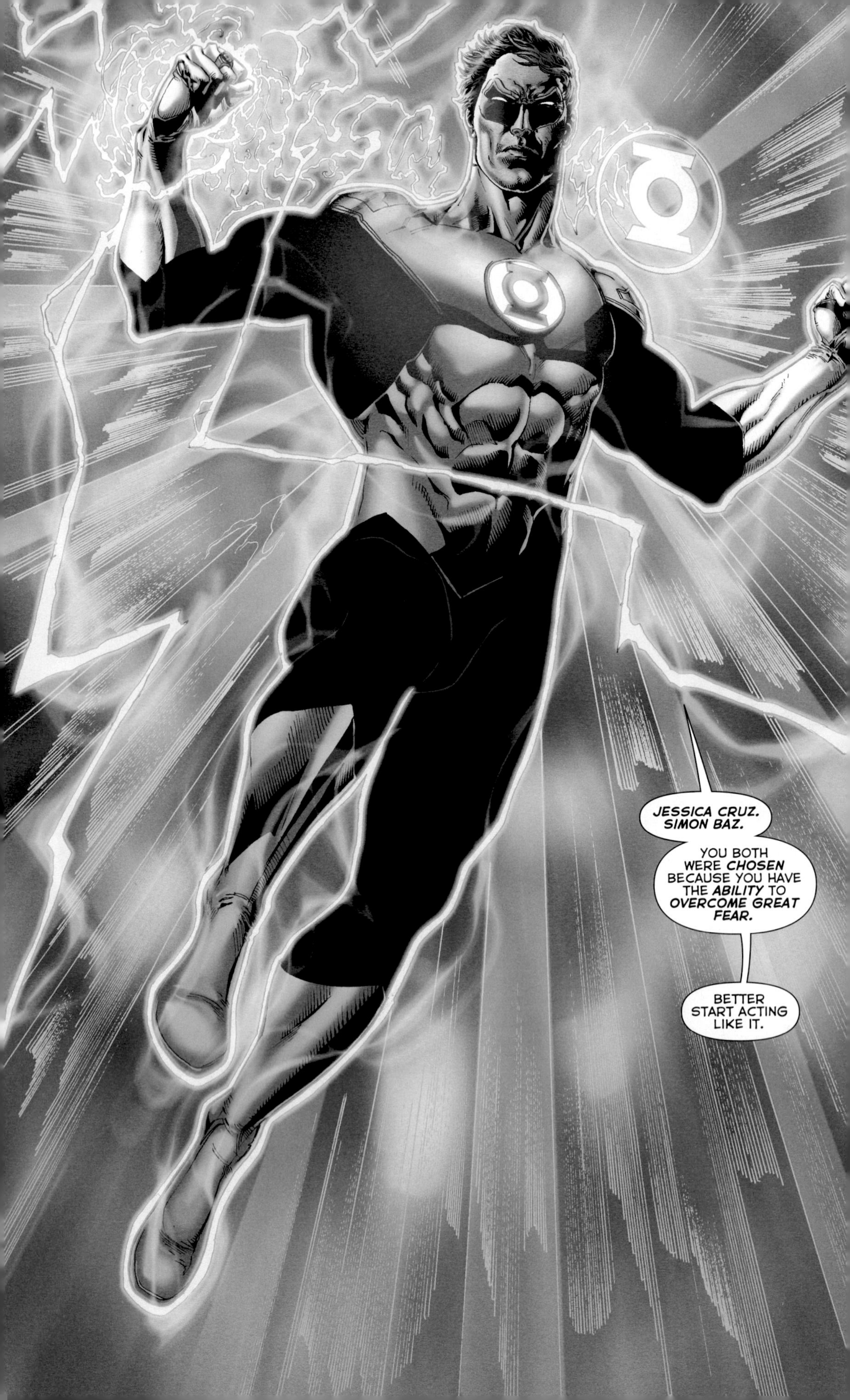
JESSICA CRUZ. SIMON BAZ.
YOU BOTH WERE CHOSEN BECAUSE YOU HAVE THE ABILITY TO OVERCOME GREAT FEAR.
BETTER START ACTING LIKE IT.

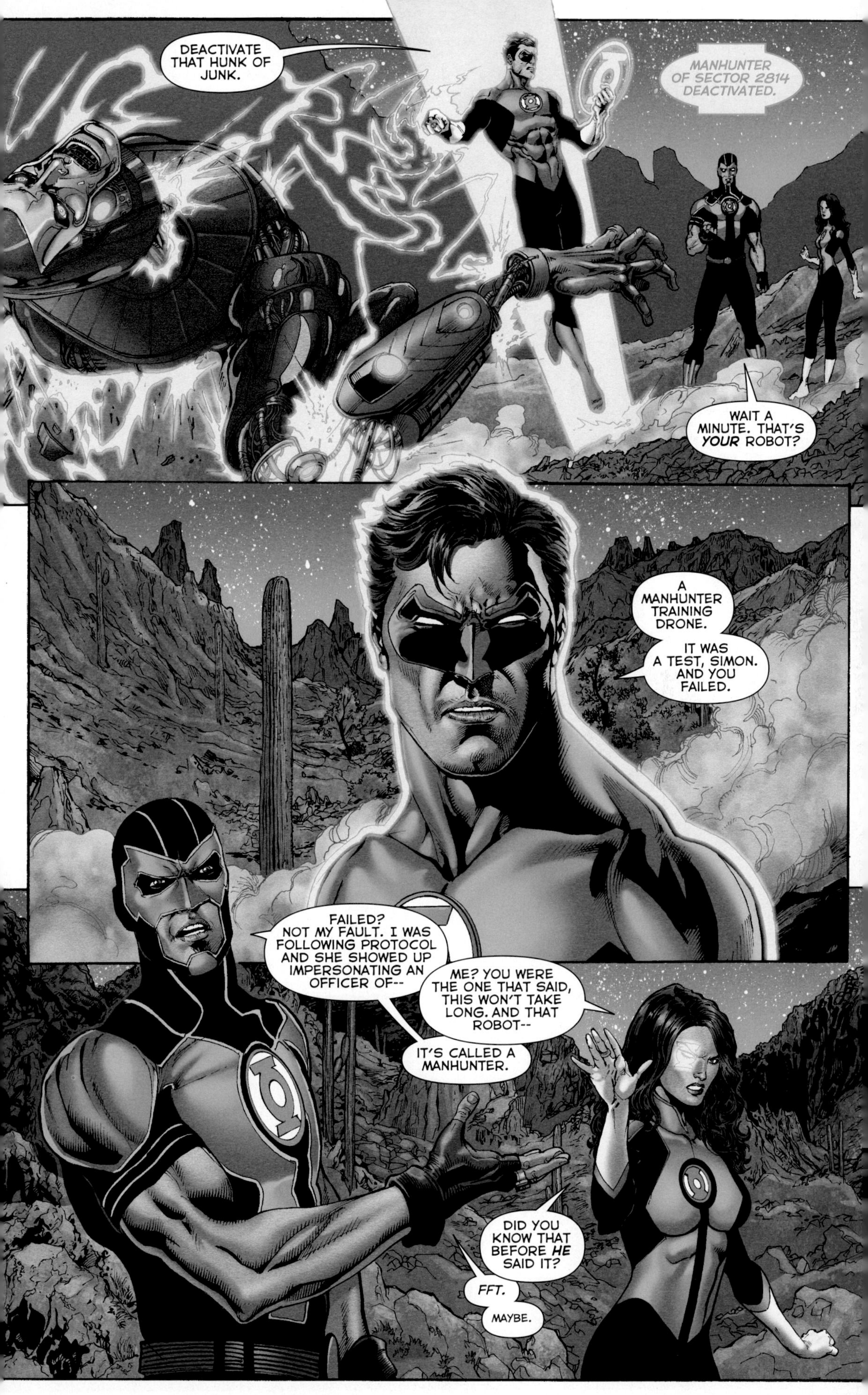
DEACTIVATE THAT HUNK OF JUNK.
MANHUNTER OF SECTOR 2814 DEACTIVATED.
WAIT A MINUTE. THAT'S *YOUR* ROBOT?
A MANHUNTER TRAINING DRONE.
IT WAS A TEST, SIMON. AND YOU FAILED.
FAILED? NOT MY FAULT. I WAS FOLLOWING PROTOCOL AND SHE SHOWED UP IMPERSONATING AN OFFICER OF--
ME? YOU WERE THE ONE THAT SAID, THIS WON'T TAKE LONG. AND THAT ROBOT--
IT'S CALLED A MANHUNTER.
DID YOU KNOW THAT BEFORE *HE* SAID IT?
FFT.
MAYBE.

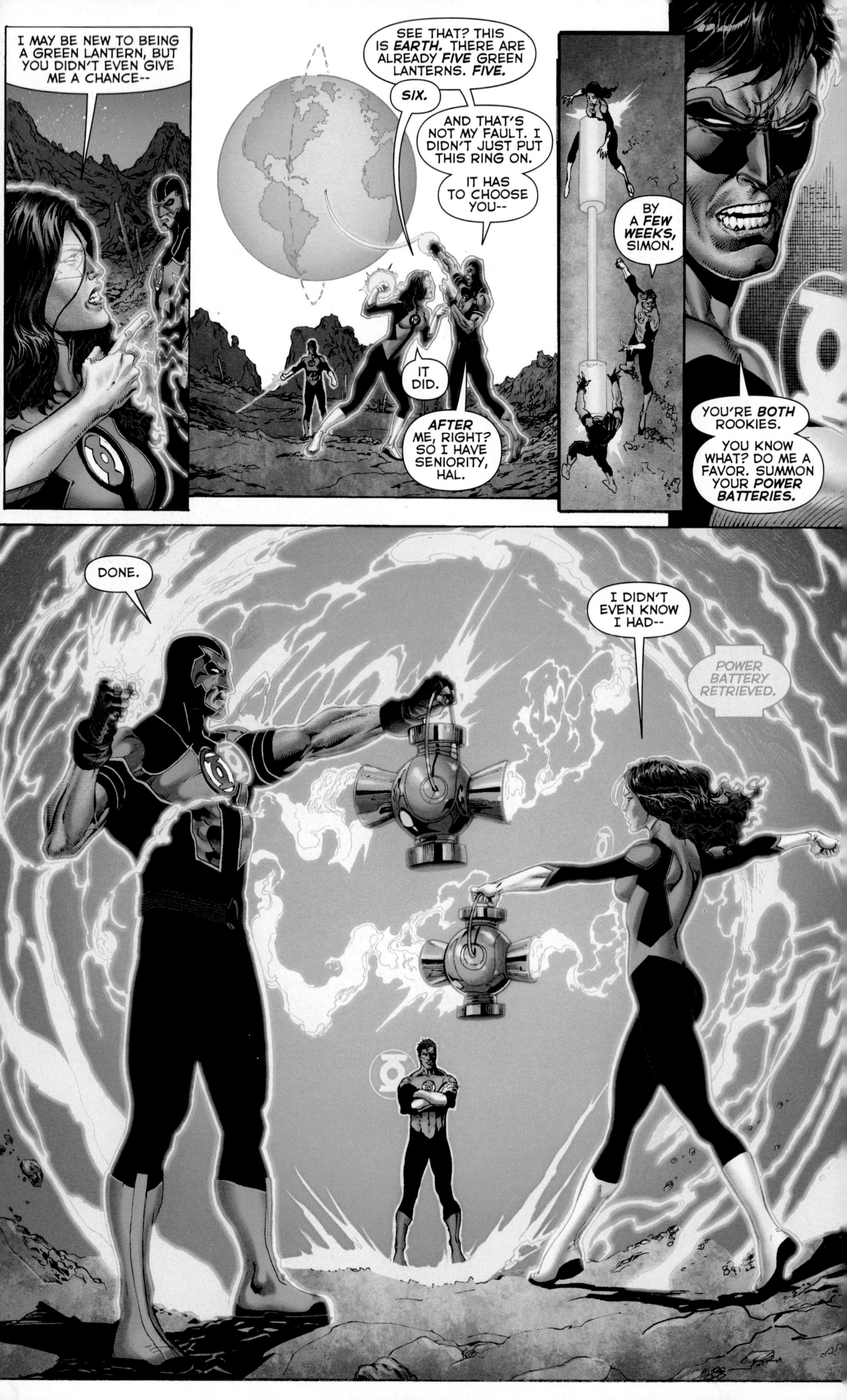
I MAY BE NEW TO BEING A GREEN LANTERN, BUT YOU DIDN'T EVEN GIVE ME A CHANCE--
SEE THAT? THIS IS EARTH. THERE ARE ALREADY FIVE GREEN LANTERNS. FIVE.
SIX.
AND THAT'S NOT MY FAULT. I DIDN'T JUST PUT THIS RING ON.
IT HAS TO CHOOSE YOU--
IT DID.
AFTER ME, RIGHT? SO I HAVE SENIORITY, HAL.
BY A FEW WEEKS, SIMON.
YOU'RE BOTH ROOKIES.
YOU KNOW WHAT? DO ME A FAVOR. SUMMON YOUR POWER BATTERIES.
DONE.
I DIDN'T EVEN KNOW I HAD--
POWER BATTERY RETRIEVED.

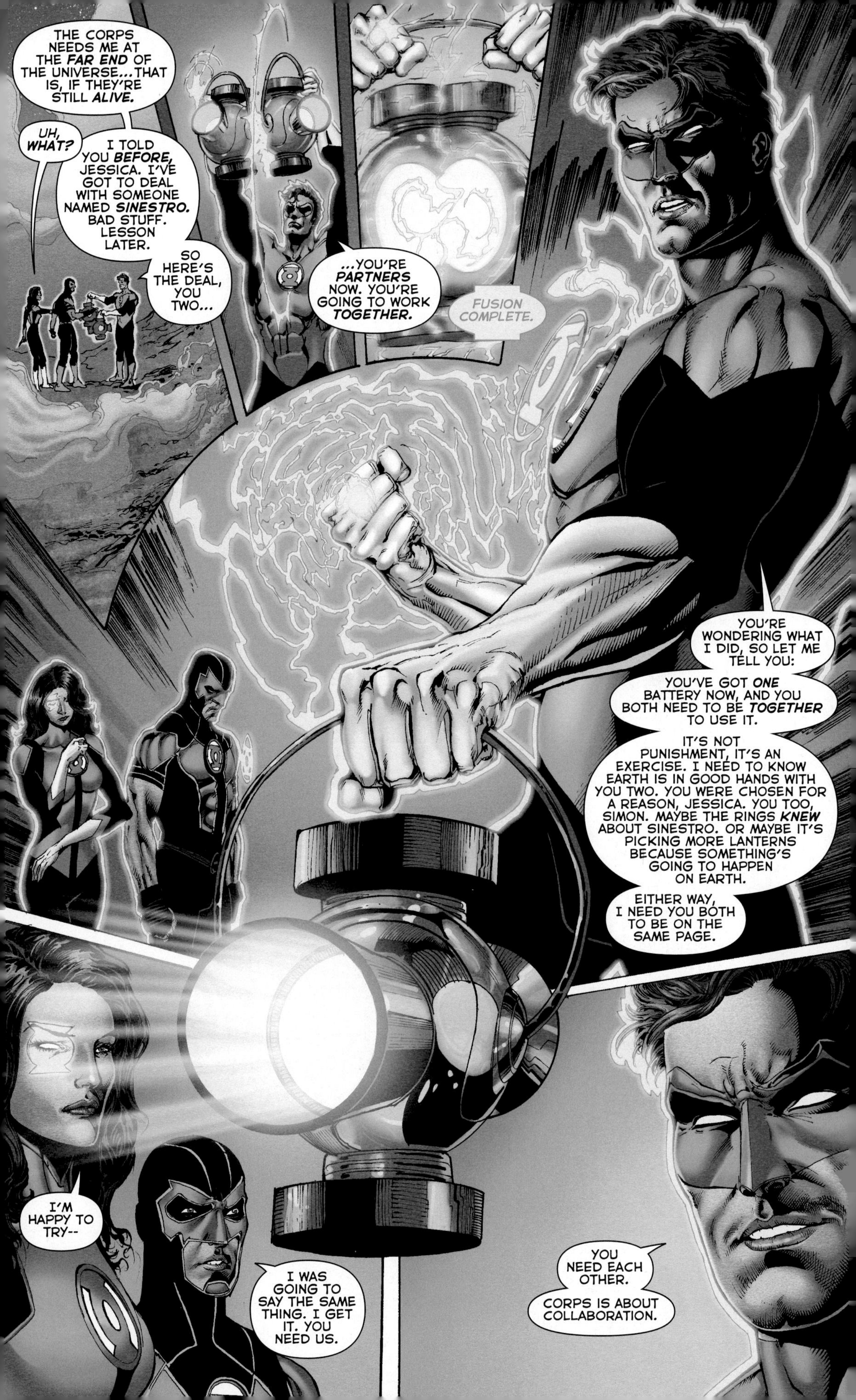
THE CORPS NEEDS ME AT THE FAR END OF THE UNIVERSE...THAT IS, IF THEY'RE STILL ALIVE.
UH, WHAT?
I TOLD YOU BEFORE, JESSICA. I'VE GOT TO DEAL WITH SOMEONE NAMED SINESTRO. BAD STUFF. LESSON LATER.
SO HERE'S THE DEAL, YOU TWO...
...YOU'RE PARTNERS NOW. YOU'RE GOING TO WORK TOGETHER.
FUSION COMPLETE.
YOU'RE WONDERING WHAT I DID, SO LET ME TELL YOU:
YOU'VE GOT ONE BATTERY NOW, AND YOU BOTH NEED TO BE TOGETHER TO USE IT.
IT'S NOT PUNISHMENT, IT'S AN EXERCISE. I NEED TO KNOW EARTH IS IN GOOD HANDS WITH YOU TWO. YOU WERE CHOSEN FOR A REASON, JESSICA. YOU TOO, SIMON. MAYBE THE RINGS KNEW ABOUT SINESTRO. OR MAYBE IT'S PICKING MORE LANTERNS BECAUSE SOMETHING'S GOING TO HAPPEN ON EARTH.
EITHER WAY, I NEED YOU BOTH TO BE ON THE SAME PAGE.
I'M HAPPY TO TRY--
I WAS GOING TO SAY THE SAME THING. I GET IT. YOU NEED US.
YOU NEED EACH OTHER.
CORPS IS ABOUT COLLABORATION.

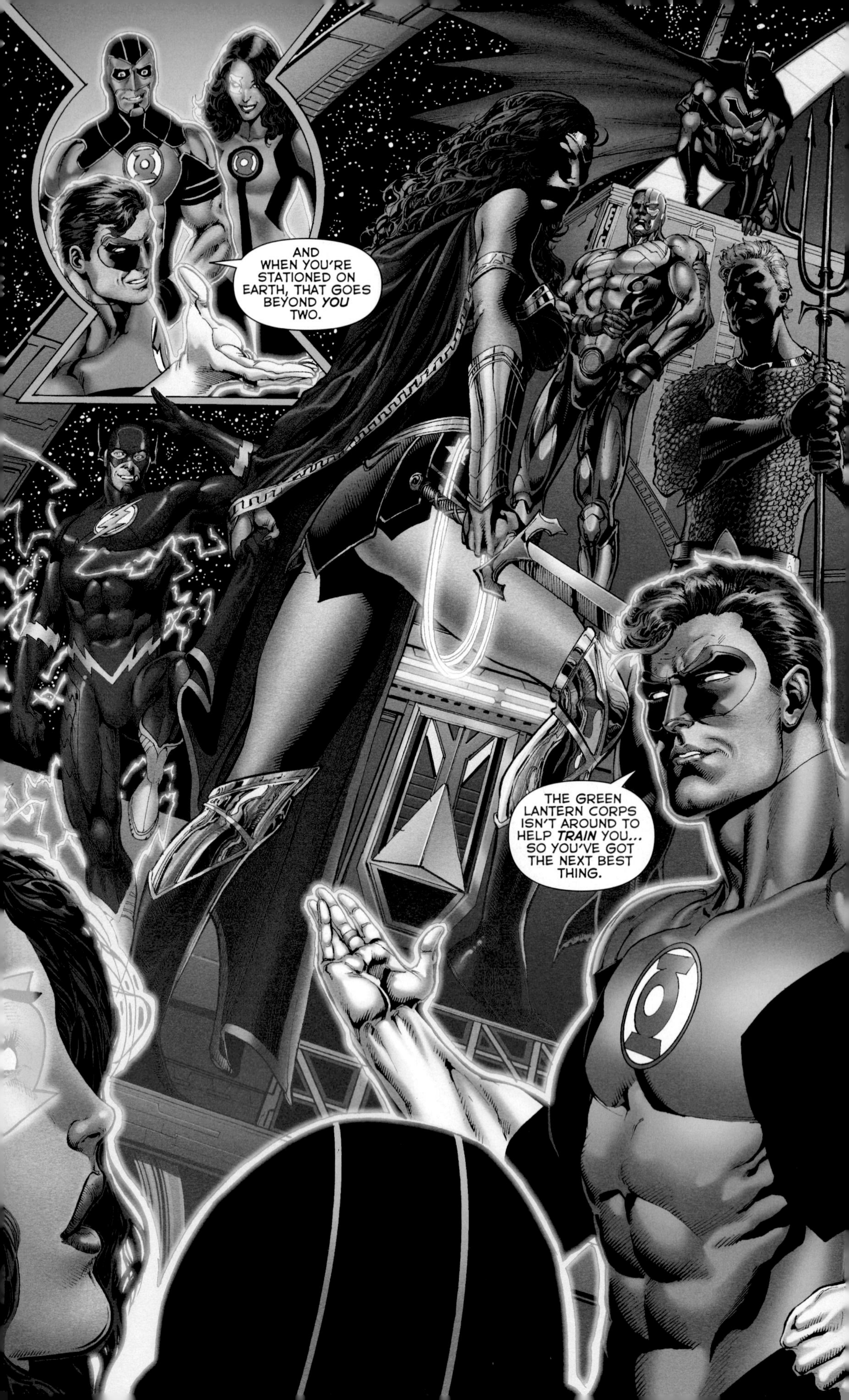
AND WHEN YOU'RE STATIONED ON EARTH, THAT GOES BEYOND *YOU* TWO.
THE GREEN LANTERN CORPS ISN'T AROUND TO HELP *TRAIN* YOU... SO YOU'VE GOT THE NEXT BEST THING.

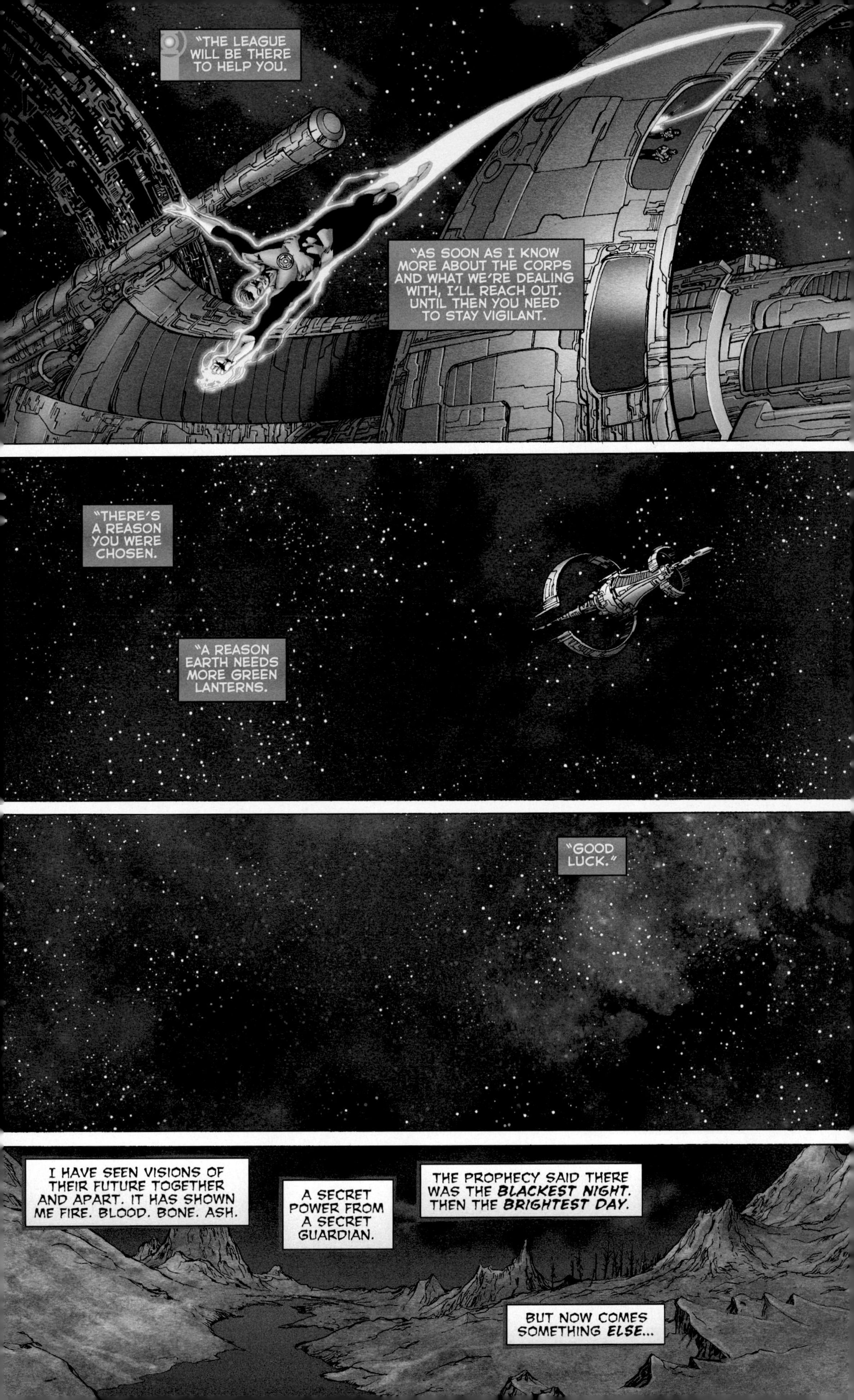
"THE LEAGUE WILL BE THERE TO HELP YOU.
"AS SOON AS I KNOW MORE ABOUT THE CORPS AND WHAT WE'RE DEALING WITH, I'LL REACH OUT. UNTIL THEN YOU NEED TO STAY VIGILANT.
"THERE'S A REASON YOU WERE CHOSEN.
"A REASON EARTH NEEDS MORE GREEN LANTERNS.
"GOOD LUCK."
I HAVE SEEN VISIONS OF THEIR FUTURE TOGETHER AND APART. IT HAS SHOWN ME FIRE. BLOOD. BONE. ASH.
A SECRET POWER FROM A SECRET GUARDIAN.
THE PROPHECY SAID THERE WAS THE *BLACKEST NIGHT*. THEN THE *BRIGHTEST DAY*.
BUT NOW COMES SOMETHING *ELSE*...

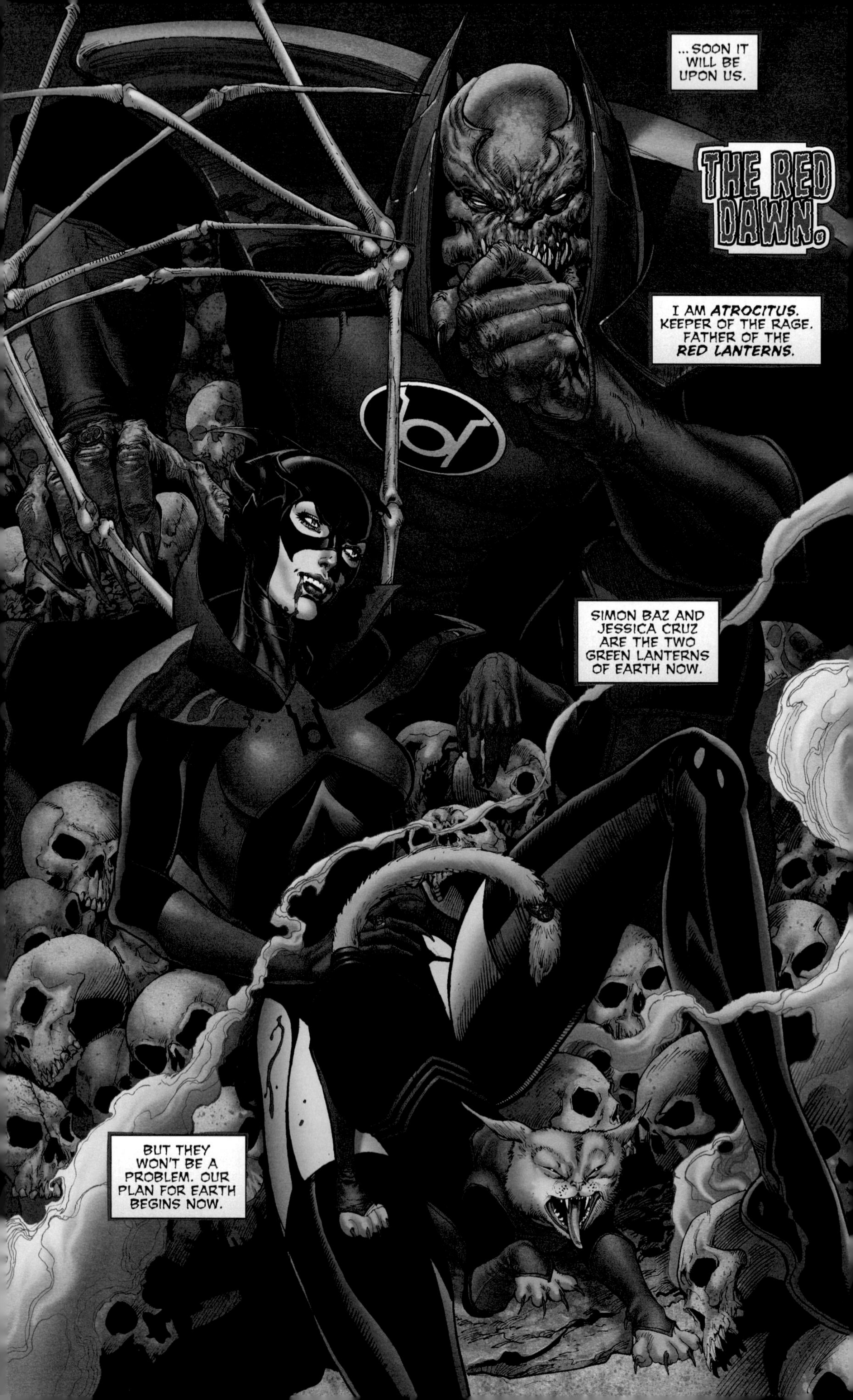
...SOON IT WILL BE UPON US.
THE RED DAWN.
I AM ATROCITUS. KEEPER OF THE RAGE. FATHER OF THE RED LANTERNS.
SIMON BAZ AND JESSICA CRUZ ARE THE TWO GREEN LANTERNS OF EARTH NOW.
BUT THEY WON'T BE A PROBLEM. OUR PLAN FOR EARTH BEGINS NOW.

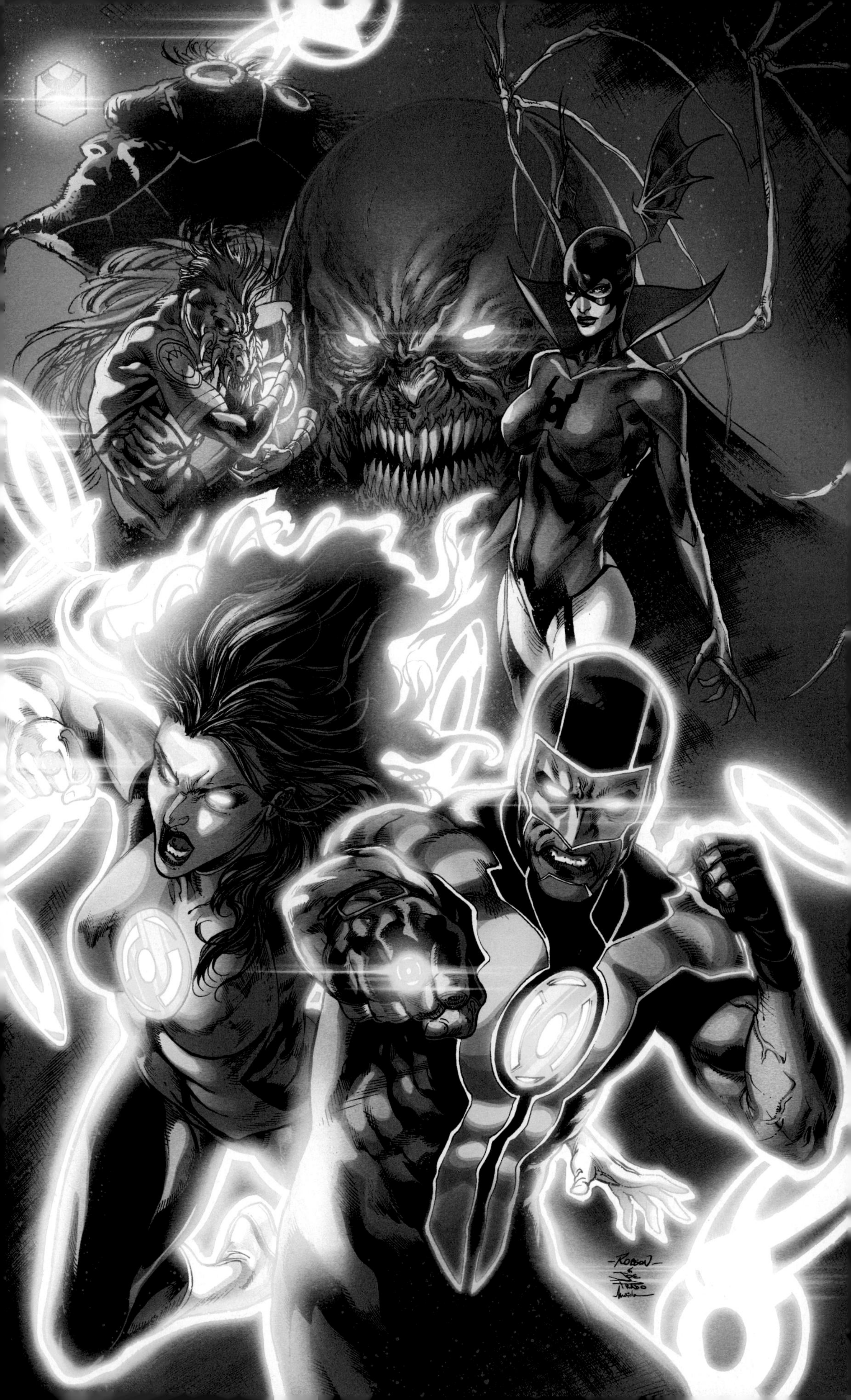

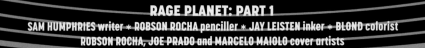

RAGE PLANET: PART 1

SAM HUMPHRIES writer ∗ ROBSON ROCHA penciller ∗ JAY LEISTEN inker ∗ BLOND colorist
ROBSON ROCHA, JOE PRADO and MARCELO MAIOLO cover artists

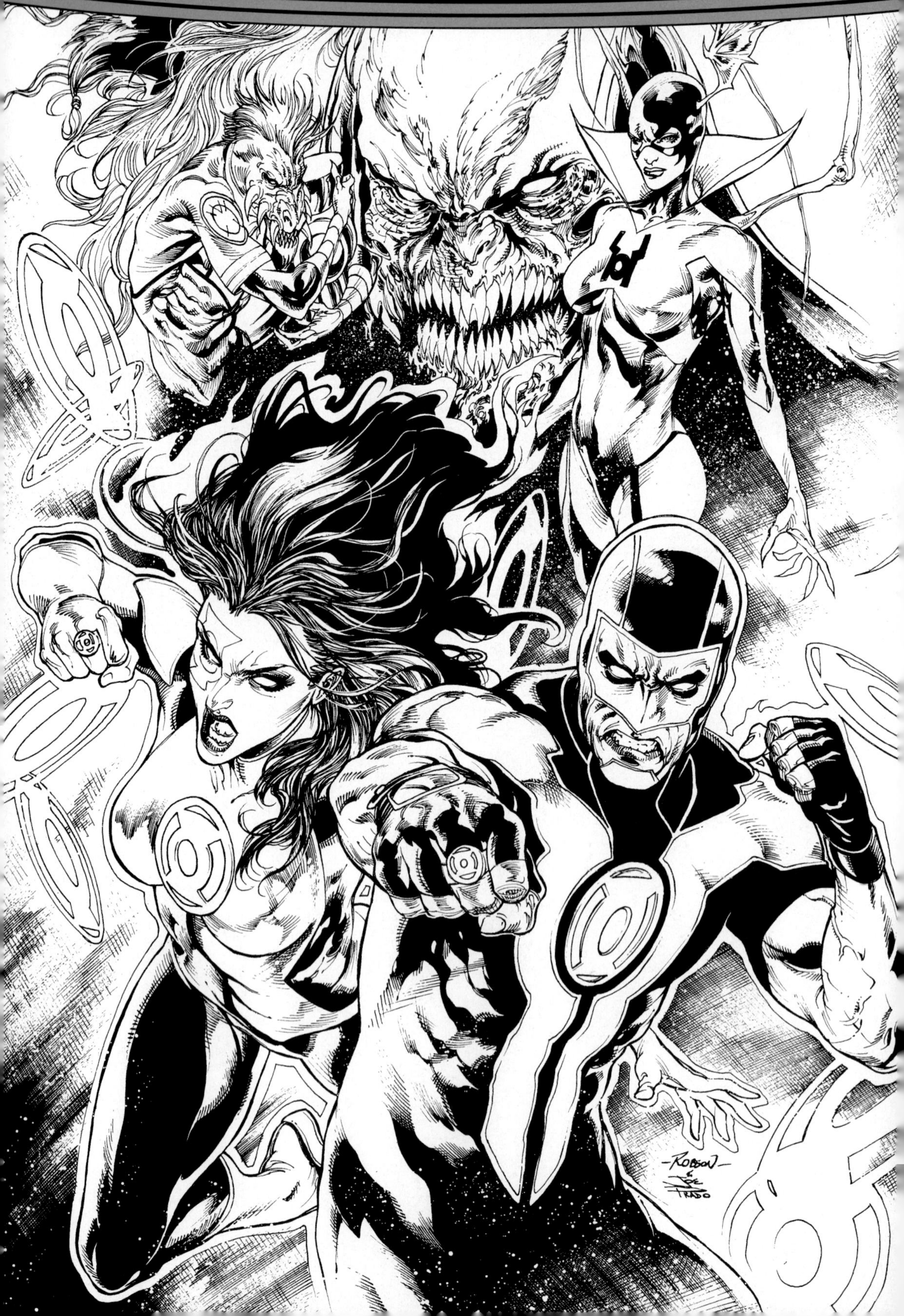

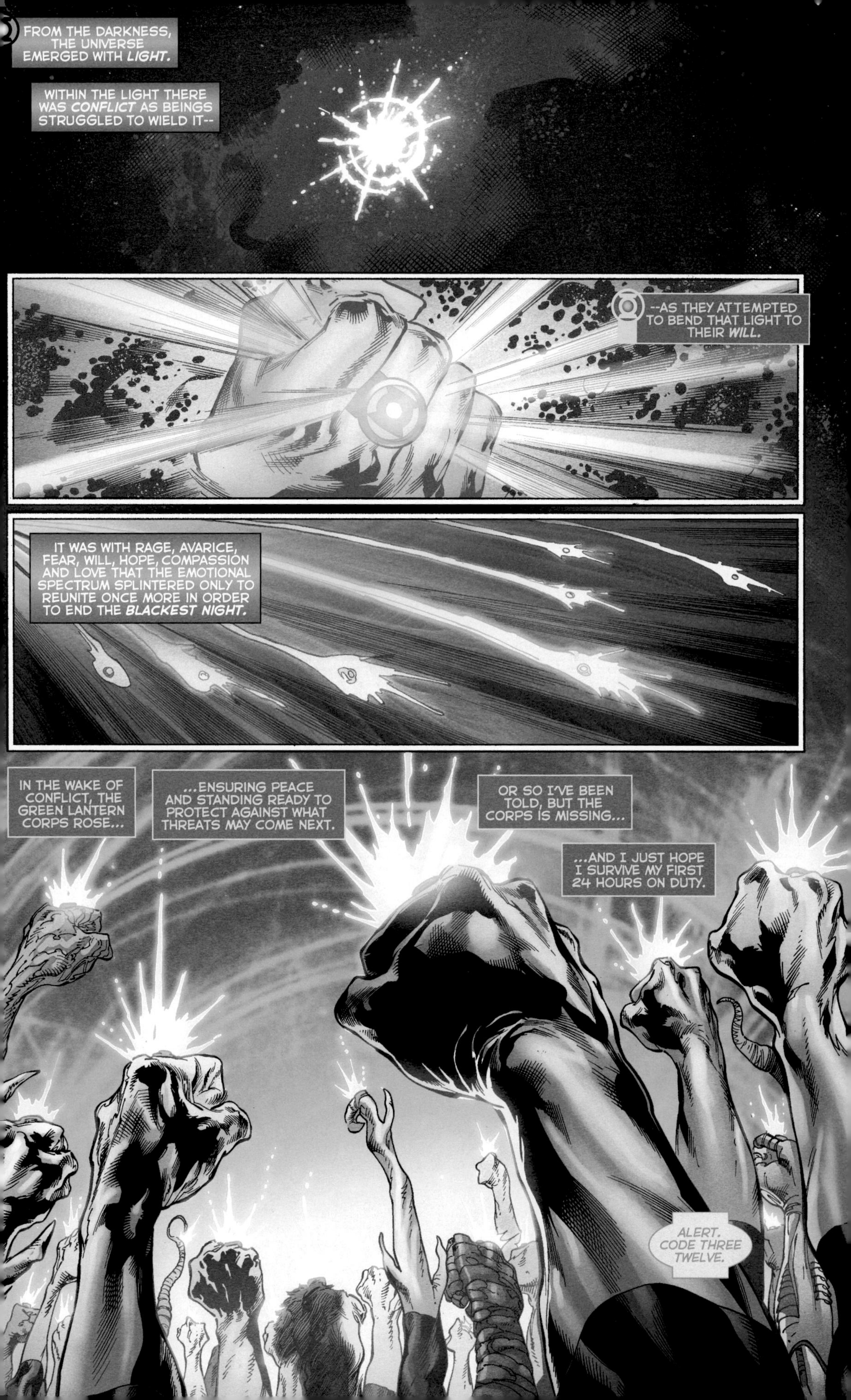

FROM THE DARKNESS, THE UNIVERSE EMERGED WITH *LIGHT.*
WITHIN THE LIGHT THERE WAS *CONFLICT* AS BEINGS STRUGGLED TO WIELD IT--
--AS THEY ATTEMPTED TO BEND THAT LIGHT TO THEIR *WILL.*
IT WAS WITH RAGE, AVARICE, FEAR, WILL, HOPE, COMPASSION AND LOVE THAT THE EMOTIONAL SPECTRUM SPLINTERED ONLY TO REUNITE ONCE MORE IN ORDER TO END THE *BLACKEST NIGHT.*
IN THE WAKE OF CONFLICT, THE GREEN LANTERN CORPS ROSE...
...ENSURING PEACE AND STANDING READY TO PROTECT AGAINST WHAT THREATS MAY COME NEXT.
OR SO I'VE BEEN TOLD, BUT THE CORPS IS MISSING...
...AND I JUST HOPE I SURVIVE MY FIRST 24 HOURS ON DUTY.
ALERT. CODE THREE TWELVE.

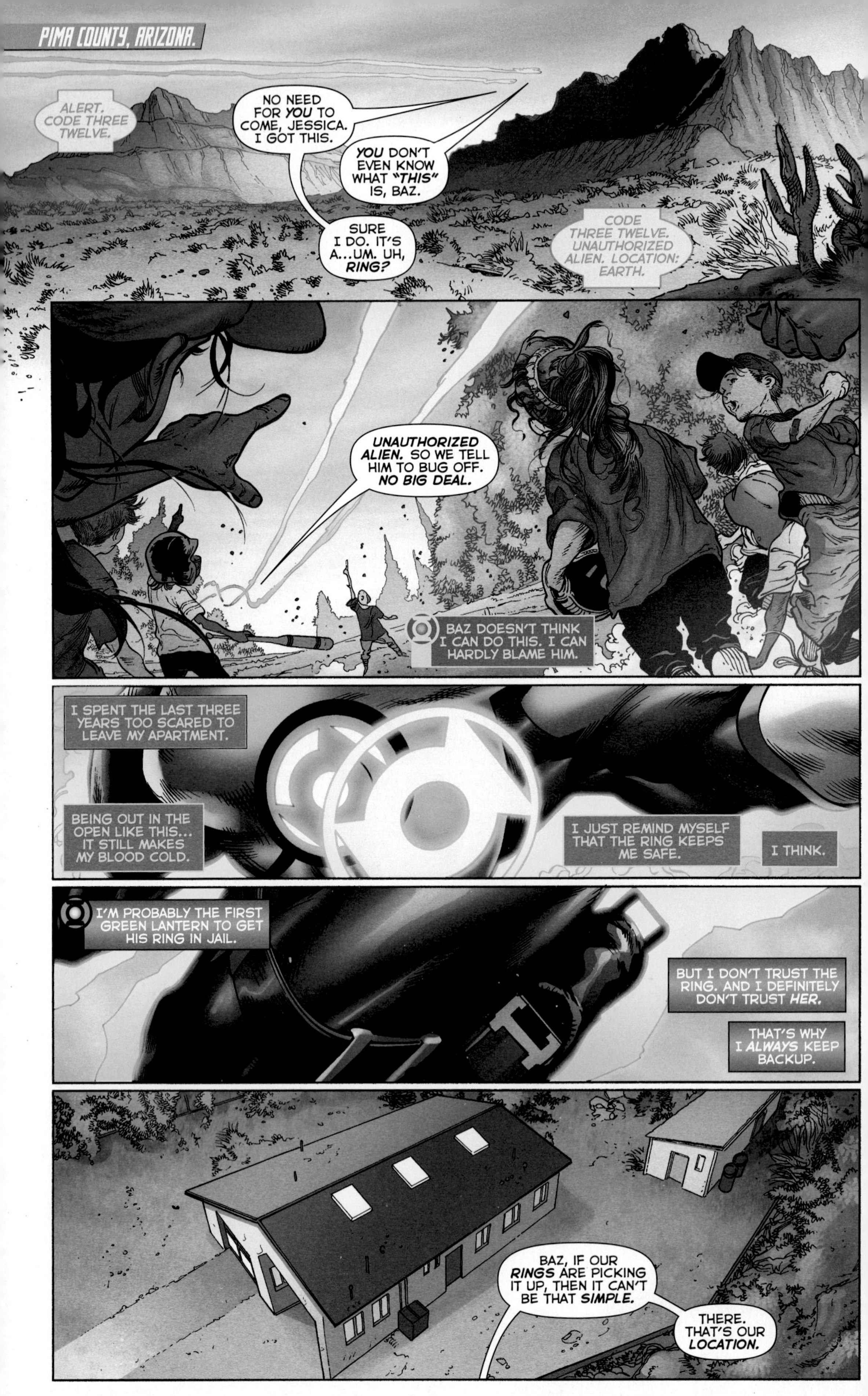
PIMA COUNTY, ARIZONA.
ALERT. CODE THREE TWELVE.
NO NEED FOR YOU TO COME, JESSICA. I GOT THIS.
YOU DON'T EVEN KNOW WHAT "THIS" IS, BAZ.
SURE I DO. IT'S A...UM. UH, RING?
CODE THREE TWELVE. UNAUTHORIZED ALIEN. LOCATION: EARTH.
UNAUTHORIZED ALIEN. SO WE TELL HIM TO BUG OFF. NO BIG DEAL.
BAZ DOESN'T THINK I CAN DO THIS. I CAN HARDLY BLAME HIM.
I SPENT THE LAST THREE YEARS TOO SCARED TO LEAVE MY APARTMENT.
BEING OUT IN THE OPEN LIKE THIS... IT STILL MAKES MY BLOOD COLD.
I JUST REMIND MYSELF THAT THE RING KEEPS ME SAFE.
I THINK.
I'M PROBABLY THE FIRST GREEN LANTERN TO GET HIS RING IN JAIL.
BUT I DON'T TRUST THE RING. AND I DEFINITELY DON'T TRUST HER.
THAT'S WHY I ALWAYS KEEP BACKUP.
BAZ, IF OUR RINGS ARE PICKING IT UP, THEN IT CAN'T BE THAT SIMPLE.
THERE. THAT'S OUR LOCATION.

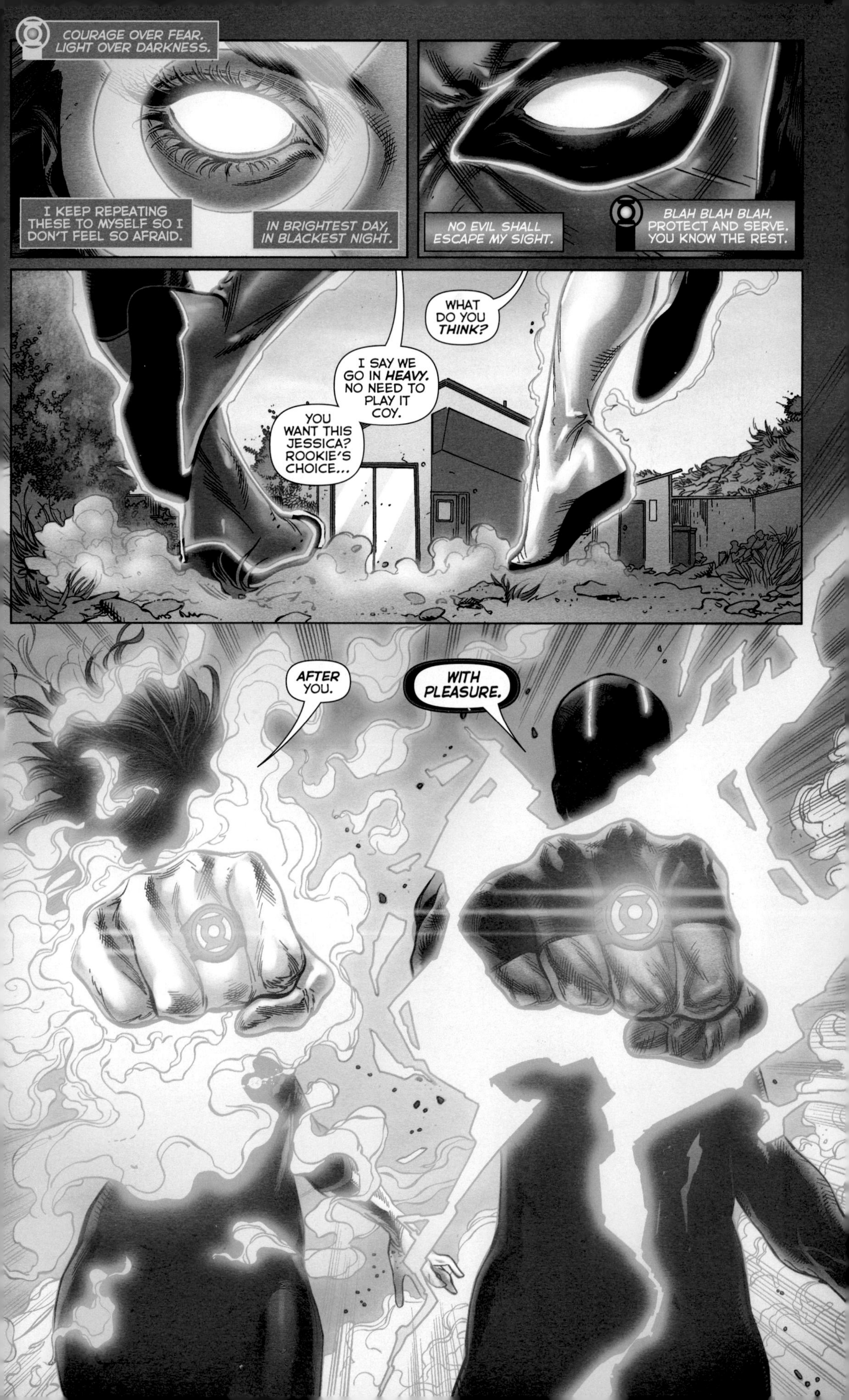
COURAGE OVER FEAR. LIGHT OVER DARKNESS.
I KEEP REPEATING THESE TO MYSELF SO I DON'T FEEL SO AFRAID.
IN BRIGHTEST DAY, IN BLACKEST NIGHT.
NO EVIL SHALL ESCAPE MY SIGHT.
BLAH BLAH BLAH. PROTECT AND SERVE. YOU KNOW THE REST.
WHAT DO YOU THINK?
I SAY WE GO IN HEAVY. NO NEED TO PLAY IT COY.
YOU WANT THIS JESSICA? ROOKIE'S CHOICE...
AFTER YOU.
WITH PLEASURE.

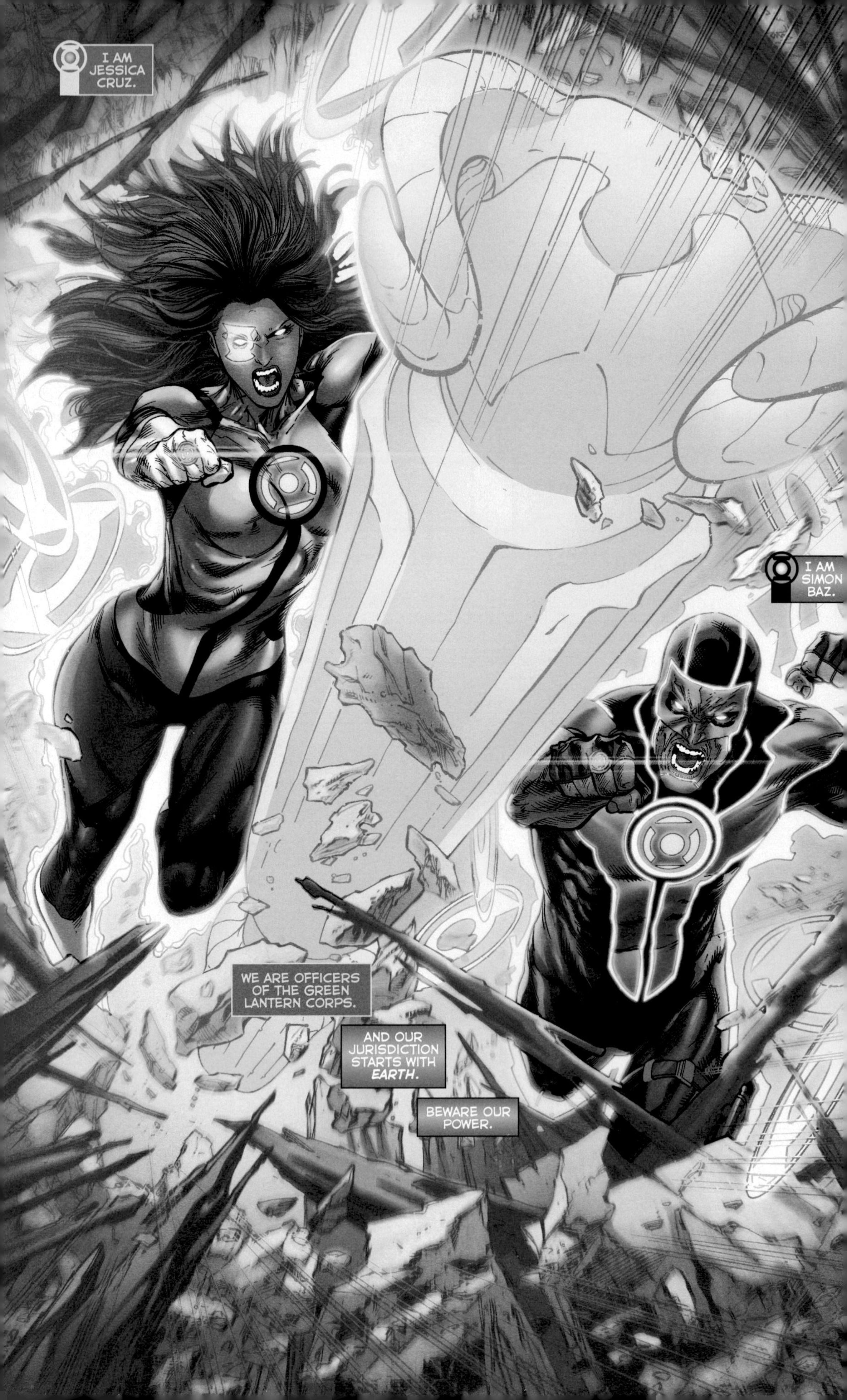
I AM JESSICA CRUZ.
I AM SIMON BAZ.
WE ARE OFFICERS OF THE GREEN LANTERN CORPS.
AND OUR JURISDICTION STARTS WITH EARTH.
BEWARE OUR POWER.

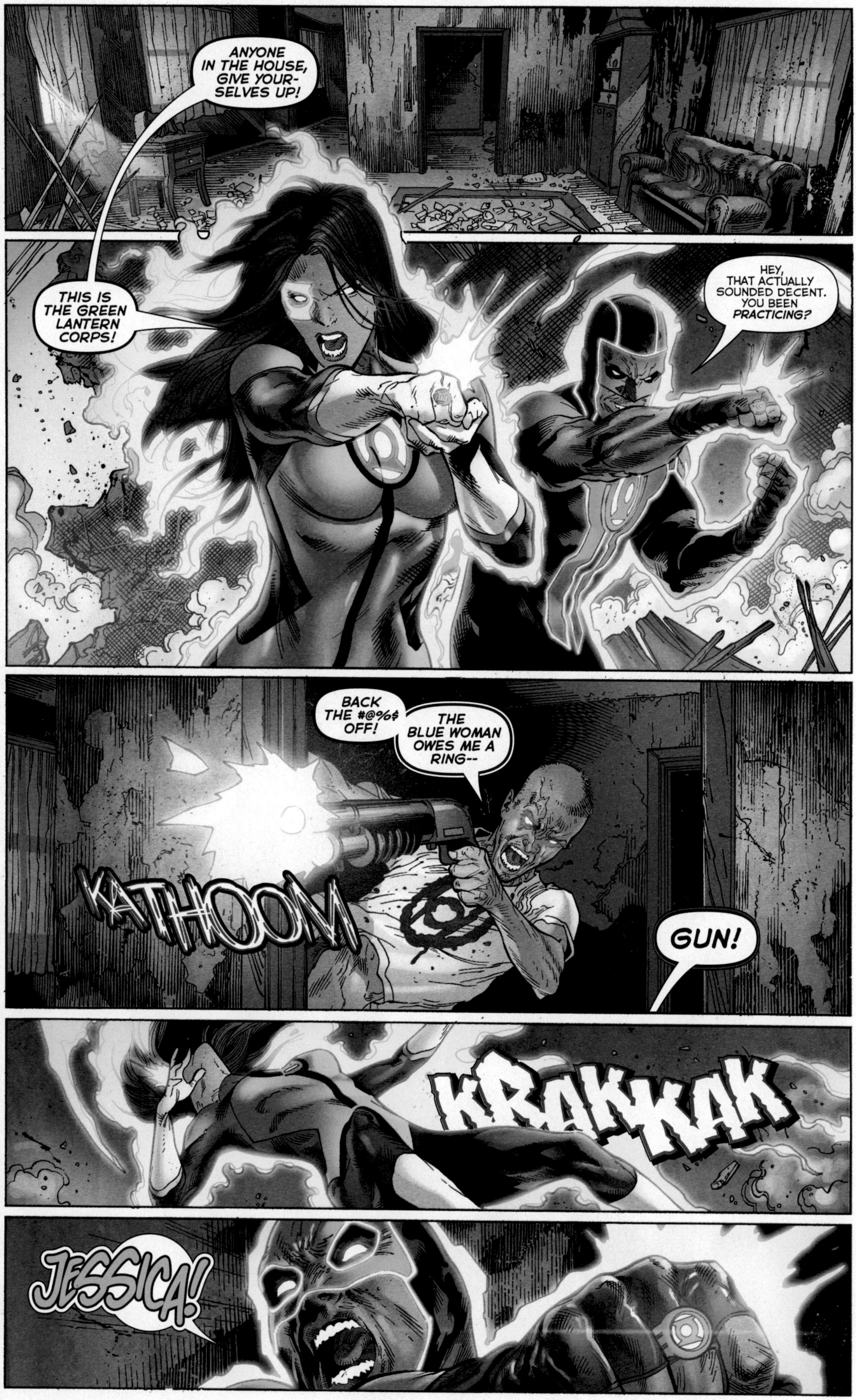

ANYONE IN THE HOUSE, GIVE YOUR-SELVES UP!
THIS IS THE GREEN LANTERN CORPS!
HEY, THAT ACTUALLY SOUNDED DECENT. YOU BEEN PRACTICING?
BACK THE #@%$ OFF!
THE BLUE WOMAN OWES ME A RING--
KATHOOM
GUN!
KRAKKAK
JESSICA!

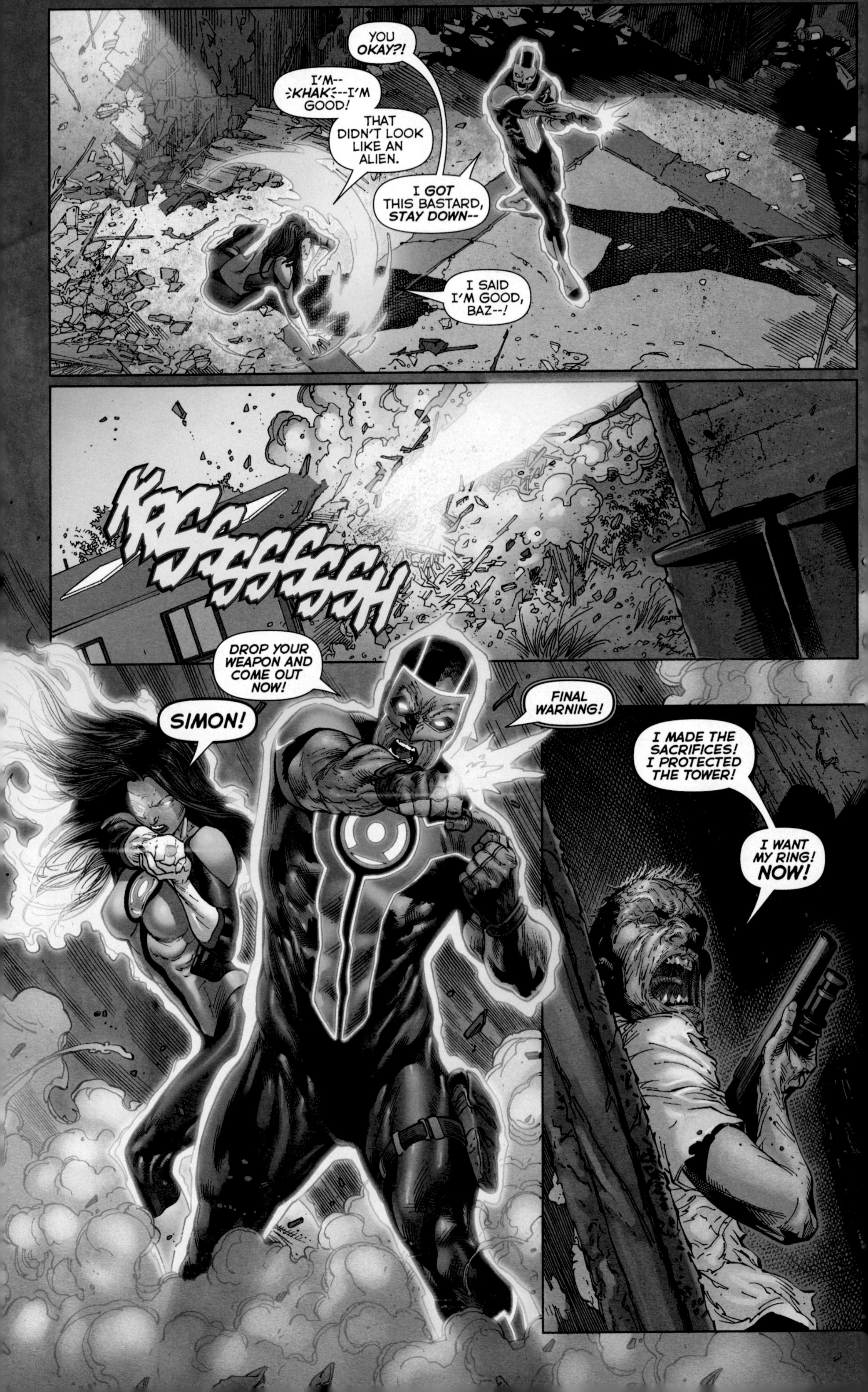
YOU OKAY?!
I'M-- KHAK--I'M GOOD!
THAT DIDN'T LOOK LIKE AN ALIEN.
I GOT THIS BASTARD, STAY DOWN--
I SAID I'M GOOD, BAZ--!
KRSSSSSSH
DROP YOUR WEAPON AND COME OUT NOW!
SIMON!
FINAL WARNING!
I MADE THE SACRIFICES! I PROTECTED THE TOWER!
I WANT MY RING! NOW!

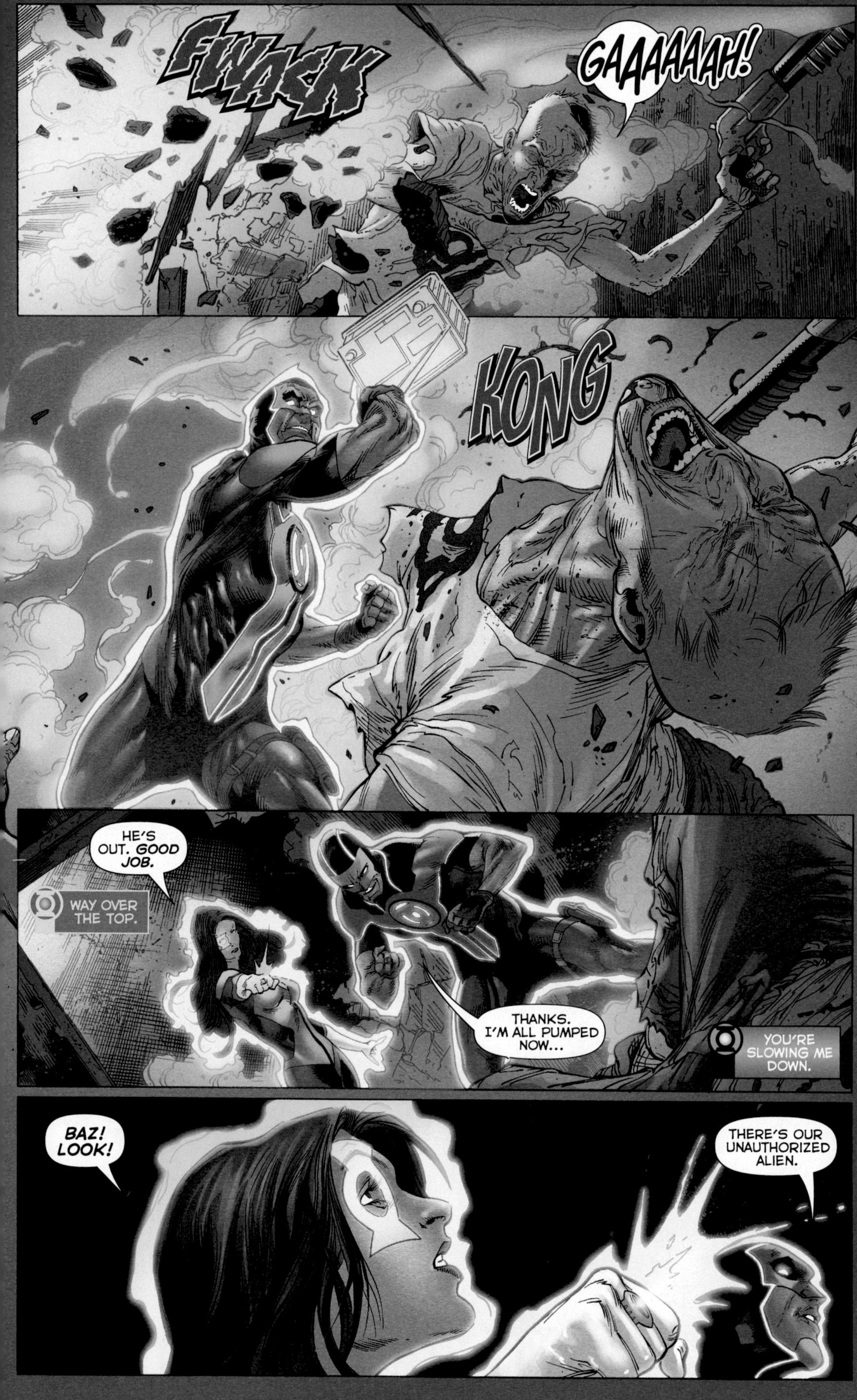
FWACK
GAAAAAAH!
KONG
HE'S OUT. GOOD JOB.
WAY OVER THE TOP.
THANKS. I'M ALL PUMPED NOW...
YOU'RE SLOWING ME DOWN.
BAZ! LOOK!
THERE'S OUR UNAUTHORIZED ALIEN.

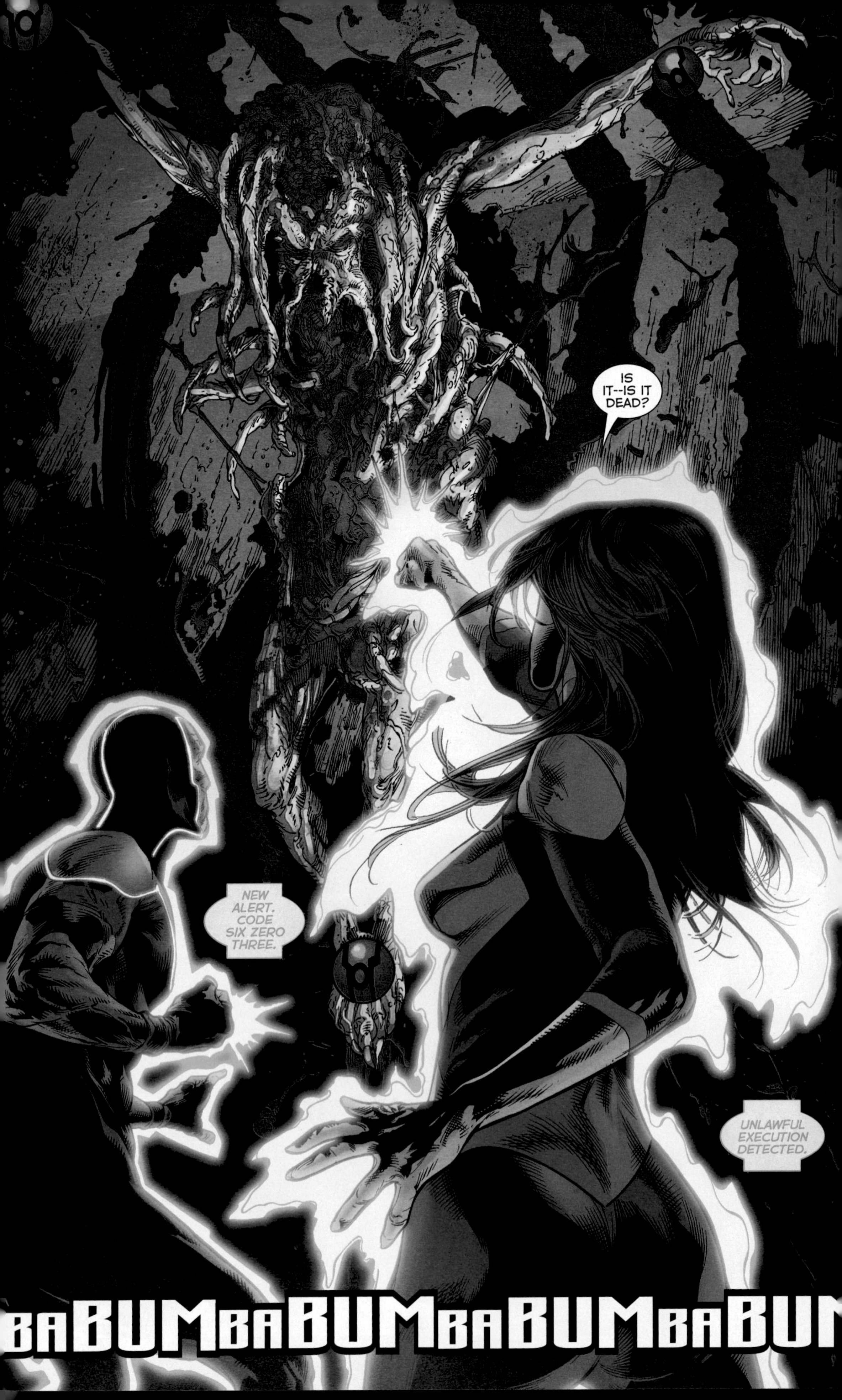
IS IT--IS IT DEAD?
NEW ALERT. CODE SIX ZERO THREE.
UNLAWFUL EXECUTION DETECTED.
BABUMBABUMBABUMBABUM

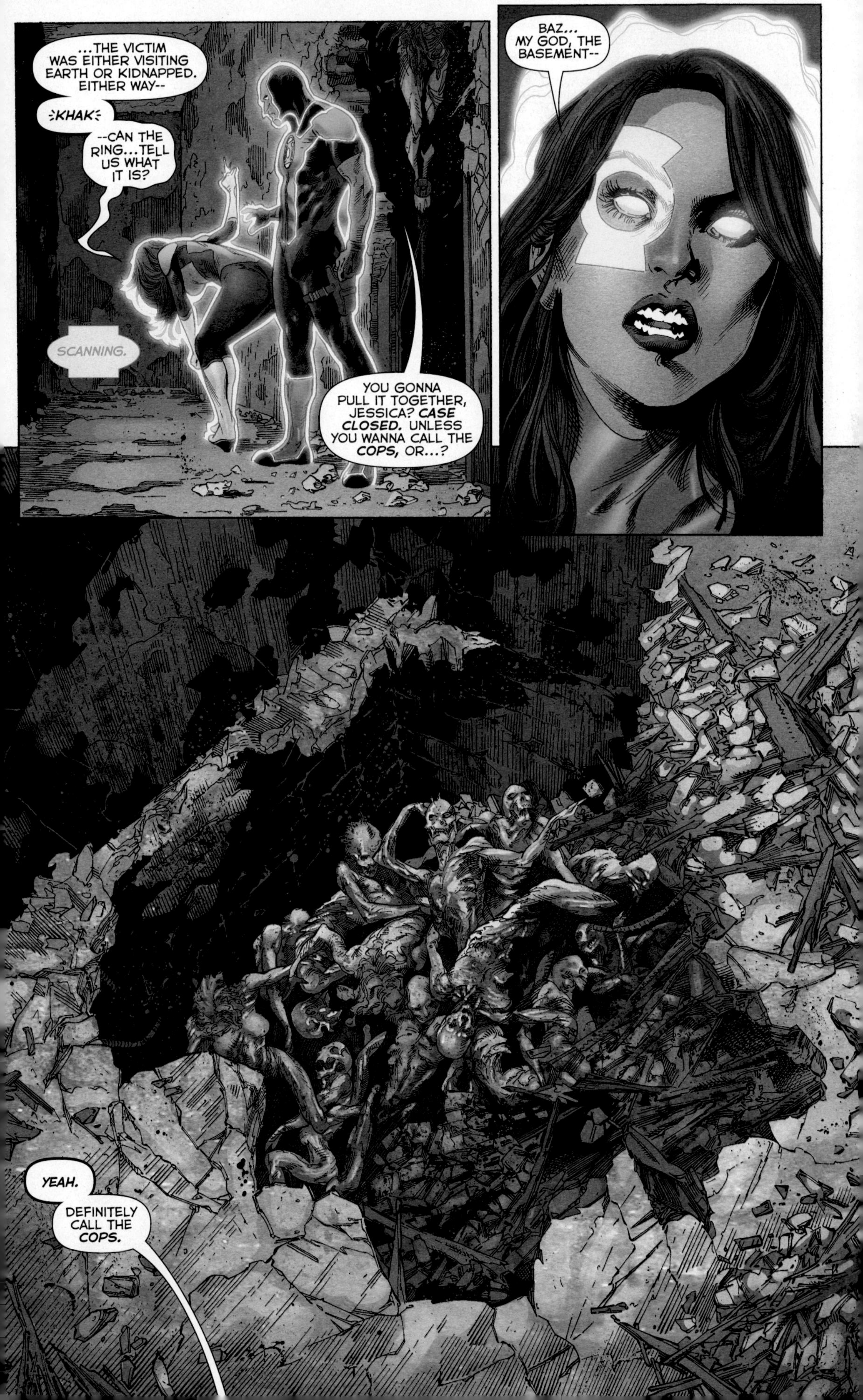
...THE VICTIM WAS EITHER VISITING EARTH OR KIDNAPPED. EITHER WAY--
KHAK
--CAN THE RING...TELL US WHAT IT IS?
SCANNING.
YOU GONNA PULL IT TOGETHER, JESSICA? CASE CLOSED. UNLESS YOU WANNA CALL THE COPS, OR...?
BAZ... MY GOD, THE BASEMENT--
YEAH.
DEFINITELY CALL THE COPS.

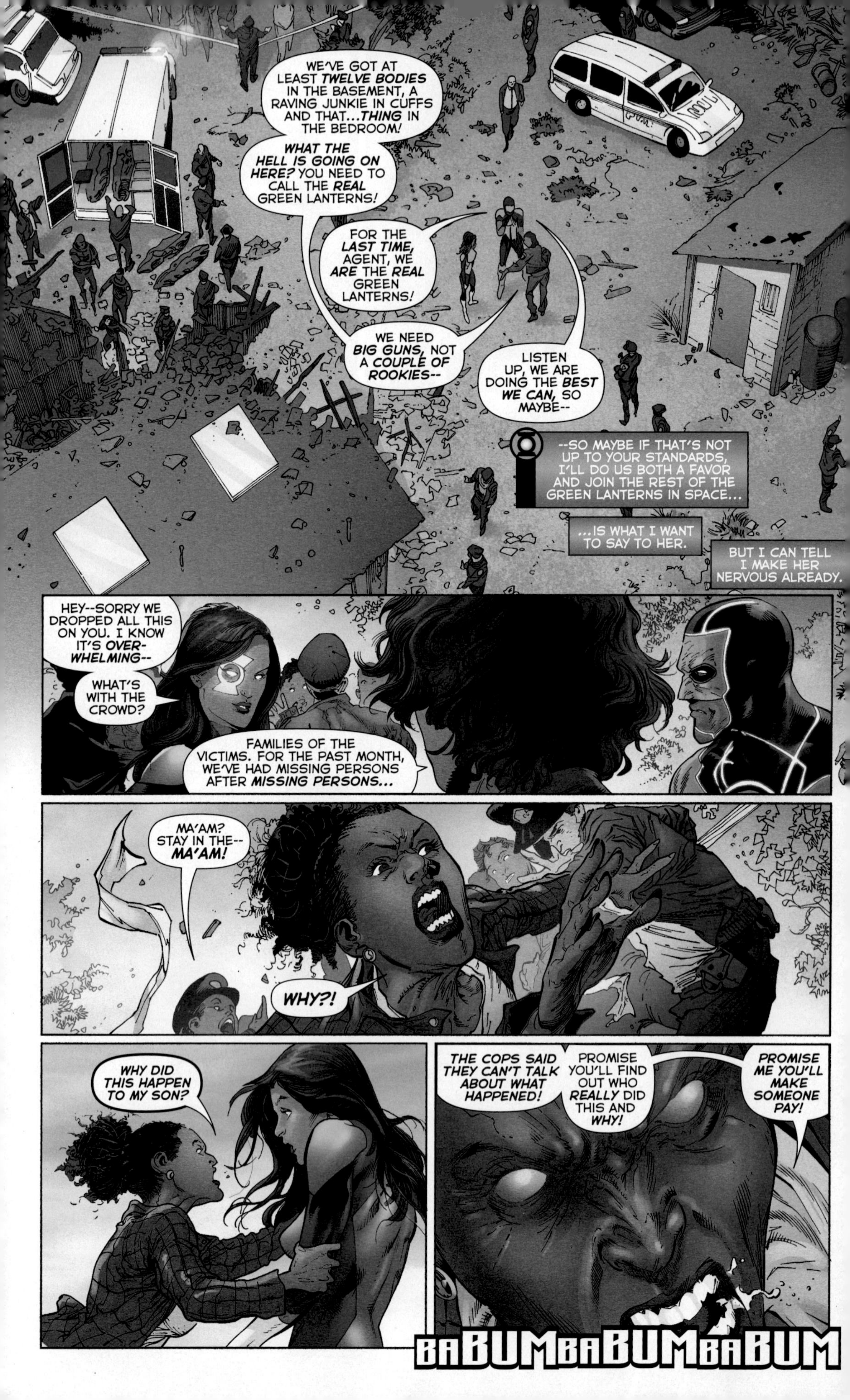
WE'VE GOT AT LEAST TWELVE BODIES IN THE BASEMENT, A RAVING JUNKIE IN CUFFS AND THAT...THING IN THE BEDROOM!
WHAT THE HELL IS GOING ON HERE? YOU NEED TO CALL THE REAL GREEN LANTERNS!
FOR THE LAST TIME, AGENT, WE ARE THE REAL GREEN LANTERNS!
WE NEED BIG GUNS, NOT A COUPLE OF ROOKIES--
LISTEN UP, WE ARE DOING THE BEST WE CAN, SO MAYBE--
--SO MAYBE IF THAT'S NOT UP TO YOUR STANDARDS, I'LL DO US BOTH A FAVOR AND JOIN THE REST OF THE GREEN LANTERNS IN SPACE...
...IS WHAT I WANT TO SAY TO HER.
BUT I CAN TELL I MAKE HER NERVOUS ALREADY.
HEY--SORRY WE DROPPED ALL THIS ON YOU. I KNOW IT'S OVER-WHELMING--
WHAT'S WITH THE CROWD?
FAMILIES OF THE VICTIMS. FOR THE PAST MONTH, WE'VE HAD MISSING PERSONS AFTER MISSING PERSONS...
MA'AM? STAY IN THE-- MA'AM!
WHY?!
WHY DID THIS HAPPEN TO MY SON?
THE COPS SAID THEY CAN'T TALK ABOUT WHAT HAPPENED!
PROMISE YOU'LL FIND OUT WHO REALLY DID THIS AND WHY!
PROMISE ME YOU'LL MAKE SOMEONE PAY!
BABUMBABUMBABUM

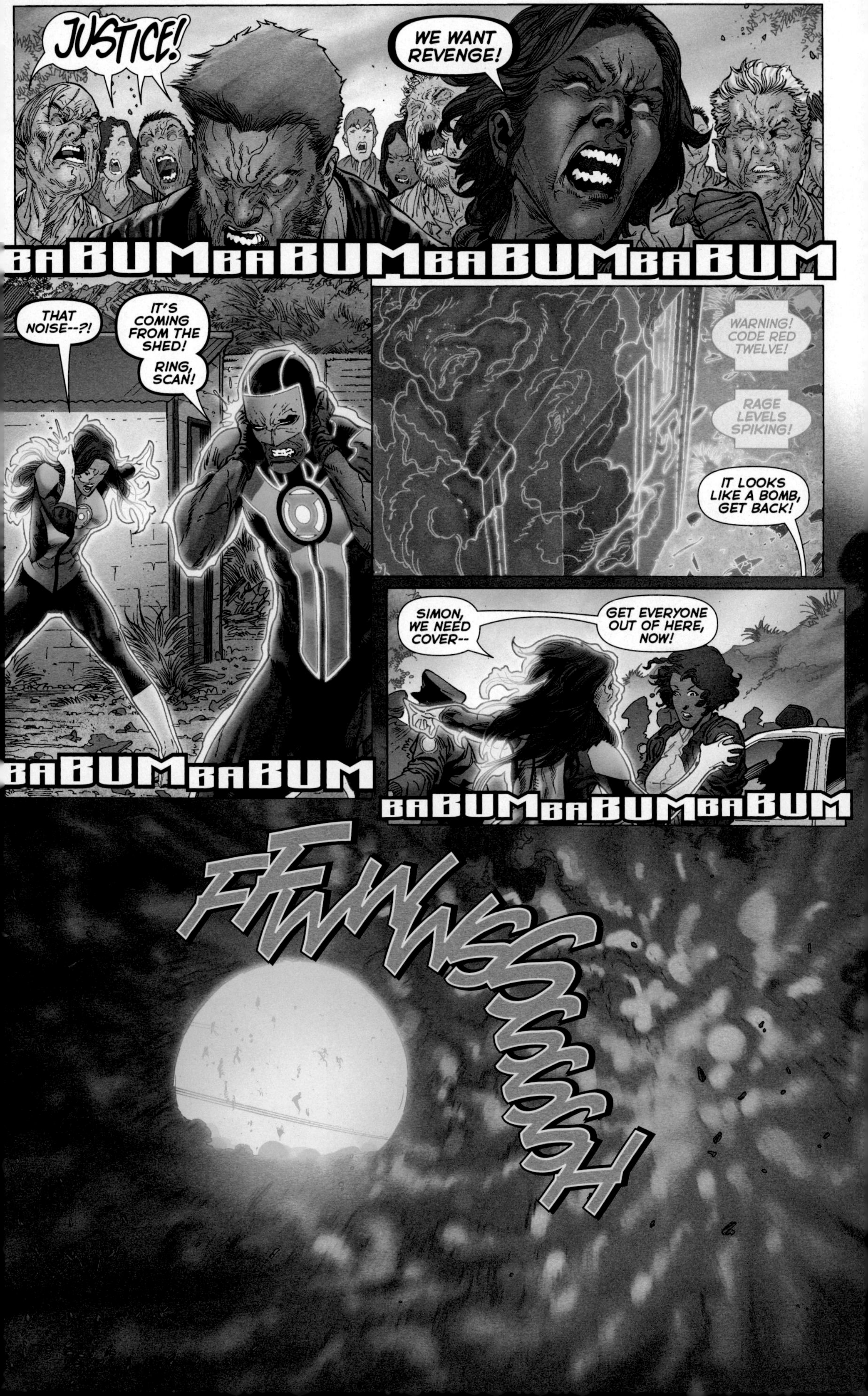
JUSTICE!
WE WANT REVENGE!
BABUMBABUMBABUMBABUM
THAT NOISE--?!
IT'S COMING FROM THE SHED!
RING, SCAN!
WARNING! CODE RED TWELVE!
RAGE LEVELS SPIKING!
IT LOOKS LIKE A BOMB, GET BACK!
BABUMBABUM
SIMON, WE NEED COVER--
GET EVERYONE OUT OF HERE, NOW!
BABUMBABUMBABUM
FFWWWSSSSSSSH

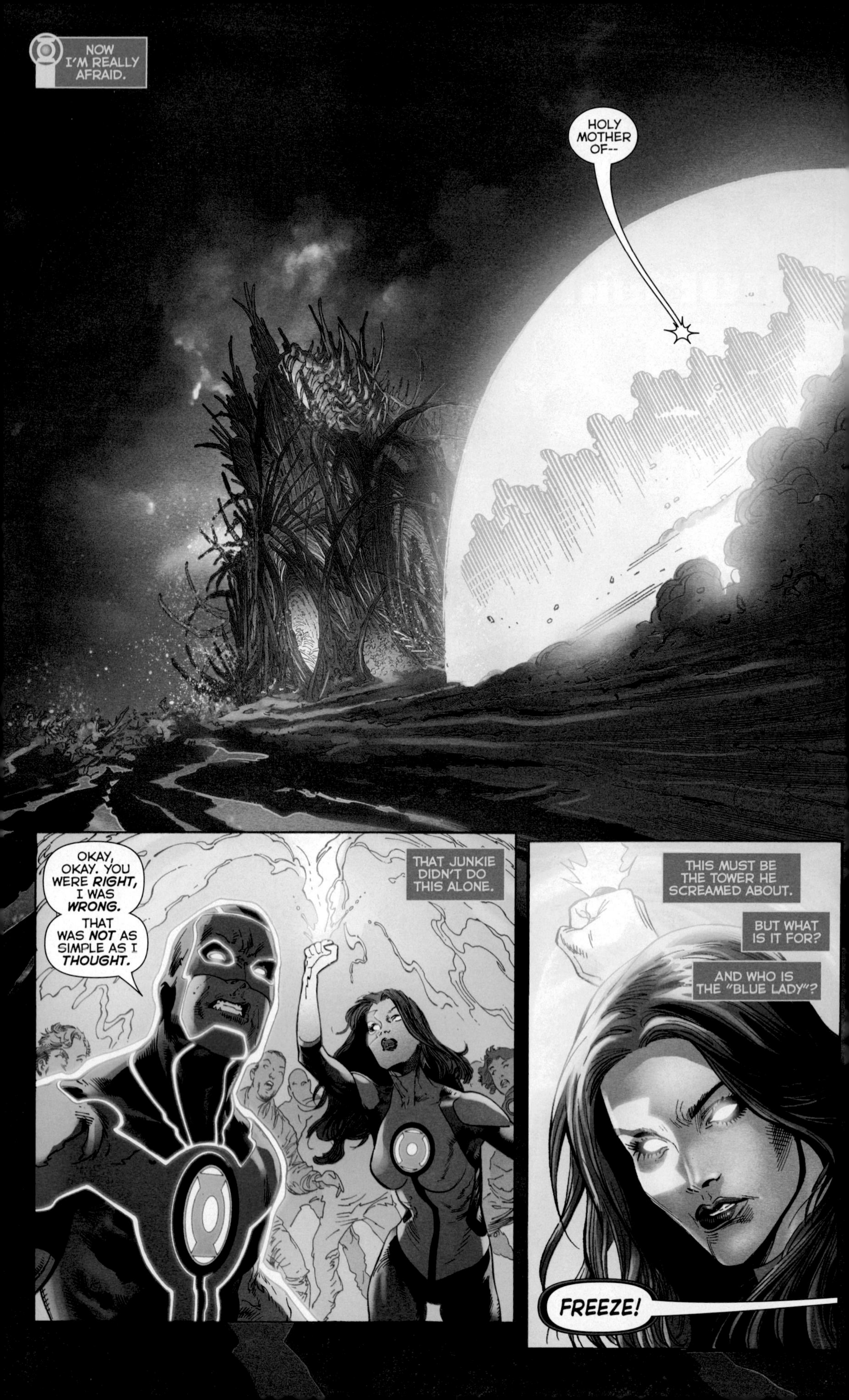
NOW I'M REALLY AFRAID.
HOLY MOTHER OF--
OKAY, OKAY. YOU WERE RIGHT, I WAS WRONG. THAT WAS NOT AS SIMPLE AS I THOUGHT.
THAT JUNKIE DIDN'T DO THIS ALONE.
THIS MUST BE THE TOWER HE SCREAMED ABOUT.
BUT WHAT IS IT FOR?
AND WHO IS THE "BLUE LADY"?
FREEZE!

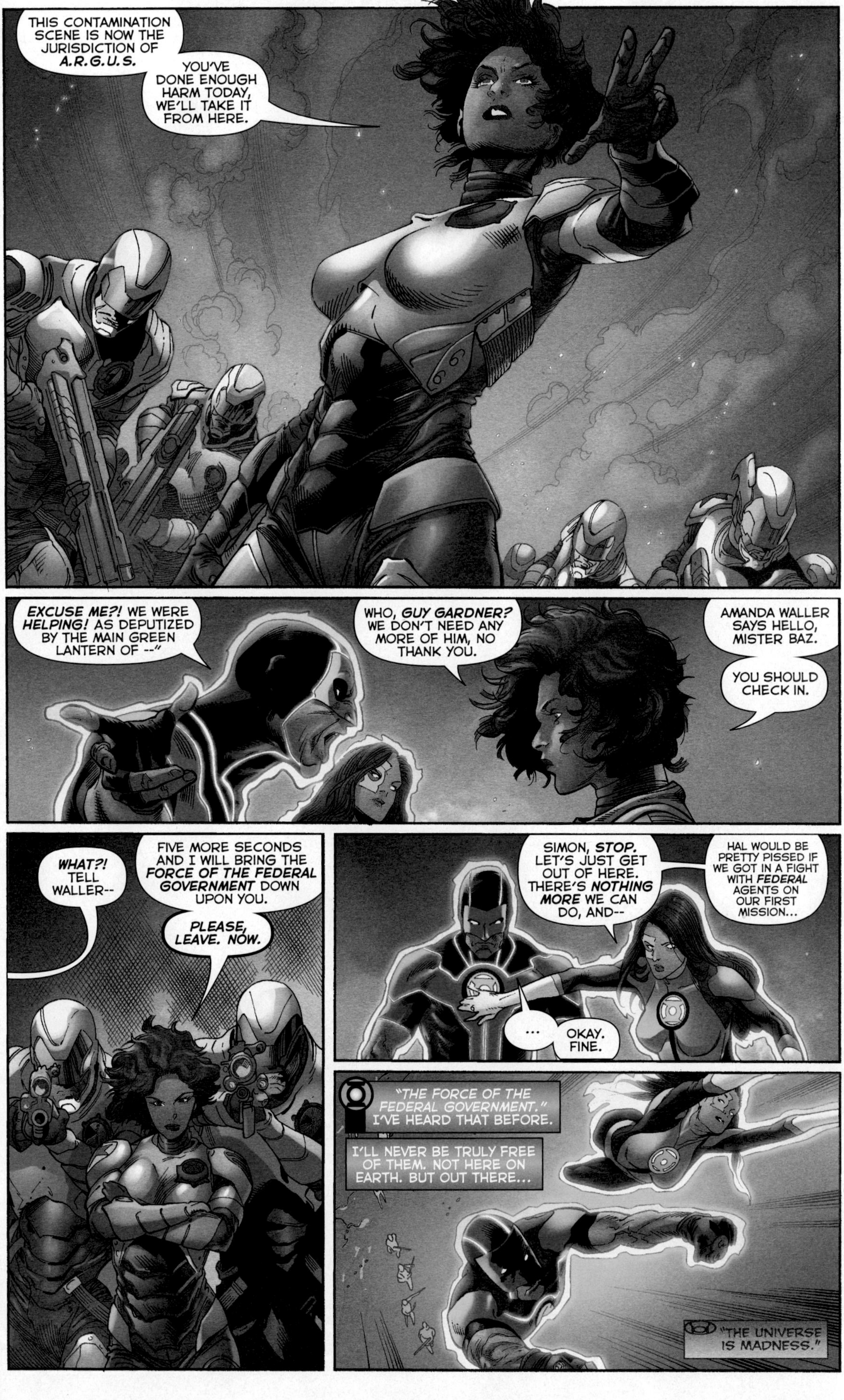
THIS CONTAMINATION SCENE IS NOW THE JURISDICTION OF A.R.G.U.S.
YOU'VE DONE ENOUGH HARM TODAY, WE'LL TAKE IT FROM HERE.
EXCUSE ME?! WE WERE HELPING! AS DEPUTIZED BY THE MAIN GREEN LANTERN OF --"
WHO, GUY GARDNER? WE DON'T NEED ANY MORE OF HIM, NO THANK YOU.
AMANDA WALLER SAYS HELLO, MISTER BAZ.
YOU SHOULD CHECK IN.
WHAT?! TELL WALLER--
FIVE MORE SECONDS AND I WILL BRING THE FORCE OF THE FEDERAL GOVERNMENT DOWN UPON YOU.
PLEASE, LEAVE. NOW.
SIMON, STOP. LET'S JUST GET OUT OF HERE. THERE'S NOTHING MORE WE CAN DO, AND--
HAL WOULD BE PRETTY PISSED IF WE GOT IN A FIGHT WITH FEDERAL AGENTS ON OUR FIRST MISSION...
...
OKAY. FINE.
"THE FORCE OF THE FEDERAL GOVERNMENT." I'VE HEARD THAT BEFORE.
I'LL NEVER BE TRULY FREE OF THEM. NOT HERE ON EARTH. BUT OUT THERE...
"THE UNIVERSE IS MADNESS."

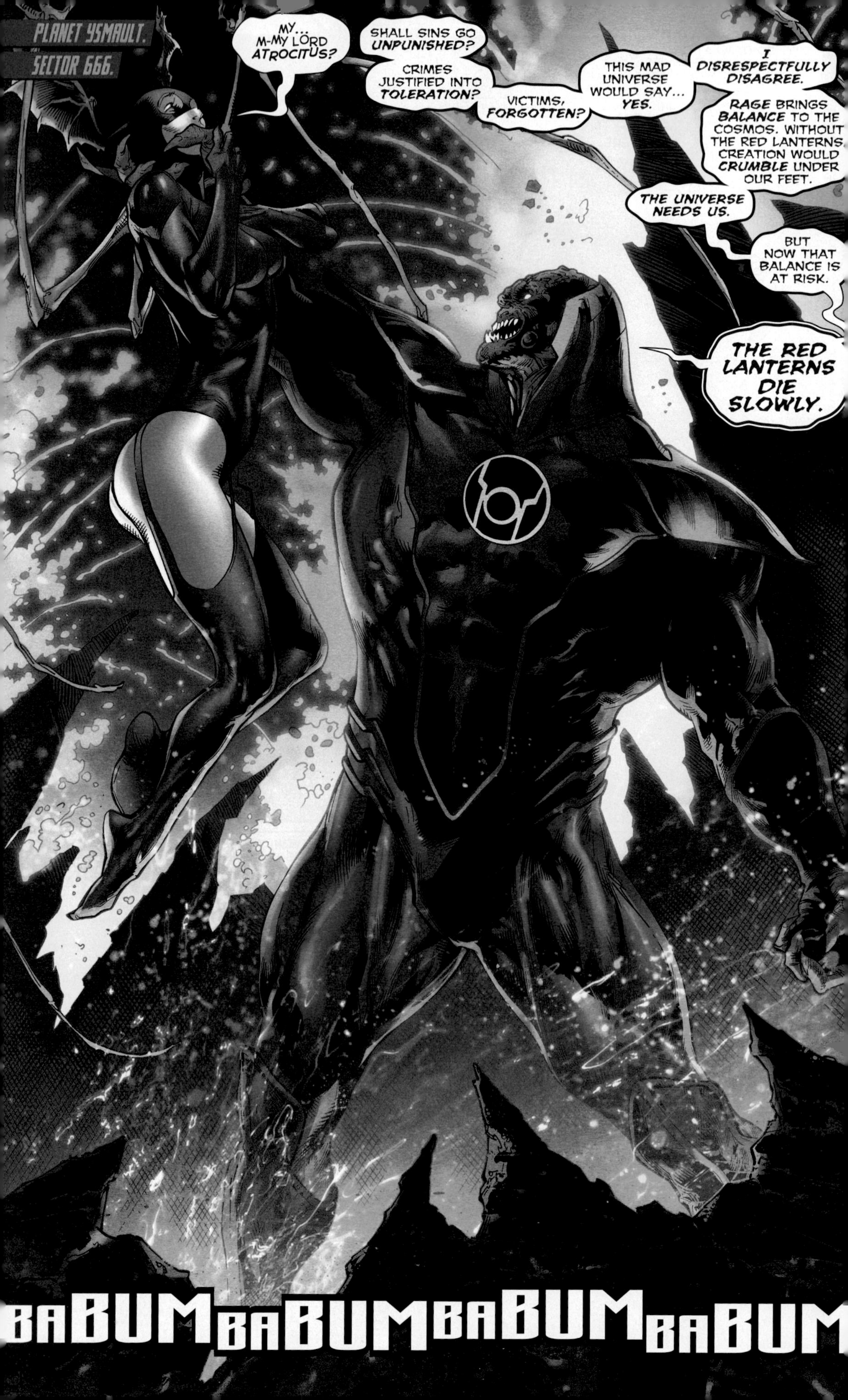
PLANET YSMAULT.
SECTOR 666.
MY... M-MY LORD ATROCITUS?
SHALL SINS GO UNPUNISHED?
CRIMES JUSTIFIED INTO TOLERATION?
VICTIMS, FORGOTTEN?
THIS MAD UNIVERSE WOULD SAY... YES.
I DISRESPECTFULLY DISAGREE.
RAGE BRINGS BALANCE TO THE COSMOS. WITHOUT THE RED LANTERNS, CREATION WOULD CRUMBLE UNDER OUR FEET.
THE UNIVERSE NEEDS US.
BUT NOW THAT BALANCE IS AT RISK.
THE RED LANTERNS DIE SLOWLY.
BABUMBABUMBABUMBABUM

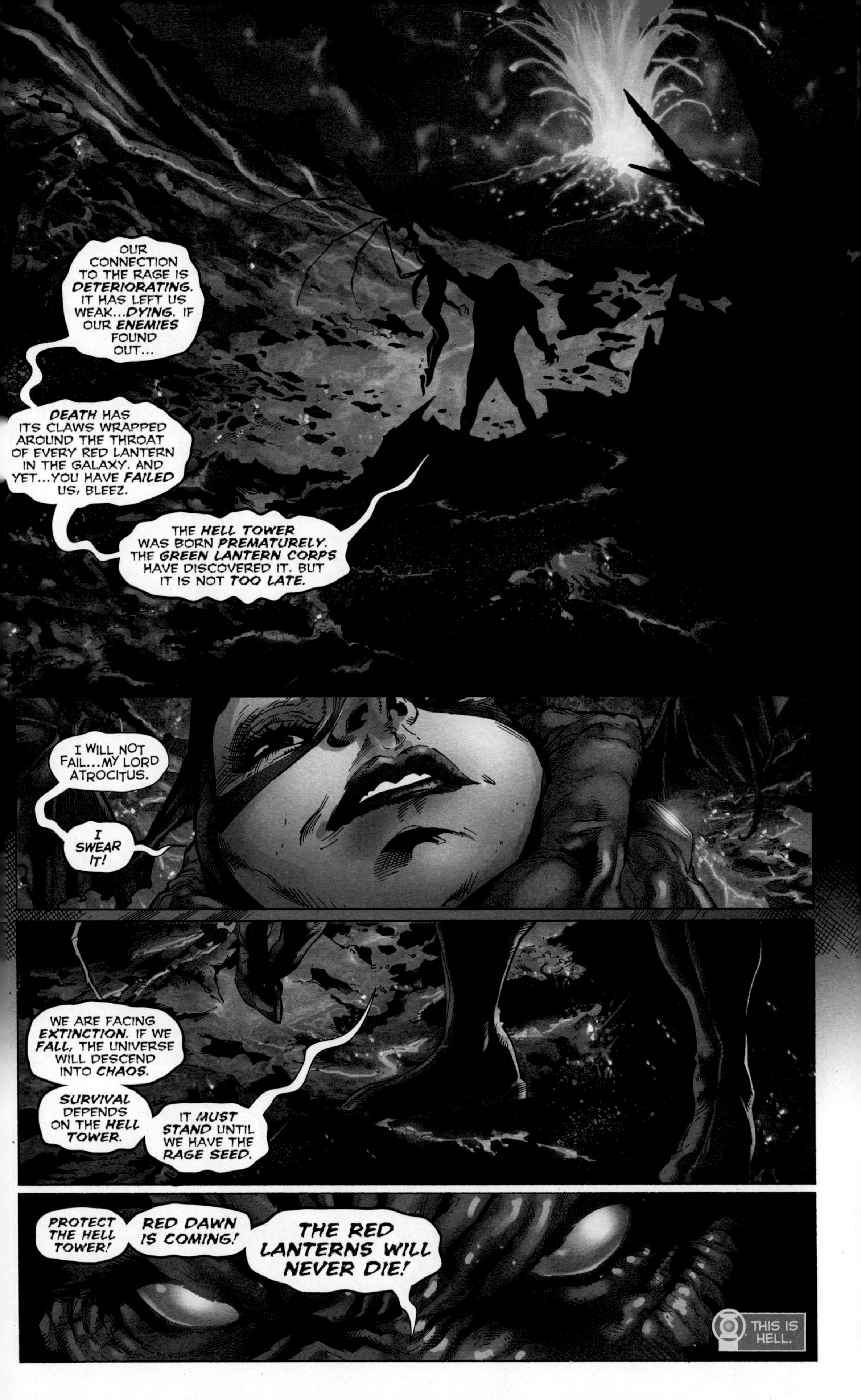
OUR CONNECTION TO THE RAGE IS DETERIORATING. IT HAS LEFT US WEAK...DYING. IF OUR ENEMIES FOUND OUT...
DEATH HAS ITS CLAWS WRAPPED AROUND THE THROAT OF EVERY RED LANTERN IN THE GALAXY. AND YET...YOU HAVE FAILED US, BLEEZ.
THE HELL TOWER WAS BORN PREMATURELY. THE GREEN LANTERN CORPS HAVE DISCOVERED IT. BUT IT IS NOT TOO LATE.
I WILL NOT FAIL...MY LORD ATROCITUS.
I SWEAR IT!
WE ARE FACING EXTINCTION. IF WE FALL, THE UNIVERSE WILL DESCEND INTO CHAOS.
SURVIVAL DEPENDS ON THE HELL TOWER.
IT MUST STAND UNTIL WE HAVE THE RAGE SEED.
PROTECT THE HELL TOWER!
RED DAWN IS COMING!
THE RED LANTERNS WILL NEVER DIE!
THIS IS HELL.

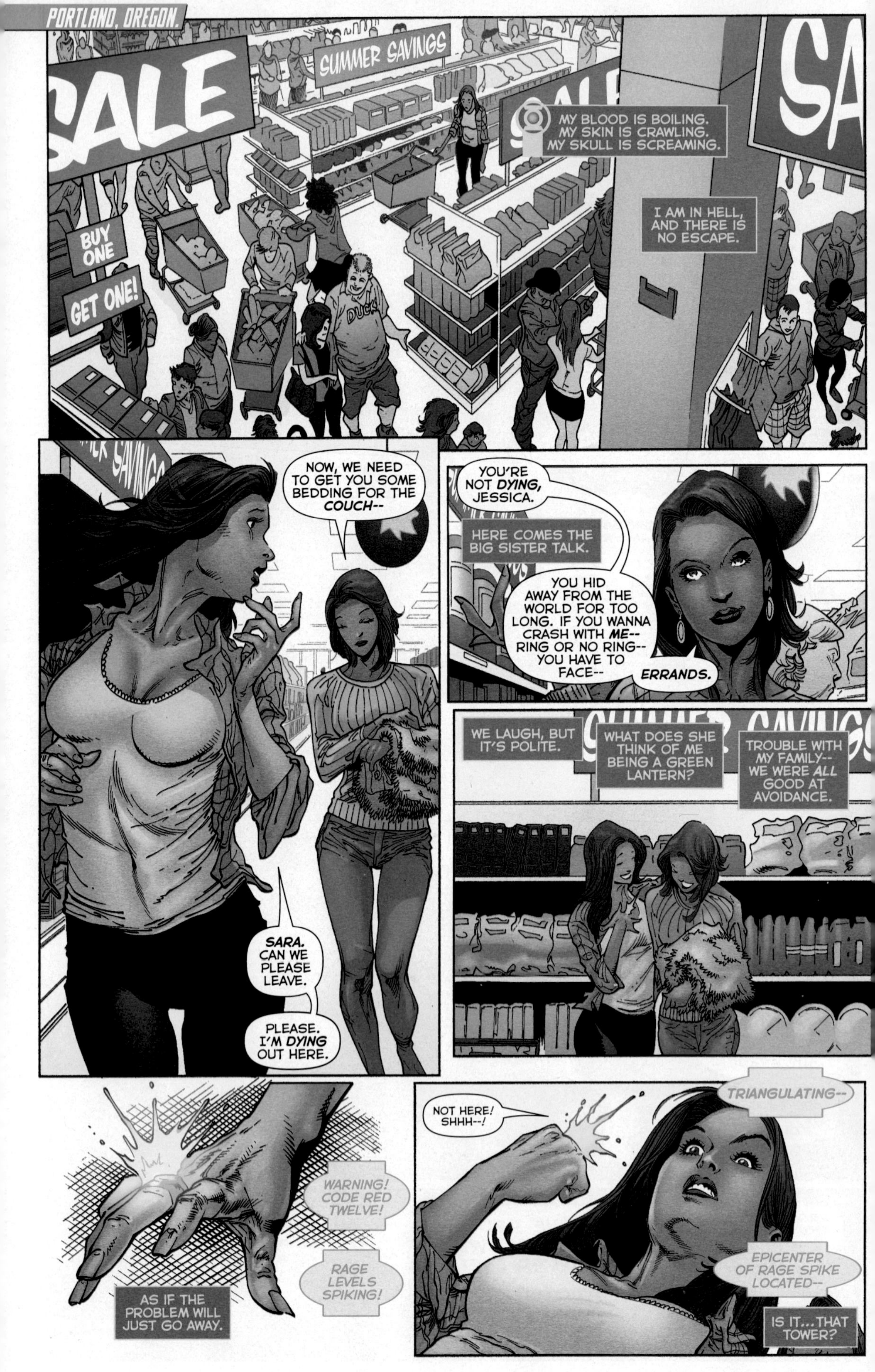
PORTLAND, OREGON.
SALE
SUMMER SAVINGS
BUY ONE
GET ONE!
DUCK
SALE
MY BLOOD IS BOILING. MY SKIN IS CRAWLING. MY SKULL IS SCREAMING.
I AM IN HELL, AND THERE IS NO ESCAPE.
NOW, WE NEED TO GET YOU SOME BEDDING FOR THE COUCH--
SARA. CAN WE PLEASE LEAVE.
PLEASE. I'M DYING OUT HERE.
YOU'RE NOT DYING, JESSICA.
HERE COMES THE BIG SISTER TALK.
YOU HID AWAY FROM THE WORLD FOR TOO LONG. IF YOU WANNA CRASH WITH ME-- RING OR NO RING-- YOU HAVE TO FACE--
ERRANDS.
WE LAUGH, BUT IT'S POLITE.
WHAT DOES SHE THINK OF ME BEING A GREEN LANTERN?
TROUBLE WITH MY FAMILY-- WE WERE ALL GOOD AT AVOIDANCE.
WARNING! CODE RED TWELVE!
RAGE LEVELS SPIKING!
AS IF THE PROBLEM WILL JUST GO AWAY.
NOT HERE! SHHH--!
TRIANGULATING--
EPICENTER OF RAGE SPIKE LOCATED--
IS IT...THAT TOWER?

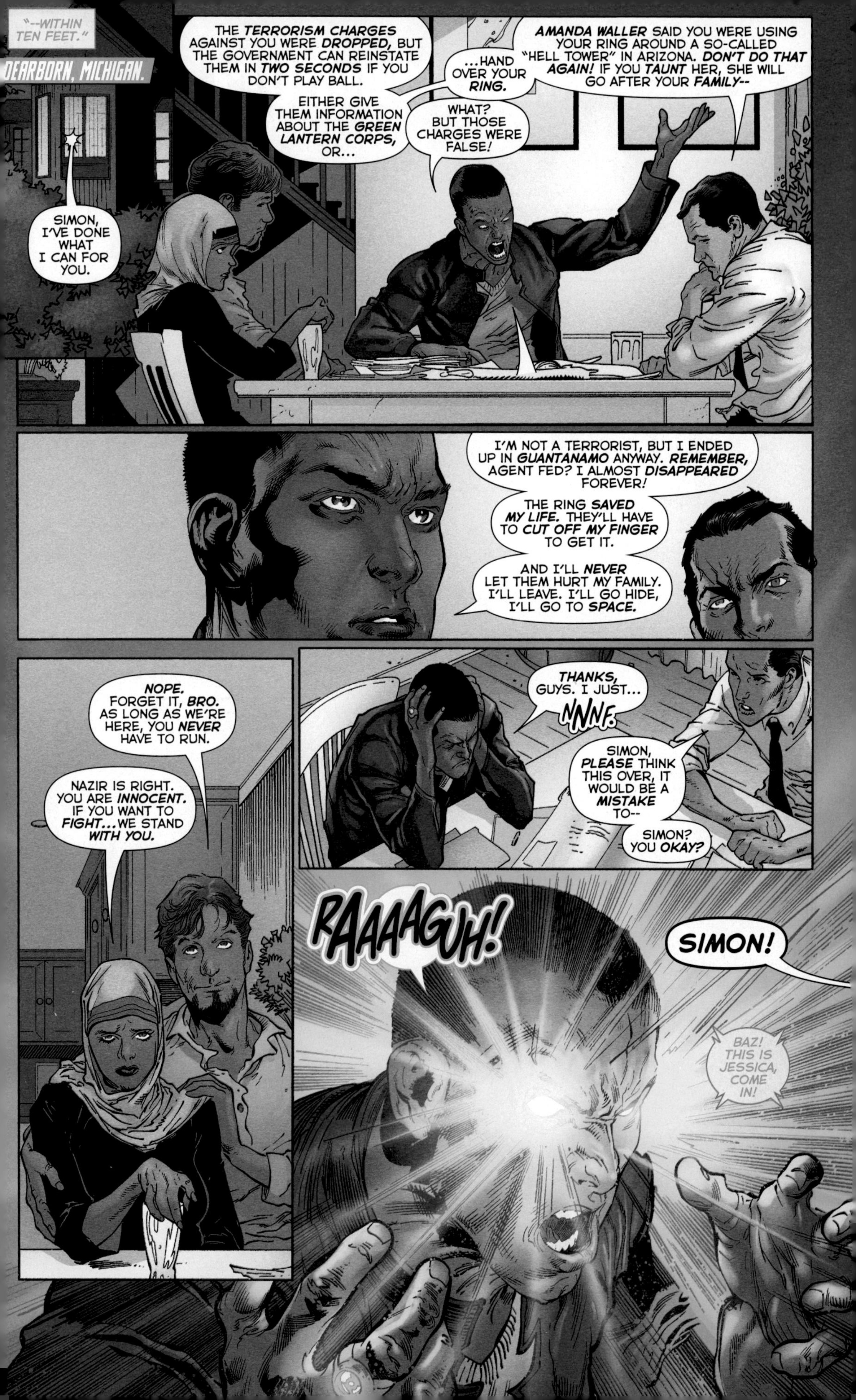
"--WITHIN TEN FEET."
DEARBORN, MICHIGAN.
THE TERRORISM CHARGES AGAINST YOU WERE DROPPED, BUT THE GOVERNMENT CAN REINSTATE THEM IN TWO SECONDS IF YOU DON'T PLAY BALL.
EITHER GIVE THEM INFORMATION ABOUT THE GREEN LANTERN CORPS, OR...
...HAND OVER YOUR RING.
WHAT? BUT THOSE CHARGES WERE FALSE!
AMANDA WALLER SAID YOU WERE USING YOUR RING AROUND A SO-CALLED "HELL TOWER" IN ARIZONA. DON'T DO THAT AGAIN! IF YOU TAUNT HER, SHE WILL GO AFTER YOUR FAMILY--
SIMON, I'VE DONE WHAT I CAN FOR YOU.
I'M NOT A TERRORIST, BUT I ENDED UP IN GUANTANAMO ANYWAY. REMEMBER, AGENT FED? I ALMOST DISAPPEARED FOREVER!
THE RING SAVED MY LIFE. THEY'LL HAVE TO CUT OFF MY FINGER TO GET IT.
AND I'LL NEVER LET THEM HURT MY FAMILY. I'LL LEAVE. I'LL GO HIDE, I'LL GO TO SPACE.
NOPE. FORGET IT, BRO. AS LONG AS WE'RE HERE, YOU NEVER HAVE TO RUN.
NAZIR IS RIGHT. YOU ARE INNOCENT. IF YOU WANT TO FIGHT...WE STAND WITH YOU.
THANKS, GUYS. I JUST...
NNNF.
SIMON, PLEASE THINK THIS OVER, IT WOULD BE A MISTAKE TO--
SIMON? YOU OKAY?
RAAAAGUH!
SIMON!
BAZ! THIS IS JESSICA, COME IN!

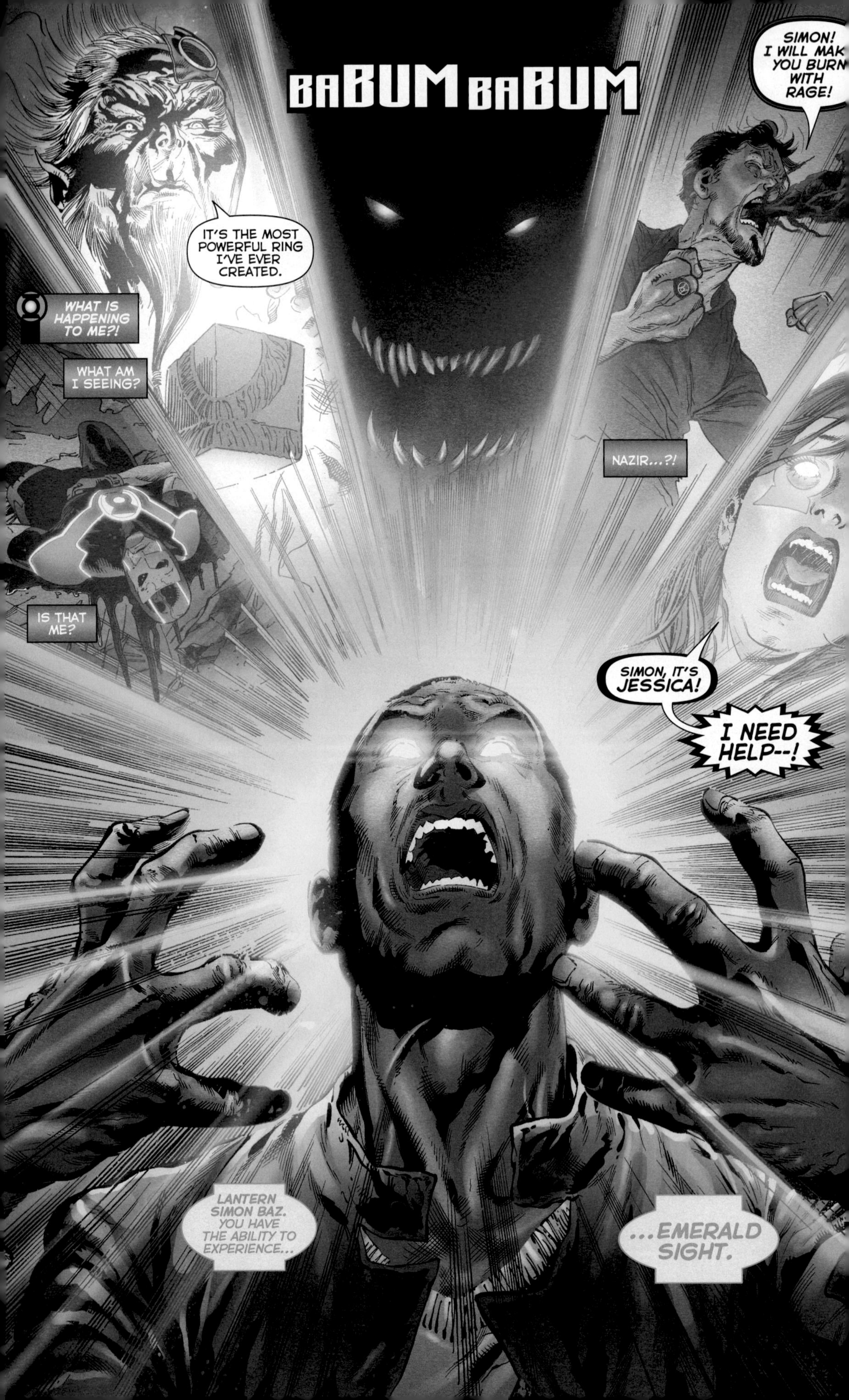
BABUM BABUM
IT'S THE MOST POWERFUL RING I'VE EVER CREATED.
SIMON! I WILL MAK YOU BURN WITH RAGE!
WHAT IS HAPPENING TO ME?!
WHAT AM I SEEING?
NAZIR...?!
IS THAT ME?
SIMON, IT'S JESSICA!
I NEED HELP--!
LANTERN SIMON BAZ. YOU HAVE THE ABILITY TO EXPERIENCE...
...EMERALD SIGHT.

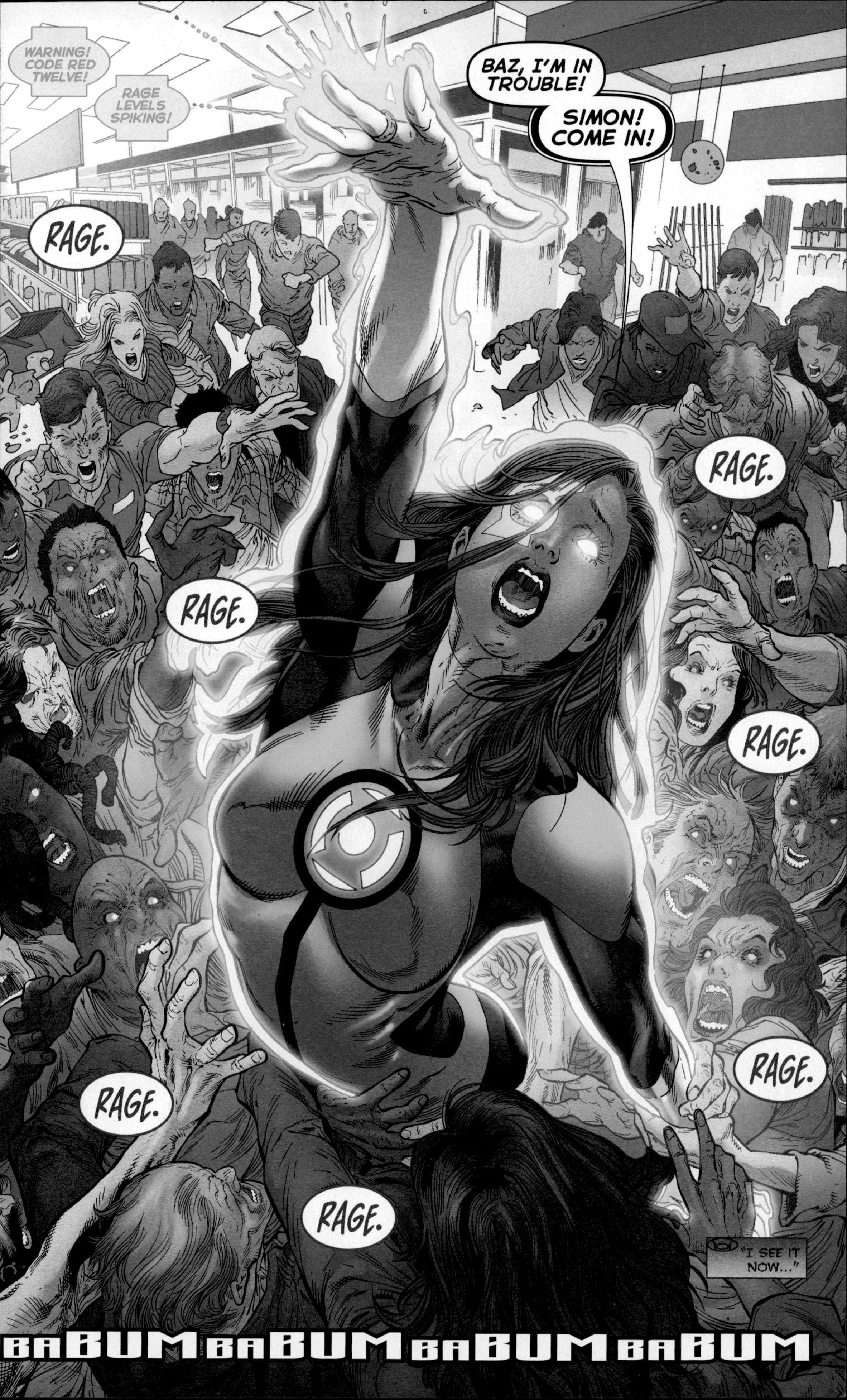
WARNING! CODE RED TWELVE!
RAGE LEVELS SPIKING!
BAZ, I'M IN TROUBLE!
SIMON! COME IN!
RAGE.
RAGE.
RAGE.
RAGE.
RAGE.
RAGE.
RAGE.
"I SEE IT NOW..."
BABUM BABUM BABUM BABUM

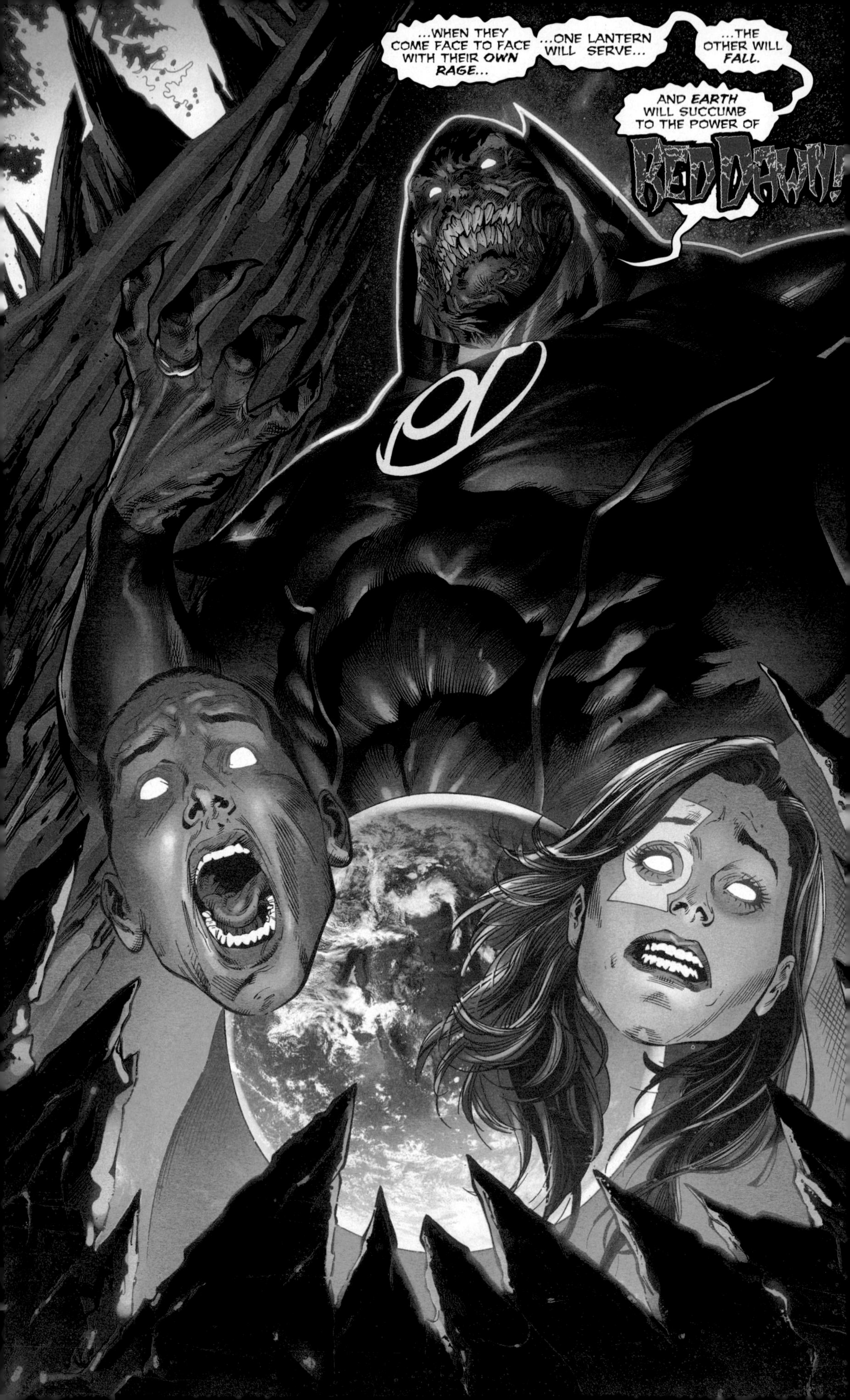

...WHEN THEY COME FACE TO FACE WITH THEIR OWN RAGE...
...ONE LANTERN WILL SERVE...
...THE OTHER WILL FALL.
AND EARTH WILL SUCCUMB TO THE POWER OF
RED DAWN!

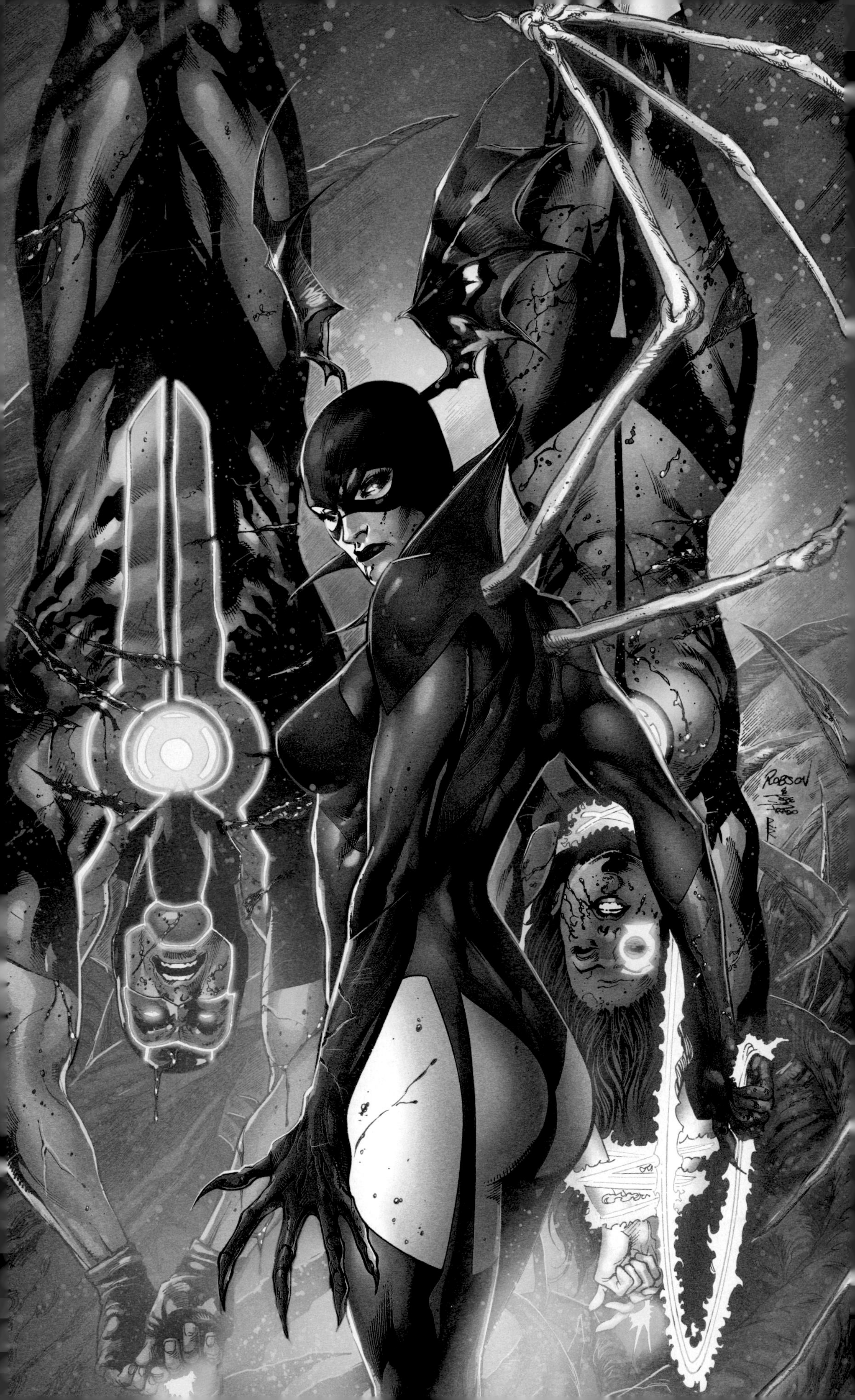

RAGE PLANET: PART 2

SAM HUMPHRIES writer * ROBSON ROCHA penciller * JAY LEISTEN inker
BLOND colorist * ROBSON ROCHA, JOE PRADO and ROD REIS cover artists

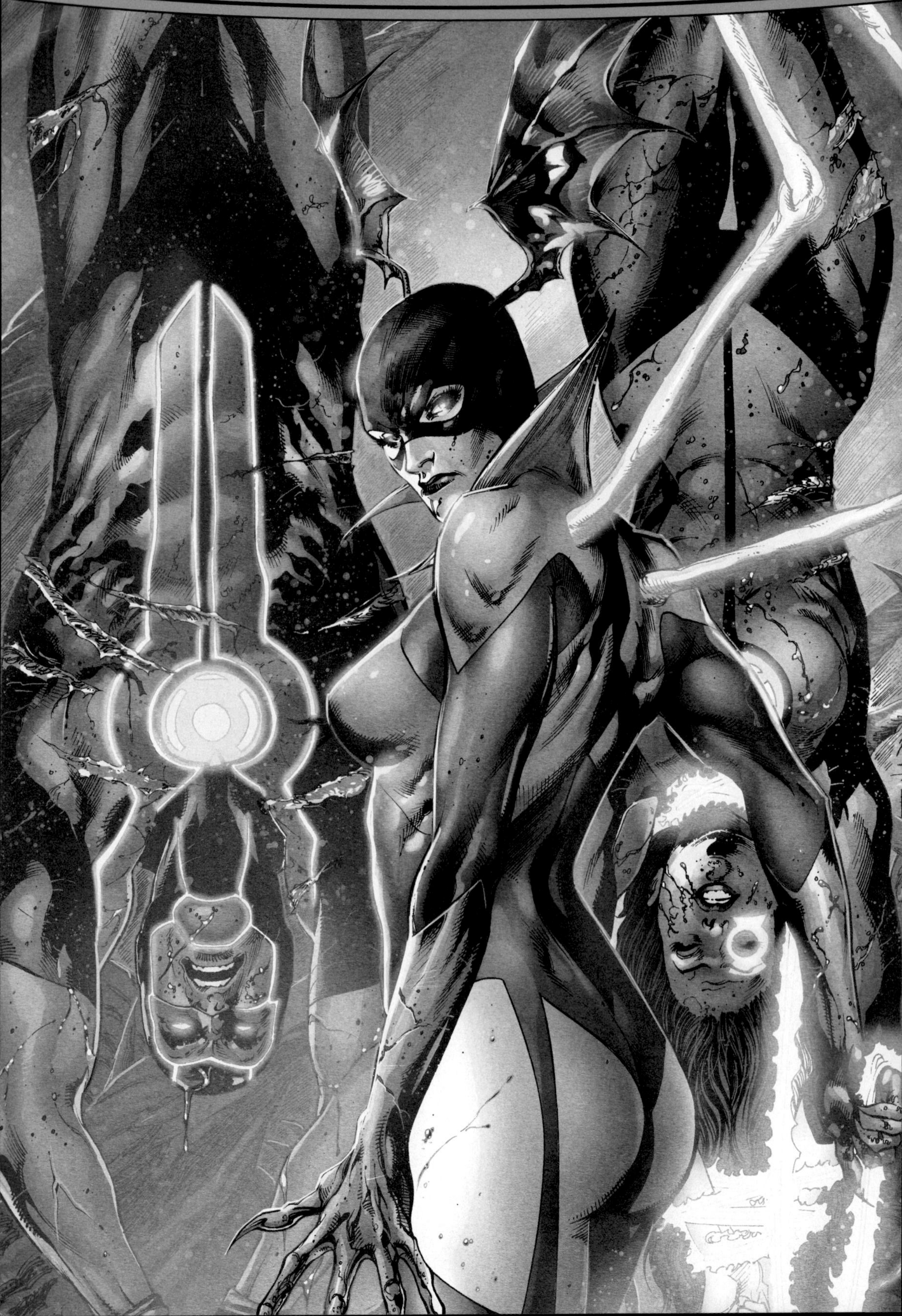

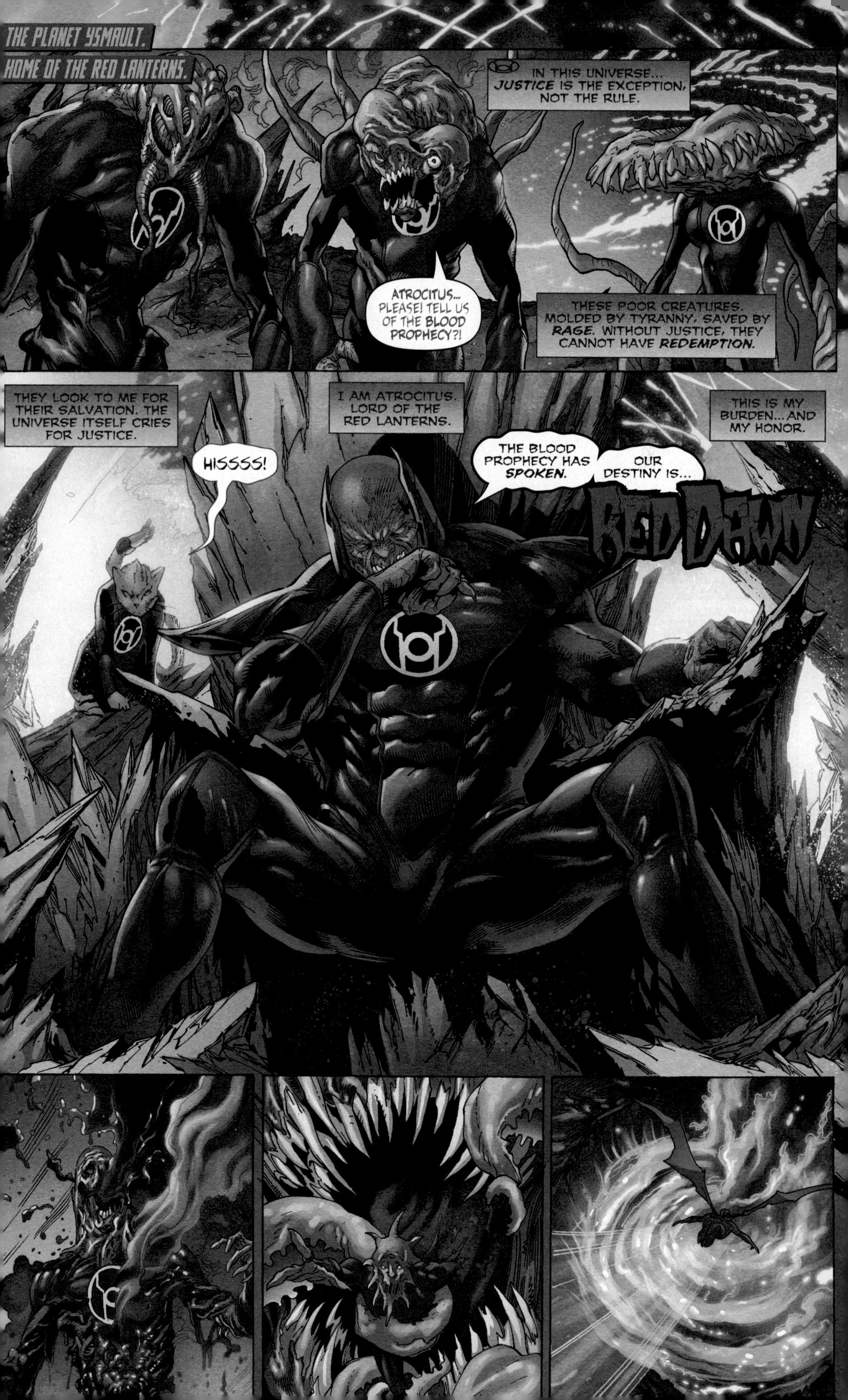
THE PLANET YSMAULT.
HOME OF THE RED LANTERNS.
IN THIS UNIVERSE... JUSTICE IS THE EXCEPTION, NOT THE RULE.
ATROCITUS... PLEASE! TELL US OF THE BLOOD PROPHECY?!
THESE POOR CREATURES. MOLDED BY TYRANNY, SAVED BY RAGE. WITHOUT JUSTICE, THEY CANNOT HAVE REDEMPTION.
THEY LOOK TO ME FOR THEIR SALVATION. THE UNIVERSE ITSELF CRIES FOR JUSTICE.
I AM ATROCITUS. LORD OF THE RED LANTERNS.
THIS IS MY BURDEN... AND MY HONOR.
HISSSS!
THE BLOOD PROPHECY HAS SPOKEN.
OUR DESTINY IS...
RED DAWN

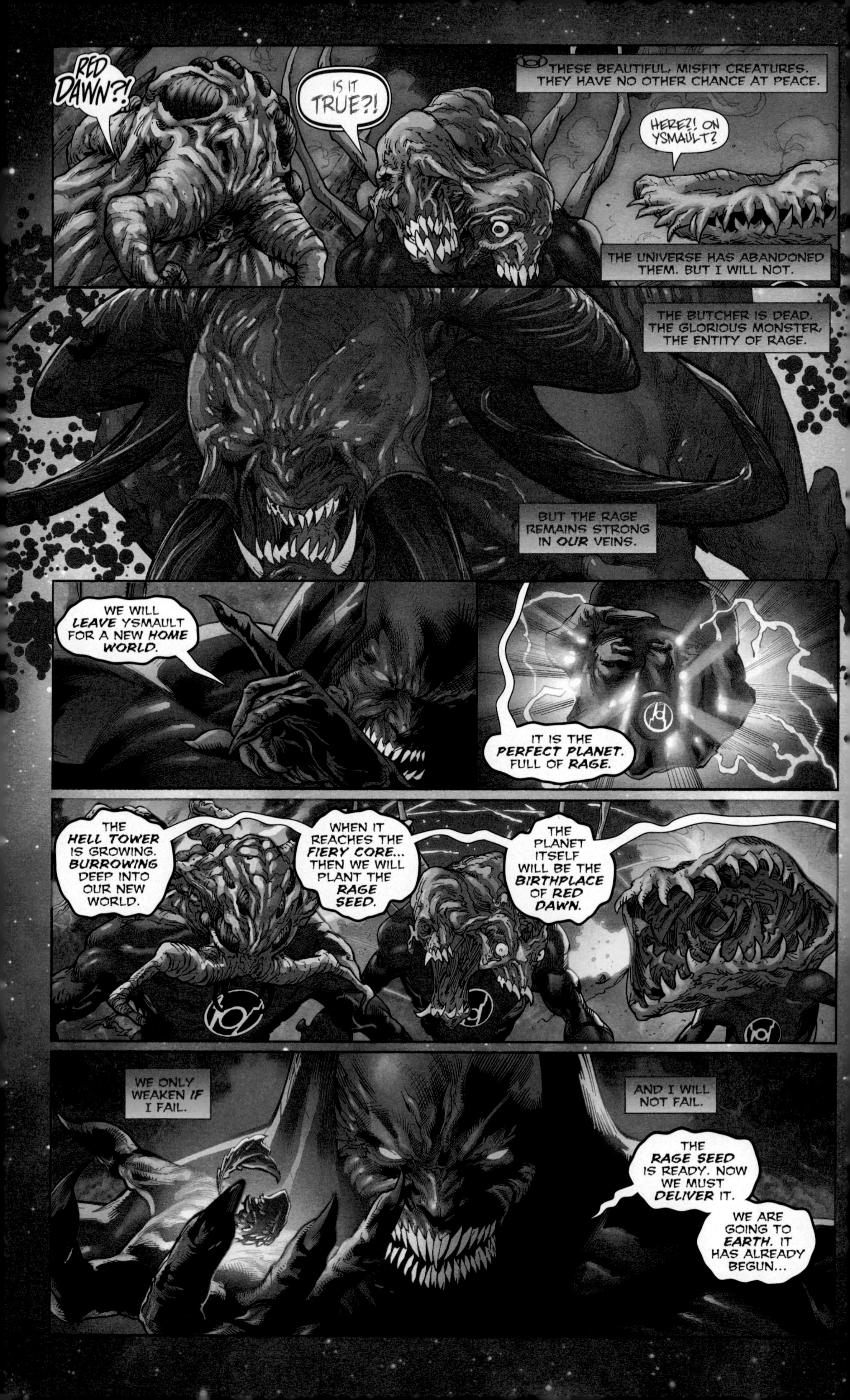
RED DAWN?!
IS IT TRUE?!
THESE BEAUTIFUL, MISFIT CREATURES. THEY HAVE NO OTHER CHANCE AT PEACE.
HERE?! ON YSMAULT?
THE UNIVERSE HAS ABANDONED THEM. BUT I WILL NOT.
THE BUTCHER IS DEAD. THE GLORIOUS MONSTER, THE ENTITY OF RAGE.
BUT THE RAGE REMAINS STRONG IN OUR VEINS.
WE WILL LEAVE YSMAULT FOR A NEW HOME WORLD.
IT IS THE PERFECT PLANET. FULL OF RAGE.
THE HELL TOWER IS GROWING. BURROWING DEEP INTO OUR NEW WORLD.
WHEN IT REACHES THE FIERY CORE... THEN WE WILL PLANT THE RAGE SEED.
THE PLANET ITSELF WILL BE THE BIRTHPLACE OF RED DAWN.
WE ONLY WEAKEN IF I FAIL.
AND I WILL NOT FAIL.
THE RAGE SEED IS READY. NOW WE MUST DELIVER IT.
WE ARE GOING TO EARTH. IT HAS ALREADY BEGUN...

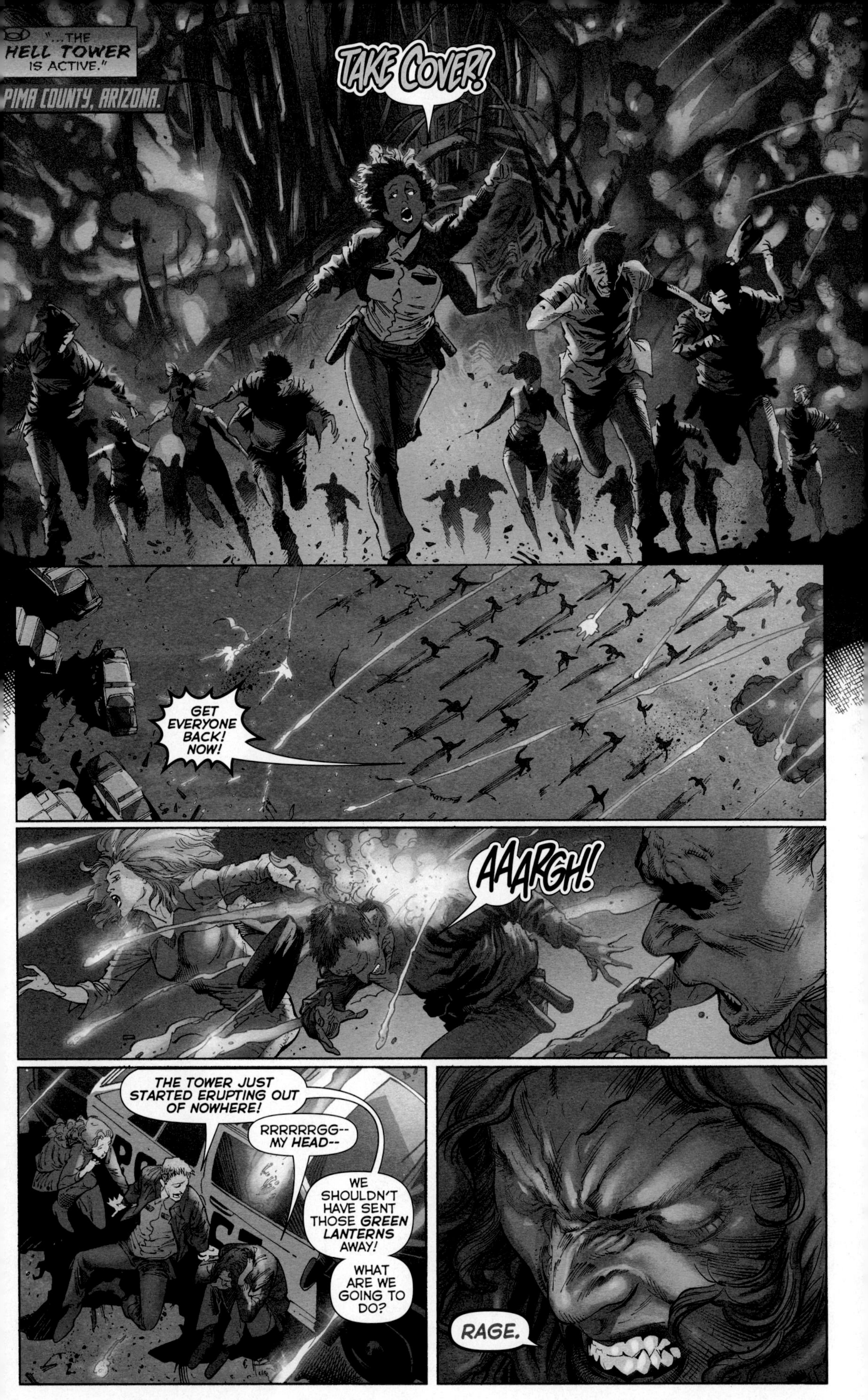
"...THE HELL TOWER IS ACTIVE."
PIMA COUNTY, ARIZONA.
TAKE COVER!
GET EVERYONE BACK! NOW!
AAARGH!
THE TOWER JUST STARTED ERUPTING OUT OF NOWHERE!
RRRRRRGG-- MY HEAD--
WE SHOULDN'T HAVE SENT THOSE GREEN LANTERNS AWAY!
WHAT ARE WE GOING TO DO?
RAGE.

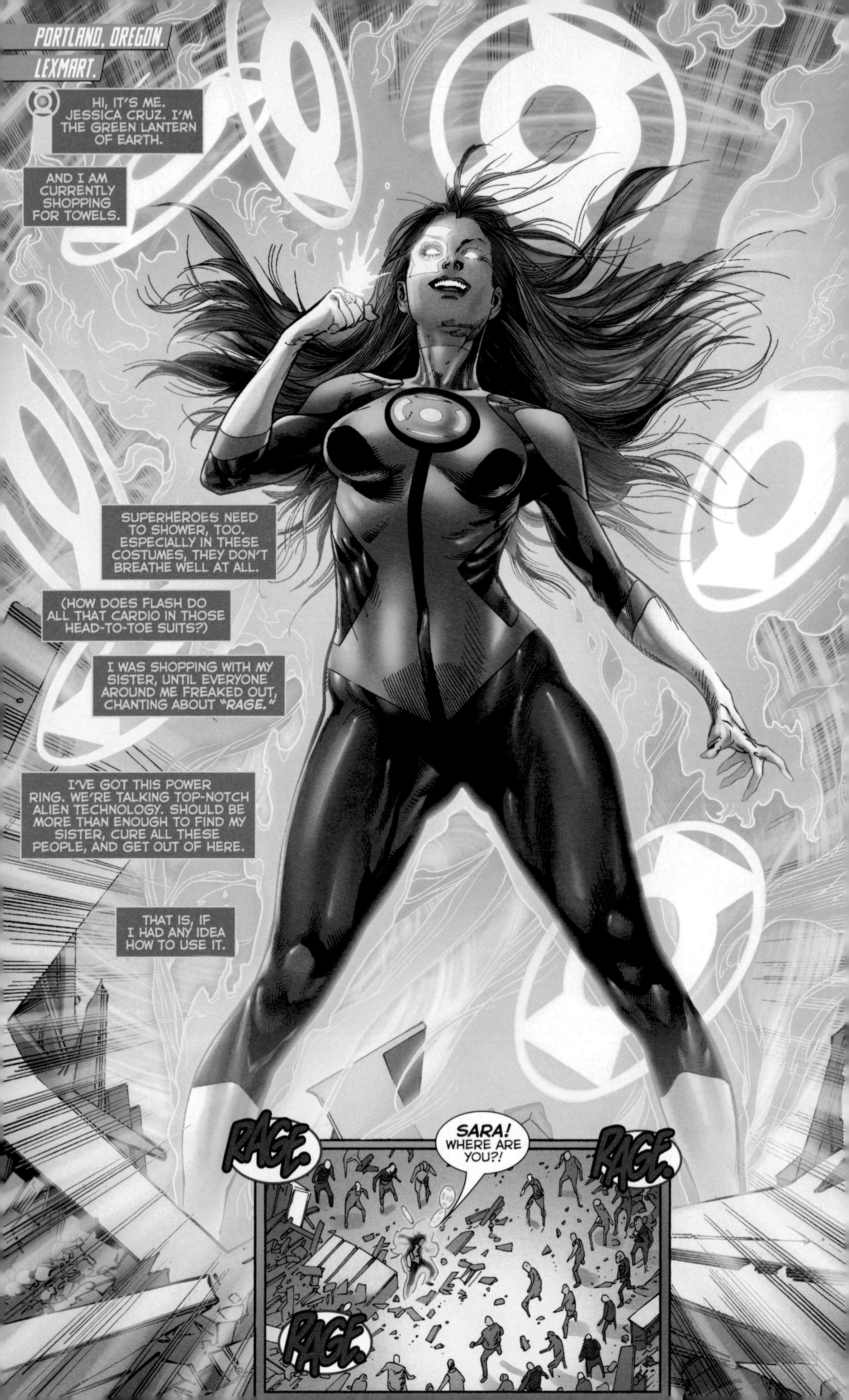
PORTLAND, OREGON.
LEXMART.
HI, IT'S ME. JESSICA CRUZ. I'M THE GREEN LANTERN OF EARTH.
AND I AM CURRENTLY SHOPPING FOR TOWELS.
SUPERHEROES NEED TO SHOWER, TOO. ESPECIALLY IN THESE COSTUMES, THEY DON'T BREATHE WELL AT ALL.
(HOW DOES FLASH DO ALL THAT CARDIO IN THOSE HEAD-TO-TOE SUITS?)
I WAS SHOPPING WITH MY SISTER, UNTIL EVERYONE AROUND ME FREAKED OUT, CHANTING ABOUT "RAGE."
I'VE GOT THIS POWER RING. WE'RE TALKING TOP-NOTCH ALIEN TECHNOLOGY. SHOULD BE MORE THAN ENOUGH TO FIND MY SISTER, CURE ALL THESE PEOPLE, AND GET OUT OF HERE.
THAT IS, IF I HAD ANY IDEA HOW TO USE IT.
RAGE.
SARA! WHERE ARE YOU?!
RAGE.
RAGE.

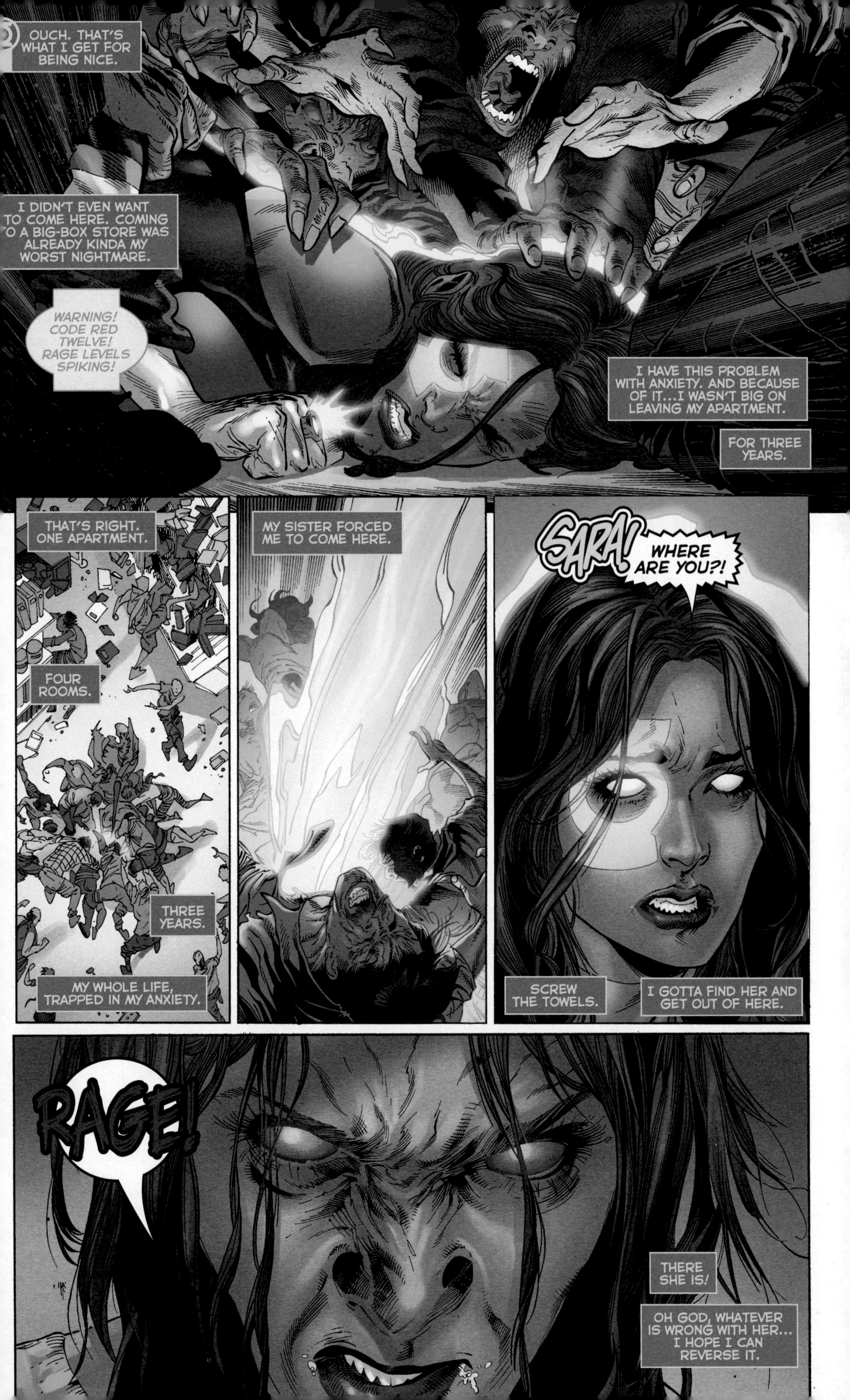

OUCH. THAT'S WHAT I GET FOR BEING NICE.
I DIDN'T EVEN WANT TO COME HERE. COMING O A BIG-BOX STORE WAS ALREADY KINDA MY WORST NIGHTMARE.
WARNING! CODE RED TWELVE! RAGE LEVELS SPIKING!
I HAVE THIS PROBLEM WITH ANXIETY. AND BECAUSE OF IT...I WASN'T BIG ON LEAVING MY APARTMENT.
FOR THREE YEARS.
THAT'S RIGHT. ONE APARTMENT.
FOUR ROOMS.
THREE YEARS.
MY WHOLE LIFE, TRAPPED IN MY ANXIETY.
MY SISTER FORCED ME TO COME HERE.
SARA! WHERE ARE YOU?!
SCREW THE TOWELS.
I GOTTA FIND HER AND GET OUT OF HERE.
RAGE!
THERE SHE IS!
OH GOD, WHATEVER IS WRONG WITH HER... I HOPE I CAN REVERSE IT.

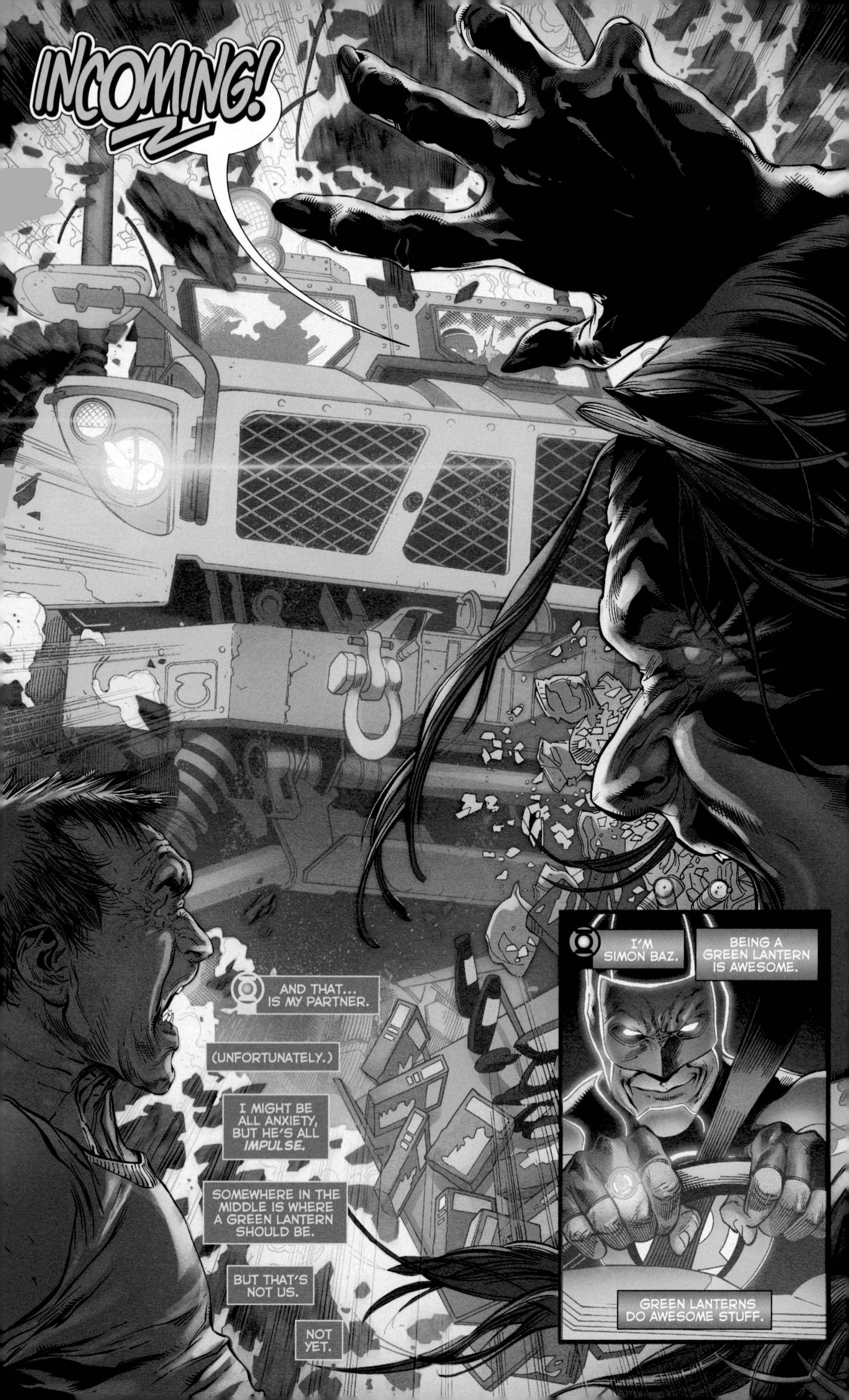
INCOMING!
AND THAT... IS MY PARTNER.
(UNFORTUNATELY.)
I MIGHT BE ALL ANXIETY, BUT HE'S ALL *IMPULSE.*
SOMEWHERE IN THE MIDDLE IS WHERE A GREEN LANTERN SHOULD BE.
BUT THAT'S NOT US.
NOT YET.
I'M SIMON BAZ.
BEING A GREEN LANTERN IS AWESOME.
GREEN LANTERNS DO AWESOME STUFF.

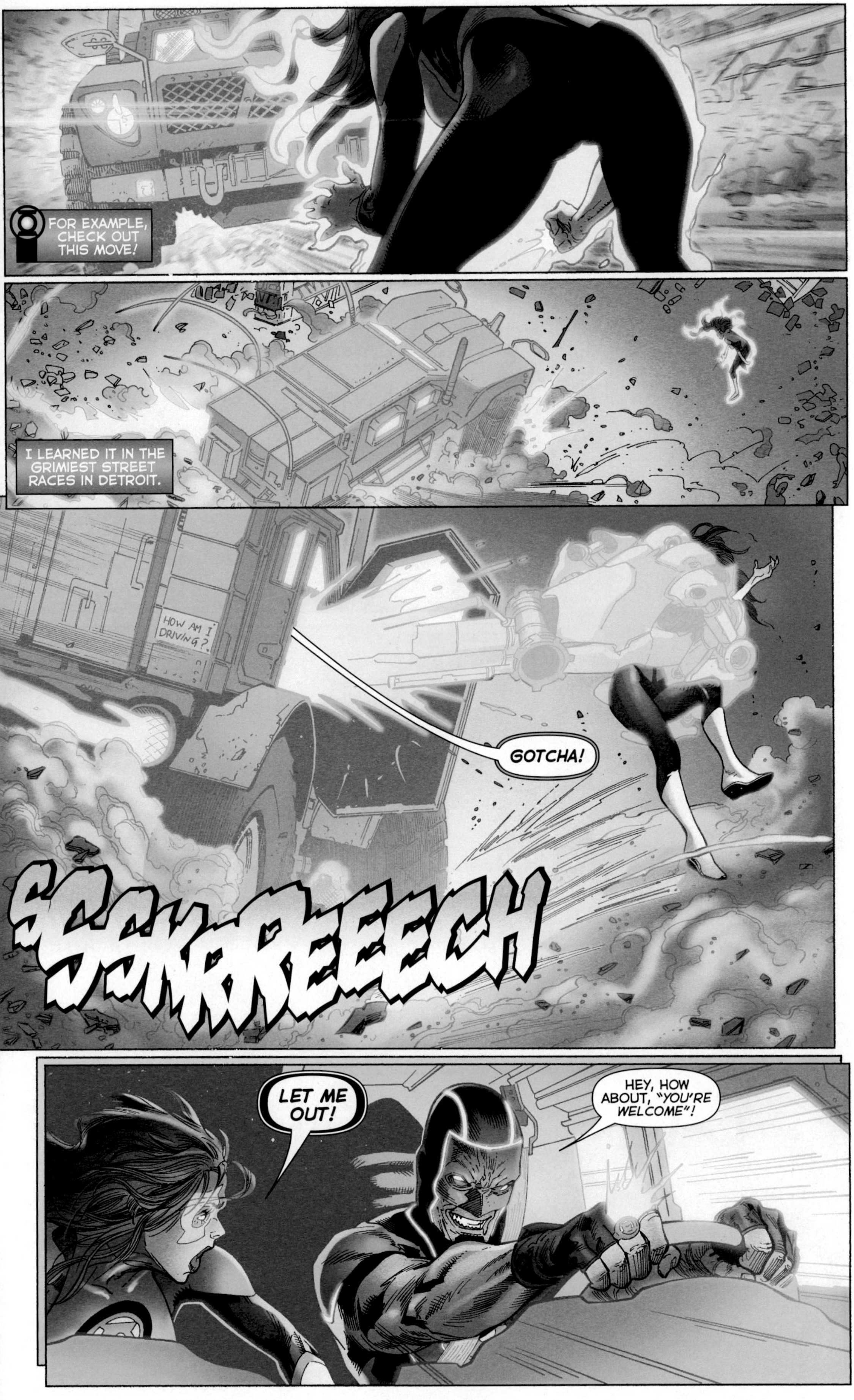
FOR EXAMPLE, CHECK OUT THIS MOVE!
I LEARNED IT IN THE GRIMIEST STREET RACES IN DETROIT.
HOW AM I DRIVING?
GOTCHA!
SSKKREEECH
LET ME OUT!
HEY, HOW ABOUT, "YOU'RE WELCOME"!

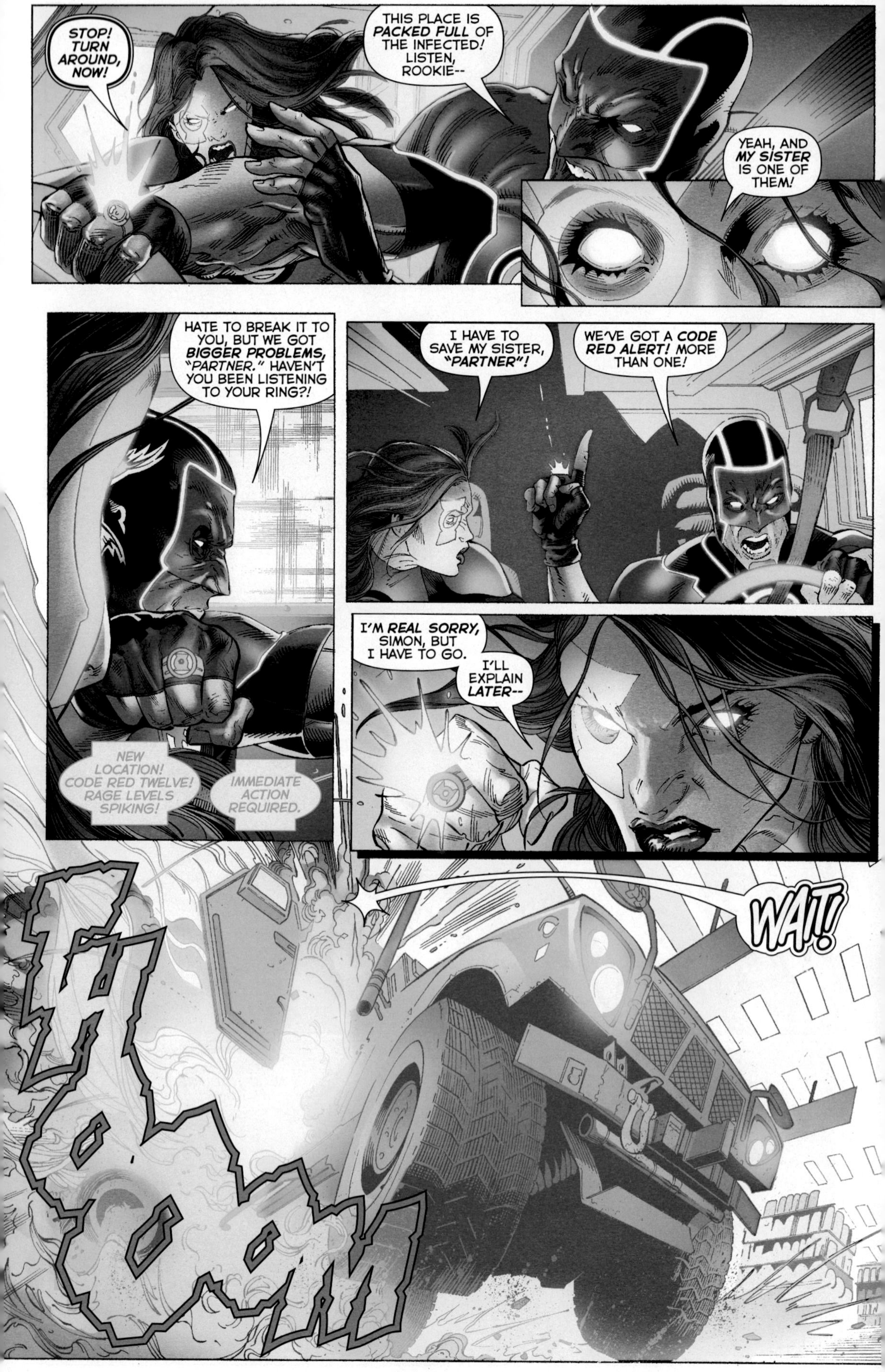
STOP! TURN AROUND, NOW!
THIS PLACE IS PACKED FULL OF THE INFECTED! LISTEN, ROOKIE--
YEAH, AND MY SISTER IS ONE OF THEM!
HATE TO BREAK IT TO YOU, BUT WE GOT BIGGER PROBLEMS, "PARTNER." HAVEN'T YOU BEEN LISTENING TO YOUR RING?!
NEW LOCATION! CODE RED TWELVE! RAGE LEVELS SPIKING!
IMMEDIATE ACTION REQUIRED.
I HAVE TO SAVE MY SISTER, "PARTNER"!
WE'VE GOT A CODE RED ALERT! MORE THAN ONE!
I'M REAL SORRY, SIMON, BUT I HAVE TO GO.
I'LL EXPLAIN LATER--
WAIT!

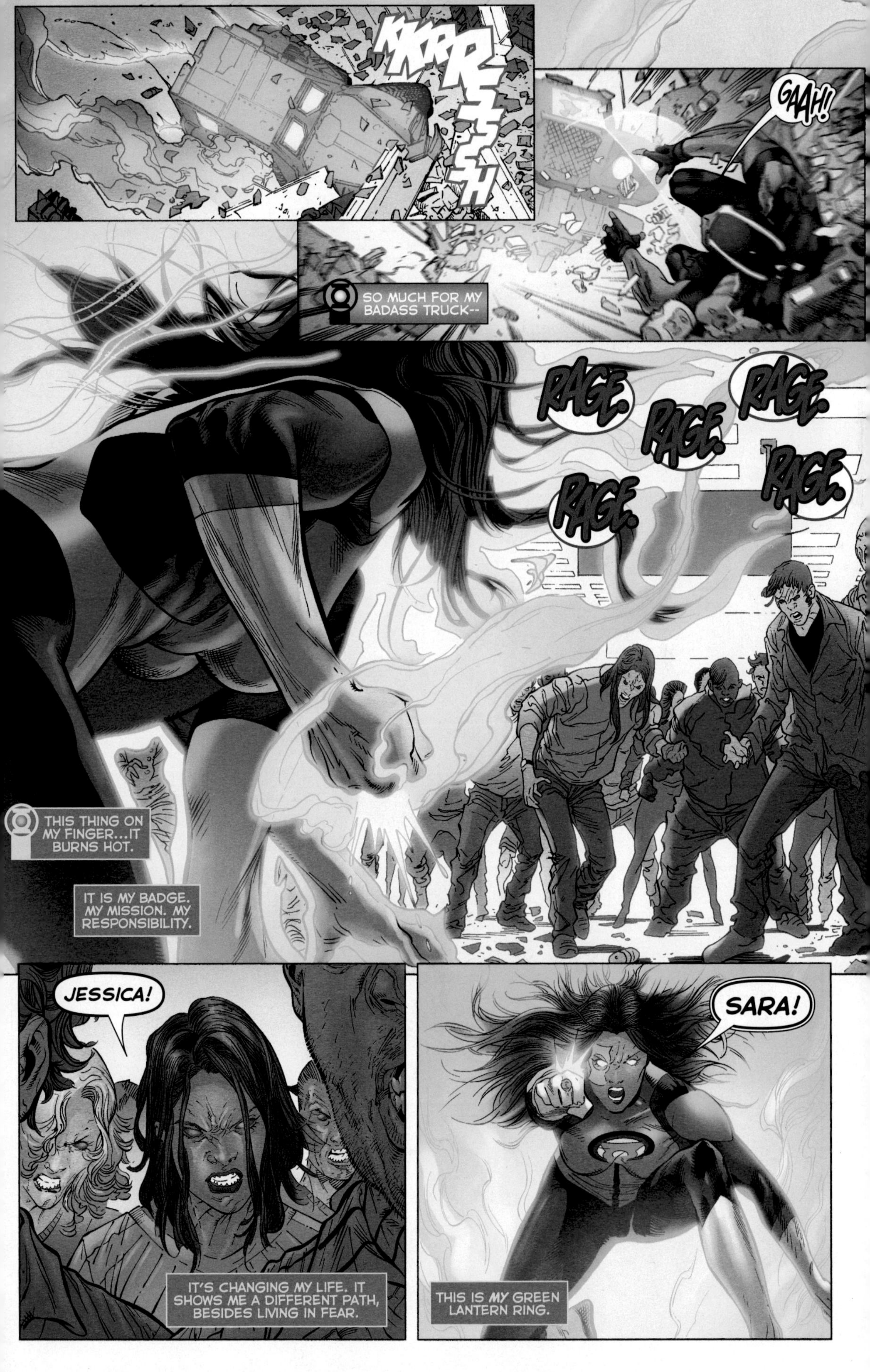
KKORRESSHH
GAAH!
SO MUCH FOR MY BADASS TRUCK--
RAGE.
RAGE.
RAGE.
RAGE.
RAGE.
THIS THING ON MY FINGER...IT BURNS HOT.
IT IS MY BADGE. MY MISSION. MY RESPONSIBILITY.
JESSICA!
IT'S CHANGING MY LIFE. IT SHOWS ME A DIFFERENT PATH, BESIDES LIVING IN FEAR.
SARA!
THIS IS *MY* GREEN LANTERN RING.

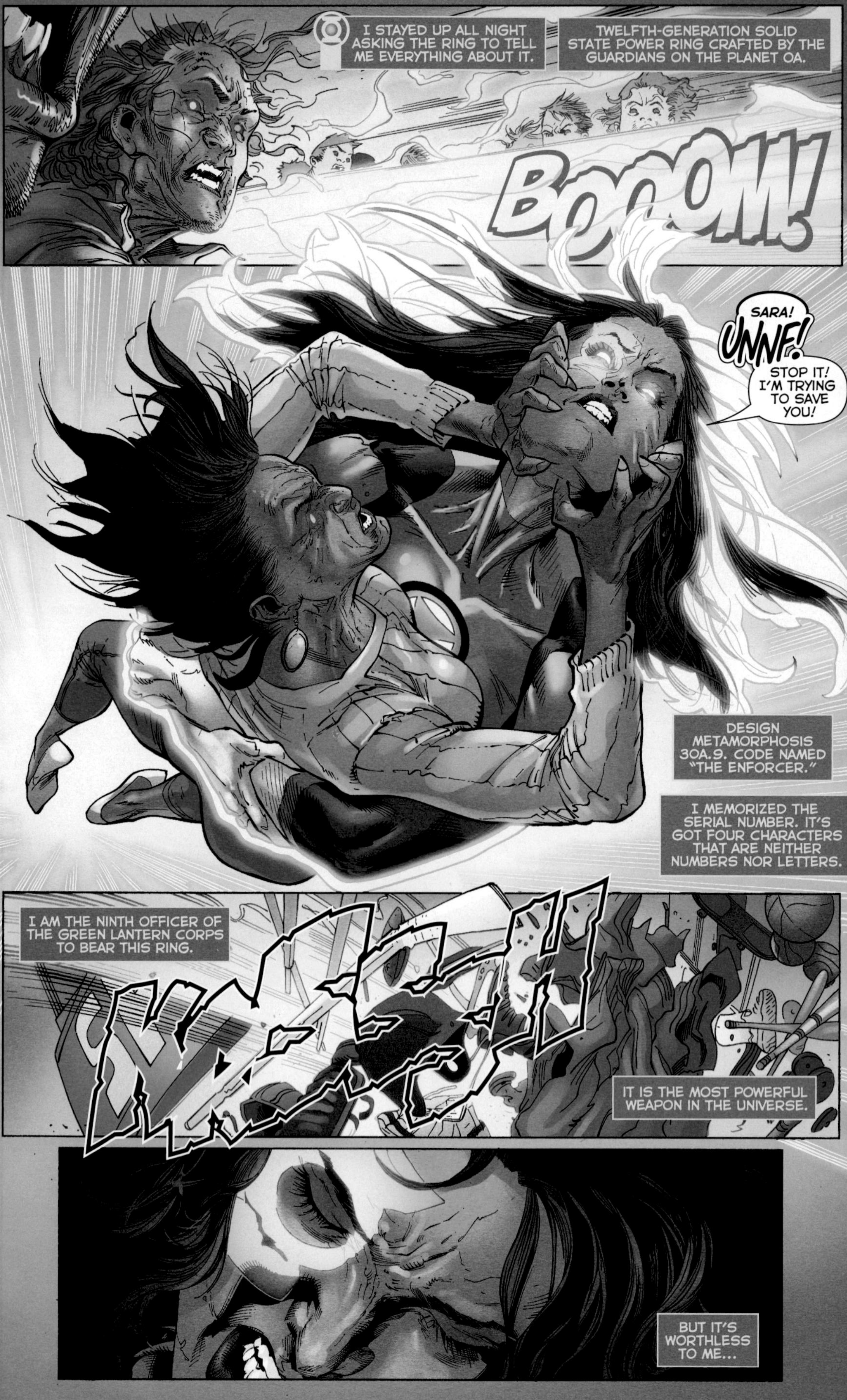
I STAYED UP ALL NIGHT ASKING THE RING TO TELL ME EVERYTHING ABOUT IT.
TWELFTH-GENERATION SOLID STATE POWER RING CRAFTED BY THE GUARDIANS ON THE PLANET OA.
BOOOOM!
SARA!
UNNF!
STOP IT! I'M TRYING TO SAVE YOU!
DESIGN METAMORPHOSIS 30A.9. CODE NAMED "THE ENFORCER."
I MEMORIZED THE SERIAL NUMBER. IT'S GOT FOUR CHARACTERS THAT ARE NEITHER NUMBERS NOR LETTERS.
I AM THE NINTH OFFICER OF THE GREEN LANTERN CORPS TO BEAR THIS RING.
IT IS THE MOST POWERFUL WEAPON IN THE UNIVERSE.
BUT IT'S WORTHLESS TO ME...

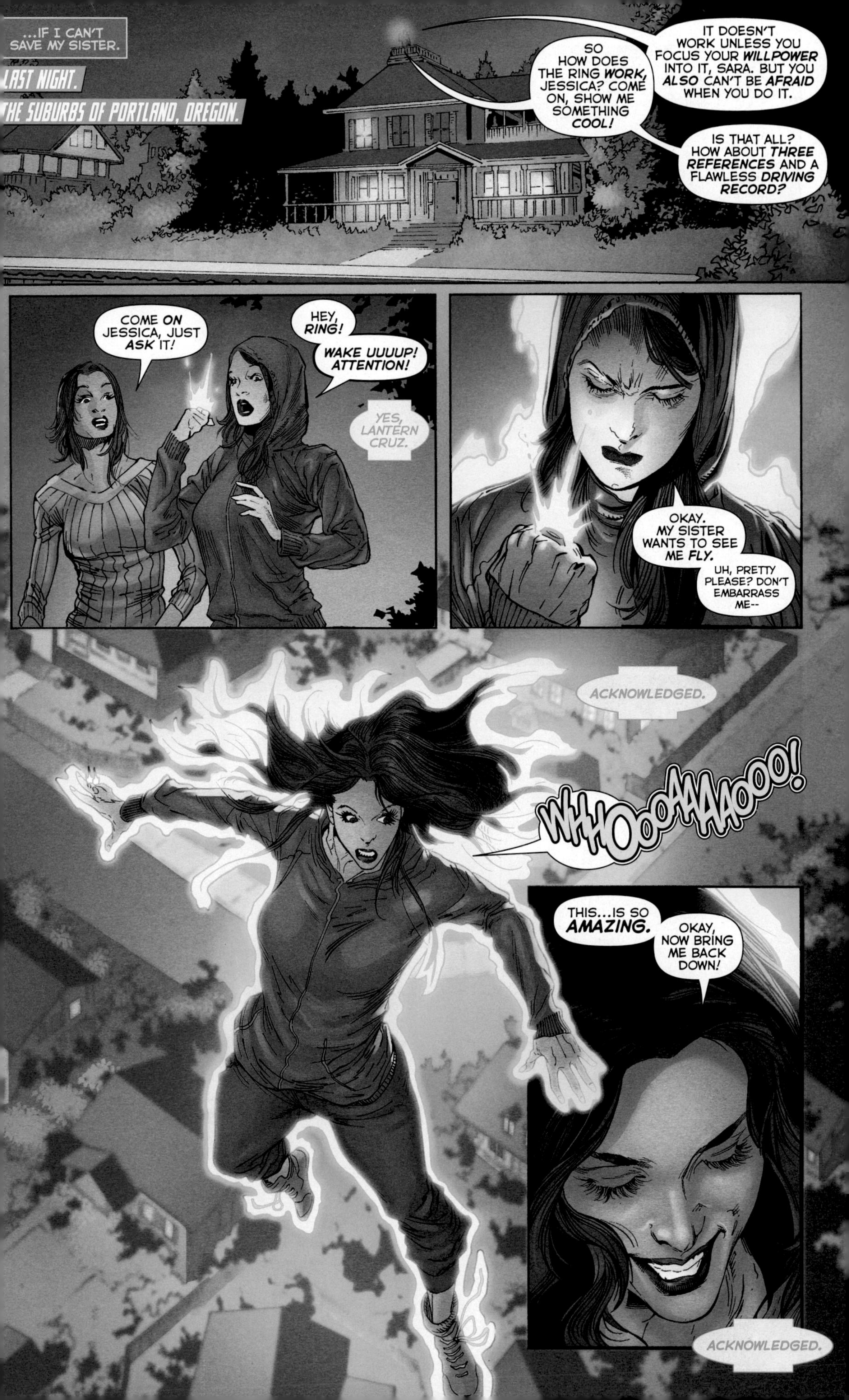
...IF I CAN'T SAVE MY SISTER.
LAST NIGHT.
THE SUBURBS OF PORTLAND, OREGON.
SO HOW DOES THE RING WORK, JESSICA? COME ON, SHOW ME SOMETHING COOL!
IT DOESN'T WORK UNLESS YOU FOCUS YOUR WILLPOWER INTO IT, SARA. BUT YOU ALSO CAN'T BE AFRAID WHEN YOU DO IT.
IS THAT ALL? HOW ABOUT THREE REFERENCES AND A FLAWLESS DRIVING RECORD?
COME ON JESSICA, JUST ASK IT!
HEY, RING!
WAKE UUUUP! ATTENTION!
YES, LANTERN CRUZ.
OKAY. MY SISTER WANTS TO SEE ME FLY.
UH, PRETTY PLEASE? DON'T EMBARRASS ME--
ACKNOWLEDGED.
WHHOOoAAAAOOO!
THIS...IS SO AMAZING.
OKAY, NOW BRING ME BACK DOWN!
ACKNOWLEDGED.

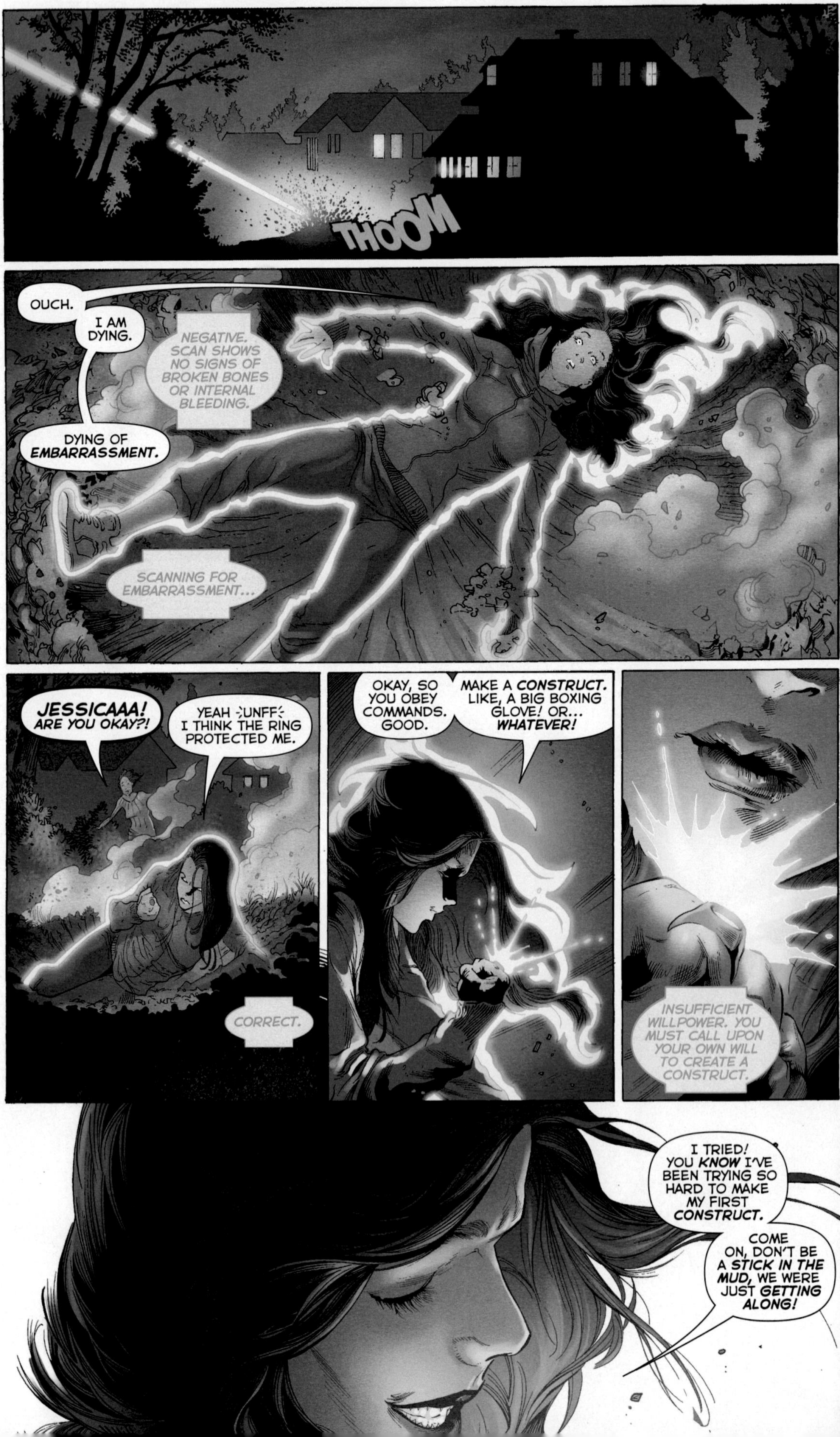

THOOM
OUCH.
I AM DYING.
NEGATIVE. SCAN SHOWS NO SIGNS OF BROKEN BONES OR INTERNAL BLEEDING.
DYING OF EMBARRASSMENT.
SCANNING FOR EMBARRASSMENT...
JESSICAAA! ARE YOU OKAY?!
YEAH -UNFF- I THINK THE RING PROTECTED ME.
CORRECT.
OKAY, SO YOU OBEY COMMANDS. GOOD.
MAKE A CONSTRUCT. LIKE, A BIG BOXING GLOVE! OR... WHATEVER!
INSUFFICIENT WILLPOWER. YOU MUST CALL UPON YOUR OWN WILL TO CREATE A CONSTRUCT.
I TRIED! YOU KNOW I'VE BEEN TRYING SO HARD TO MAKE MY FIRST CONSTRUCT.
COME ON, DON'T BE A STICK IN THE MUD, WE WERE JUST GETTING ALONG!

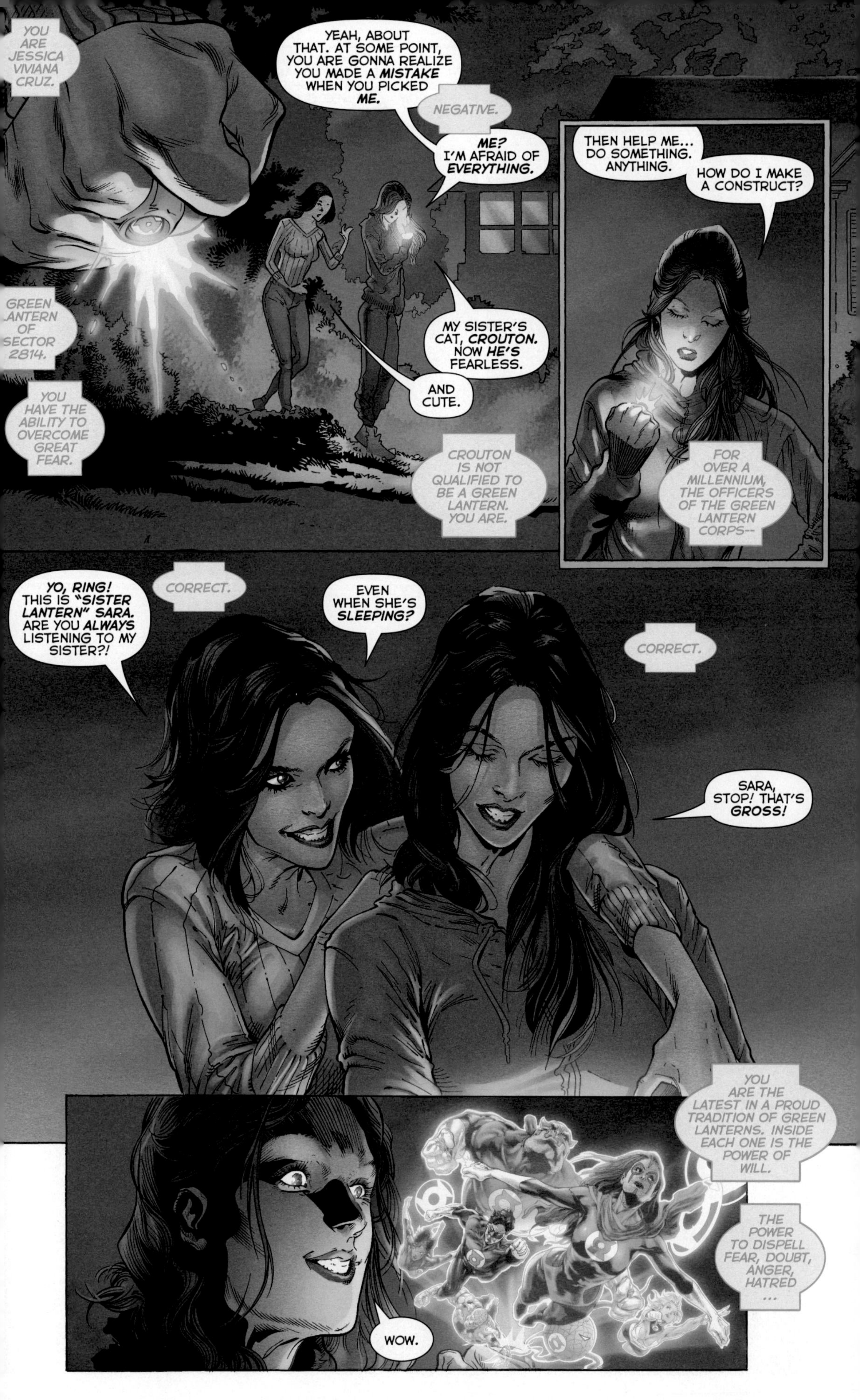
YOU ARE JESSICA VIVIANA CRUZ.
GREEN LANTERN OF SECTOR 2814.
YEAH, ABOUT THAT. AT SOME POINT, YOU ARE GONNA REALIZE YOU MADE A **MISTAKE** WHEN YOU PICKED **ME.**
NEGATIVE.
YOU HAVE THE ABILITY TO OVERCOME GREAT FEAR.
ME? I'M AFRAID OF **EVERYTHING.**
MY SISTER'S CAT, **CROUTON.** NOW **HE'S** FEARLESS.
AND CUTE.
CROUTON IS NOT QUALIFIED TO BE A GREEN LANTERN. YOU ARE.
THEN HELP ME... DO SOMETHING. ANYTHING.
HOW DO I MAKE A CONSTRUCT?
FOR OVER A MILLENNIUM, THE OFFICERS OF THE GREEN LANTERN CORPS--
YO, RING! THIS IS **"SISTER LANTERN" SARA.** ARE YOU **ALWAYS** LISTENING TO MY SISTER?!
CORRECT.
EVEN WHEN SHE'S **SLEEPING?**
CORRECT.
SARA, STOP! THAT'S **GROSS!**
YOU ARE THE LATEST IN A PROUD TRADITION OF GREEN LANTERNS. INSIDE EACH ONE IS THE POWER OF WILL.
THE POWER TO DISPELL FEAR, DOUBT, ANGER, HATRED ...
WOW.

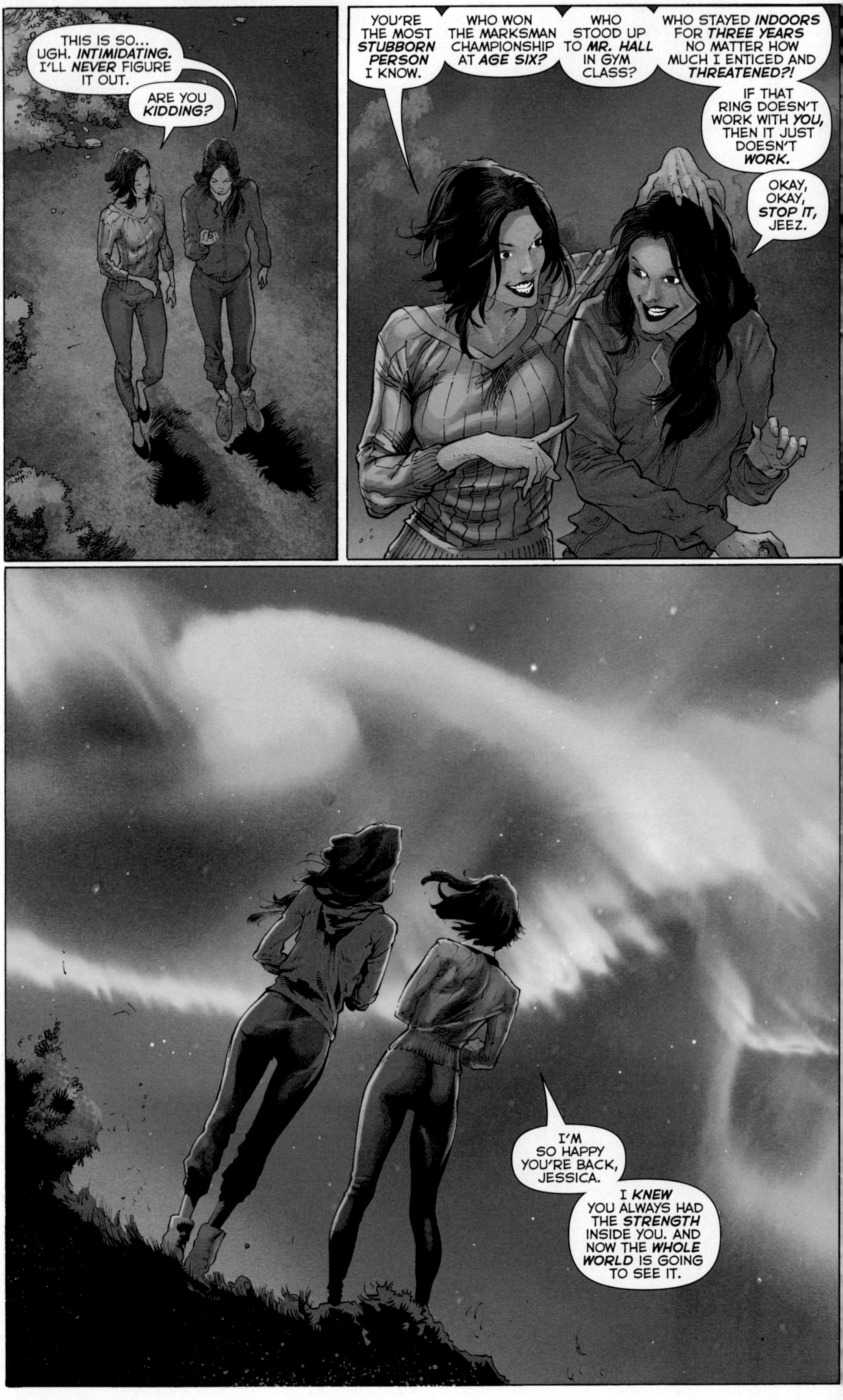
THIS IS SO... UGH. INTIMIDATING. I'LL NEVER FIGURE IT OUT.
ARE YOU KIDDING?
YOU'RE THE MOST STUBBORN PERSON I KNOW.
WHO WON THE MARKSMAN CHAMPIONSHIP AT AGE SIX?
WHO STOOD UP TO MR. HALL IN GYM CLASS?
WHO STAYED INDOORS FOR THREE YEARS NO MATTER HOW MUCH I ENTICED AND THREATENED?!
IF THAT RING DOESN'T WORK WITH YOU, THEN IT JUST DOESN'T WORK.
OKAY, OKAY, STOP IT, JEEZ.
I'M SO HAPPY YOU'RE BACK, JESSICA.
I KNEW YOU ALWAYS HAD THE STRENGTH INSIDE YOU. AND NOW THE WHOLE WORLD IS GOING TO SEE IT.

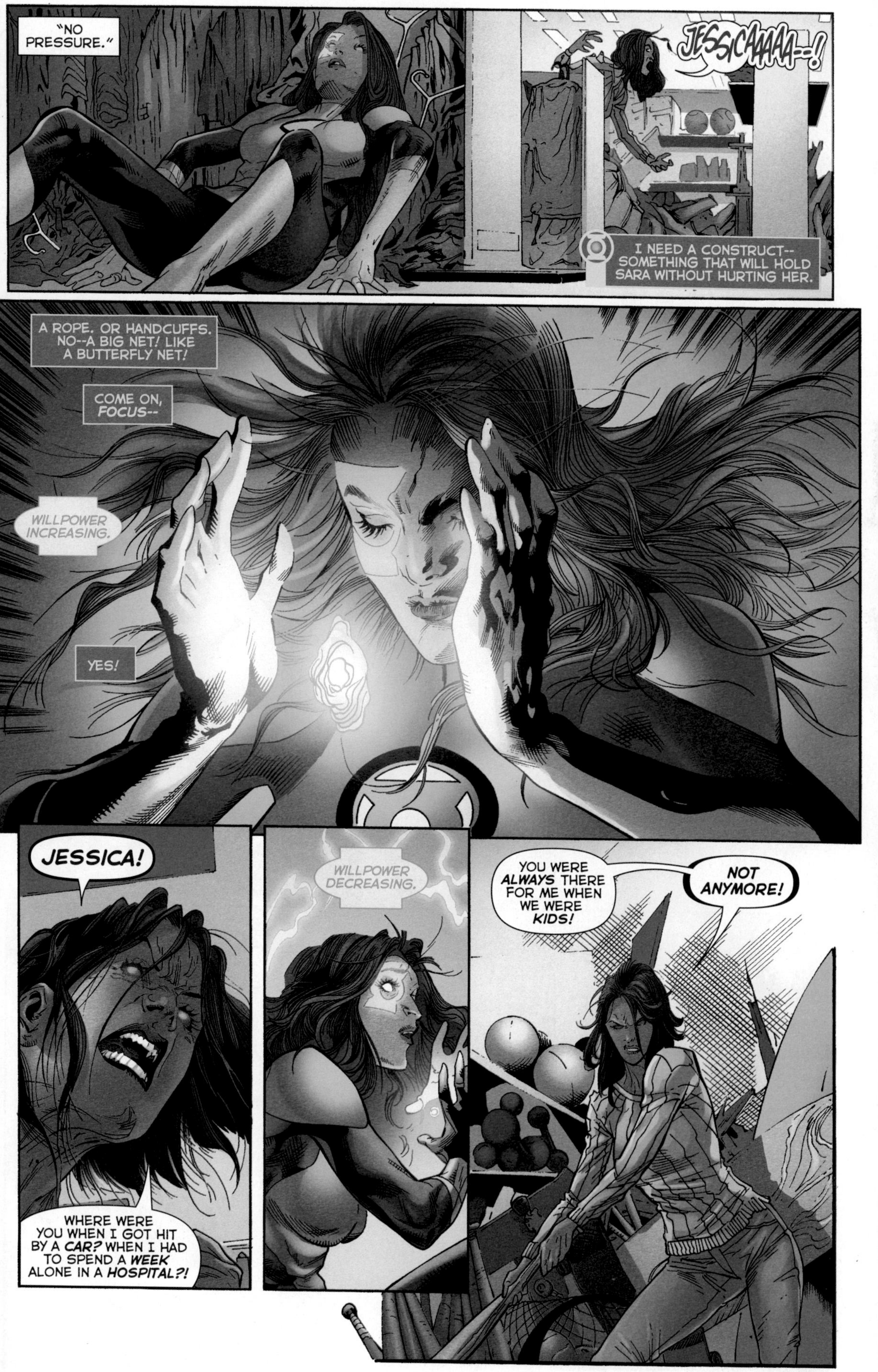
"NO PRESSURE."
JESSICAAAAA--!
I NEED A CONSTRUCT-- SOMETHING THAT WILL HOLD SARA WITHOUT HURTING HER.
A ROPE. OR HANDCUFFS. NO--A BIG NET! LIKE A BUTTERFLY NET!
COME ON, FOCUS--
WILLPOWER INCREASING.
YES!
JESSICA!
WHERE WERE YOU WHEN I GOT HIT BY A CAR? WHEN I HAD TO SPEND A WEEK ALONE IN A HOSPITAL?!
WILLPOWER DECREASING.
YOU WERE ALWAYS THERE FOR ME WHEN WE WERE KIDS!
NOT ANYMORE!

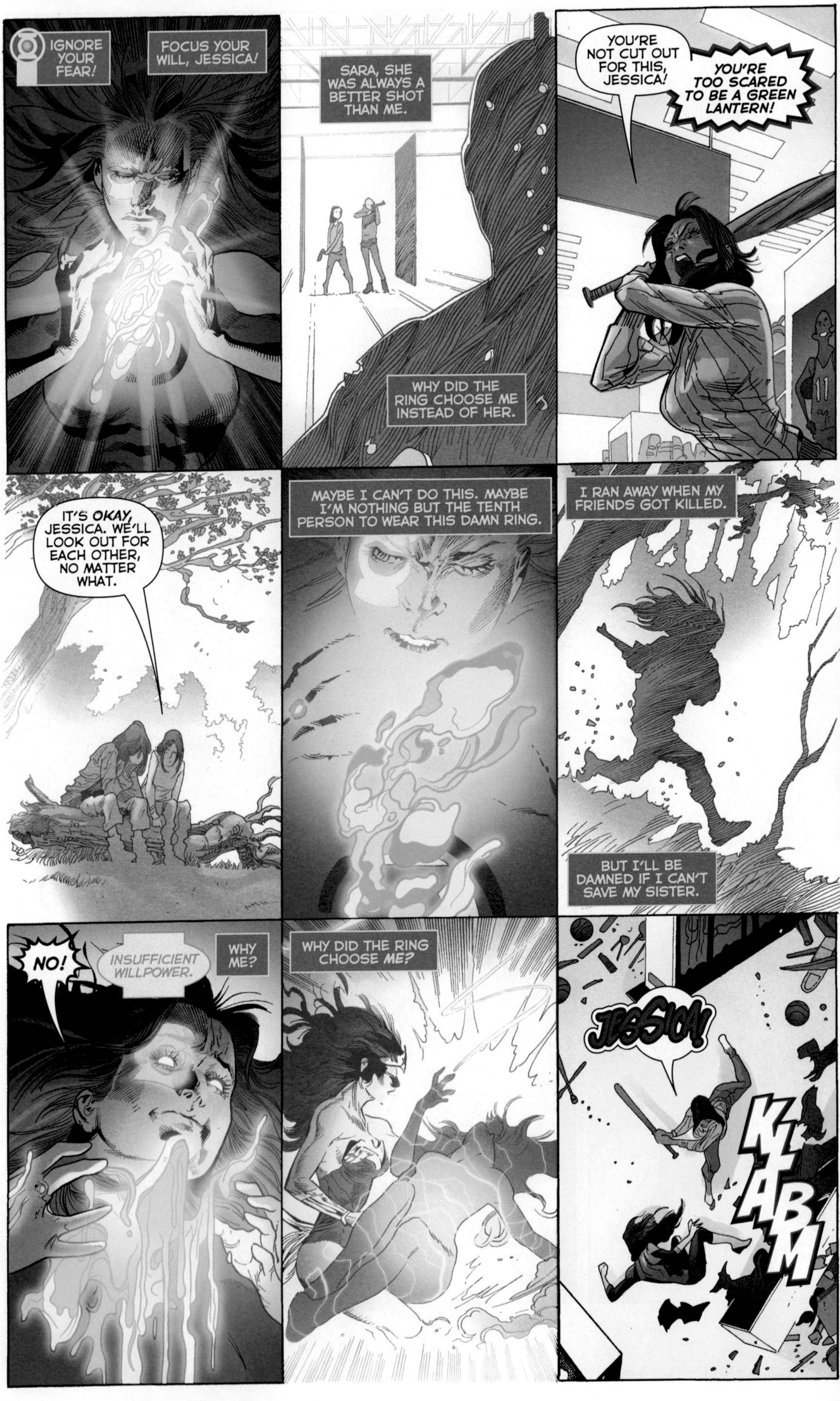
IGNORE YOUR FEAR!
FOCUS YOUR WILL, JESSICA!
SARA, SHE WAS ALWAYS A BETTER SHOT THAN ME.
WHY DID THE RING CHOOSE ME INSTEAD OF HER.
YOU'RE NOT CUT OUT FOR THIS, JESSICA!
YOU'RE TOO SCARED TO BE A GREEN LANTERN!
IT'S OKAY, JESSICA. WE'LL LOOK OUT FOR EACH OTHER, NO MATTER WHAT.
MAYBE I CAN'T DO THIS. MAYBE I'M NOTHING BUT THE TENTH PERSON TO WEAR THIS DAMN RING.
I RAN AWAY WHEN MY FRIENDS GOT KILLED.
BUT I'LL BE DAMNED IF I CAN'T SAVE MY SISTER.
NO!
INSUFFICIENT WILLPOWER.
WHY ME?
WHY DID THE RING CHOOSE ME?
JESSICA!
KTABM

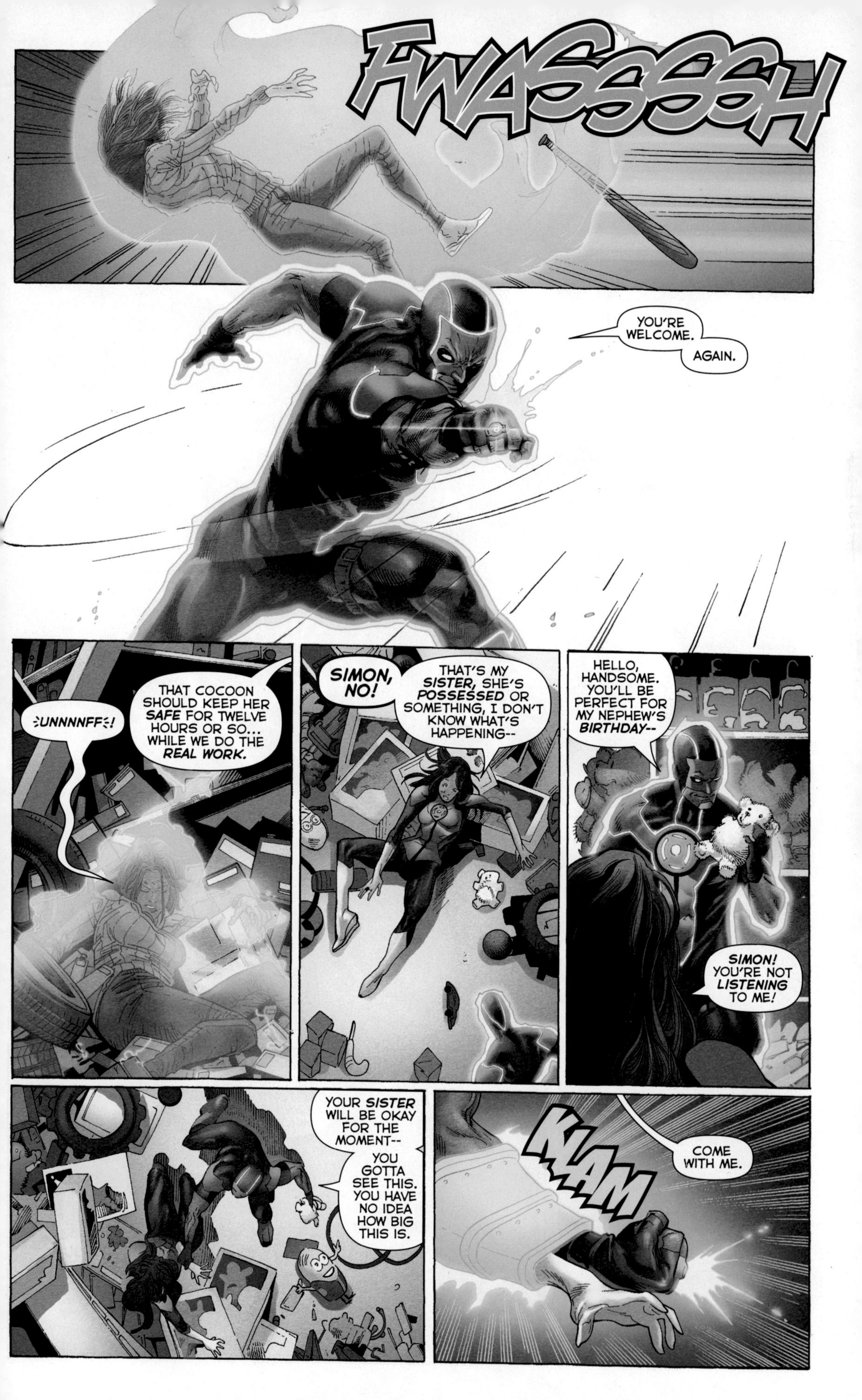
FWASSSSH
YOU'RE WELCOME.
AGAIN.
UNNNNFF!
THAT COCOON SHOULD KEEP HER *SAFE* FOR TWELVE HOURS OR SO... WHILE WE DO THE *REAL WORK.*
SIMON, NO!
THAT'S MY *SISTER,* SHE'S *POSSESSED* OR SOMETHING, I DON'T KNOW WHAT'S HAPPENING--
HELLO, HANDSOME. YOU'LL BE PERFECT FOR MY NEPHEW'S *BIRTHDAY--*
SIMON! YOU'RE NOT *LISTENING* TO ME!
YOUR *SISTER* WILL BE OKAY FOR THE MOMENT--
YOU GOTTA SEE THIS. YOU HAVE NO IDEA HOW BIG THIS IS.
KLAM
COME WITH ME.

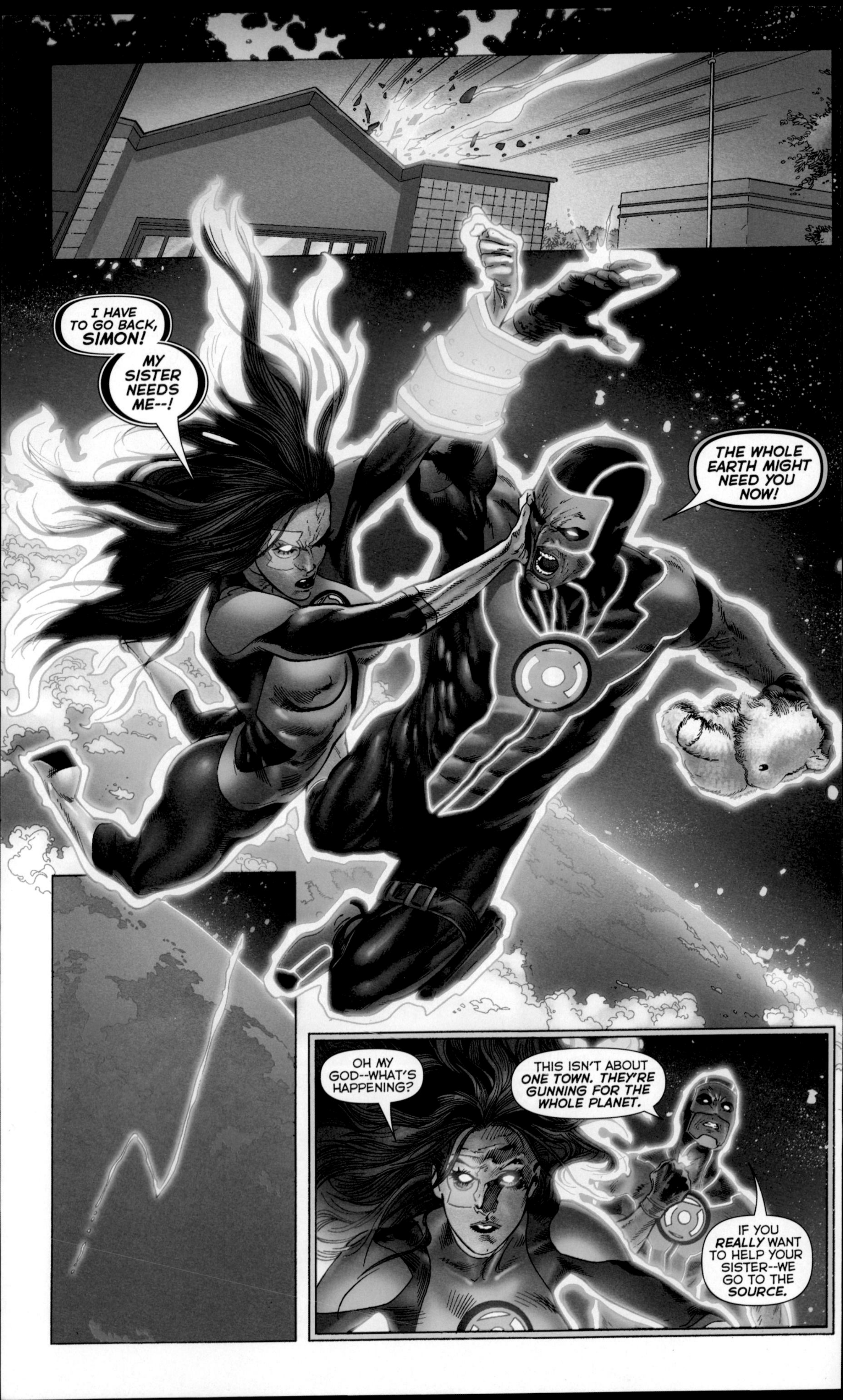
I HAVE TO GO BACK, SIMON!
MY SISTER NEEDS ME--!
THE WHOLE EARTH MIGHT NEED YOU NOW!
OH MY GOD--WHAT'S HAPPENING?
THIS ISN'T ABOUT ONE TOWN. THEY'RE GUNNING FOR THE WHOLE PLANET.
IF YOU REALLY WANT TO HELP YOUR SISTER--WE GO TO THE SOURCE.

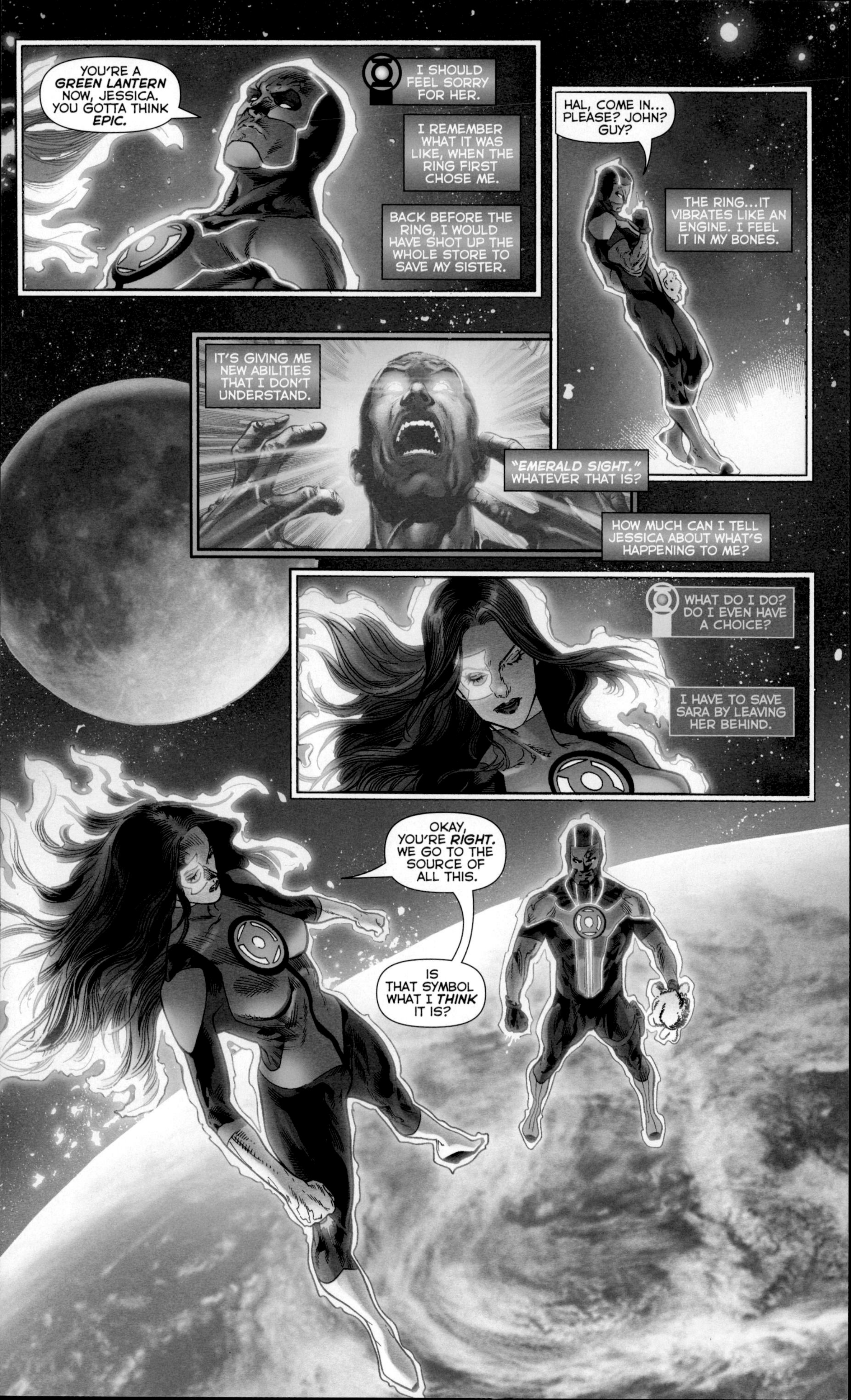
YOU'RE A GREEN LANTERN NOW, JESSICA. YOU GOTTA THINK EPIC.
I SHOULD FEEL SORRY FOR HER.
I REMEMBER WHAT IT WAS LIKE, WHEN THE RING FIRST CHOSE ME.
BACK BEFORE THE RING, I WOULD HAVE SHOT UP THE WHOLE STORE TO SAVE MY SISTER.
HAL, COME IN... PLEASE? JOHN? GUY?
THE RING...IT VIBRATES LIKE AN ENGINE. I FEEL IT IN MY BONES.
IT'S GIVING ME NEW ABILITIES THAT I DON'T UNDERSTAND.
"EMERALD SIGHT." WHATEVER THAT IS?
HOW MUCH CAN I TELL JESSICA ABOUT WHAT'S HAPPENING TO ME?
WHAT DO I DO? DO I EVEN HAVE A CHOICE?
I HAVE TO SAVE SARA BY LEAVING HER BEHIND.
OKAY, YOU'RE RIGHT. WE GO TO THE SOURCE OF ALL THIS.
IS THAT SYMBOL WHAT I THINK IT IS?

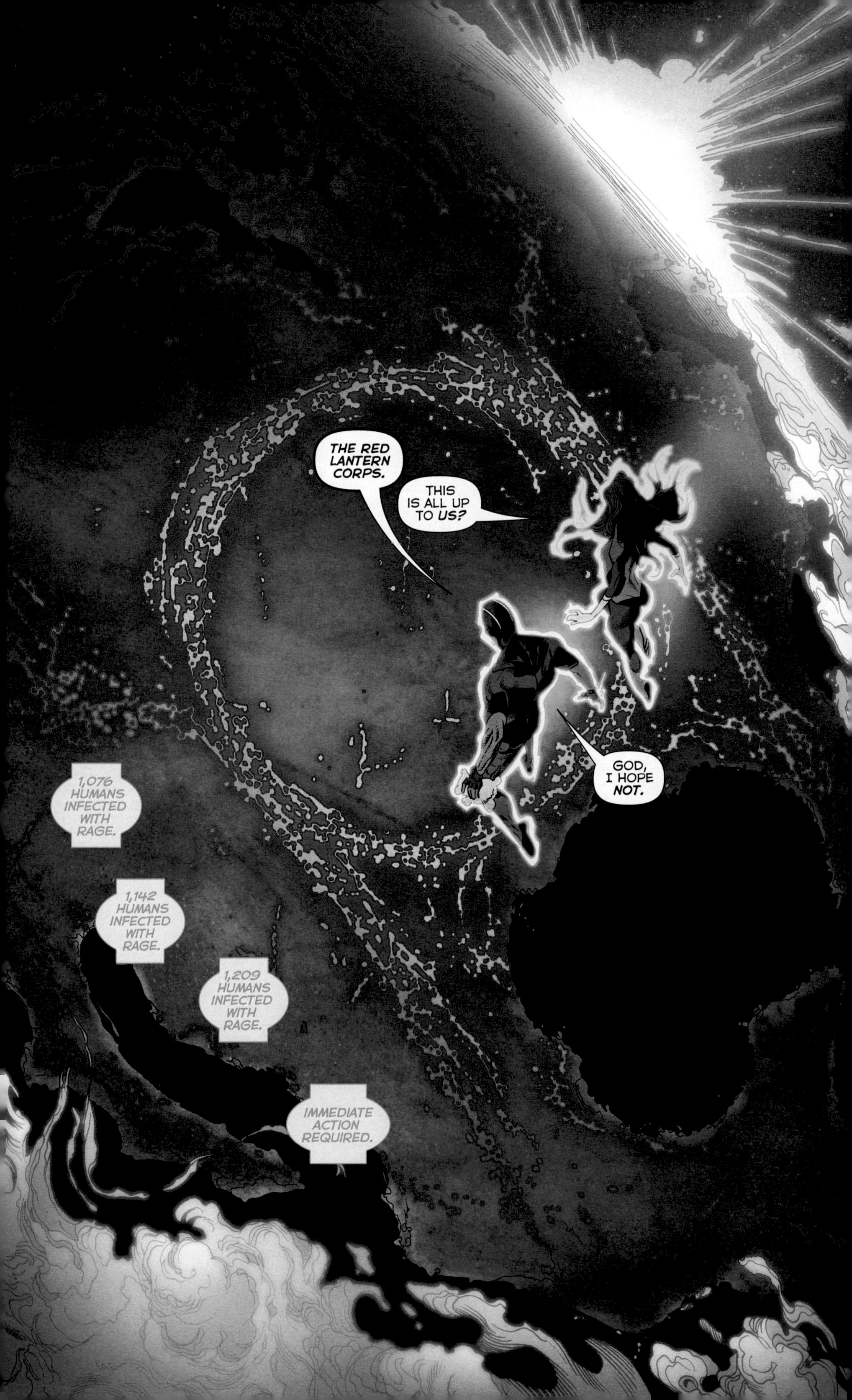
THE RED LANTERN CORPS.
THIS IS ALL UP TO US?
GOD, I HOPE NOT.
1,076 HUMANS INFECTED WITH RAGE.
1,142 HUMANS INFECTED WITH RAGE.
1,209 HUMANS INFECTED WITH RAGE.
IMMEDIATE ACTION REQUIRED.

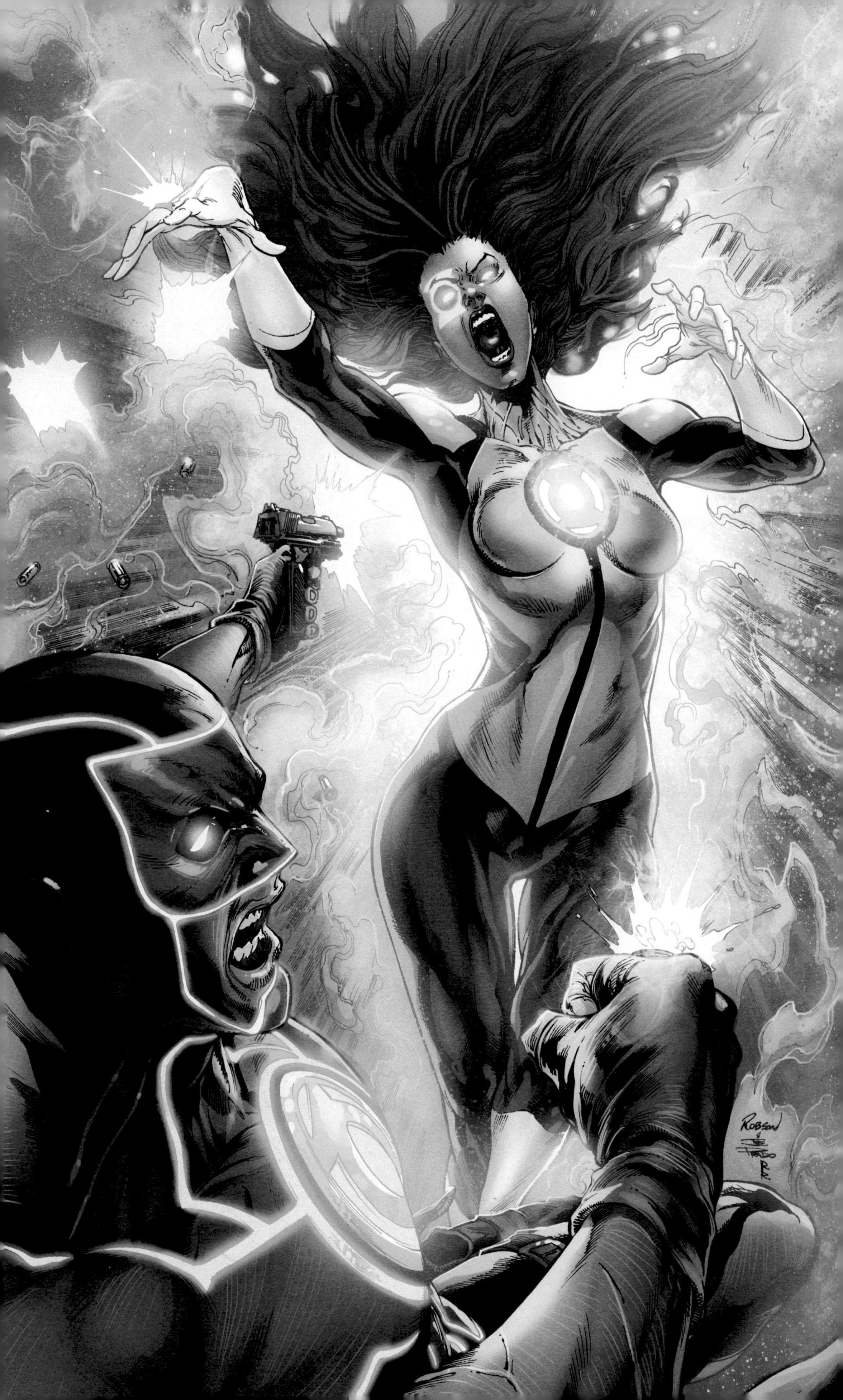

RAGE PLANET: PART 3

SAM HUMPHRIES writer * ROBSON ROCHA, TOM DERENICK, JACK HERBERT and NEIL EDWARDS pencillers
JAY LEISTEN, TOM PALMER, JACK HERBERT and KEITH CHAMPAGNE inkers * HI-FI colorist
ROBSON ROCHA, JOE PRADO and ROD REIS cover artists

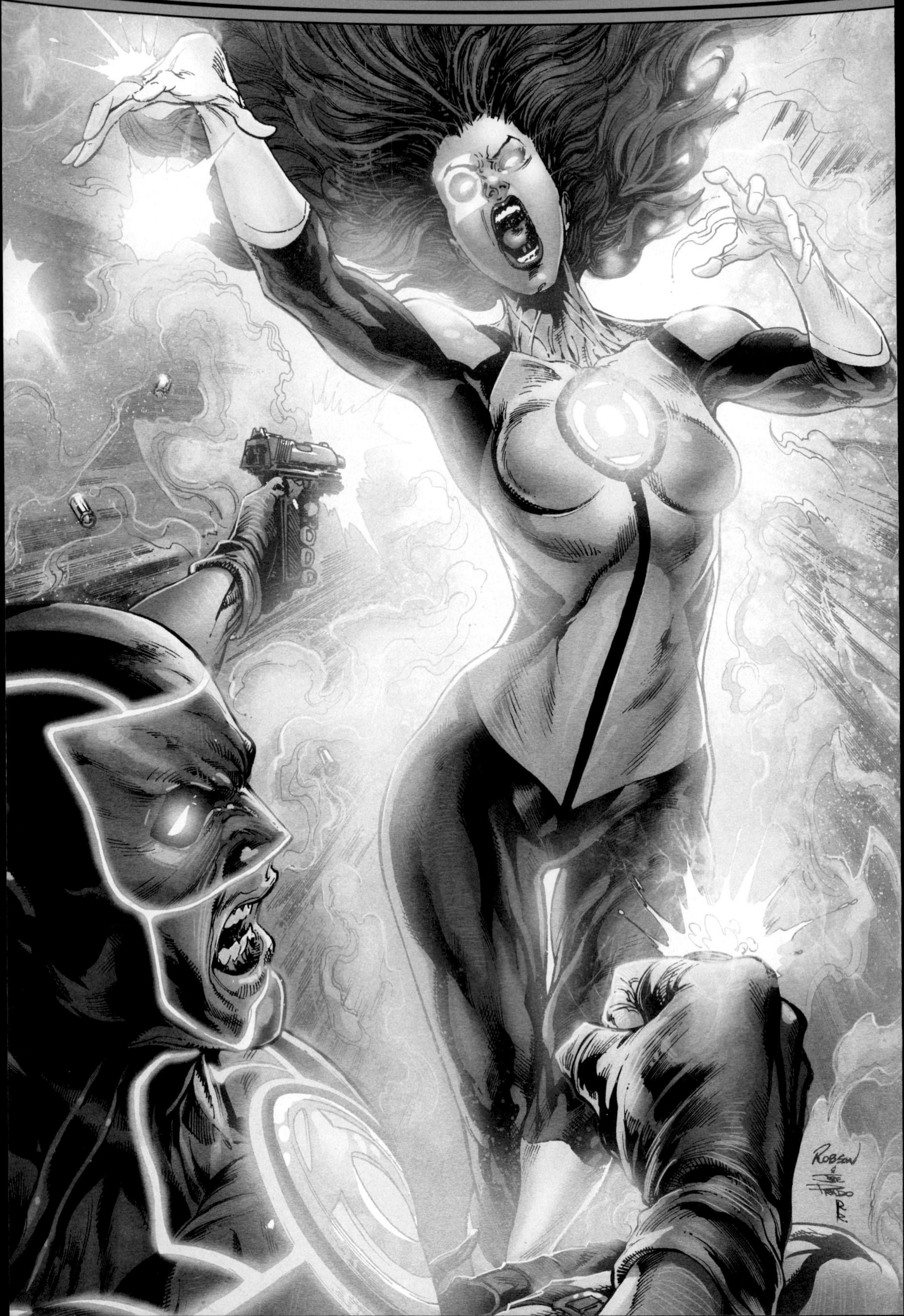

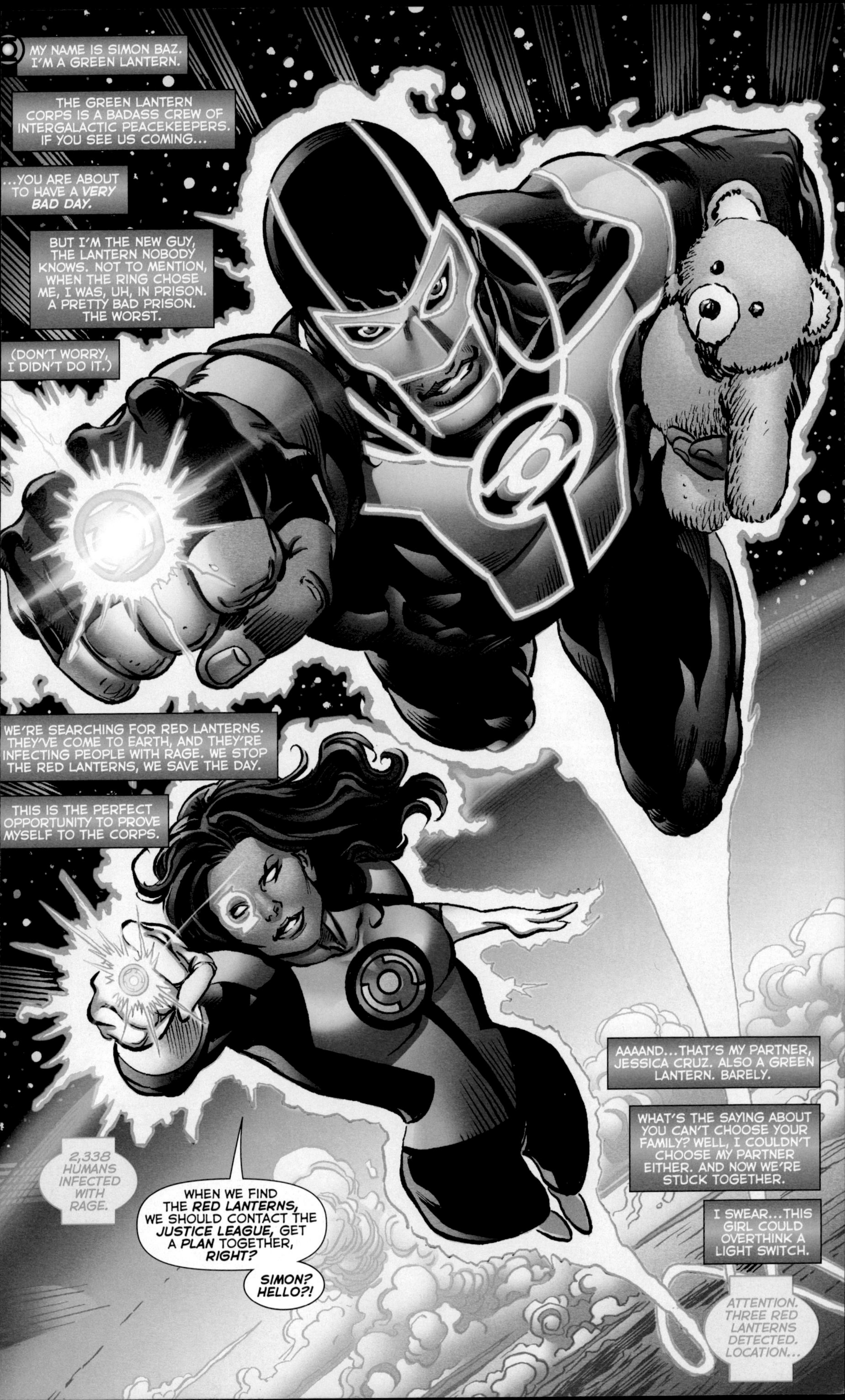
MY NAME IS SIMON BAZ. I'M A GREEN LANTERN.
THE GREEN LANTERN CORPS IS A BADASS CREW OF INTERGALACTIC PEACEKEEPERS. IF YOU SEE US COMING...
...YOU ARE ABOUT TO HAVE A VERY BAD DAY.
BUT I'M THE NEW GUY, THE LANTERN NOBODY KNOWS. NOT TO MENTION, WHEN THE RING CHOSE ME, I WAS, UH, IN PRISON. A PRETTY BAD PRISON. THE WORST.
(DON'T WORRY, I DIDN'T DO IT.)
WE'RE SEARCHING FOR RED LANTERNS. THEY'VE COME TO EARTH, AND THEY'RE INFECTING PEOPLE WITH RAGE. WE STOP THE RED LANTERNS, WE SAVE THE DAY.
THIS IS THE PERFECT OPPORTUNITY TO PROVE MYSELF TO THE CORPS.
AAAAND...THAT'S MY PARTNER, JESSICA CRUZ. ALSO A GREEN LANTERN. BARELY.
WHAT'S THE SAYING ABOUT YOU CAN'T CHOOSE YOUR FAMILY? WELL, I COULDN'T CHOOSE MY PARTNER EITHER. AND NOW WE'RE STUCK TOGETHER.
I SWEAR...THIS GIRL COULD OVERTHINK A LIGHT SWITCH.
2,338 HUMANS INFECTED WITH RAGE.
WHEN WE FIND THE RED LANTERNS, WE SHOULD CONTACT THE JUSTICE LEAGUE, GET A PLAN TOGETHER, RIGHT?
SIMON? HELLO?!
ATTENTION. THREE RED LANTERNS DETECTED. LOCATION...

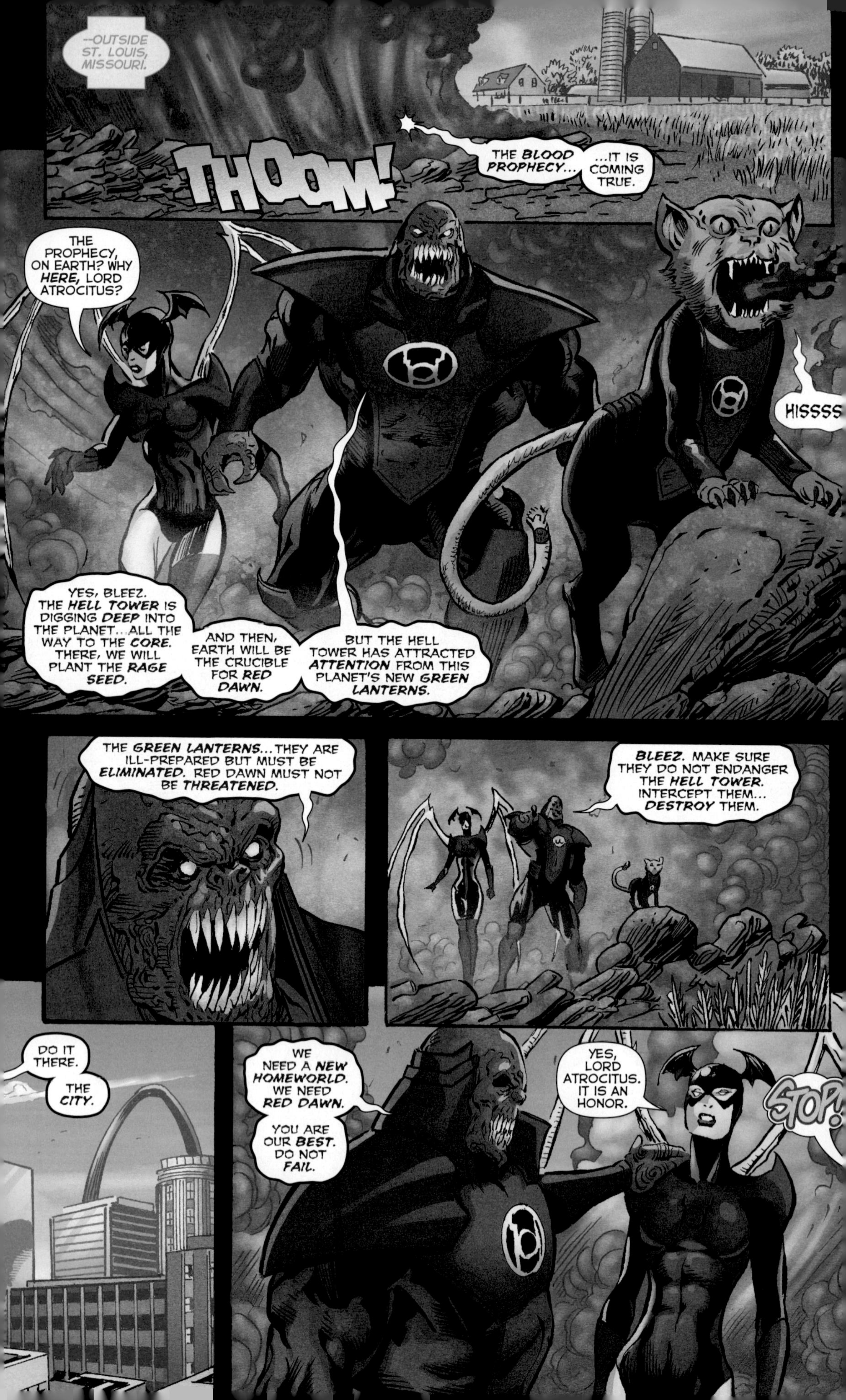
--OUTSIDE ST. LOUIS, MISSOURI.
THOOOM!
THE BLOOD PROPHECY...
...IT IS COMING TRUE.
THE PROPHECY, ON EARTH? WHY HERE, LORD ATROCITUS?
HISSSS
YES, BLEEZ. THE HELL TOWER IS DIGGING DEEP INTO THE PLANET...ALL THE WAY TO THE CORE. THERE, WE WILL PLANT THE RAGE SEED.
AND THEN, EARTH WILL BE THE CRUCIBLE FOR RED DAWN.
BUT THE HELL TOWER HAS ATTRACTED ATTENTION FROM THIS PLANET'S NEW GREEN LANTERNS.
THE GREEN LANTERNS...THEY ARE ILL-PREPARED BUT MUST BE ELIMINATED. RED DAWN MUST NOT BE THREATENED.
BLEEZ. MAKE SURE THEY DO NOT ENDANGER THE HELL TOWER. INTERCEPT THEM... DESTROY THEM.
DO IT THERE.
THE CITY.
WE NEED A NEW HOMEWORLD. WE NEED RED DAWN.
YOU ARE OUR BEST. DO NOT FAIL.
YES, LORD ATROCITUS. IT IS AN HONOR.
STOP!

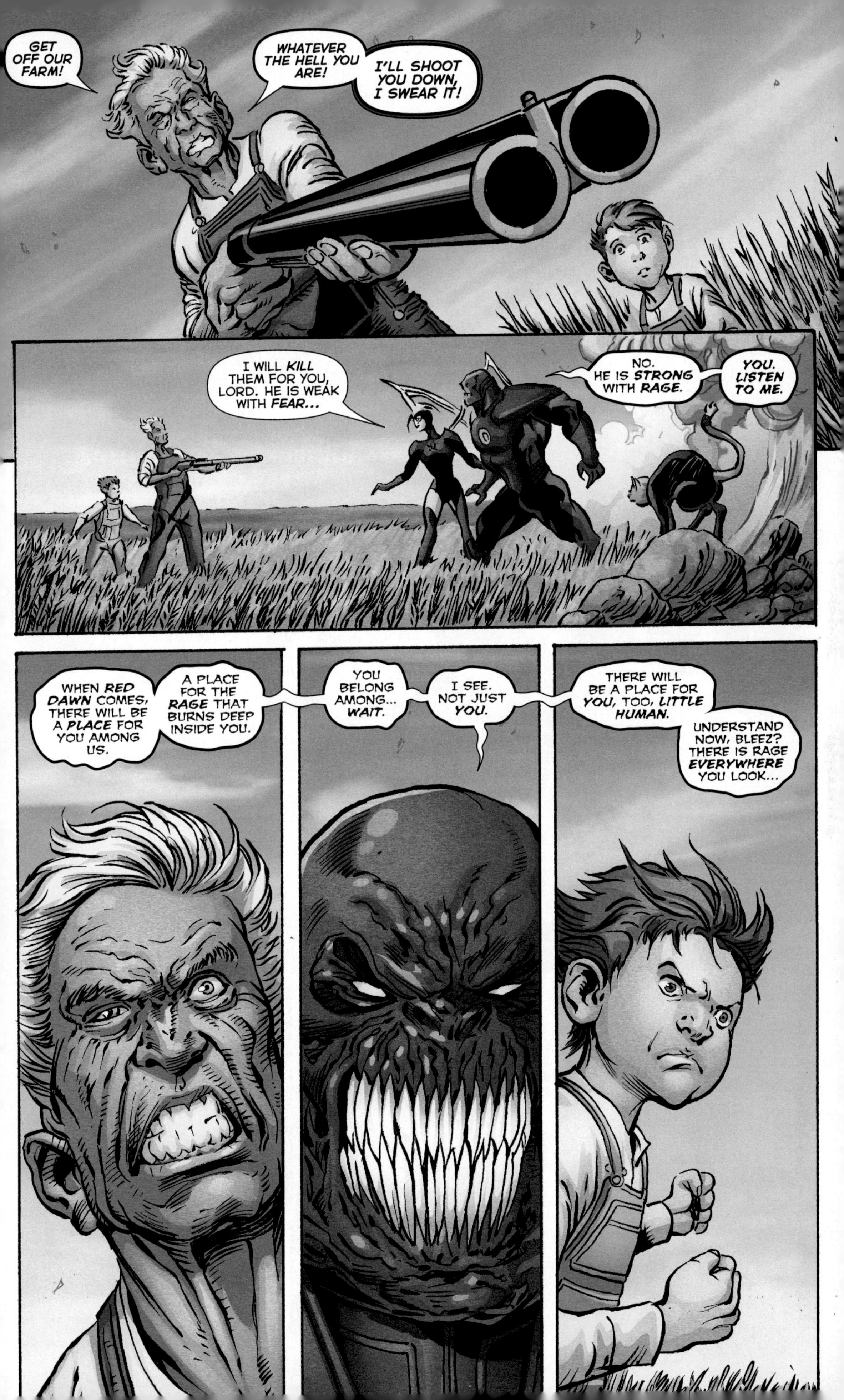
GET OFF OUR FARM!
WHATEVER THE HELL YOU ARE!
I'LL SHOOT YOU DOWN, I SWEAR IT!
I WILL KILL THEM FOR YOU, LORD. HE IS WEAK WITH FEAR...
NO. HE IS STRONG WITH RAGE.
YOU. LISTEN TO ME.
WHEN RED DAWN COMES, THERE WILL BE A PLACE FOR YOU AMONG US.
A PLACE FOR THE RAGE THAT BURNS DEEP INSIDE YOU.
YOU BELONG AMONG... WAIT.
I SEE. NOT JUST YOU.
THERE WILL BE A PLACE FOR YOU, TOO, LITTLE HUMAN.
UNDERSTAND NOW, BLEEZ? THERE IS RAGE EVERYWHERE YOU LOOK...

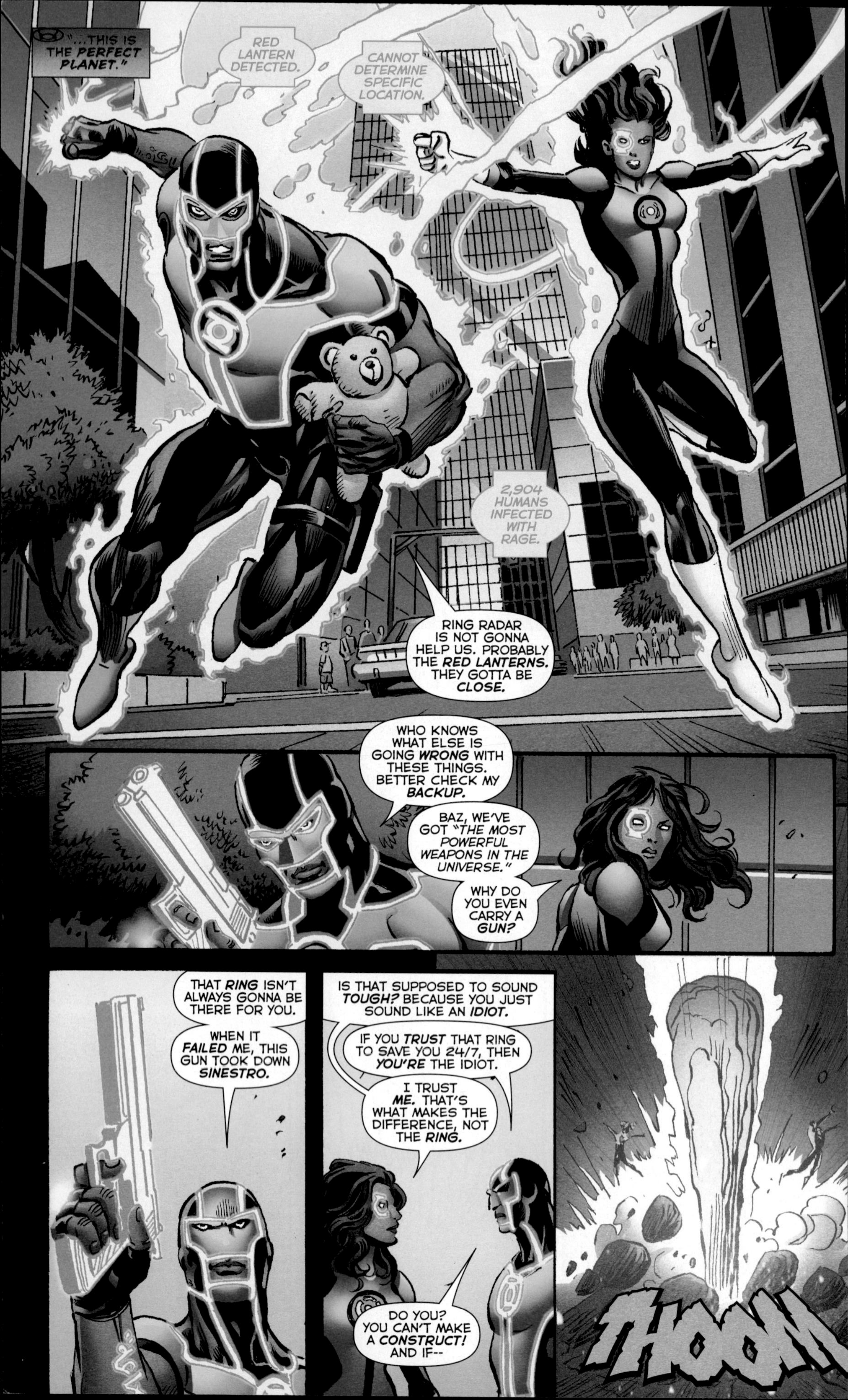
"...THIS IS THE PERFECT PLANET."
RED LANTERN DETECTED.
CANNOT DETERMINE SPECIFIC LOCATION.
2,904 HUMANS INFECTED WITH RAGE.
RING RADAR IS NOT GONNA HELP US. PROBABLY THE RED LANTERNS. THEY GOTTA BE CLOSE.
WHO KNOWS WHAT ELSE IS GOING WRONG WITH THESE THINGS. BETTER CHECK MY BACKUP.
BAZ, WE'VE GOT "THE MOST POWERFUL WEAPONS IN THE UNIVERSE."
WHY DO YOU EVEN CARRY A GUN?
THAT RING ISN'T ALWAYS GONNA BE THERE FOR YOU.
WHEN IT FAILED ME, THIS GUN TOOK DOWN SINESTRO.
IS THAT SUPPOSED TO SOUND TOUGH? BECAUSE YOU JUST SOUND LIKE AN IDIOT.
IF YOU TRUST THAT RING TO SAVE YOU 24/7, THEN YOU'RE THE IDIOT.
I TRUST ME. THAT'S WHAT MAKES THE DIFFERENCE, NOT THE RING.
DO YOU? YOU CAN'T MAKE A CONSTRUCT! AND IF--
THOOM

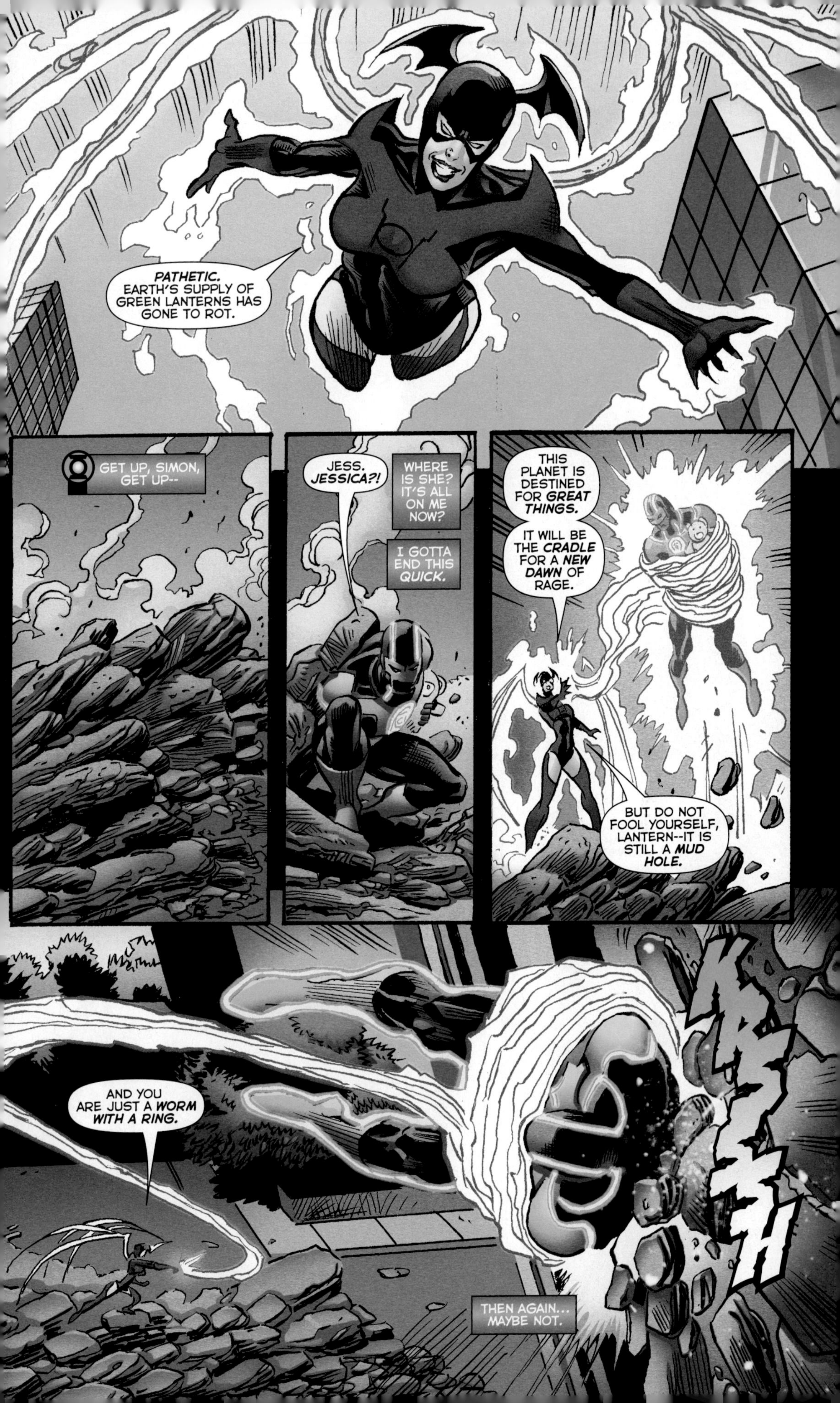
PATHETIC. EARTH'S SUPPLY OF GREEN LANTERNS HAS GONE TO ROT.
GET UP, SIMON, GET UP--
JESS. JESSICA?!
WHERE IS SHE? IT'S ALL ON ME NOW?
I GOTTA END THIS QUICK.
THIS PLANET IS DESTINED FOR GREAT THINGS.
IT WILL BE THE CRADLE FOR A NEW DAWN OF RAGE.
BUT DO NOT FOOL YOURSELF, LANTERN--IT IS STILL A MUD HOLE.
AND YOU ARE JUST A WORM WITH A RING.
KRSSH
THEN AGAIN... MAYBE NOT.

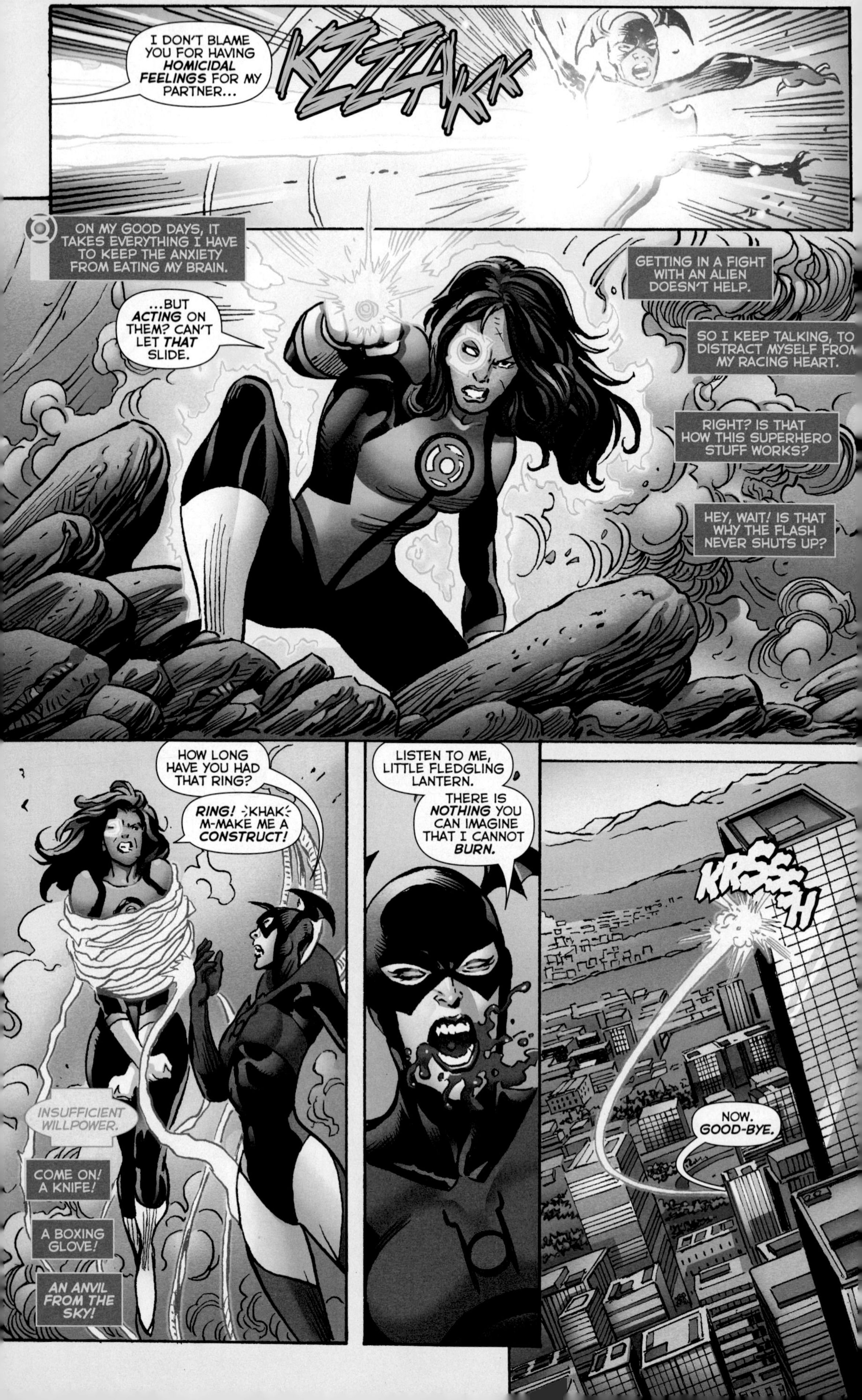

I DON'T BLAME YOU FOR HAVING HOMICIDAL FEELINGS FOR MY PARTNER...
KZZZAKK
ON MY GOOD DAYS, IT TAKES EVERYTHING I HAVE TO KEEP THE ANXIETY FROM EATING MY BRAIN.
...BUT ACTING ON THEM? CAN'T LET THAT SLIDE.
GETTING IN A FIGHT WITH AN ALIEN DOESN'T HELP.
SO I KEEP TALKING, TO DISTRACT MYSELF FROM MY RACING HEART.
RIGHT? IS THAT HOW THIS SUPERHERO STUFF WORKS?
HEY, WAIT! IS THAT WHY THE FLASH NEVER SHUTS UP?
HOW LONG HAVE YOU HAD THAT RING?
RING! KHAK M-MAKE ME A CONSTRUCT!
INSUFFICIENT WILLPOWER.
COME ON! A KNIFE!
A BOXING GLOVE!
AN ANVIL FROM THE SKY!
LISTEN TO ME, LITTLE FLEDGLING LANTERN.
THERE IS NOTHING YOU CAN IMAGINE THAT I CANNOT BURN.
KRSSSH
NOW. GOOD-BYE.

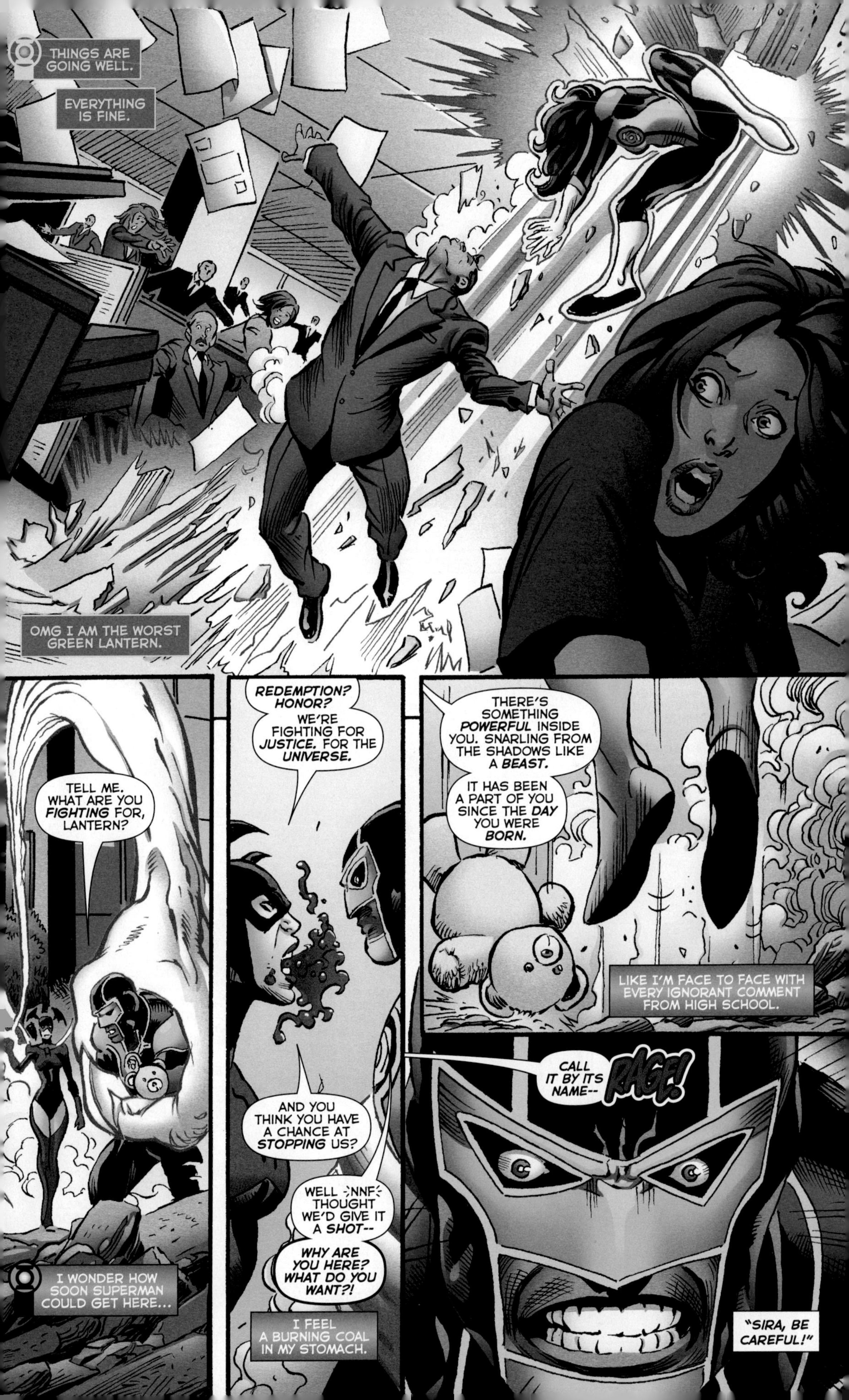
THINGS ARE GOING WELL.
EVERYTHING IS FINE.
OMG I AM THE WORST GREEN LANTERN.
TELL ME. WHAT ARE YOU FIGHTING FOR, LANTERN?
I WONDER HOW SOON SUPERMAN COULD GET HERE...
REDEMPTION? HONOR? WE'RE FIGHTING FOR JUSTICE. FOR THE UNIVERSE.
AND YOU THINK YOU HAVE A CHANCE AT STOPPING US?
WELL -NNF- THOUGHT WE'D GIVE IT A SHOT--
WHY ARE YOU HERE? WHAT DO YOU WANT?!
I FEEL A BURNING COAL IN MY STOMACH.
THERE'S SOMETHING POWERFUL INSIDE YOU. SNARLING FROM THE SHADOWS LIKE A BEAST.
IT HAS BEEN A PART OF YOU SINCE THE DAY YOU WERE BORN.
LIKE I'M FACE TO FACE WITH EVERY IGNORANT COMMENT FROM HIGH SCHOOL.
CALL IT BY ITS NAME-- RAGE!
"SIRA, BE CAREFUL!"

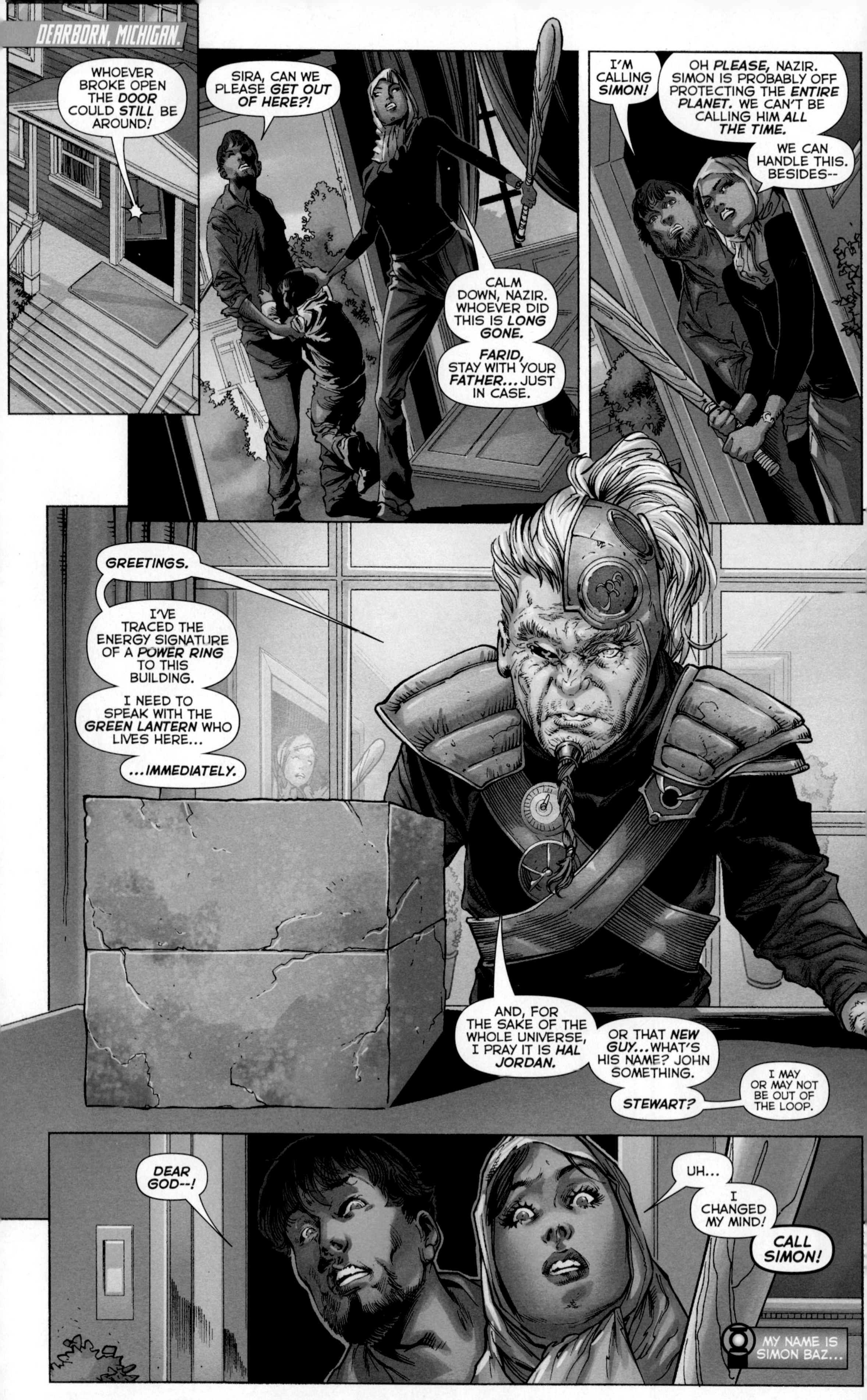
DEARBORN, MICHIGAN.
WHOEVER BROKE OPEN THE DOOR COULD STILL BE AROUND!
SIRA, CAN WE PLEASE GET OUT OF HERE?!
CALM DOWN, NAZIR. WHOEVER DID THIS IS LONG GONE.
FARID, STAY WITH YOUR FATHER... JUST IN CASE.
I'M CALLING SIMON!
OH PLEASE, NAZIR. SIMON IS PROBABLY OFF PROTECTING THE ENTIRE PLANET. WE CAN'T BE CALLING HIM ALL THE TIME.
WE CAN HANDLE THIS. BESIDES--
GREETINGS.
I'VE TRACED THE ENERGY SIGNATURE OF A POWER RING TO THIS BUILDING.
I NEED TO SPEAK WITH THE GREEN LANTERN WHO LIVES HERE...
...IMMEDIATELY.
AND, FOR THE SAKE OF THE WHOLE UNIVERSE, I PRAY IT IS HAL JORDAN.
OR THAT NEW GUY...WHAT'S HIS NAME? JOHN SOMETHING.
STEWART?
I MAY OR MAY NOT BE OUT OF THE LOOP.
DEAR GOD--!
UH...
I CHANGED MY MIND!
CALL SIMON!
MY NAME IS SIMON BAZ...

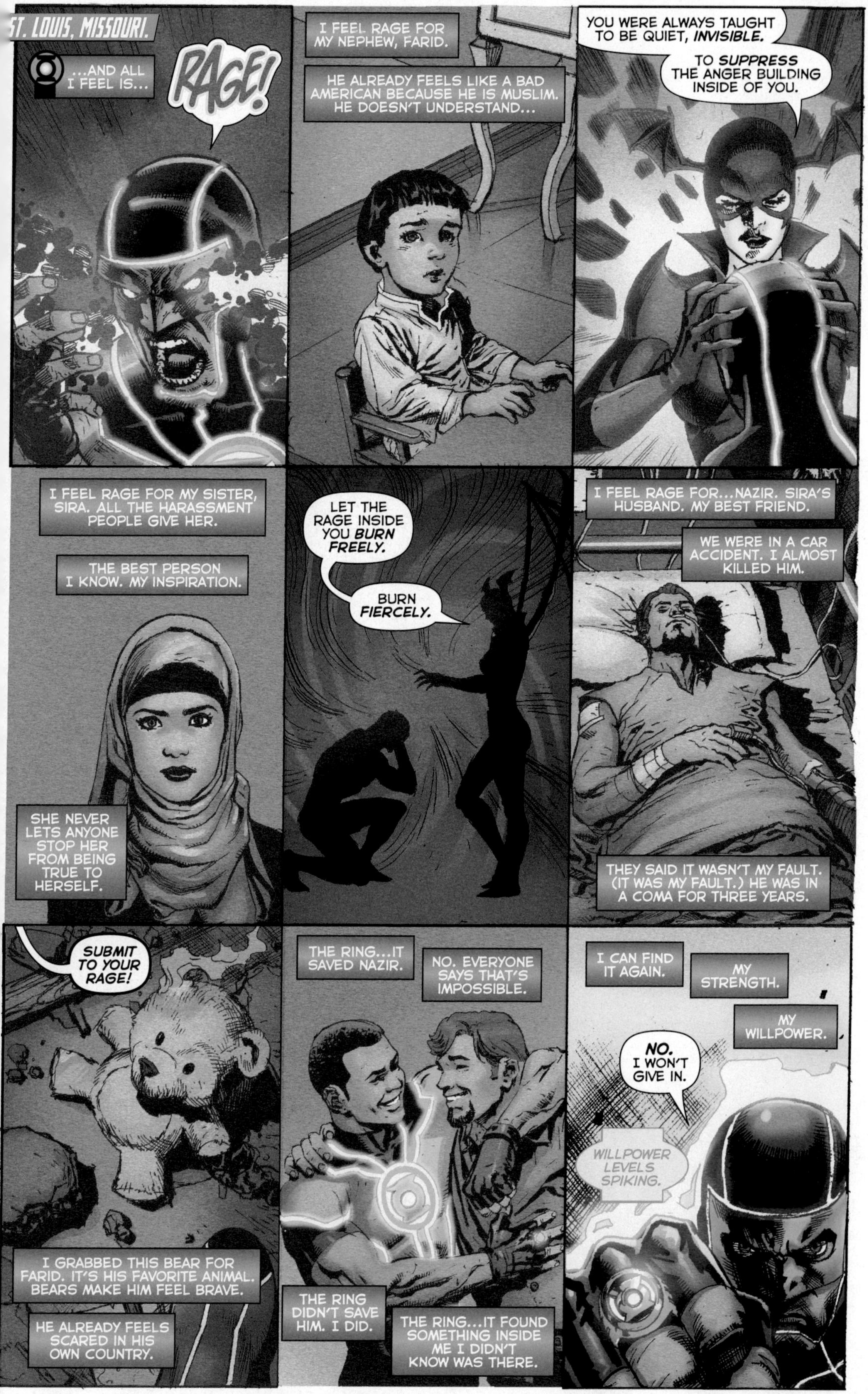
ST. LOUIS, MISSOURI.
...AND ALL I FEEL IS...
RAGE!
I FEEL RAGE FOR MY NEPHEW, FARID.
HE ALREADY FEELS LIKE A BAD AMERICAN BECAUSE HE IS MUSLIM. HE DOESN'T UNDERSTAND...
YOU WERE ALWAYS TAUGHT TO BE QUIET, INVISIBLE.
TO SUPPRESS THE ANGER BUILDING INSIDE OF YOU.
I FEEL RAGE FOR MY SISTER, SIRA. ALL THE HARASSMENT PEOPLE GIVE HER.
THE BEST PERSON I KNOW. MY INSPIRATION.
SHE NEVER LETS ANYONE STOP HER FROM BEING TRUE TO HERSELF.
LET THE RAGE INSIDE YOU BURN FREELY.
BURN FIERCELY.
I FEEL RAGE FOR...NAZIR. SIRA'S HUSBAND. MY BEST FRIEND.
WE WERE IN A CAR ACCIDENT. I ALMOST KILLED HIM.
THEY SAID IT WASN'T MY FAULT. (IT WAS MY FAULT.) HE WAS IN A COMA FOR THREE YEARS.
SUBMIT TO YOUR RAGE!
I GRABBED THIS BEAR FOR FARID. IT'S HIS FAVORITE ANIMAL. BEARS MAKE HIM FEEL BRAVE.
HE ALREADY FEELS SCARED IN HIS OWN COUNTRY.
THE RING...IT SAVED NAZIR.
NO. EVERYONE SAYS THAT'S IMPOSSIBLE.
THE RING DIDN'T SAVE HIM. I DID.
THE RING...IT FOUND SOMETHING INSIDE ME I DIDN'T KNOW WAS THERE.
I CAN FIND IT AGAIN.
MY STRENGTH.
MY WILLPOWER.
NO. I WON'T GIVE IN.
WILLPOWER LEVELS SPIKING.

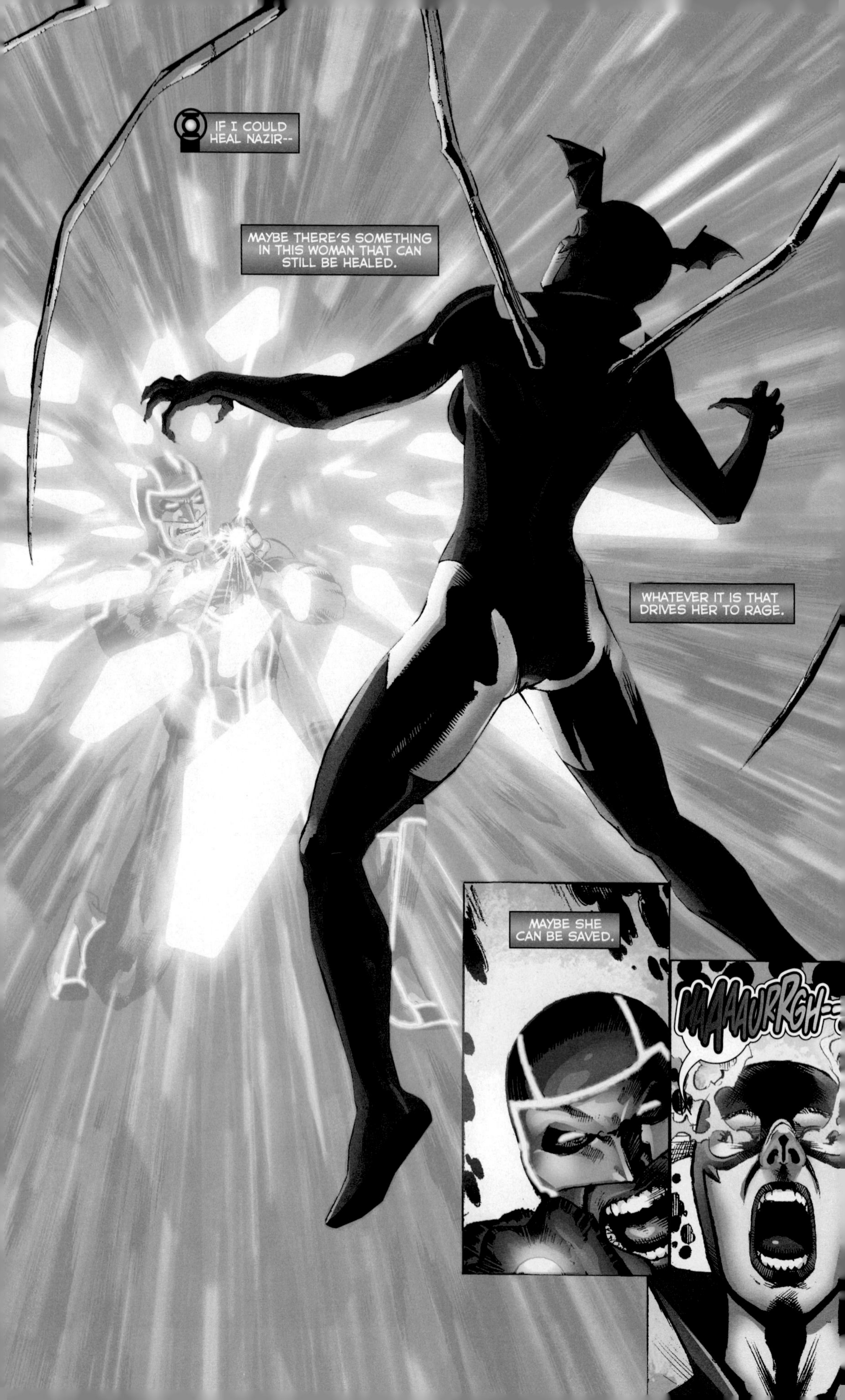
IF I COULD HEAL NAZIR--
MAYBE THERE'S SOMETHING IN THIS WOMAN THAT CAN STILL BE HEALED.
WHATEVER IT IS THAT DRIVES HER TO RAGE.
MAYBE SHE CAN BE SAVED.
HAAAAURRGH--

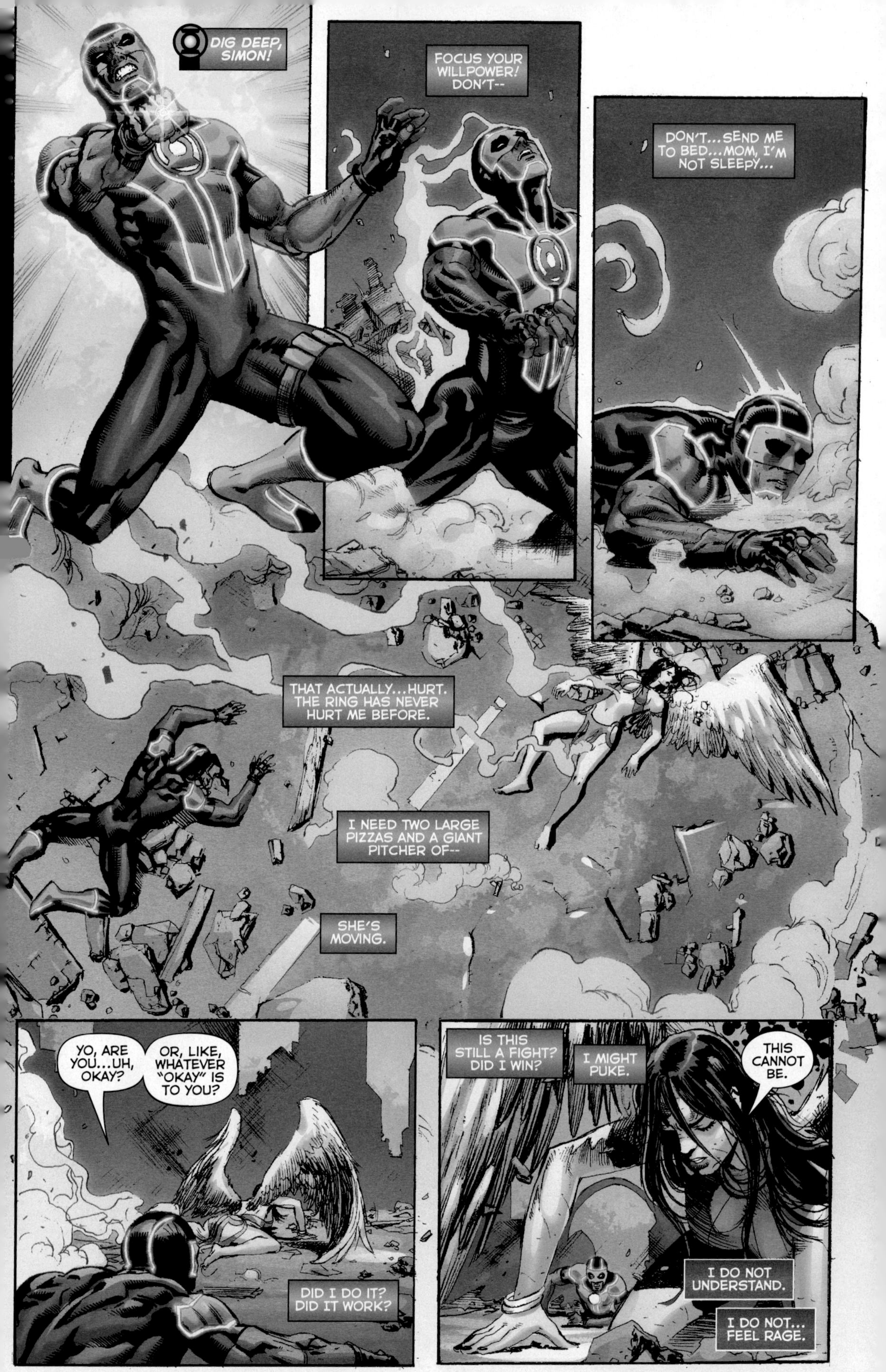
DIG DEEP, SIMON!
FOCUS YOUR WILLPOWER! DON'T--
DON'T...SEND ME TO BED...MOM, I'M NOT SLEEPY...
THAT ACTUALLY...HURT. THE RING HAS NEVER HURT ME BEFORE.
I NEED TWO LARGE PIZZAS AND A GIANT PITCHER OF--
SHE'S MOVING.
YO, ARE YOU...UH, OKAY?
OR, LIKE, WHATEVER "OKAY" IS TO YOU?
DID I DO IT? DID IT WORK?
IS THIS STILL A FIGHT? DID I WIN?
I MIGHT PUKE.
THIS CANNOT BE.
I DO NOT UNDERSTAND.
I DO NOT... FEEL RAGE.

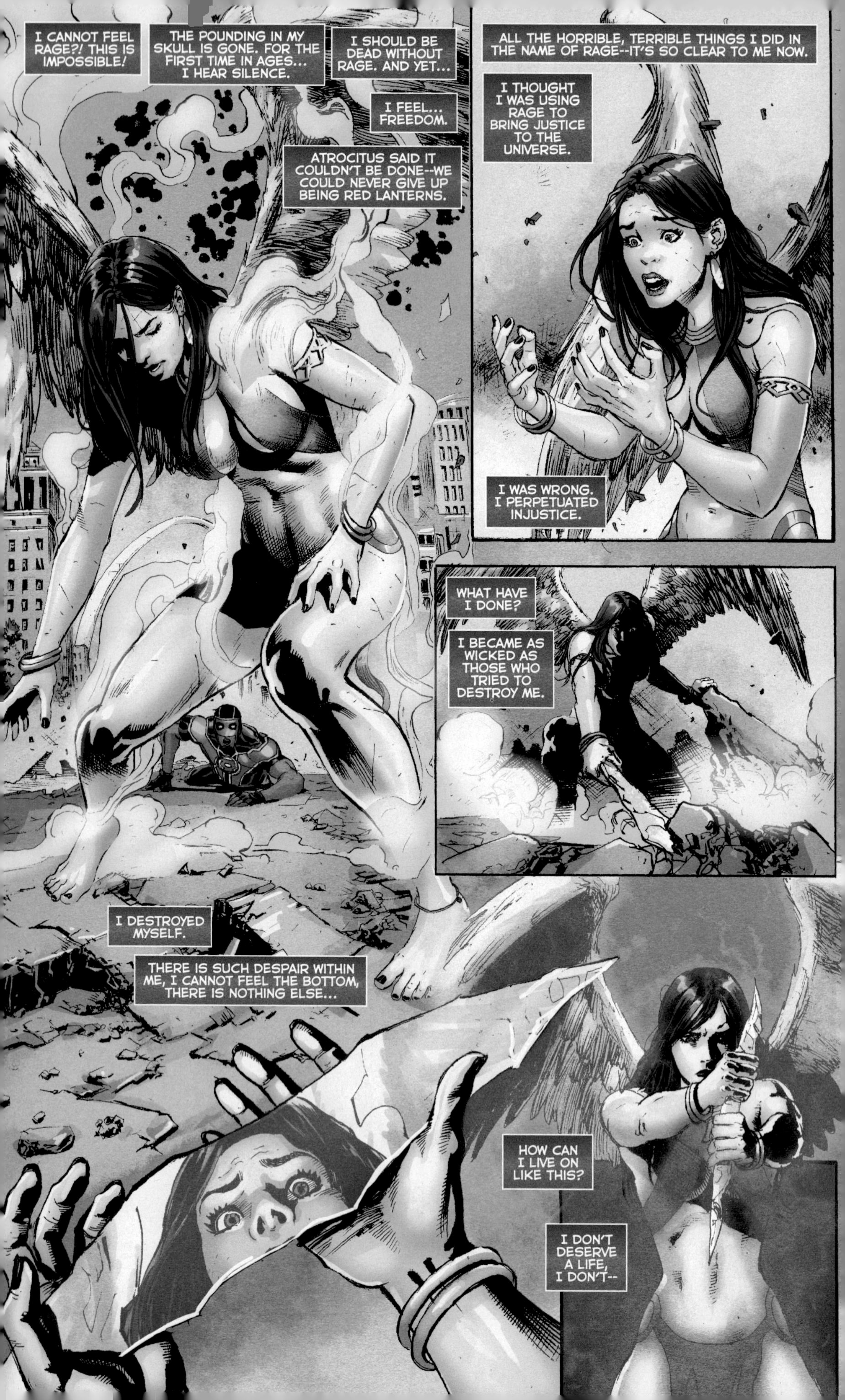
I CANNOT FEEL RAGE?! THIS IS IMPOSSIBLE!
THE POUNDING IN MY SKULL IS GONE. FOR THE FIRST TIME IN AGES... I HEAR SILENCE.
I SHOULD BE DEAD WITHOUT RAGE. AND YET...
I FEEL... FREEDOM.
ATROCITUS SAID IT COULDN'T BE DONE--WE COULD NEVER GIVE UP BEING RED LANTERNS.
ALL THE HORRIBLE, TERRIBLE THINGS I DID IN THE NAME OF RAGE--IT'S SO CLEAR TO ME NOW.
I THOUGHT I WAS USING RAGE TO BRING JUSTICE TO THE UNIVERSE.
I WAS WRONG. I PERPETUATED INJUSTICE.
WHAT HAVE I DONE?
I BECAME AS WICKED AS THOSE WHO TRIED TO DESTROY ME.
I DESTROYED MYSELF.
THERE IS SUCH DESPAIR WITHIN ME, I CANNOT FEEL THE BOTTOM, THERE IS NOTHING ELSE...
HOW CAN I LIVE ON LIKE THIS?
I DON'T DESERVE A LIFE, I DON'T--

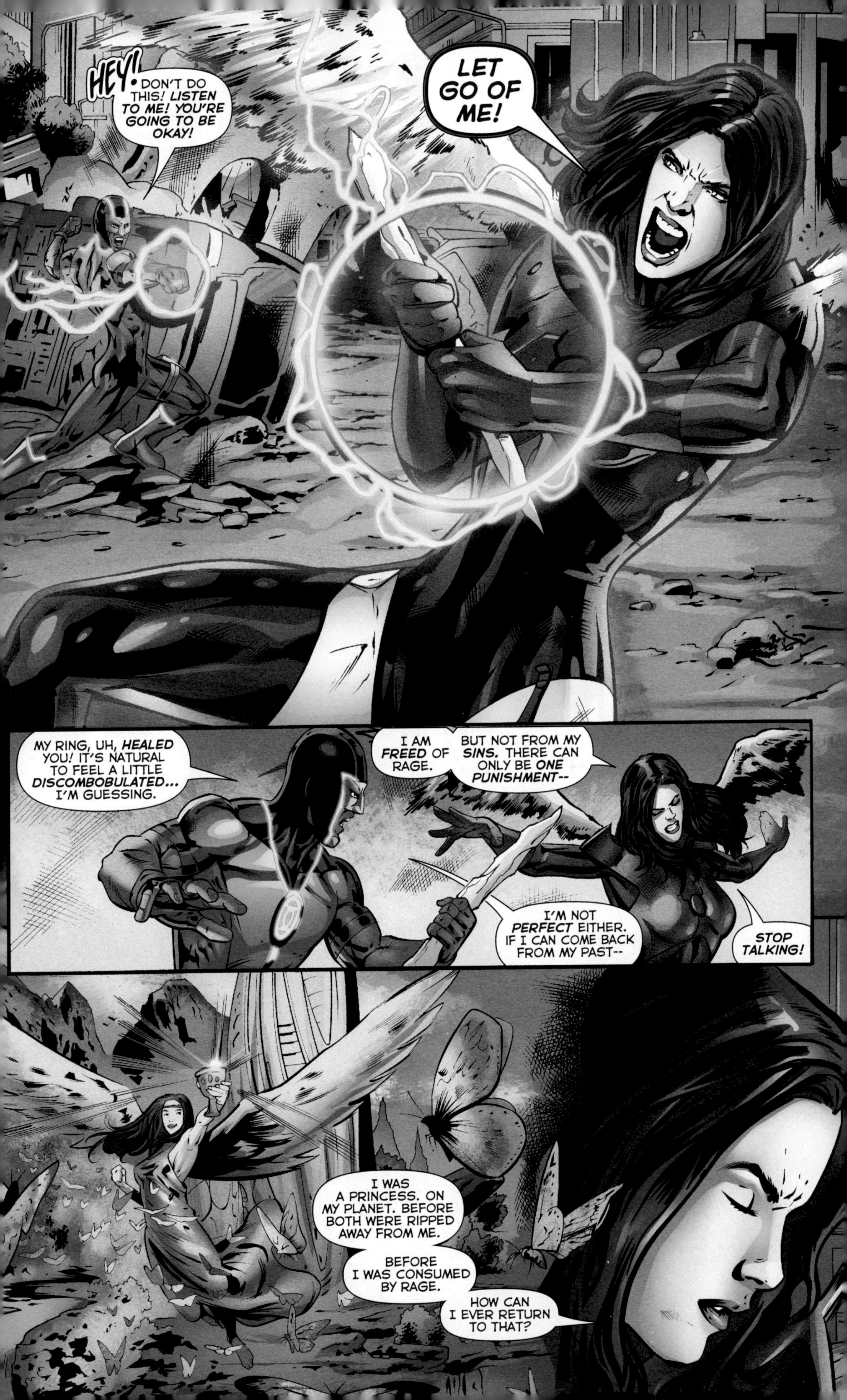
HEY!
DON'T DO THIS! LISTEN TO ME! YOU'RE GOING TO BE OKAY!
LET GO OF ME!
MY RING, UH, HEALED YOU! IT'S NATURAL TO FEEL A LITTLE DISCOMBOBULATED... I'M GUESSING.
I AM FREED OF RAGE.
BUT NOT FROM MY SINS. THERE CAN ONLY BE ONE PUNISHMENT--
I'M NOT PERFECT EITHER. IF I CAN COME BACK FROM MY PAST--
STOP TALKING!
I WAS A PRINCESS. ON MY PLANET. BEFORE BOTH WERE RIPPED AWAY FROM ME.
BEFORE I WAS CONSUMED BY RAGE.
HOW CAN I EVER RETURN TO THAT?

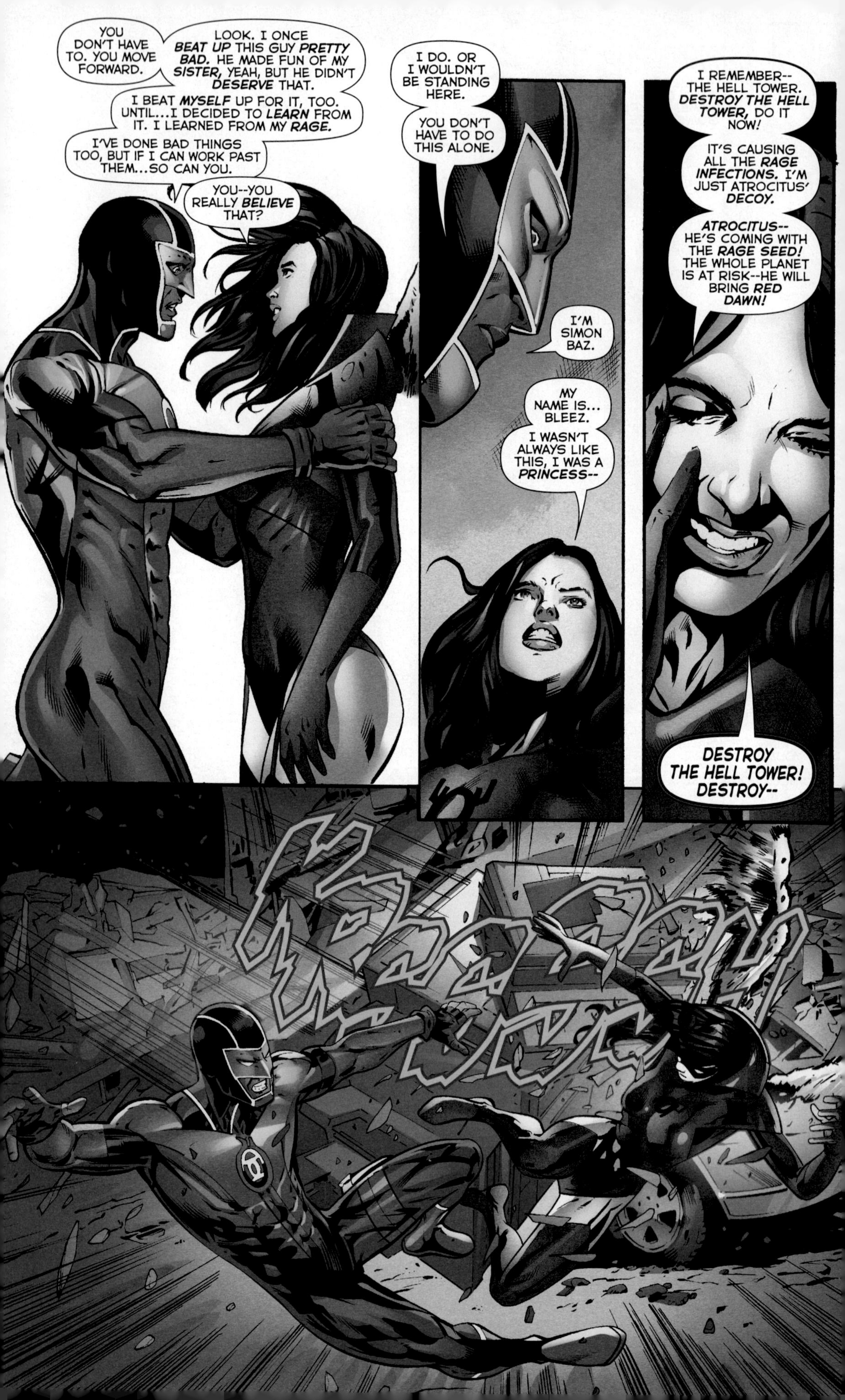
YOU DON'T HAVE TO. YOU MOVE FORWARD.
LOOK. I ONCE BEAT UP THIS GUY PRETTY BAD. HE MADE FUN OF MY SISTER, YEAH, BUT HE DIDN'T DESERVE THAT.
I BEAT MYSELF UP FOR IT, TOO. UNTIL...I DECIDED TO LEARN FROM IT. I LEARNED FROM MY RAGE.
I'VE DONE BAD THINGS TOO, BUT IF I CAN WORK PAST THEM...SO CAN YOU.
YOU--YOU REALLY BELIEVE THAT?
I DO. OR I WOULDN'T BE STANDING HERE.
YOU DON'T HAVE TO DO THIS ALONE.
I'M SIMON BAZ.
MY NAME IS... BLEEZ.
I WASN'T ALWAYS LIKE THIS, I WAS A PRINCESS--
I REMEMBER-- THE HELL TOWER. DESTROY THE HELL TOWER, DO IT NOW!
IT'S CAUSING ALL THE RAGE INFECTIONS. I'M JUST ATROCITUS' DECOY.
ATROCITUS-- HE'S COMING WITH THE RAGE SEED! THE WHOLE PLANET IS AT RISK--HE WILL BRING RED DAWN!
DESTROY THE HELL TOWER! DESTROY--

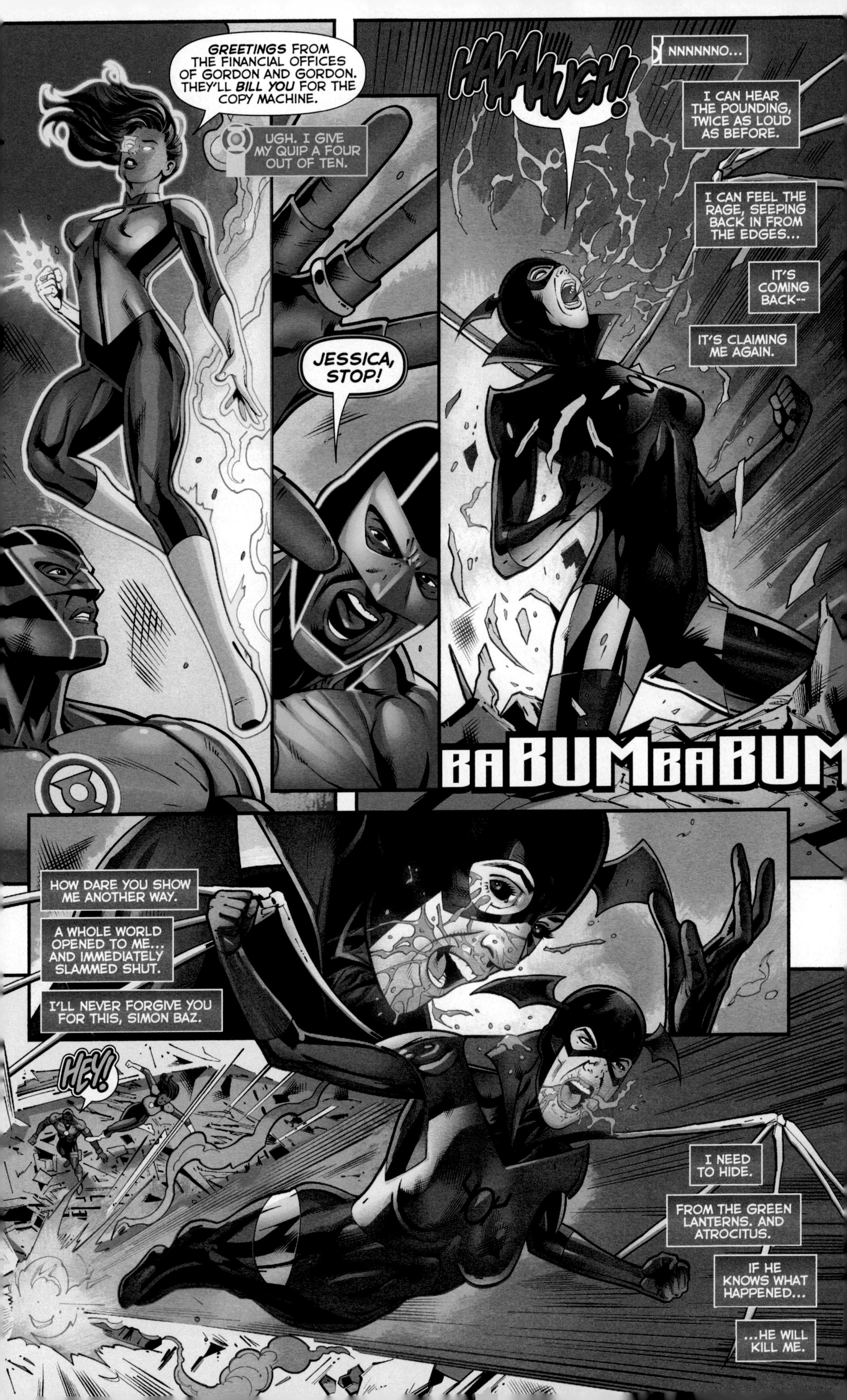

GREETINGS FROM THE FINANCIAL OFFICES OF GORDON AND GORDON. THEY'LL BILL YOU FOR THE COPY MACHINE.
UGH. I GIVE MY QUIP A FOUR OUT OF TEN.
JESSICA, STOP!
HAAAAAUGH!
NNNNNNO...
I CAN HEAR THE POUNDING, TWICE AS LOUD AS BEFORE.
I CAN FEEL THE RAGE, SEEPING BACK IN FROM THE EDGES...
IT'S COMING BACK--
IT'S CLAIMING ME AGAIN.
BABUMBABUM
HOW DARE YOU SHOW ME ANOTHER WAY.
A WHOLE WORLD OPENED TO ME... AND IMMEDIATELY SLAMMED SHUT.
I'LL NEVER FORGIVE YOU FOR THIS, SIMON BAZ.
HEY!
I NEED TO HIDE.
FROM THE GREEN LANTERNS. AND ATROCITUS.
IF HE KNOWS WHAT HAPPENED...
...HE WILL KILL ME.

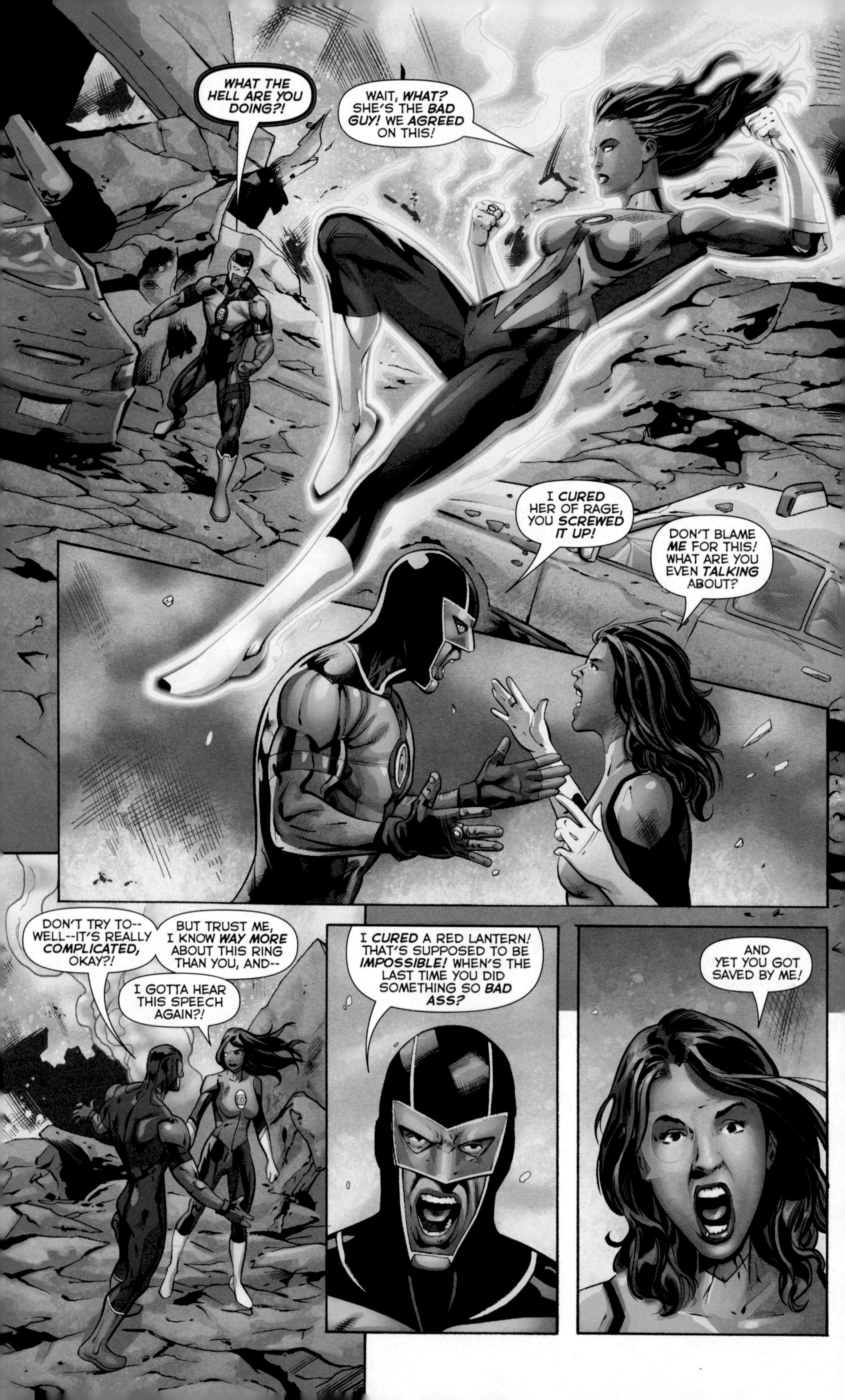

WHAT THE HELL ARE YOU DOING?!
WAIT, WHAT? SHE'S THE BAD GUY! WE AGREED ON THIS!
I CURED HER OF RAGE, YOU SCREWED IT UP!
DON'T BLAME ME FOR THIS! WHAT ARE YOU EVEN TALKING ABOUT?
DON'T TRY TO-- WELL--IT'S REALLY COMPLICATED, OKAY?!
BUT TRUST ME, I KNOW WAY MORE ABOUT THIS RING THAN YOU, AND--
I GOTTA HEAR THIS SPEECH AGAIN?!
I CURED A RED LANTERN! THAT'S SUPPOSED TO BE IMPOSSIBLE! WHEN'S THE LAST TIME YOU DID SOMETHING SO BAD ASS?
AND YET YOU GOT SAVED BY ME!

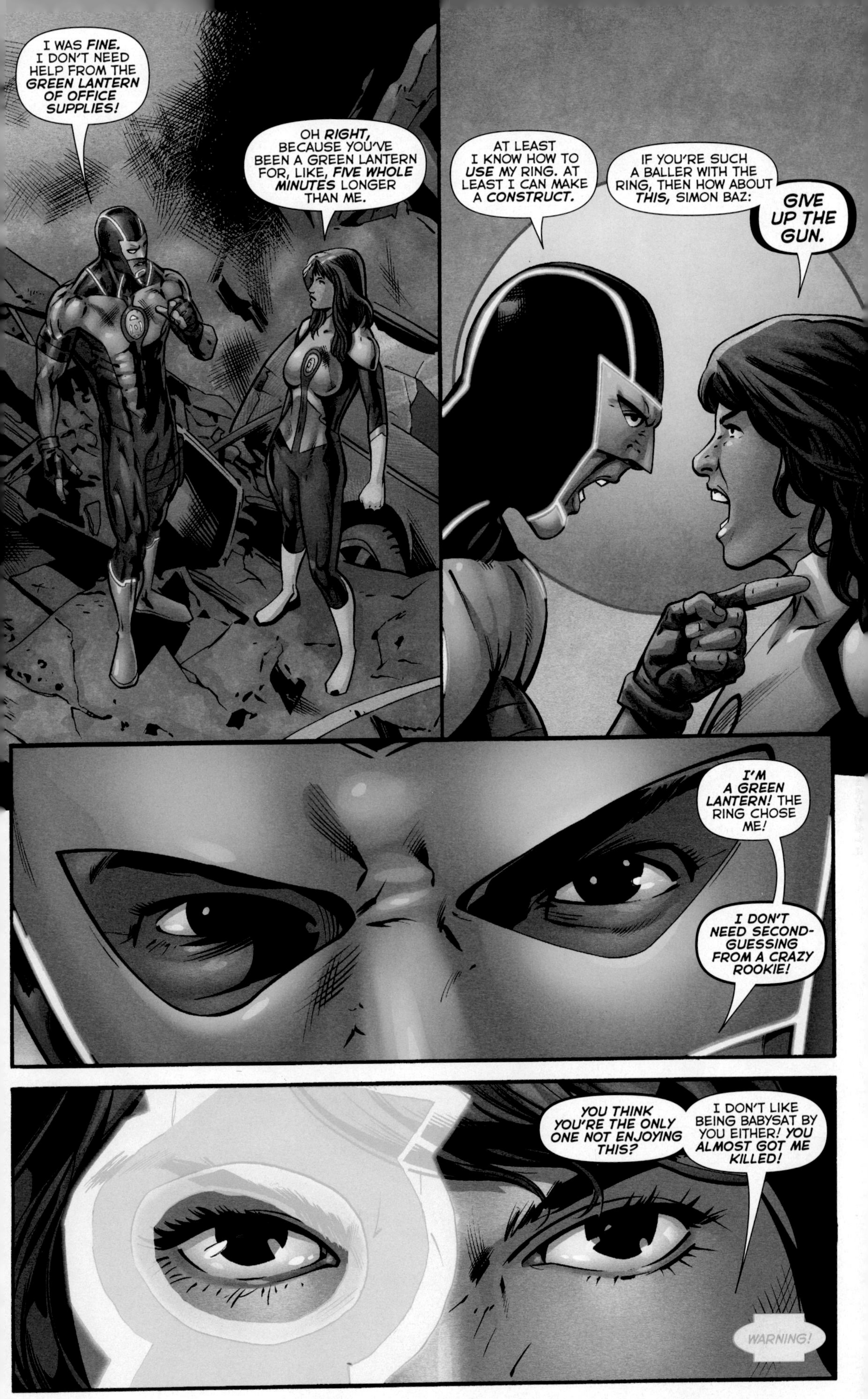
I WAS FINE. I DON'T NEED HELP FROM THE GREEN LANTERN OF OFFICE SUPPLIES!
OH RIGHT, BECAUSE YOU'VE BEEN A GREEN LANTERN FOR, LIKE, FIVE WHOLE MINUTES LONGER THAN ME.
AT LEAST I KNOW HOW TO USE MY RING. AT LEAST I CAN MAKE A CONSTRUCT.
IF YOU'RE SUCH A BALLER WITH THE RING, THEN HOW ABOUT THIS, SIMON BAZ:
GIVE UP THE GUN.
I'M A GREEN LANTERN! THE RING CHOSE ME!
I DON'T NEED SECOND-GUESSING FROM A CRAZY ROOKIE!
YOU THINK YOU'RE THE ONLY ONE NOT ENJOYING THIS?
I DON'T LIKE BEING BABYSAT BY YOU EITHER! YOU ALMOST GOT ME KILLED!
WARNING!

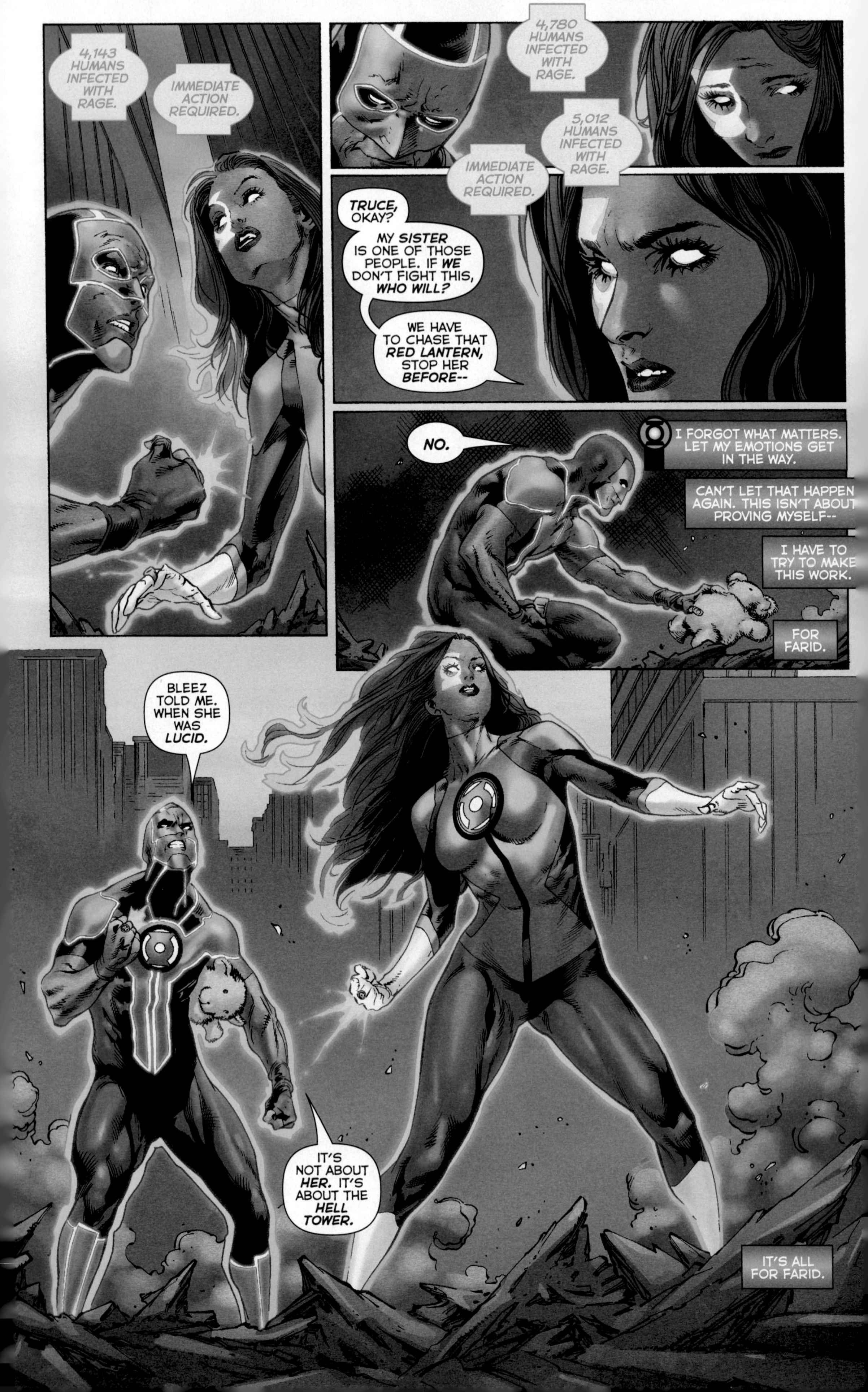

4,143 HUMANS INFECTED WITH RAGE.
IMMEDIATE ACTION REQUIRED.
4,780 HUMANS INFECTED WITH RAGE.
5,012 HUMANS INFECTED WITH RAGE.
IMMEDIATE ACTION REQUIRED.
TRUCE, OKAY?
MY SISTER IS ONE OF THOSE PEOPLE. IF WE DON'T FIGHT THIS, WHO WILL?
WE HAVE TO CHASE THAT RED LANTERN, STOP HER BEFORE--
NO.
I FORGOT WHAT MATTERS. LET MY EMOTIONS GET IN THE WAY.
CAN'T LET THAT HAPPEN AGAIN. THIS ISN'T ABOUT PROVING MYSELF--
I HAVE TO TRY TO MAKE THIS WORK.
FOR FARID.
BLEEZ TOLD ME. WHEN SHE WAS LUCID.
IT'S NOT ABOUT HER. IT'S ABOUT THE HELL TOWER.
IT'S ALL FOR FARID.

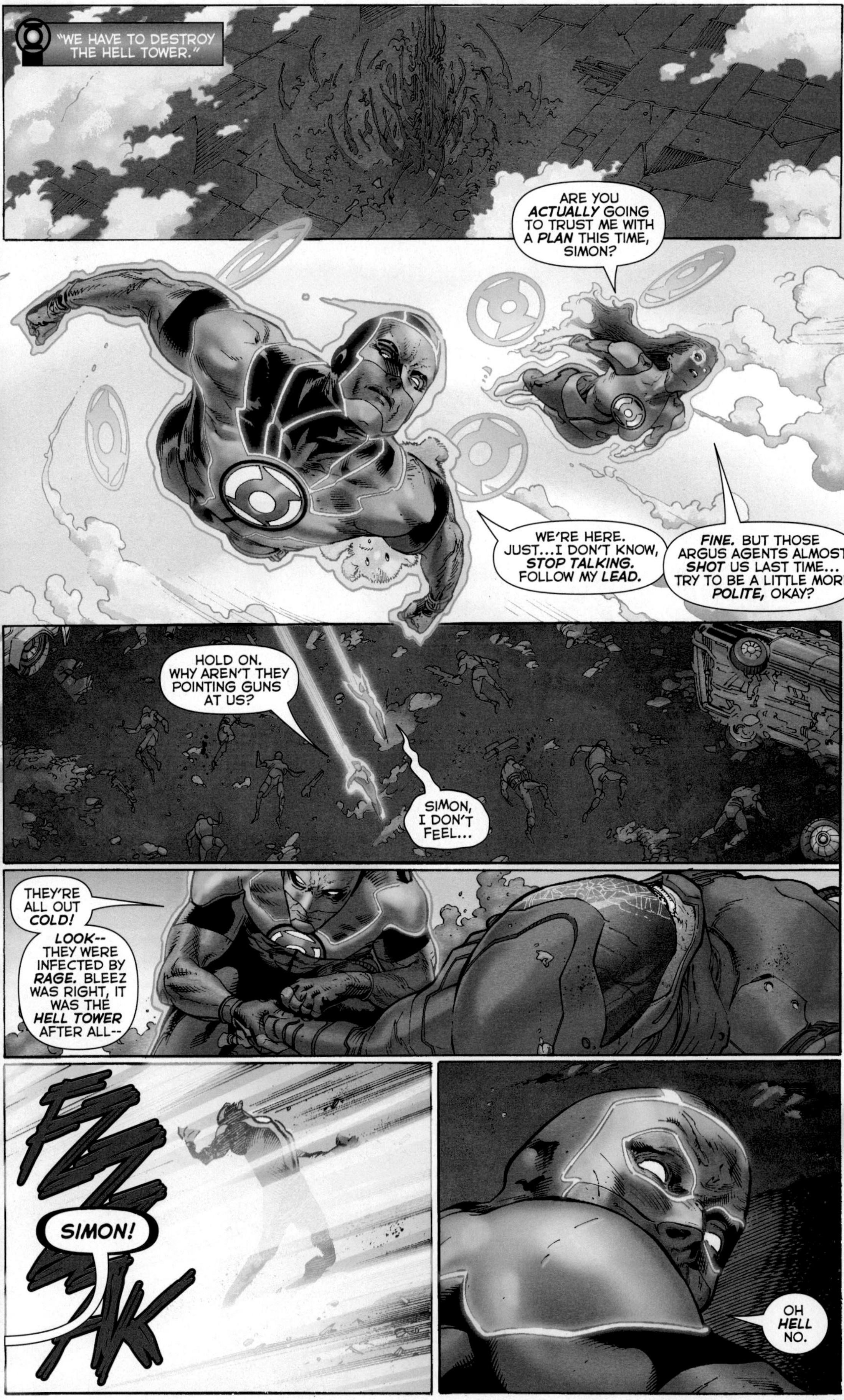
"WE HAVE TO DESTROY THE HELL TOWER."
ARE YOU ACTUALLY GOING TO TRUST ME WITH A PLAN THIS TIME, SIMON?
WE'RE HERE. JUST...I DON'T KNOW, STOP TALKING. FOLLOW MY LEAD.
FINE. BUT THOSE ARGUS AGENTS ALMOST SHOT US LAST TIME... TRY TO BE A LITTLE MORE POLITE, OKAY?
HOLD ON. WHY AREN'T THEY POINTING GUNS AT US?
SIMON, I DON'T FEEL...
THEY'RE ALL OUT COLD!
LOOK-- THEY WERE INFECTED BY RAGE. BLEEZ WAS RIGHT, IT WAS THE HELL TOWER AFTER ALL--
FZZ
SIMON!
SHK
OH HELL NO.

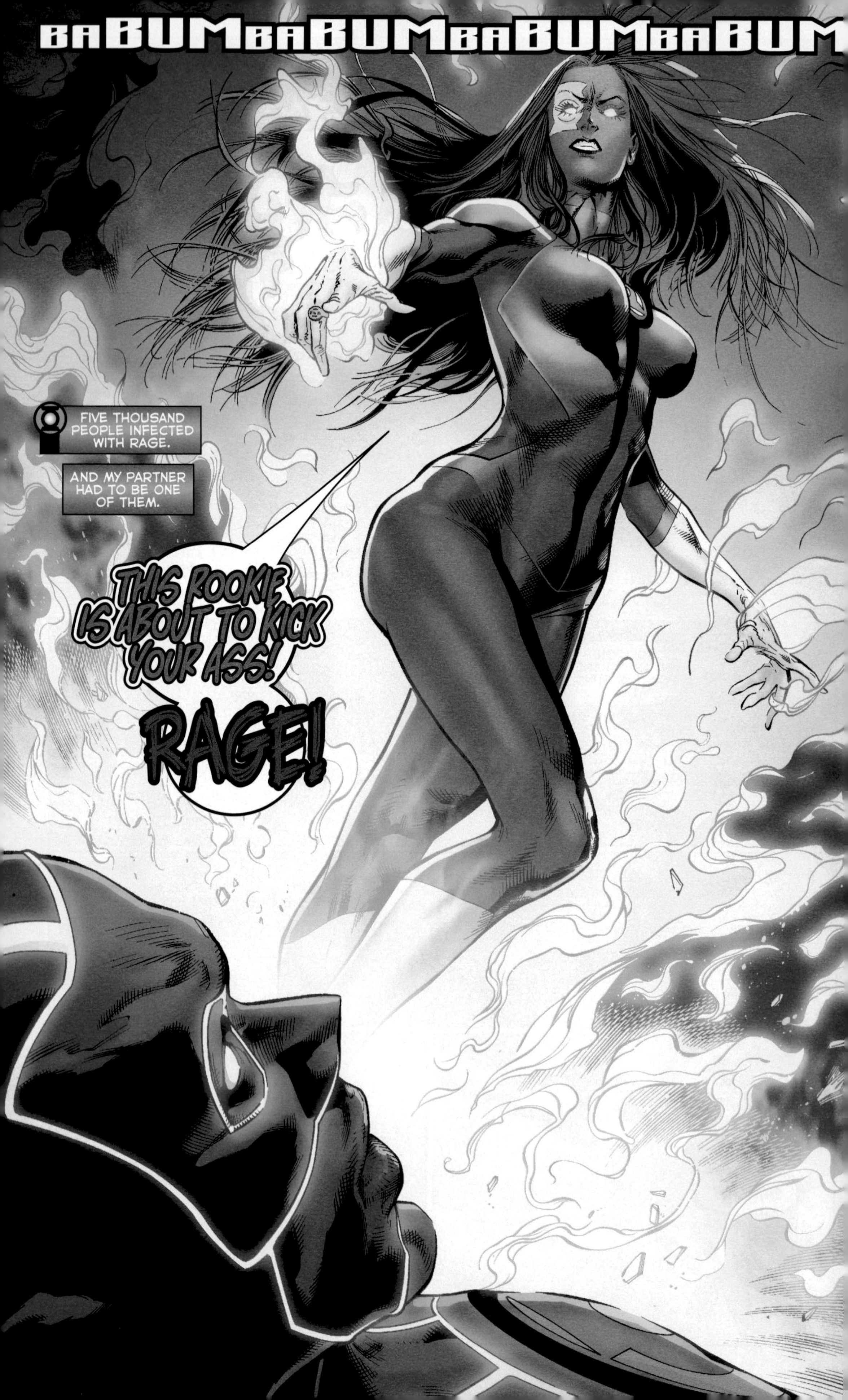

BaBUMBaBUMBaBUMBaBUM
FIVE THOUSAND PEOPLE INFECTED WITH RAGE.
AND MY PARTNER HAD TO BE ONE OF THEM.
THIS ROOKIE IS ABOUT TO KICK YOUR ASS!
RAGE!

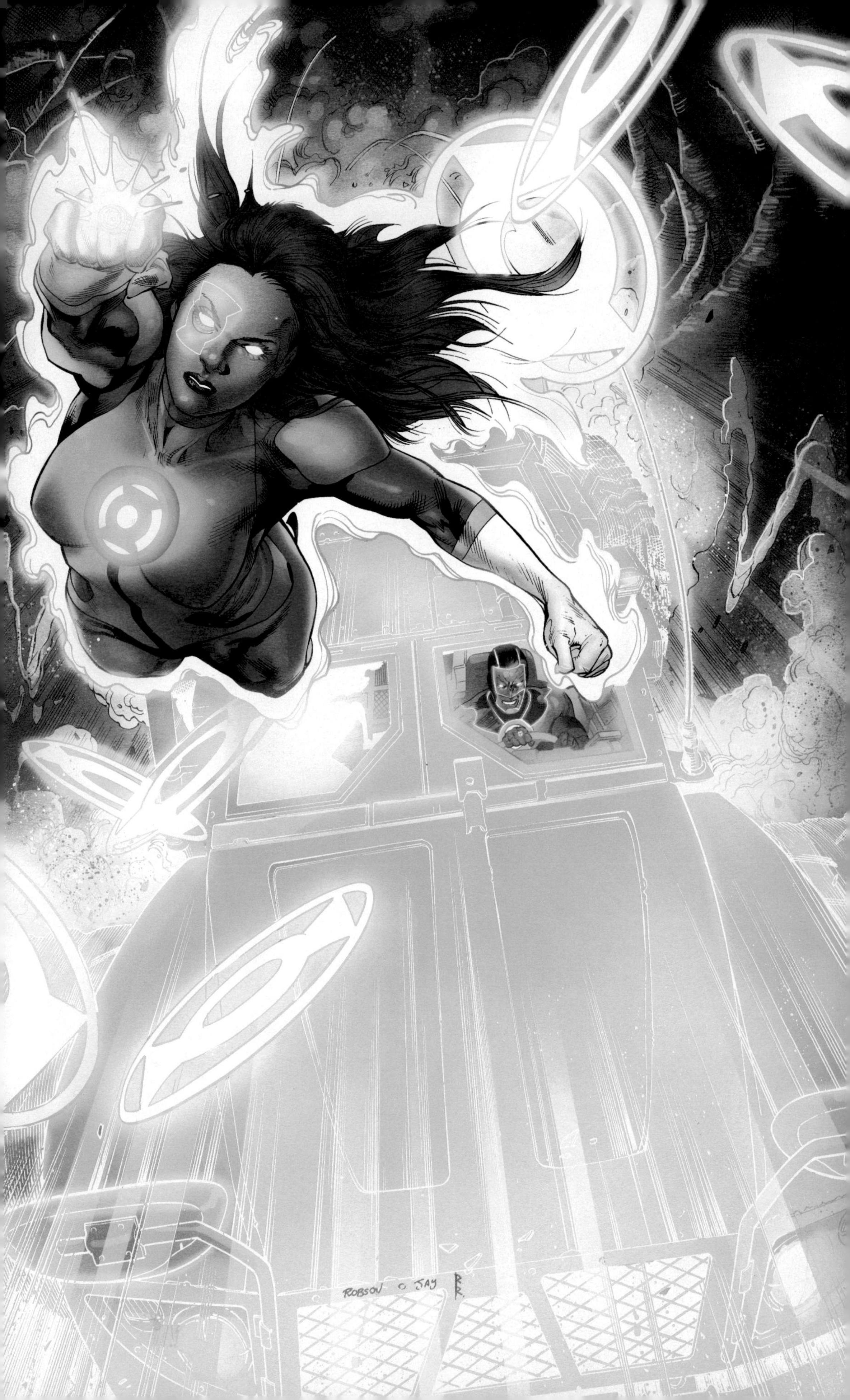
ROBSON JAY R.R.

RAGE PLANET: PART 4

SAM HUMPHRIES writer * ROBSON ROCHA, ED BENES and TOM DERENICK pencillers
JAY LEISTEN, ROB HUNTER, MARK IRWIN, VICENTE CIFUENTES, TOM PALMER and MARC DEERING inkers * BLOND colorist
ROBSON ROCHA, JAY LEISTEN and ROD REIS cover artists

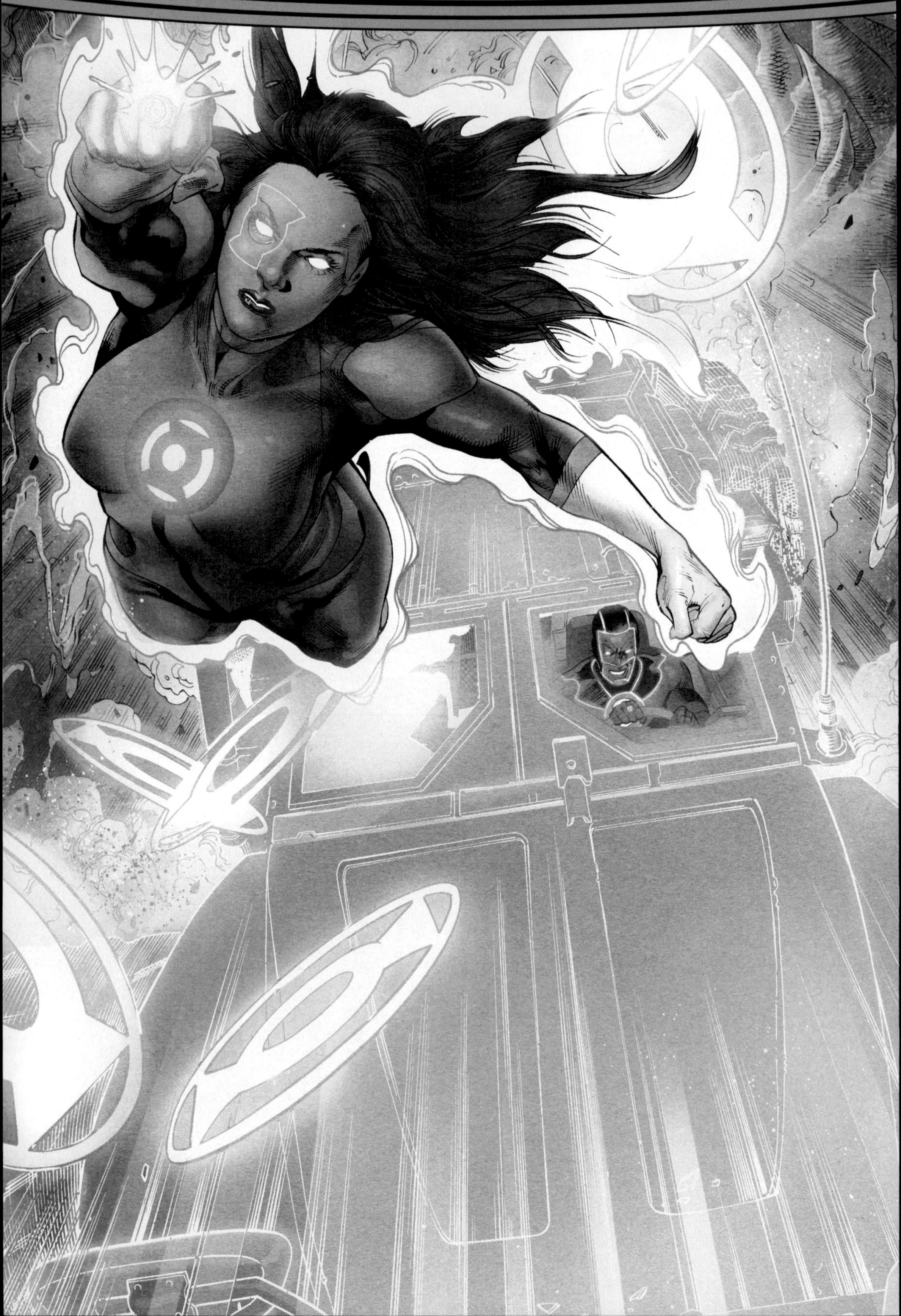

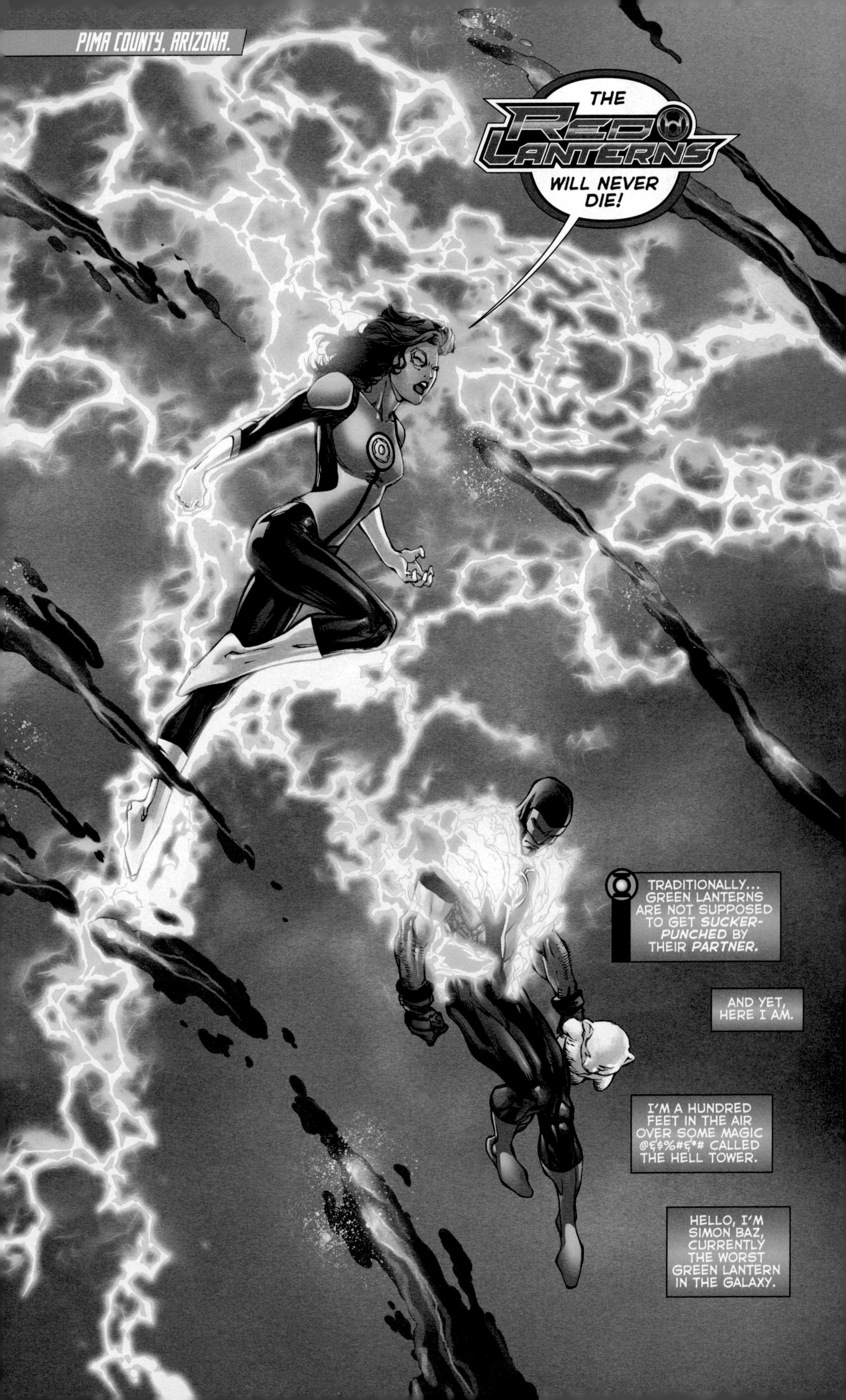
PIMA COUNTY, ARIZONA.
THE RED LANTERNS WILL NEVER DIE!
TRADITIONALLY... GREEN LANTERNS ARE NOT SUPPOSED TO GET SUCKER-PUNCHED BY THEIR PARTNER.
AND YET, HERE I AM.
I'M A HUNDRED FEET IN THE AIR OVER SOME MAGIC @&$%#&*# CALLED THE HELL TOWER.
HELLO, I'M SIMON BAZ, CURRENTLY THE WORST GREEN LANTERN IN THE GALAXY.

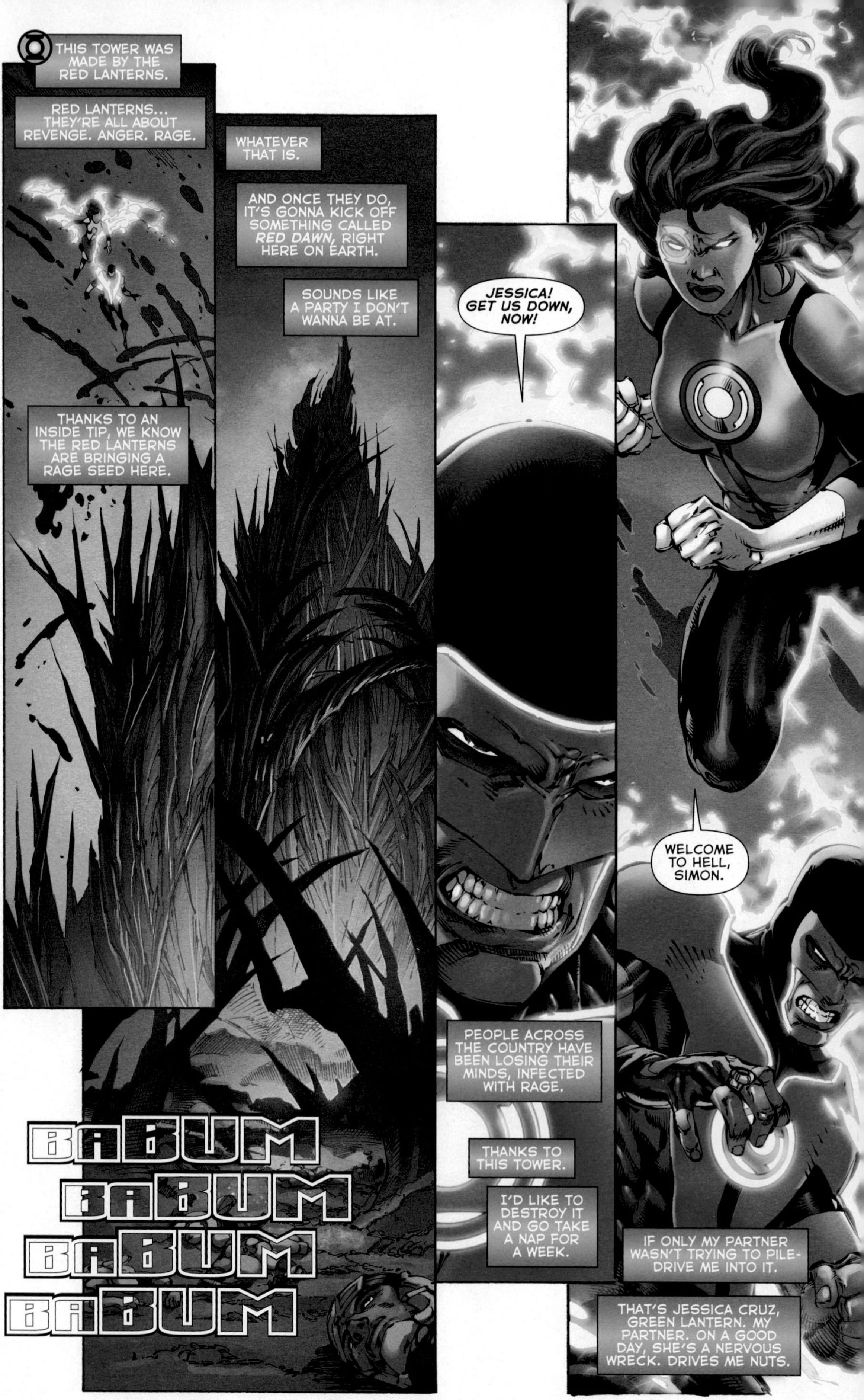
THIS TOWER WAS MADE BY THE RED LANTERNS.
RED LANTERNS... THEY'RE ALL ABOUT REVENGE. ANGER. RAGE.
THANKS TO AN INSIDE TIP, WE KNOW THE RED LANTERNS ARE BRINGING A RAGE SEED HERE.
WHATEVER THAT IS.
AND ONCE THEY DO, IT'S GONNA KICK OFF SOMETHING CALLED RED DAWN, RIGHT HERE ON EARTH.
SOUNDS LIKE A PARTY I DON'T WANNA BE AT.
BABUM BABUM BABUM BABUM
JESSICA! GET US DOWN, NOW!
PEOPLE ACROSS THE COUNTRY HAVE BEEN LOSING THEIR MINDS, INFECTED WITH RAGE.
THANKS TO THIS TOWER.
I'D LIKE TO DESTROY IT AND GO TAKE A NAP FOR A WEEK.
WELCOME TO HELL, SIMON.
IF ONLY MY PARTNER WASN'T TRYING TO PILE-DRIVE ME INTO IT.
THAT'S JESSICA CRUZ, GREEN LANTERN. MY PARTNER. ON A GOOD DAY, SHE'S A NERVOUS WRECK. DRIVES ME NUTS.

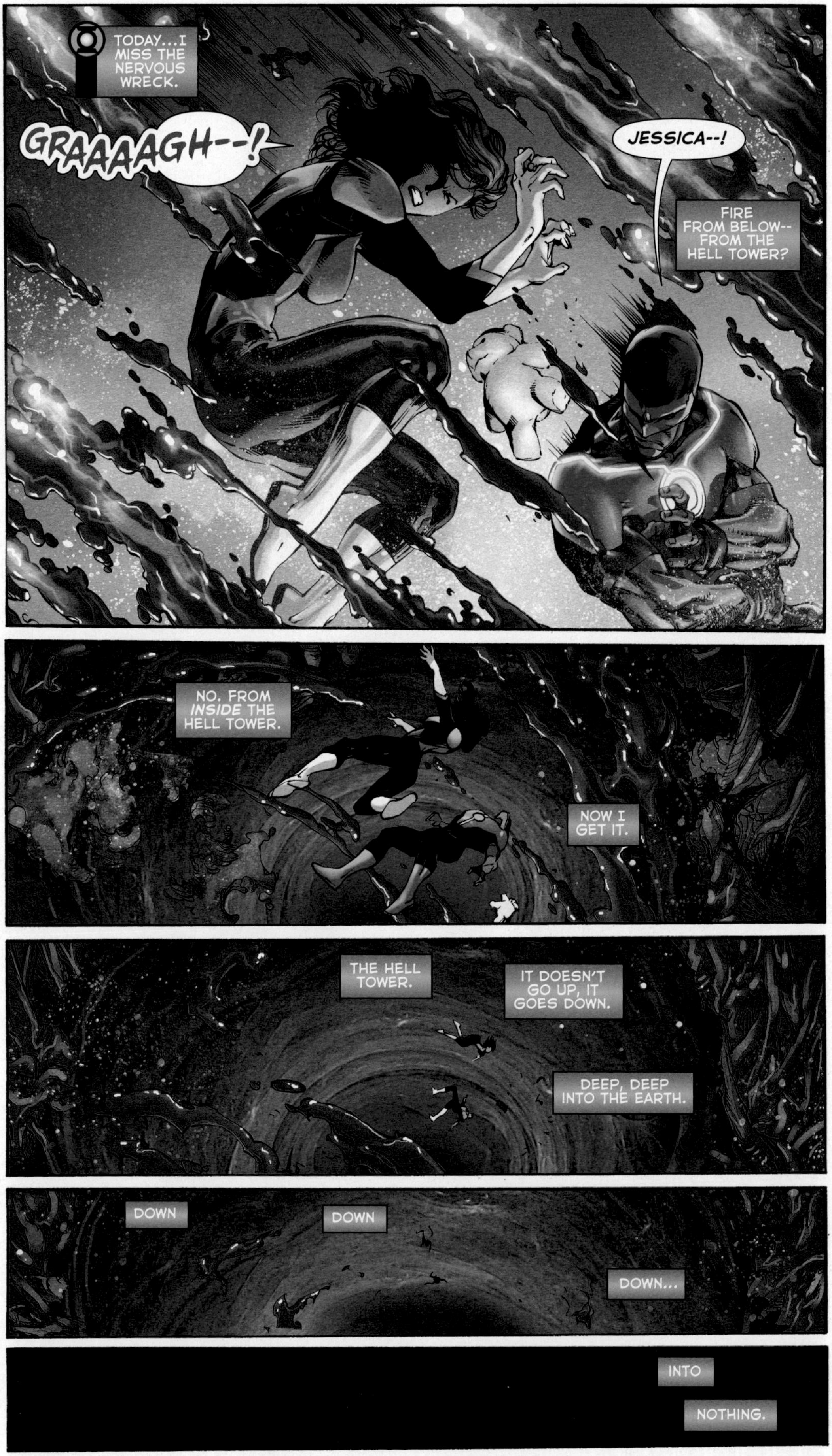
TODAY...I MISS THE NERVOUS WRECK.
GRAAAAGH--!
JESSICA--!
FIRE FROM BELOW-- FROM THE HELL TOWER?
NO. FROM *INSIDE* THE HELL TOWER.
NOW I GET IT.
THE HELL TOWER.
IT DOESN'T GO UP, IT GOES DOWN.
DEEP, DEEP INTO THE EARTH.
DOWN
DOWN
DOWN...
INTO
NOTHING.

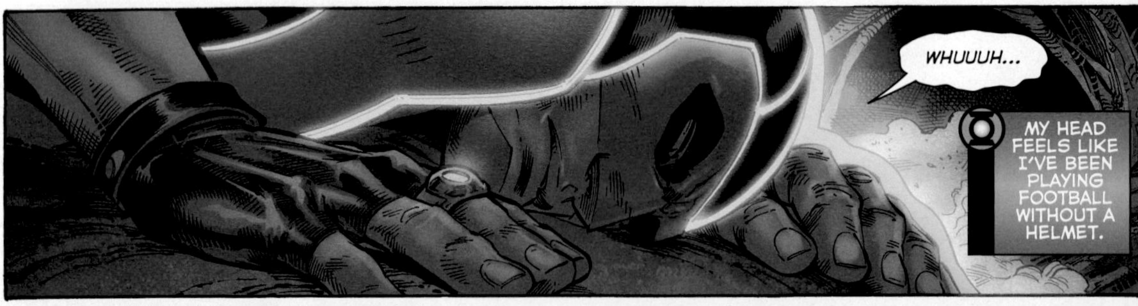
WHUUUH...
MY HEAD FEELS LIKE I'VE BEEN PLAYING FOOTBALL WITHOUT A HELMET.

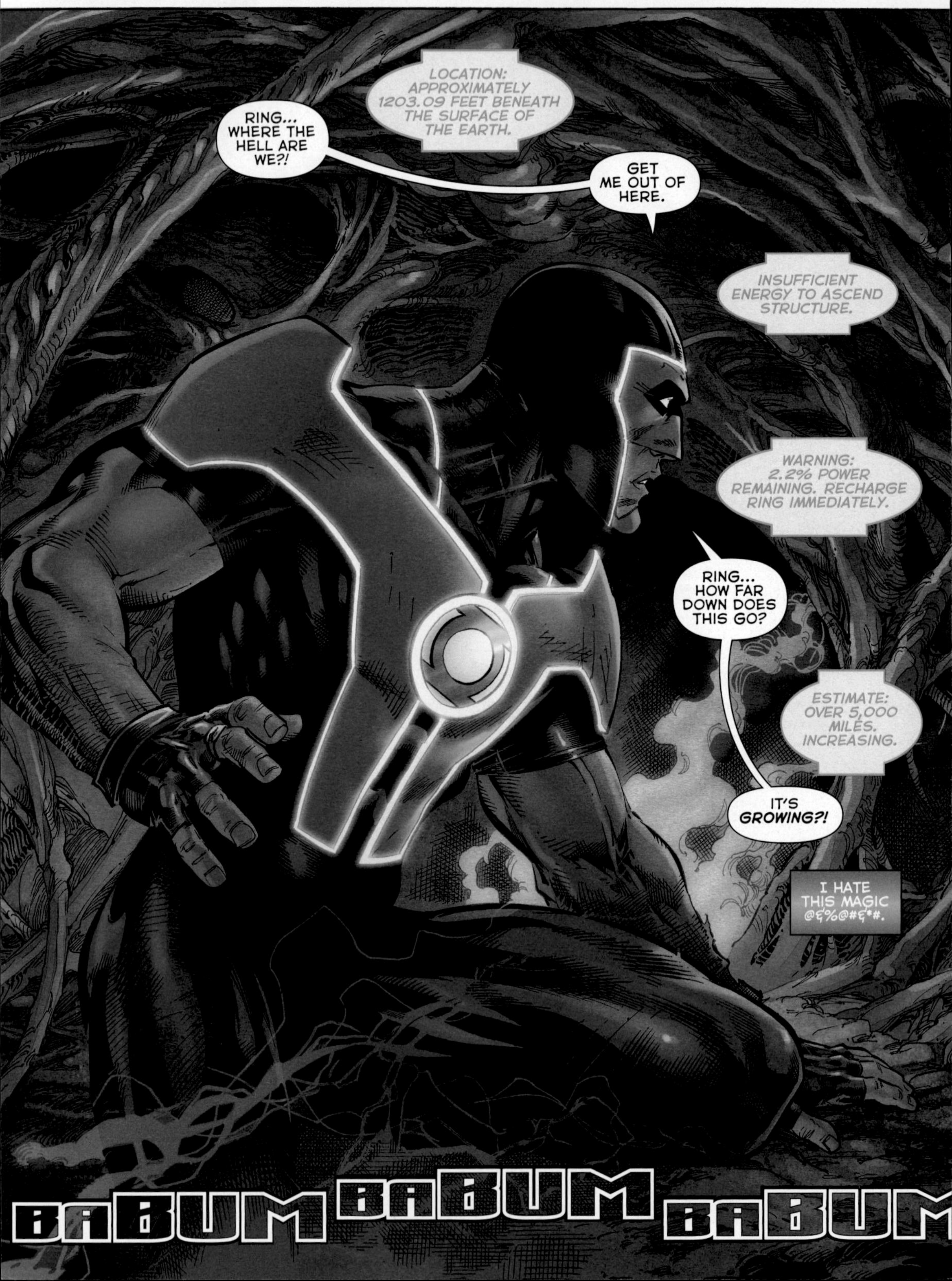
RING... WHERE THE HELL ARE WE?!
LOCATION: APPROXIMATELY 1203.09 FEET BENEATH THE SURFACE OF THE EARTH.
GET ME OUT OF HERE.
INSUFFICIENT ENERGY TO ASCEND STRUCTURE.
WARNING: 2.2% POWER REMAINING. RECHARGE RING IMMEDIATELY.
RING... HOW FAR DOWN DOES THIS GO?
ESTIMATE: OVER 5,000 MILES. INCREASING.
IT'S GROWING?!
I HATE THIS MAGIC @£%@#£*#.
BABUM BABUM BABUM

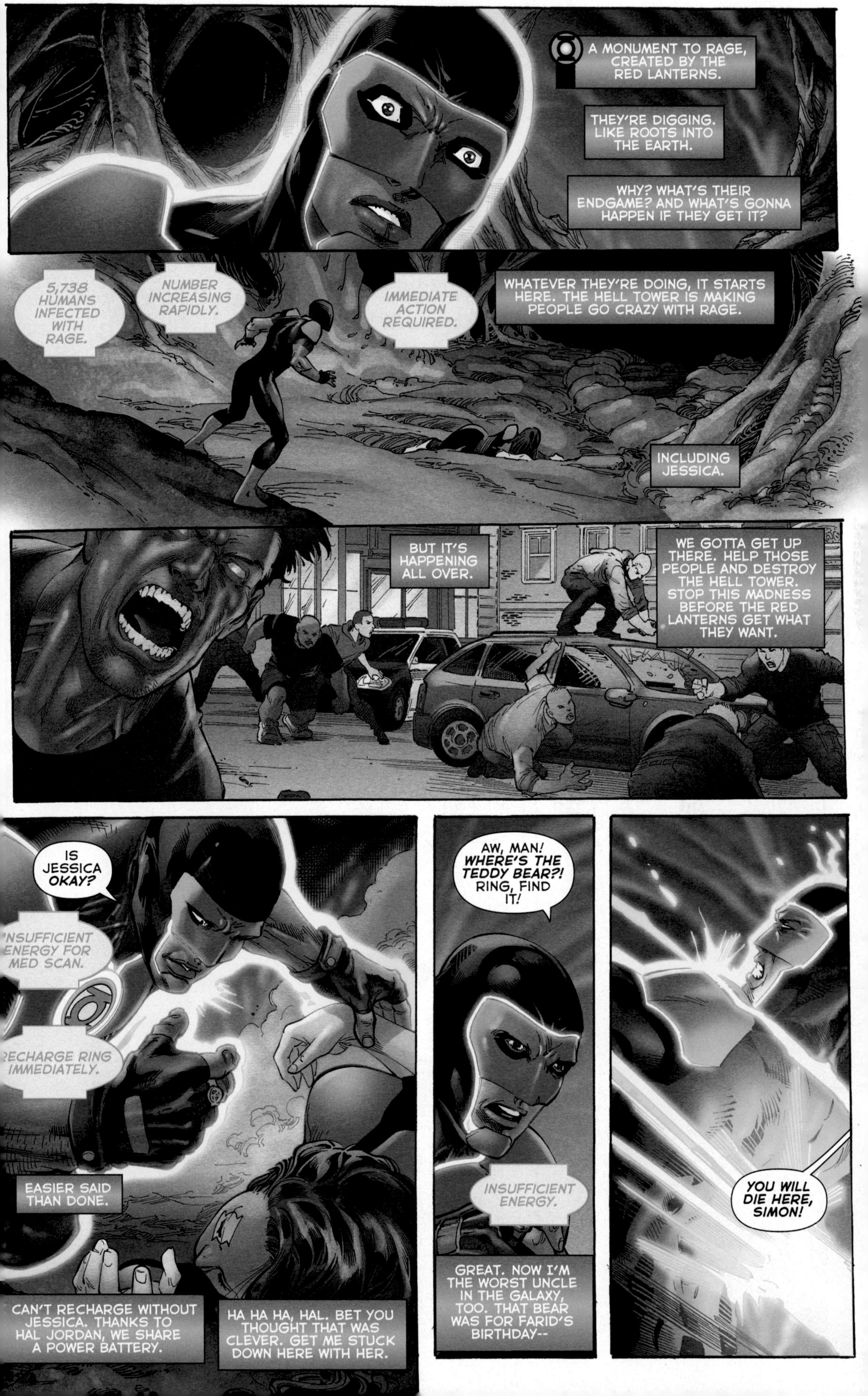
A MONUMENT TO RAGE, CREATED BY THE RED LANTERNS.
THEY'RE DIGGING. LIKE ROOTS INTO THE EARTH.
WHY? WHAT'S THEIR ENDGAME? AND WHAT'S GONNA HAPPEN IF THEY GET IT?
5,738 HUMANS INFECTED WITH RAGE.
NUMBER INCREASING RAPIDLY.
IMMEDIATE ACTION REQUIRED.
WHATEVER THEY'RE DOING, IT STARTS HERE. THE HELL TOWER IS MAKING PEOPLE GO CRAZY WITH RAGE.
INCLUDING JESSICA.
BUT IT'S HAPPENING ALL OVER.
WE GOTTA GET UP THERE. HELP THOSE PEOPLE AND DESTROY THE HELL TOWER. STOP THIS MADNESS BEFORE THE RED LANTERNS GET WHAT THEY WANT.
IS JESSICA OKAY?
INSUFFICIENT ENERGY FOR MED SCAN.
RECHARGE RING IMMEDIATELY.
EASIER SAID THAN DONE.
CAN'T RECHARGE WITHOUT JESSICA. THANKS TO HAL JORDAN, WE SHARE A POWER BATTERY.
HA HA HA, HAL. BET YOU THOUGHT THAT WAS CLEVER. GET ME STUCK DOWN HERE WITH HER.
AW, MAN! WHERE'S THE TEDDY BEAR?! RING, FIND IT!
INSUFFICIENT ENERGY.
GREAT. NOW I'M THE WORST UNCLE IN THE GALAXY, TOO. THAT BEAR WAS FOR FARID'S BIRTHDAY--
YOU WILL DIE HERE, SIMON!

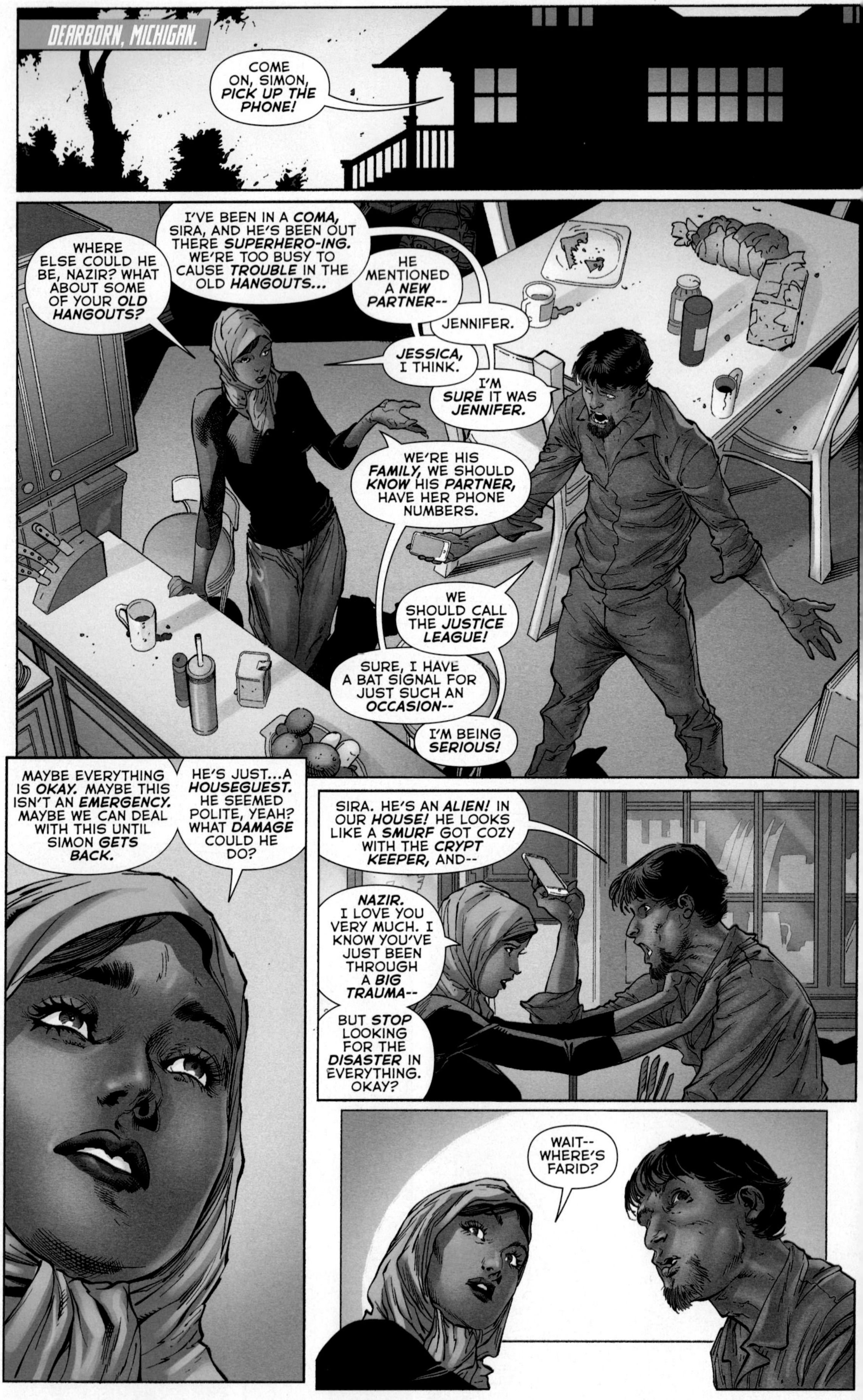
DEARBORN, MICHIGAN.
COME ON, SIMON, PICK UP THE PHONE!
WHERE ELSE COULD HE BE, NAZIR? WHAT ABOUT SOME OF YOUR OLD HANGOUTS?
I'VE BEEN IN A COMA, SIRA, AND HE'S BEEN OUT THERE SUPERHERO-ING. WE'RE TOO BUSY TO CAUSE TROUBLE IN THE OLD HANGOUTS...
HE MENTIONED A NEW PARTNER--
JENNIFER.
JESSICA, I THINK.
I'M SURE IT WAS JENNIFER.
WE'RE HIS FAMILY, WE SHOULD KNOW HIS PARTNER, HAVE HER PHONE NUMBERS.
WE SHOULD CALL THE JUSTICE LEAGUE!
SURE, I HAVE A BAT SIGNAL FOR JUST SUCH AN OCCASION--
I'M BEING SERIOUS!
MAYBE EVERYTHING IS OKAY. MAYBE THIS ISN'T AN EMERGENCY. MAYBE WE CAN DEAL WITH THIS UNTIL SIMON GETS BACK.
HE'S JUST...A HOUSEGUEST. HE SEEMED POLITE, YEAH? WHAT DAMAGE COULD HE DO?
SIRA. HE'S AN ALIEN! IN OUR HOUSE! HE LOOKS LIKE A SMURF GOT COZY WITH THE CRYPT KEEPER, AND--
NAZIR. I LOVE YOU VERY MUCH. I KNOW YOU'VE JUST BEEN THROUGH A BIG TRAUMA--
BUT STOP LOOKING FOR THE DISASTER IN EVERYTHING. OKAY?
WAIT-- WHERE'S FARID?

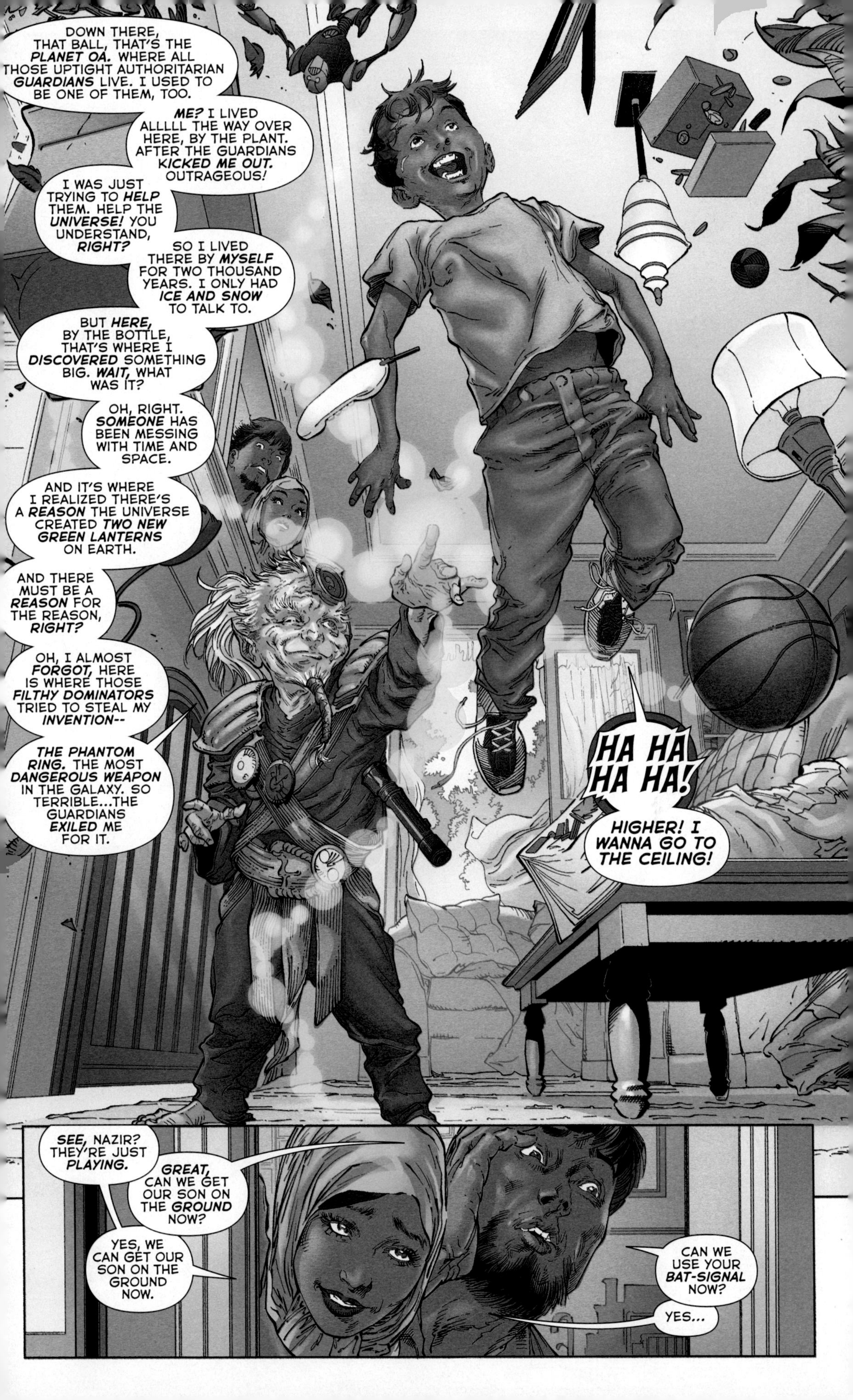
DOWN THERE, THAT BALL, THAT'S THE PLANET OA. WHERE ALL THOSE UPTIGHT AUTHORITARIAN GUARDIANS LIVE. I USED TO BE ONE OF THEM, TOO.
ME? I LIVED ALLLLL THE WAY OVER HERE, BY THE PLANT. AFTER THE GUARDIANS KICKED ME OUT. OUTRAGEOUS!
I WAS JUST TRYING TO HELP THEM. HELP THE UNIVERSE! YOU UNDERSTAND, RIGHT?
SO I LIVED THERE BY MYSELF FOR TWO THOUSAND YEARS. I ONLY HAD ICE AND SNOW TO TALK TO.
BUT HERE, BY THE BOTTLE, THAT'S WHERE I DISCOVERED SOMETHING BIG. WAIT, WHAT WAS IT?
OH, RIGHT. SOMEONE HAS BEEN MESSING WITH TIME AND SPACE.
AND IT'S WHERE I REALIZED THERE'S A REASON THE UNIVERSE CREATED TWO NEW GREEN LANTERNS ON EARTH.
AND THERE MUST BE A REASON FOR THE REASON, RIGHT?
OH, I ALMOST FORGOT, HERE IS WHERE THOSE FILTHY DOMINATORS TRIED TO STEAL MY INVENTION--
THE PHANTOM RING. THE MOST DANGEROUS WEAPON IN THE GALAXY. SO TERRIBLE...THE GUARDIANS EXILED ME FOR IT.
HA HA HA HA!
HIGHER! I WANNA GO TO THE CEILING!
SEE, NAZIR? THEY'RE JUST PLAYING.
GREAT, CAN WE GET OUR SON ON THE GROUND NOW?
YES, WE CAN GET OUR SON ON THE GROUND NOW.
CAN WE USE YOUR BAT-SIGNAL NOW?
YES...

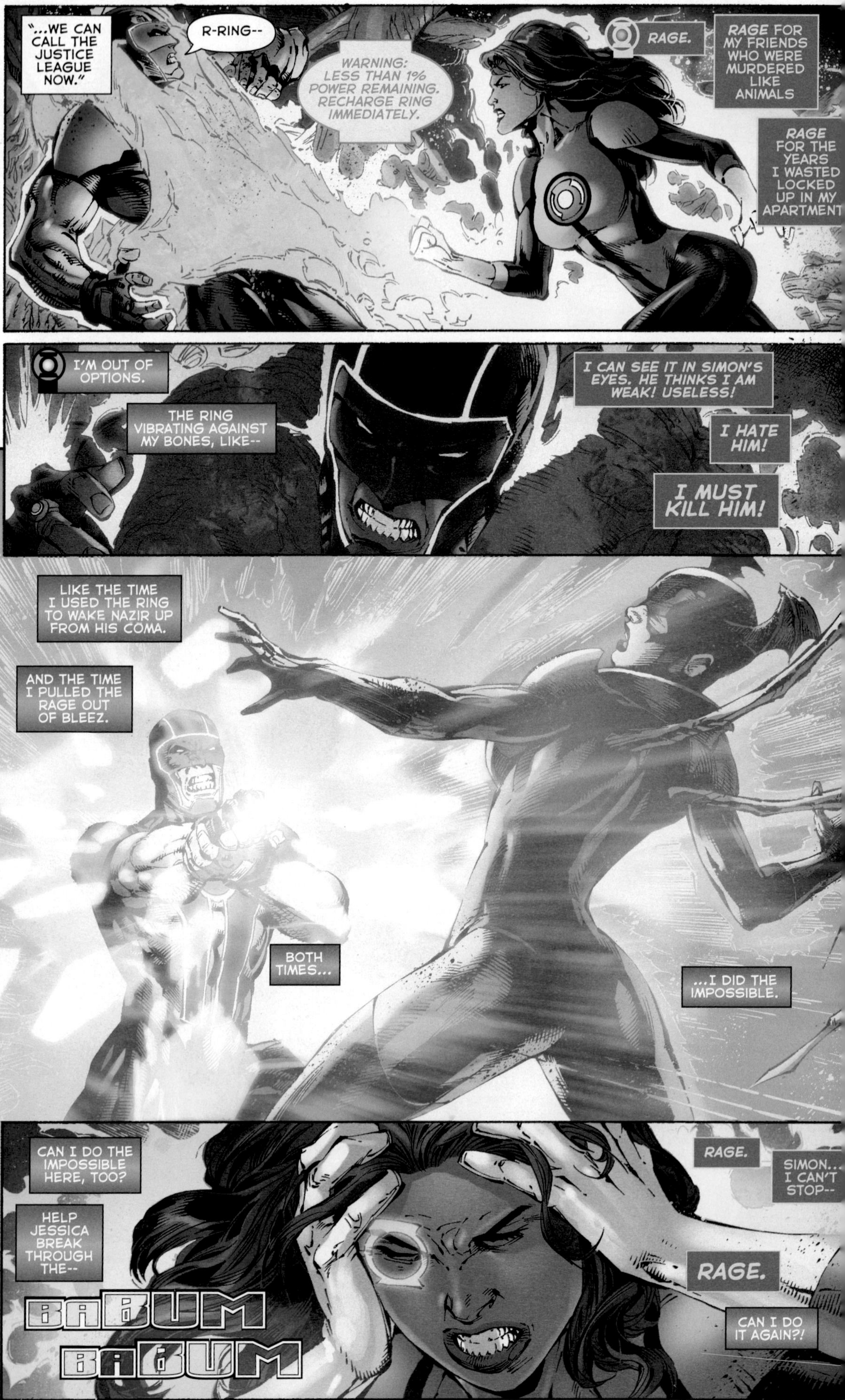
"...WE CAN CALL THE JUSTICE LEAGUE NOW."
R-RING--
WARNING: LESS THAN 1% POWER REMAINING. RECHARGE RING IMMEDIATELY.
RAGE.
RAGE FOR MY FRIENDS WHO WERE MURDERED LIKE ANIMALS
RAGE FOR THE YEARS I WASTED LOCKED UP IN MY APARTMENT
I'M OUT OF OPTIONS.
THE RING VIBRATING AGAINST MY BONES, LIKE--
I CAN SEE IT IN SIMON'S EYES. HE THINKS I AM WEAK! USELESS!
I HATE HIM!
I MUST KILL HIM!
LIKE THE TIME I USED THE RING TO WAKE NAZIR UP FROM HIS COMA.
AND THE TIME I PULLED THE RAGE OUT OF BLEEZ.
BOTH TIMES...
...I DID THE IMPOSSIBLE.
CAN I DO THE IMPOSSIBLE HERE, TOO?
HELP JESSICA BREAK THROUGH THE--
BABUM
BABUM
RAGE.
SIMON... I CAN'T STOP--
RAGE.
CAN I DO IT AGAIN?!

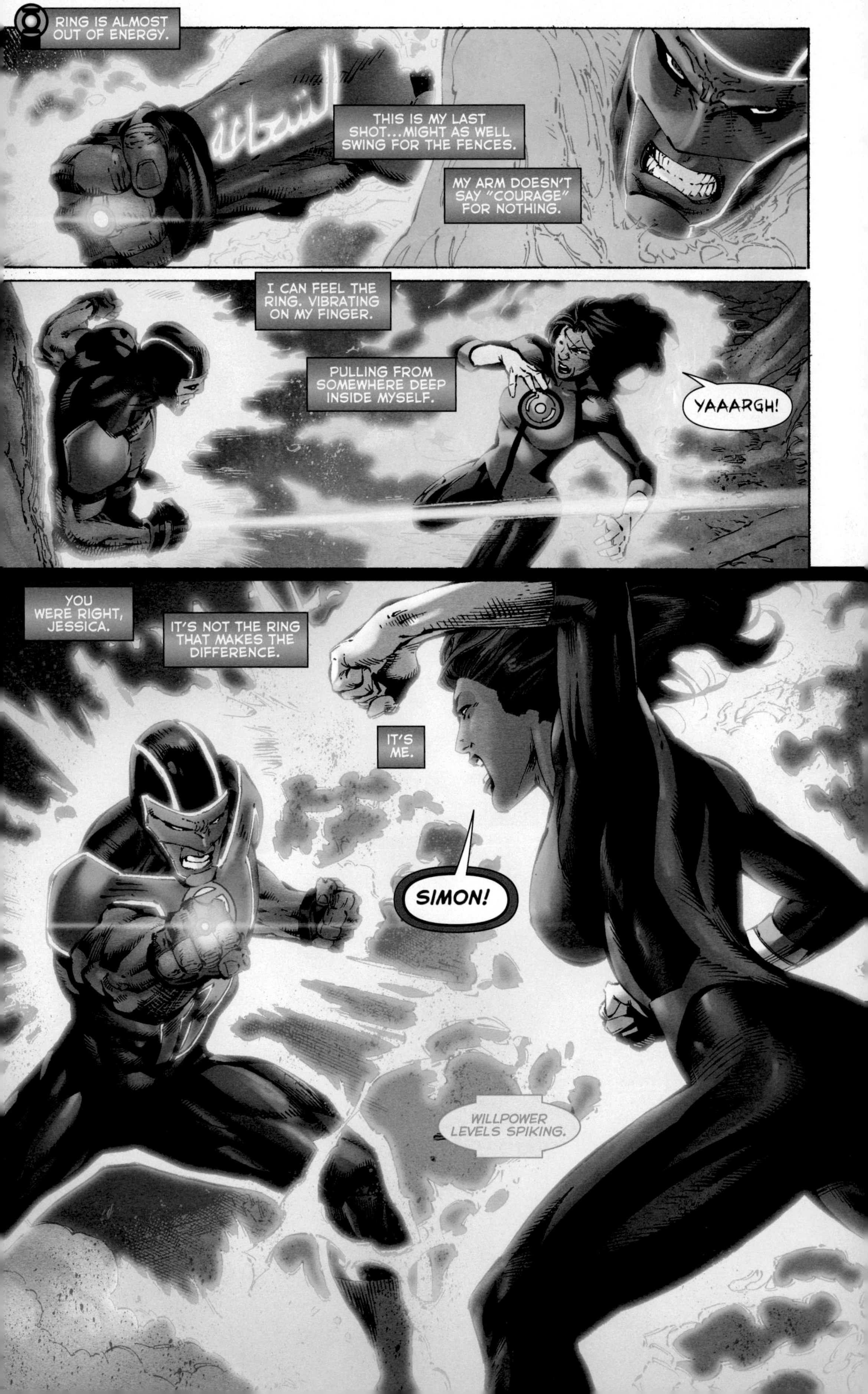
RING IS ALMOST OUT OF ENERGY.
THIS IS MY LAST SHOT...MIGHT AS WELL SWING FOR THE FENCES.
MY ARM DOESN'T SAY "COURAGE" FOR NOTHING.
I CAN FEEL THE RING. VIBRATING ON MY FINGER.
PULLING FROM SOMEWHERE DEEP INSIDE MYSELF.
YAAARGH!
YOU WERE RIGHT, JESSICA.
IT'S NOT THE RING THAT MAKES THE DIFFERENCE.
IT'S ME.
SIMON!
WILLPOWER LEVELS SPIKING.

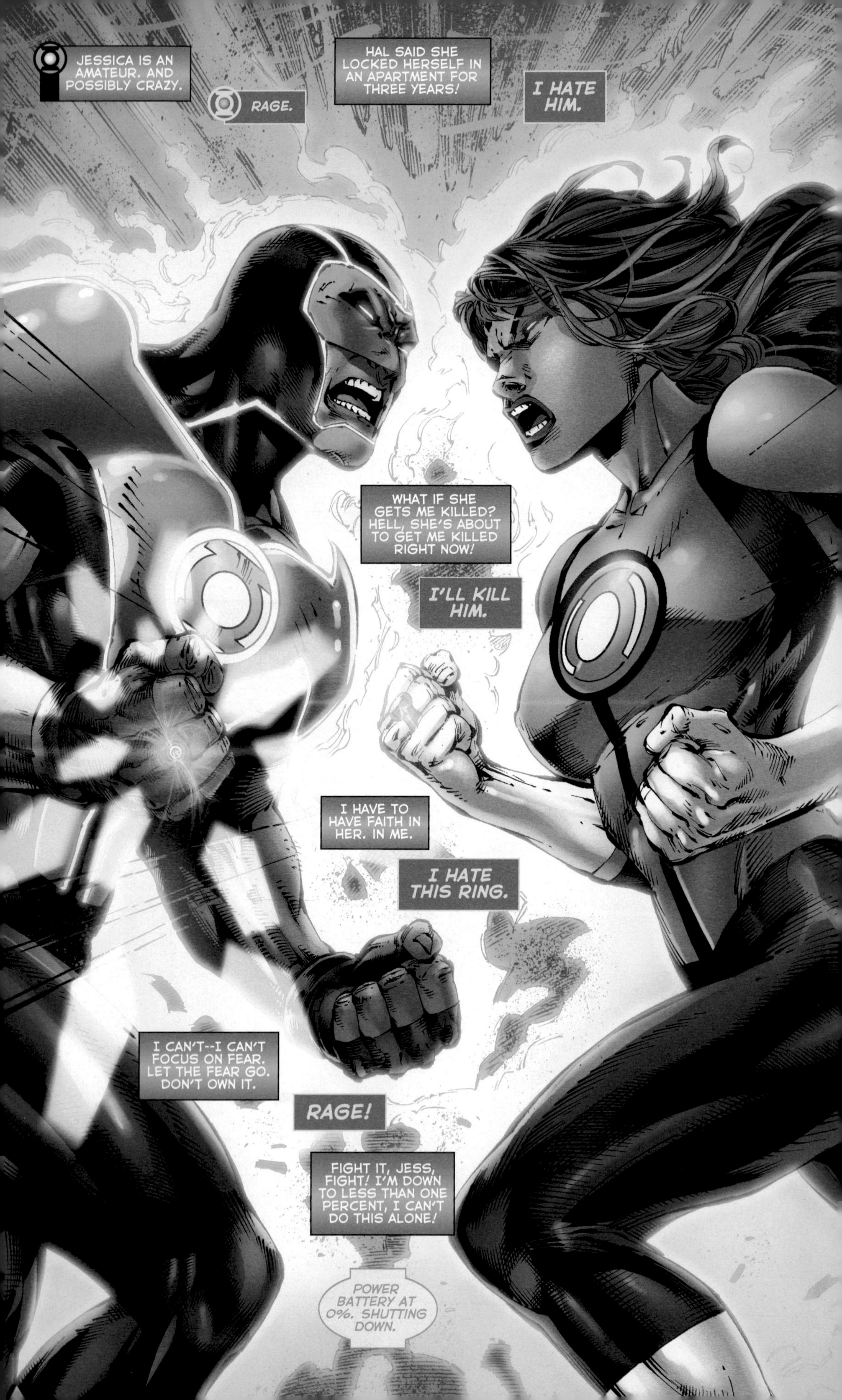

JESSICA IS AN AMATEUR. AND POSSIBLY CRAZY.
RAGE.
HAL SAID SHE LOCKED HERSELF IN AN APARTMENT FOR THREE YEARS!
I HATE HIM.
WHAT IF SHE GETS ME KILLED? HELL, SHE'S ABOUT TO GET ME KILLED RIGHT NOW!
I'LL KILL HIM.
I HAVE TO HAVE FAITH IN HER. IN ME.
I HATE THIS RING.
I CAN'T--I CAN'T FOCUS ON FEAR. LET THE FEAR GO. DON'T OWN IT.
RAGE!
FIGHT IT, JESS, FIGHT! I'M DOWN TO LESS THAN ONE PERCENT, I CAN'T DO THIS ALONE!
POWER BATTERY AT 0%. SHUTTING DOWN.

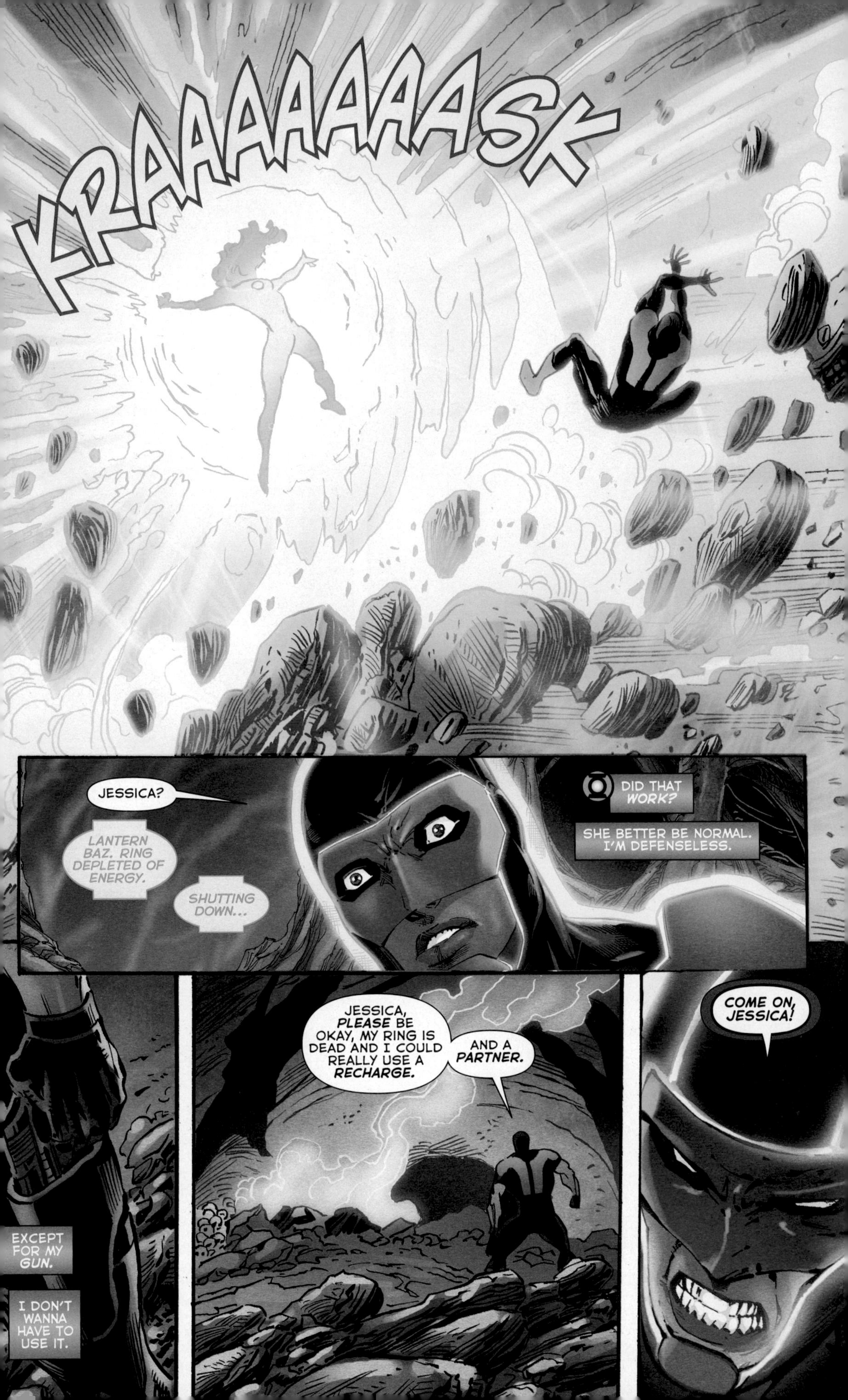
KRAAAAAASK
JESSICA?
LANTERN BAZ. RING DEPLETED OF ENERGY.
SHUTTING DOWN...
DID THAT *WORK?*
SHE BETTER BE NORMAL. I'M DEFENSELESS.
EXCEPT FOR MY *GUN.*
I DON'T WANNA HAVE TO USE IT.
JESSICA, *PLEASE* BE OKAY, MY RING IS DEAD AND I COULD REALLY USE A *RECHARGE.*
AND A *PARTNER.*
COME ON, JESSICA!

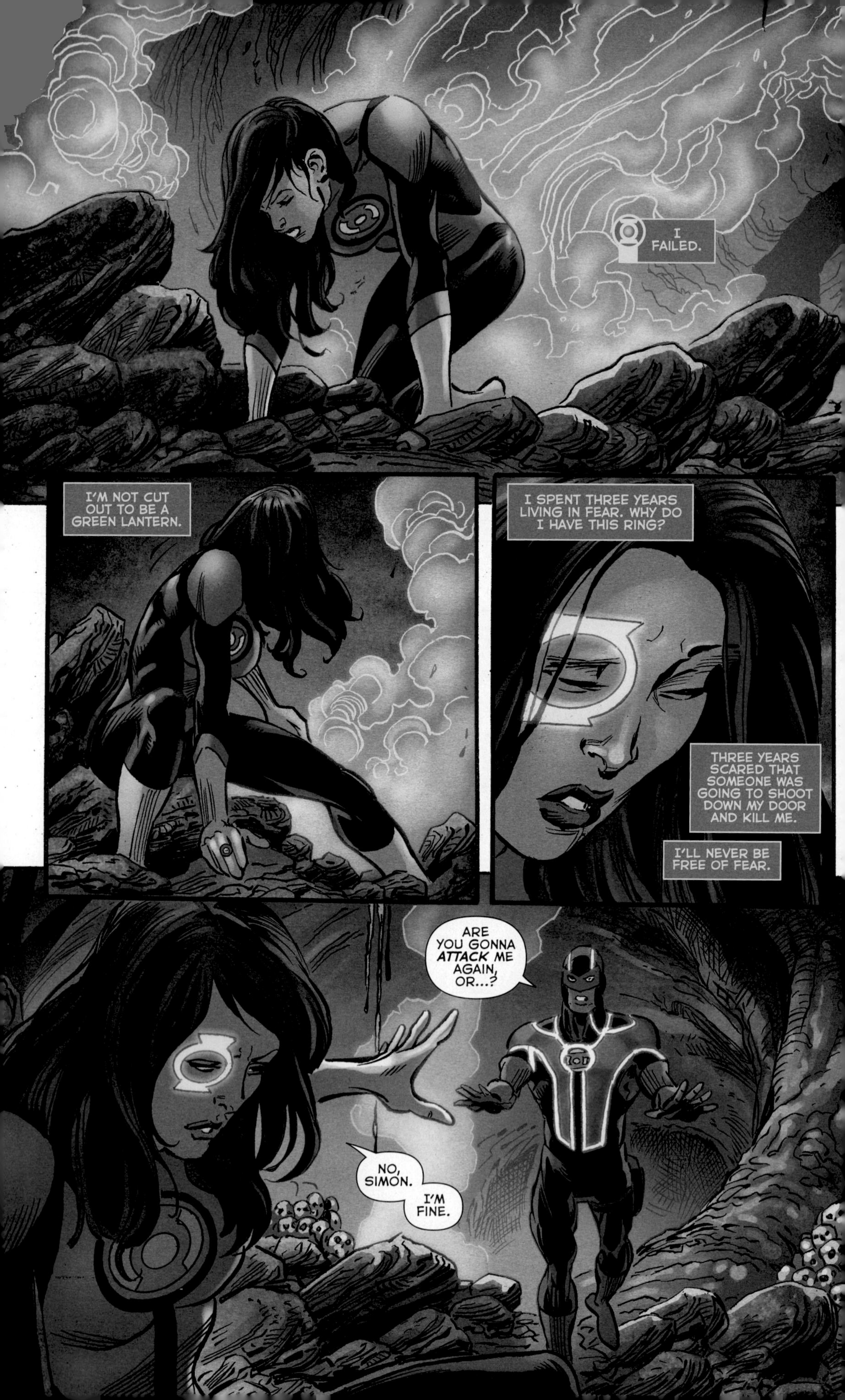
I FAILED.
I'M NOT CUT OUT TO BE A GREEN LANTERN.
I SPENT THREE YEARS LIVING IN FEAR. WHY DO I HAVE THIS RING?
THREE YEARS SCARED THAT SOMEONE WAS GOING TO SHOOT DOWN MY DOOR AND KILL ME.
I'LL NEVER BE FREE OF FEAR.
ARE YOU GONNA *ATTACK* ME AGAIN, OR...?
NO, SIMON.
I'M FINE.

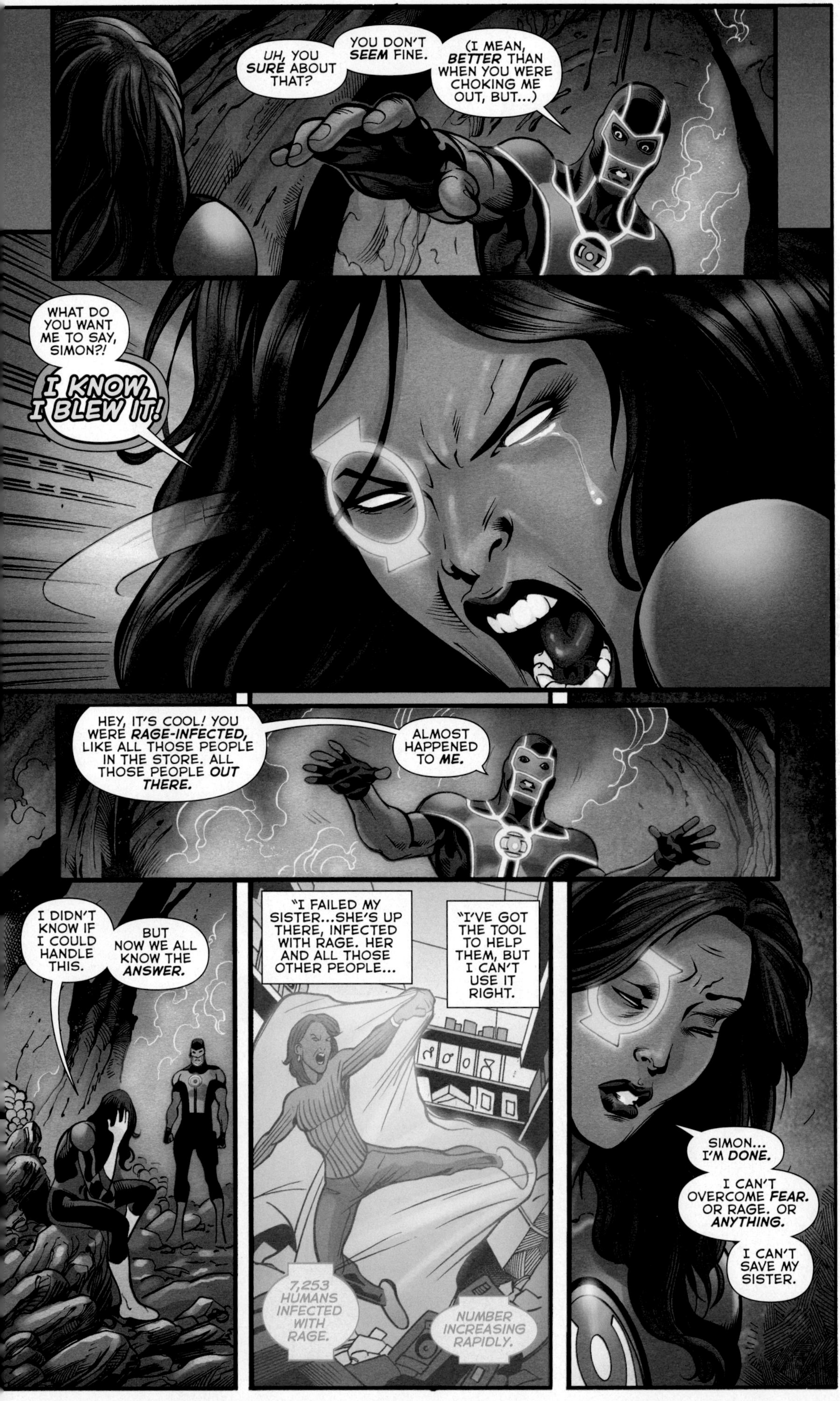
UH, YOU SURE ABOUT THAT?
YOU DON'T SEEM FINE.
(I MEAN, BETTER THAN WHEN YOU WERE CHOKING ME OUT, BUT...)
WHAT DO YOU WANT ME TO SAY, SIMON?!
I KNOW, I BLEW IT!
HEY, IT'S COOL! YOU WERE RAGE-INFECTED, LIKE ALL THOSE PEOPLE IN THE STORE. ALL THOSE PEOPLE OUT THERE.
ALMOST HAPPENED TO ME.
I DIDN'T KNOW IF I COULD HANDLE THIS.
BUT NOW WE ALL KNOW THE ANSWER.
"I FAILED MY SISTER...SHE'S UP THERE, INFECTED WITH RAGE. HER AND ALL THOSE OTHER PEOPLE...
"I'VE GOT THE TOOL TO HELP THEM, BUT I CAN'T USE IT RIGHT.
7,253 HUMANS INFECTED WITH RAGE.
NUMBER INCREASING RAPIDLY.
SIMON... I'M DONE.
I CAN'T OVERCOME FEAR. OR RAGE. OR ANYTHING.
I CAN'T SAVE MY SISTER.

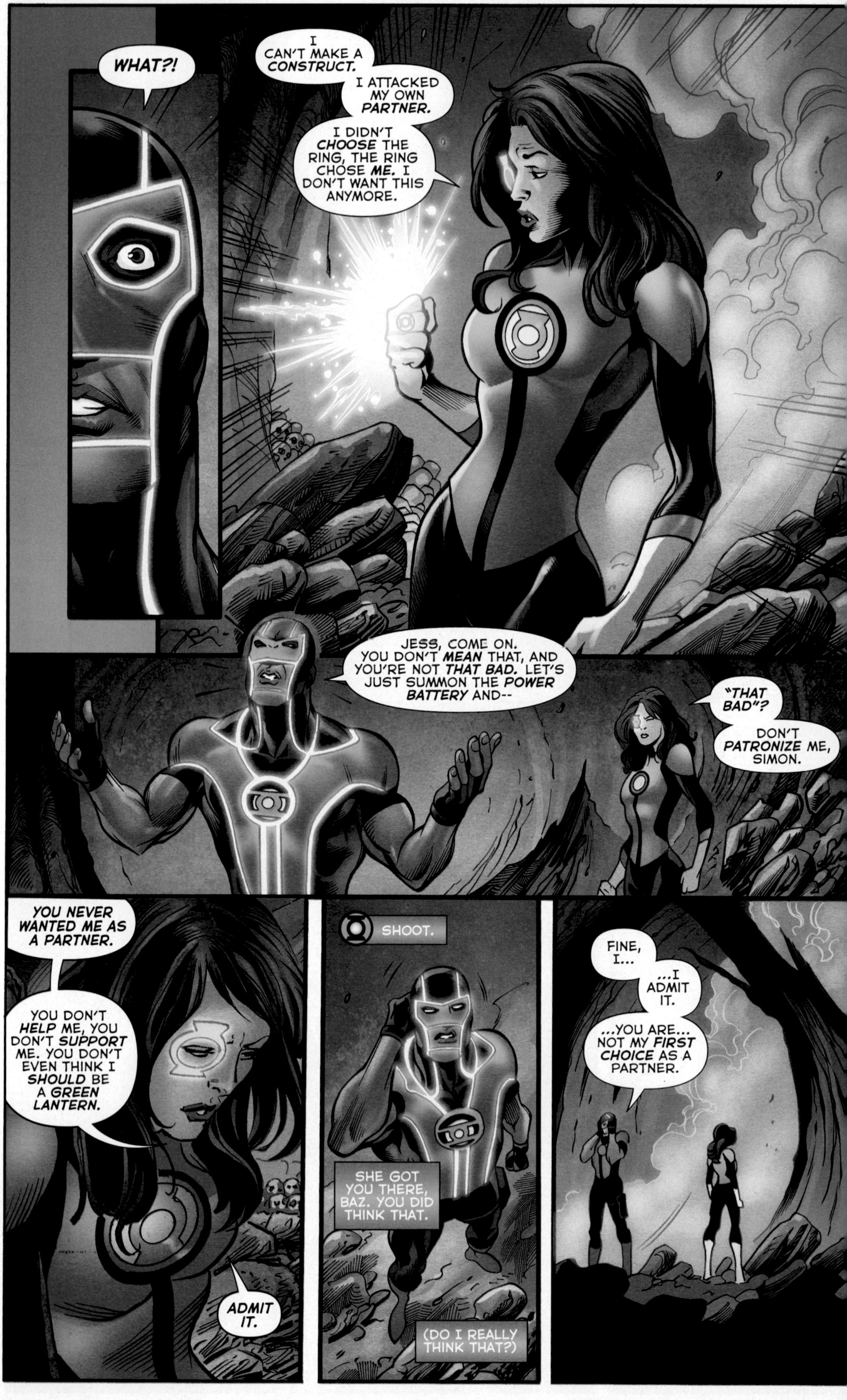
WHAT?!
I CAN'T MAKE A CONSTRUCT.
I ATTACKED MY OWN PARTNER.
I DIDN'T CHOOSE THE RING, THE RING CHOSE ME. I DON'T WANT THIS ANYMORE.
JESS, COME ON. YOU DON'T MEAN THAT, AND YOU'RE NOT THAT BAD. LET'S JUST SUMMON THE POWER BATTERY AND--
"THAT BAD"?
DON'T PATRONIZE ME, SIMON.
YOU NEVER WANTED ME AS A PARTNER.
YOU DON'T HELP ME, YOU DON'T SUPPORT ME. YOU DON'T EVEN THINK I SHOULD BE A GREEN LANTERN.
ADMIT IT.
SHOOT.
SHE GOT YOU THERE, BAZ. YOU DID THINK THAT.
(DO I REALLY THINK THAT?)
FINE, I...
...I ADMIT IT.
...YOU ARE... NOT MY FIRST CHOICE AS A PARTNER.

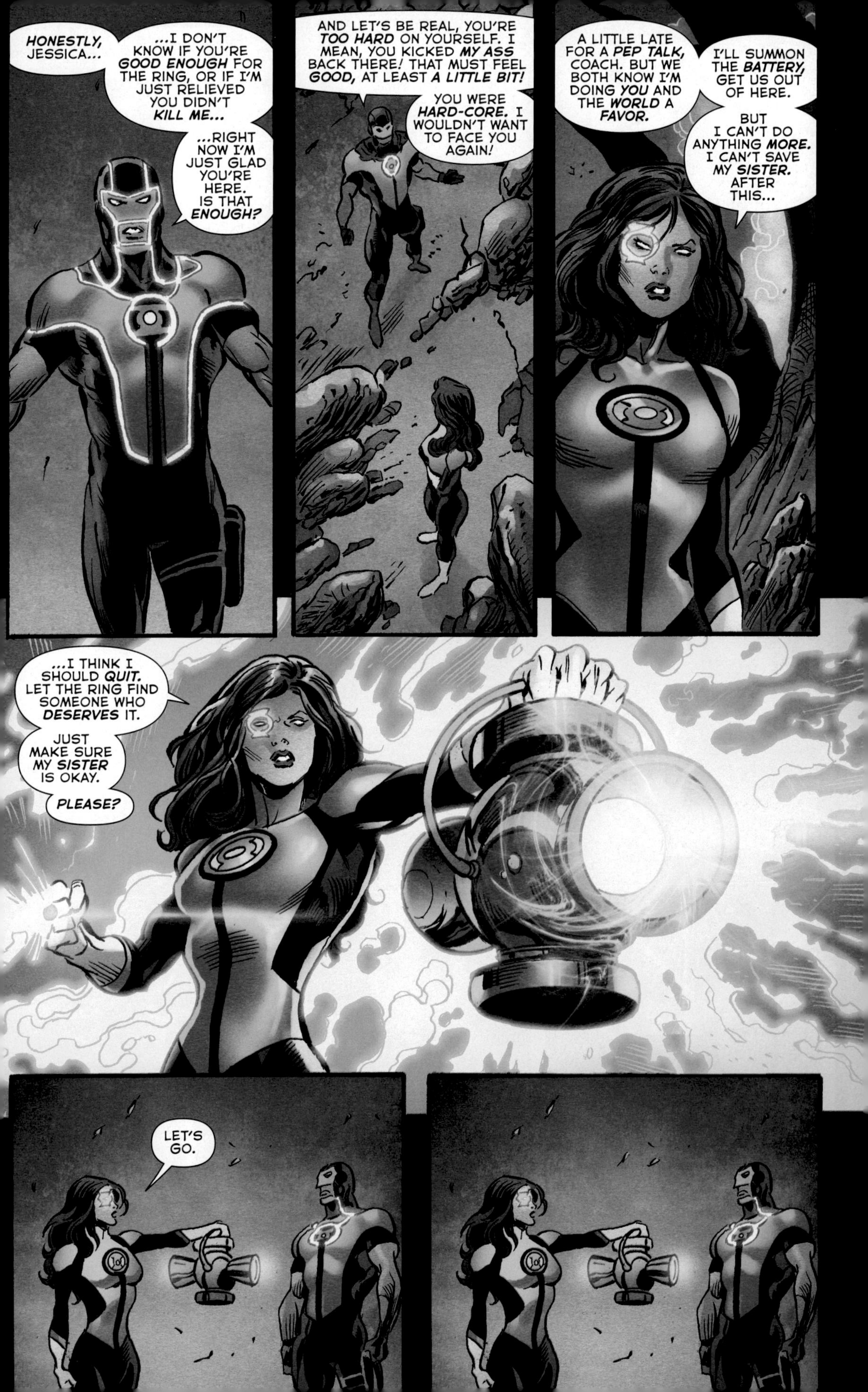
HONESTLY, JESSICA...
...I DON'T KNOW IF YOU'RE GOOD ENOUGH FOR THE RING, OR IF I'M JUST RELIEVED YOU DIDN'T KILL ME...
...RIGHT NOW I'M JUST GLAD YOU'RE HERE. IS THAT ENOUGH?
AND LET'S BE REAL, YOU'RE TOO HARD ON YOURSELF. I MEAN, YOU KICKED MY ASS BACK THERE! THAT MUST FEEL GOOD, AT LEAST A LITTLE BIT!
YOU WERE HARD-CORE. I WOULDN'T WANT TO FACE YOU AGAIN!
A LITTLE LATE FOR A PEP TALK, COACH. BUT WE BOTH KNOW I'M DOING YOU AND THE WORLD A FAVOR.
I'LL SUMMON THE BATTERY, GET US OUT OF HERE.
BUT I CAN'T DO ANYTHING MORE. I CAN'T SAVE MY SISTER. AFTER THIS...
...I THINK I SHOULD QUIT. LET THE RING FIND SOMEONE WHO DESERVES IT.
JUST MAKE SURE MY SISTER IS OKAY.
PLEASE?
LET'S GO.

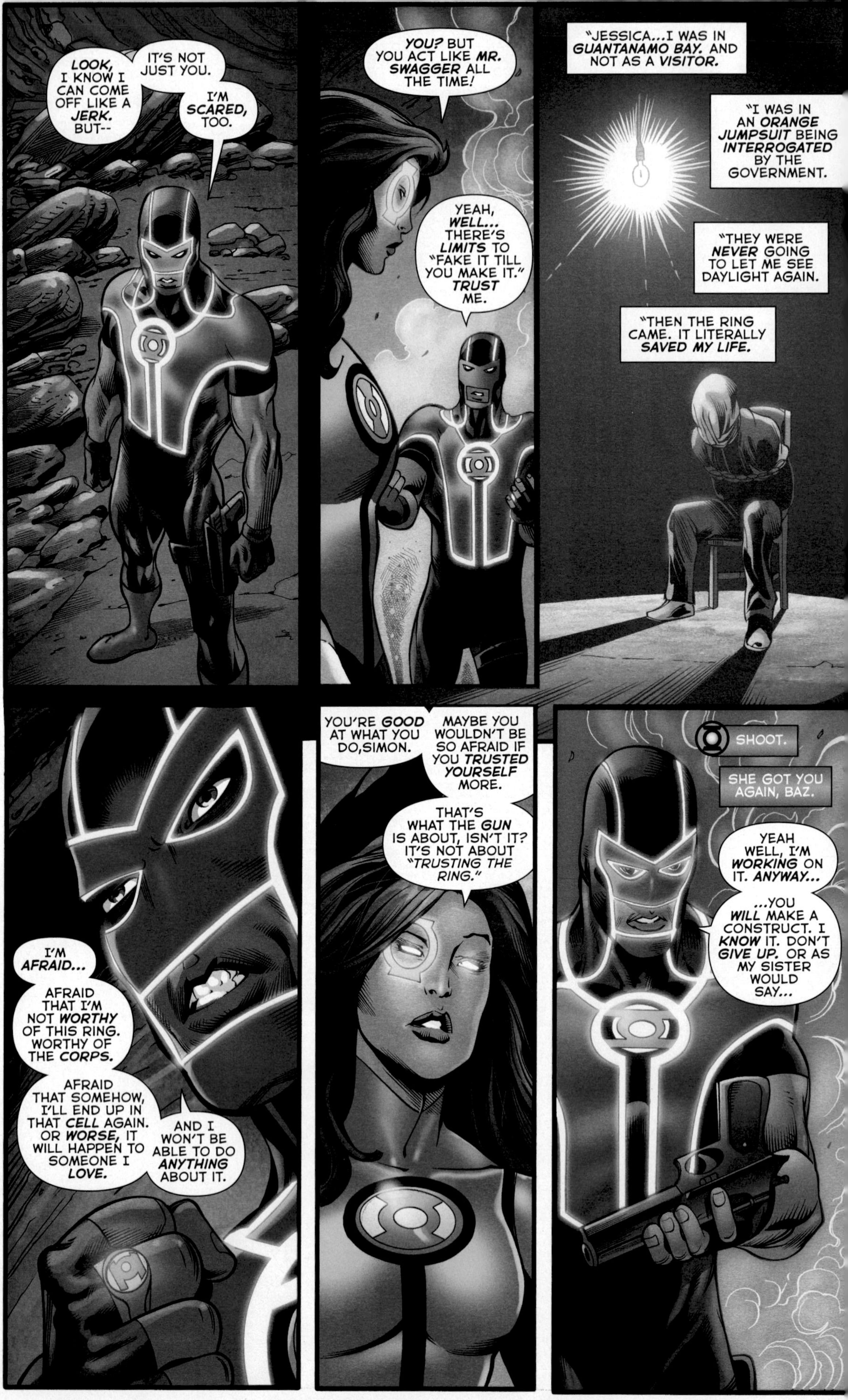
LOOK, I KNOW I CAN COME OFF LIKE A JERK. BUT--
IT'S NOT JUST YOU.
I'M SCARED, TOO.
YOU? BUT YOU ACT LIKE MR. SWAGGER ALL THE TIME!
YEAH, WELL... THERE'S LIMITS TO "FAKE IT TILL YOU MAKE IT." TRUST ME.
"JESSICA...I WAS IN GUANTANAMO BAY. AND NOT AS A VISITOR.
"I WAS IN AN ORANGE JUMPSUIT BEING INTERROGATED BY THE GOVERNMENT.
"THEY WERE NEVER GOING TO LET ME SEE DAYLIGHT AGAIN.
"THEN THE RING CAME. IT LITERALLY SAVED MY LIFE.
I'M AFRAID...
AFRAID THAT I'M NOT WORTHY OF THIS RING. WORTHY OF THE CORPS.
AFRAID THAT SOMEHOW, I'LL END UP IN THAT CELL AGAIN. OR WORSE, IT WILL HAPPEN TO SOMEONE I LOVE.
AND I WON'T BE ABLE TO DO ANYTHING ABOUT IT.
YOU'RE GOOD AT WHAT YOU DO, SIMON.
MAYBE YOU WOULDN'T BE SO AFRAID IF YOU TRUSTED YOURSELF MORE.
THAT'S WHAT THE GUN IS ABOUT, ISN'T IT? IT'S NOT ABOUT "TRUSTING THE RING."
SHOOT.
SHE GOT YOU AGAIN, BAZ.
YEAH WELL, I'M WORKING ON IT. ANYWAY...
...YOU WILL MAKE A CONSTRUCT. I KNOW IT. DON'T GIVE UP. OR AS MY SISTER WOULD SAY...

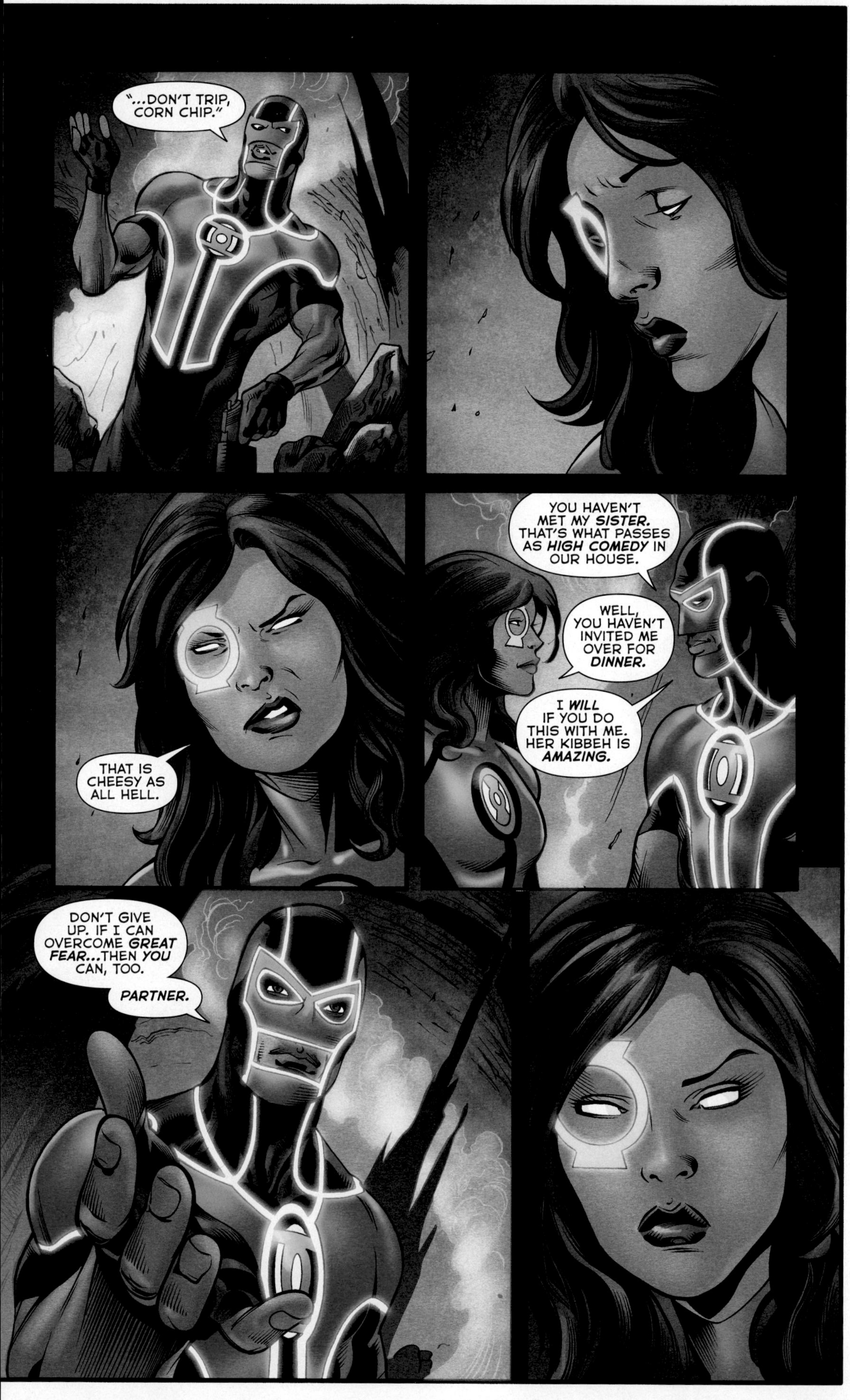
"...DON'T TRIP, CORN CHIP."
THAT IS CHEESY AS ALL HELL.
YOU HAVEN'T MET MY SISTER. THAT'S WHAT PASSES AS HIGH COMEDY IN OUR HOUSE.
WELL, YOU HAVEN'T INVITED ME OVER FOR DINNER.
I WILL IF YOU DO THIS WITH ME. HER KIBBEH IS AMAZING.
DON'T GIVE UP. IF I CAN OVERCOME GREAT FEAR...THEN YOU CAN, TOO.
PARTNER.

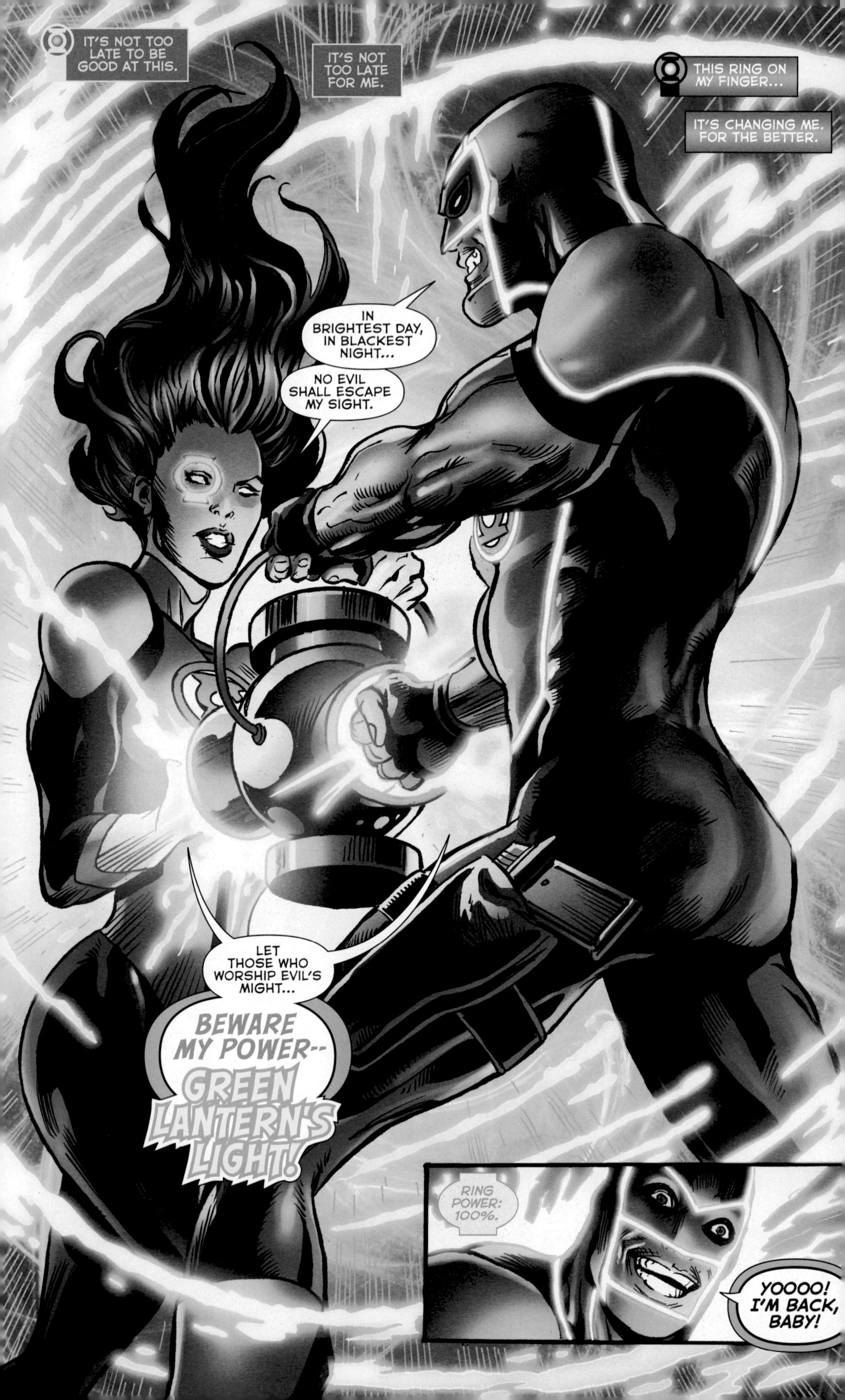
IT'S NOT TOO LATE TO BE GOOD AT THIS.
IT'S NOT TOO LATE FOR ME.
THIS RING ON MY FINGER...
IT'S CHANGING ME. FOR THE BETTER.
IN BRIGHTEST DAY, IN BLACKEST NIGHT...
NO EVIL SHALL ESCAPE MY SIGHT.
LET THOSE WHO WORSHIP EVIL'S MIGHT...
BEWARE MY POWER--
GREEN LANTERN'S LIGHT!
RING POWER: 100%.
YOOOO! I'M BACK, BABY!

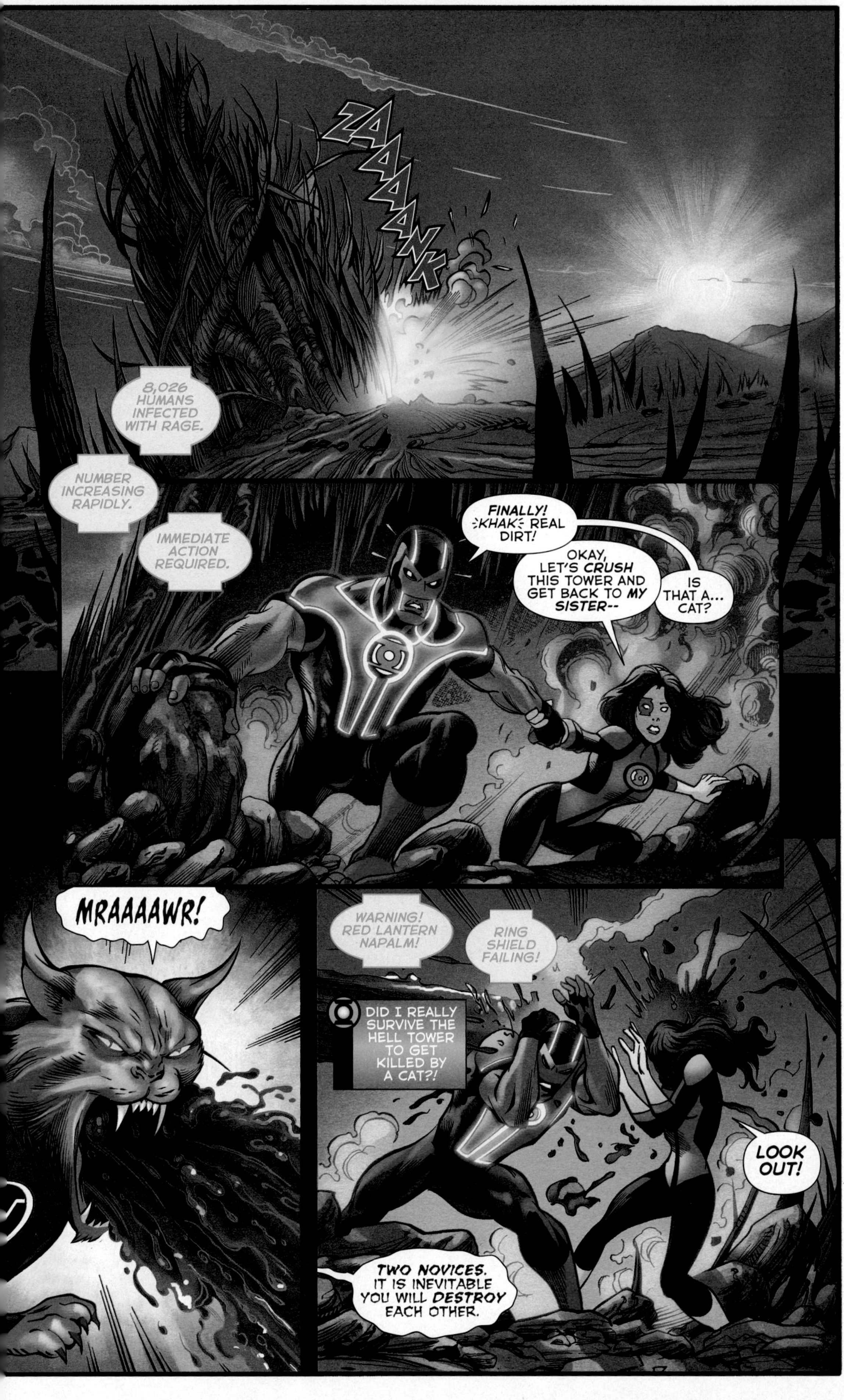
ZAAAAANK
8,026 HUMANS INFECTED WITH RAGE.
NUMBER INCREASING RAPIDLY.
IMMEDIATE ACTION REQUIRED.
FINALLY! *KHAK* REAL DIRT!
OKAY, LET'S CRUSH THIS TOWER AND GET BACK TO MY SISTER--
IS THAT A... CAT?
MRAAAAWR!
WARNING! RED LANTERN NAPALM!
RING SHIELD FAILING!
DID I REALLY SURVIVE THE HELL TOWER TO GET KILLED BY A CAT?!
LOOK OUT!
TWO NOVICES. IT IS INEVITABLE YOU WILL DESTROY EACH OTHER.

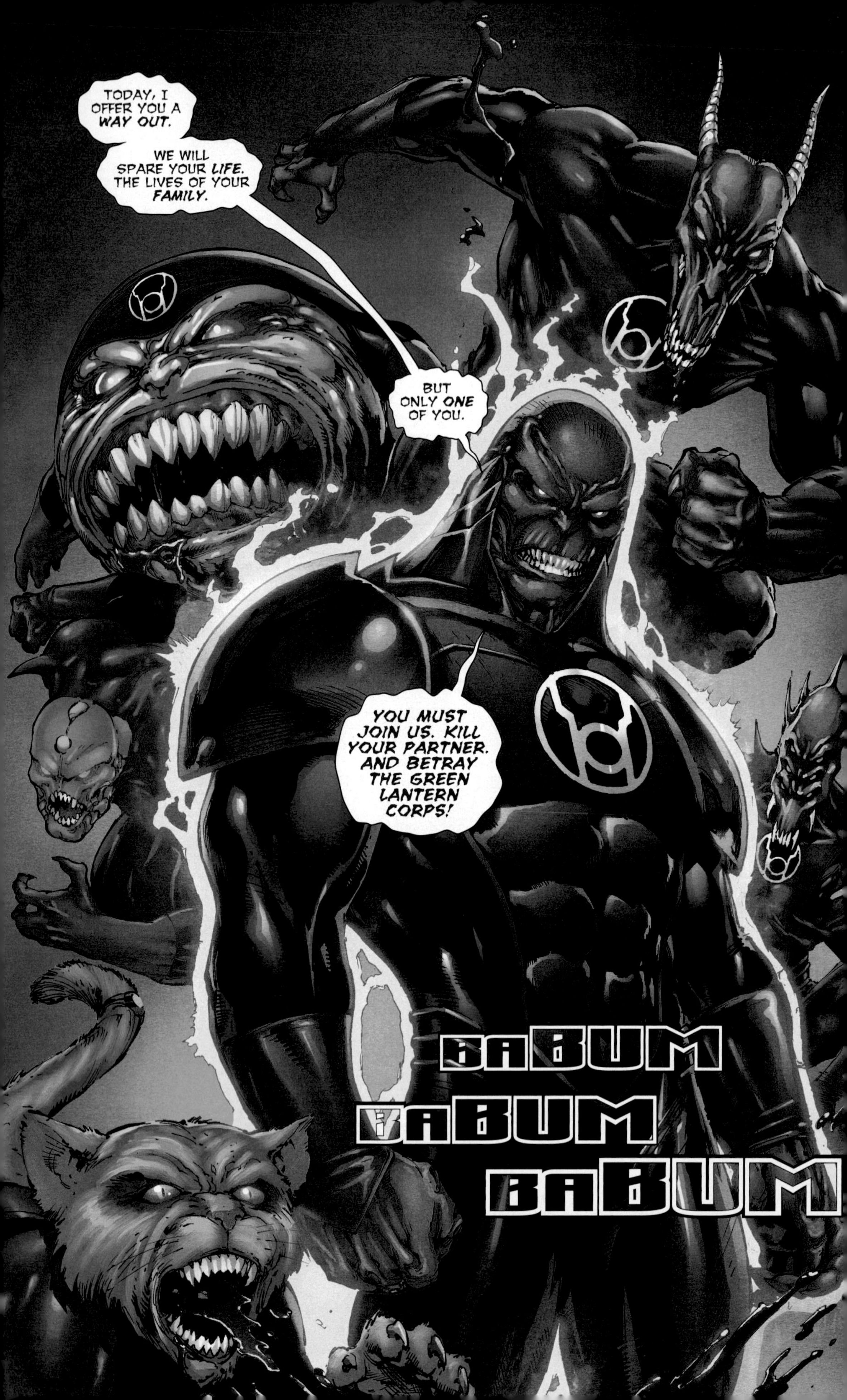

TODAY, I OFFER YOU A WAY OUT.
WE WILL SPARE YOUR LIFE. THE LIVES OF YOUR FAMILY.
BUT ONLY ONE OF YOU.
YOU MUST JOIN US. KILL YOUR PARTNER. AND BETRAY THE GREEN LANTERN CORPS!
BABUM
BABUM
BABUM

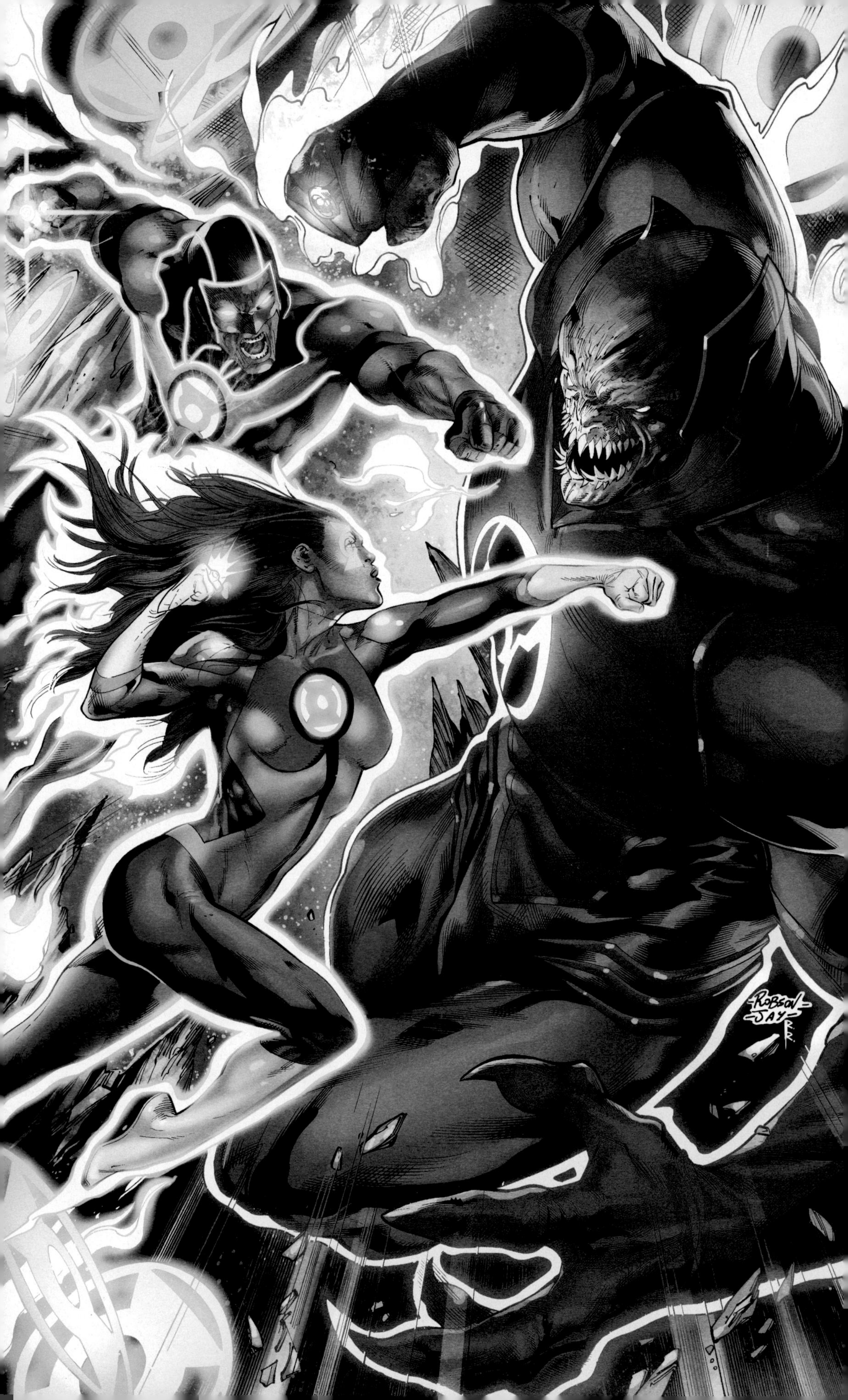
ROBSON
JAY

RAGE PLANET: PART 5

SAM HUMPHRIES writer * ROBSON ROCHA and EDUARDO PANSICA pencillers
JAY LEISTEN and JULIO FERREIRA inkers * BLOND colorist
ROBSON ROCHA, JAY LEISTEN and ROD REIS cover artists

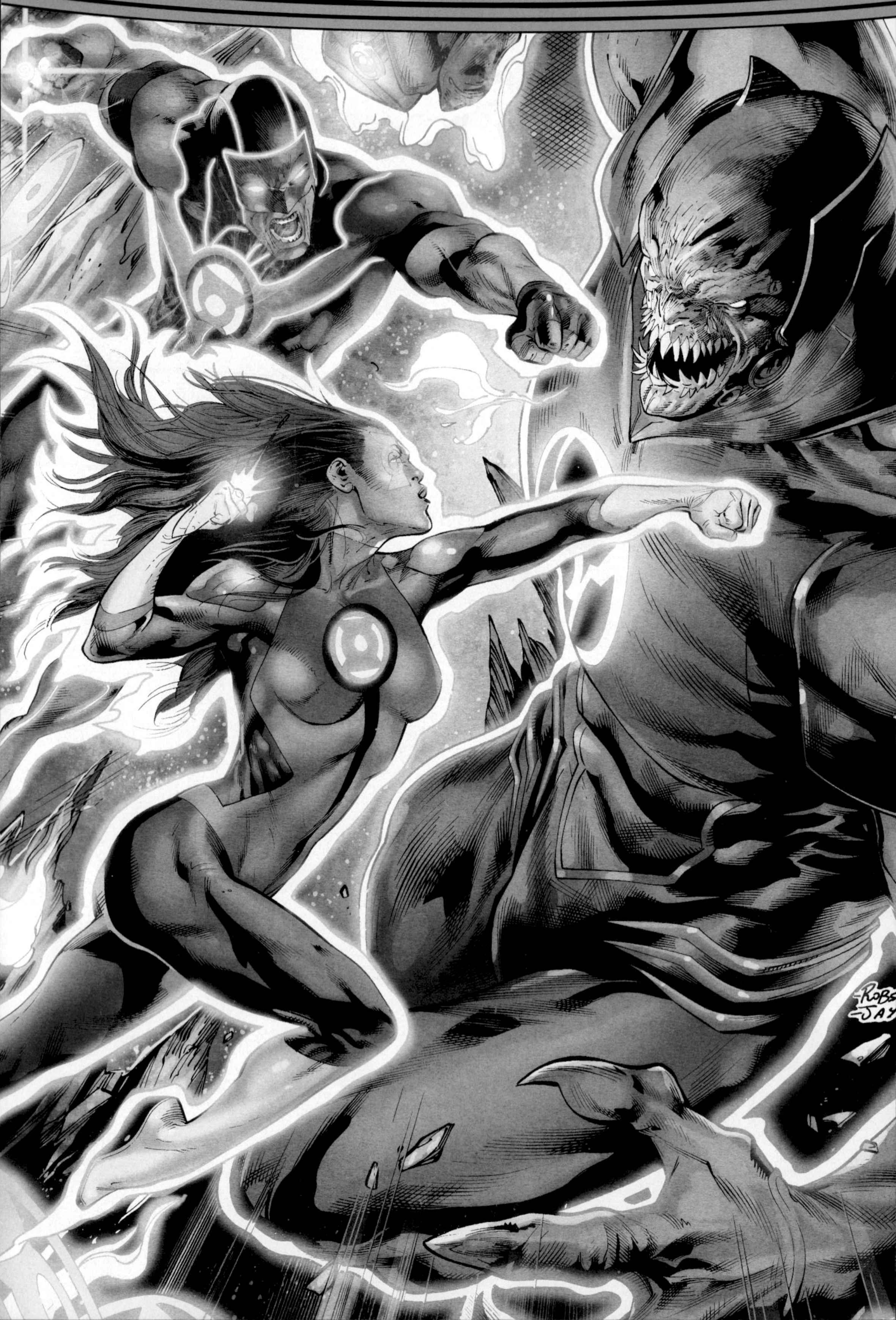

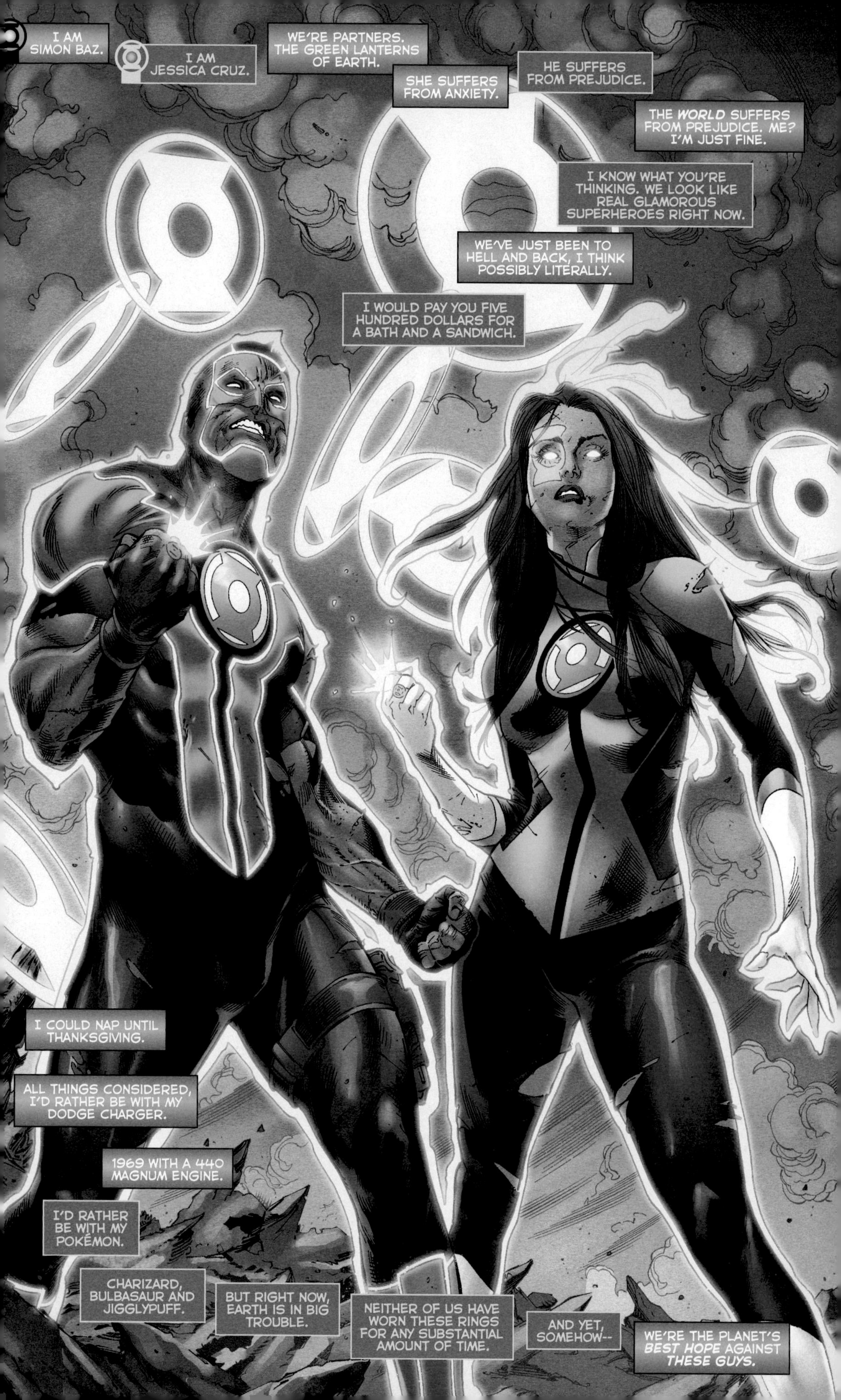
I AM SIMON BAZ.
I AM JESSICA CRUZ.
WE'RE PARTNERS. THE GREEN LANTERNS OF EARTH.
SHE SUFFERS FROM ANXIETY.
HE SUFFERS FROM PREJUDICE.
THE *WORLD* SUFFERS FROM PREJUDICE. ME? I'M JUST FINE.
I KNOW WHAT YOU'RE THINKING. WE LOOK LIKE REAL GLAMOROUS SUPERHEROES RIGHT NOW.
WE'VE JUST BEEN TO HELL AND BACK, I THINK POSSIBLY LITERALLY.
I WOULD PAY YOU FIVE HUNDRED DOLLARS FOR A BATH AND A SANDWICH.
I COULD NAP UNTIL THANKSGIVING.
ALL THINGS CONSIDERED, I'D RATHER BE WITH MY DODGE CHARGER.
1969 WITH A 440 MAGNUM ENGINE.
I'D RATHER BE WITH MY POKÉMON.
CHARIZARD, BULBASAUR AND JIGGLYPUFF.
BUT RIGHT NOW, EARTH IS IN BIG TROUBLE.
NEITHER OF US HAVE WORN THESE RINGS FOR ANY SUBSTANTIAL AMOUNT OF TIME.
AND YET, SOMEHOW--
WE'RE THE PLANET'S *BEST HOPE* AGAINST *THESE GUYS.*

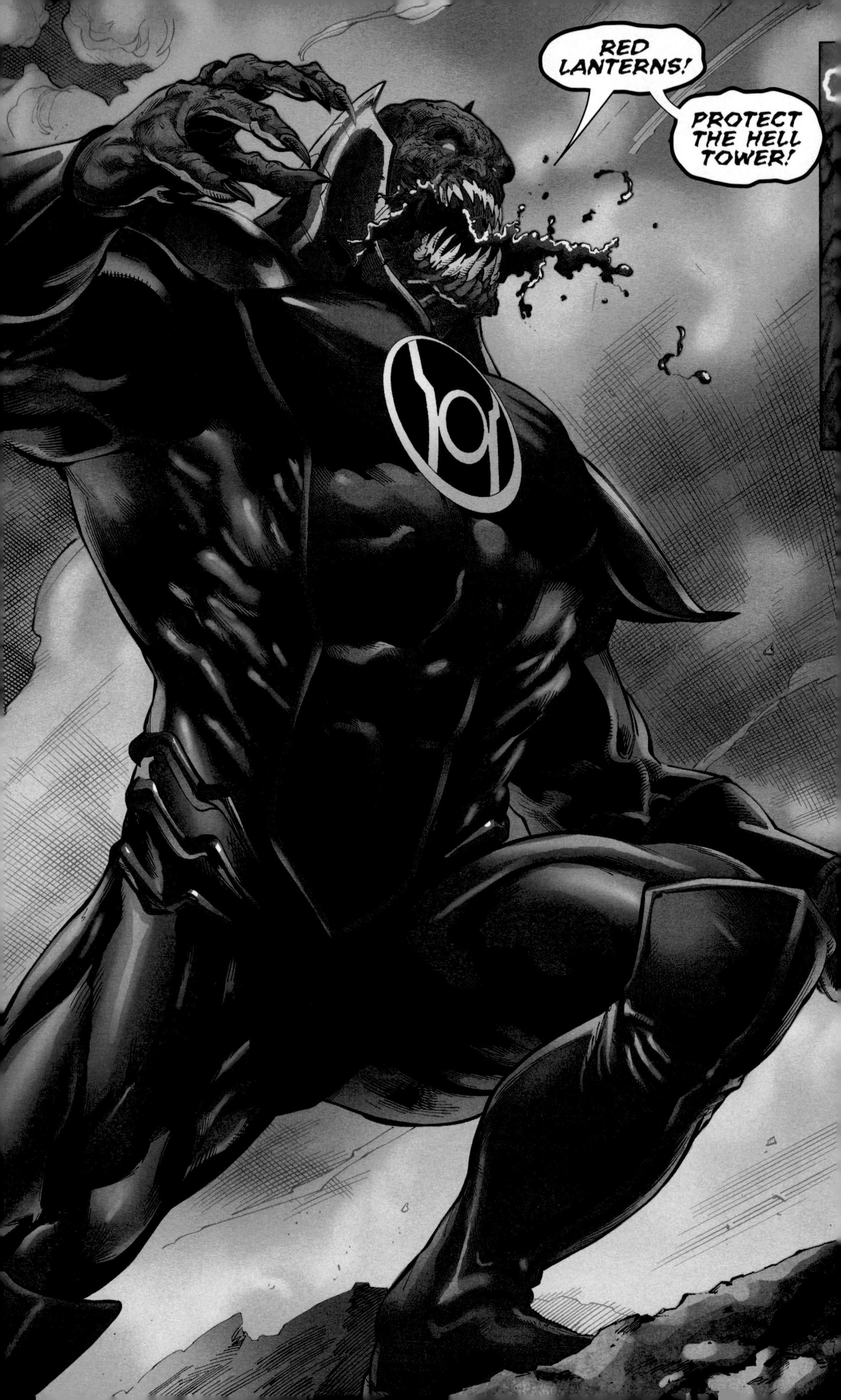
RED LANTERNS!
PROTECT THE HELL TOWER!

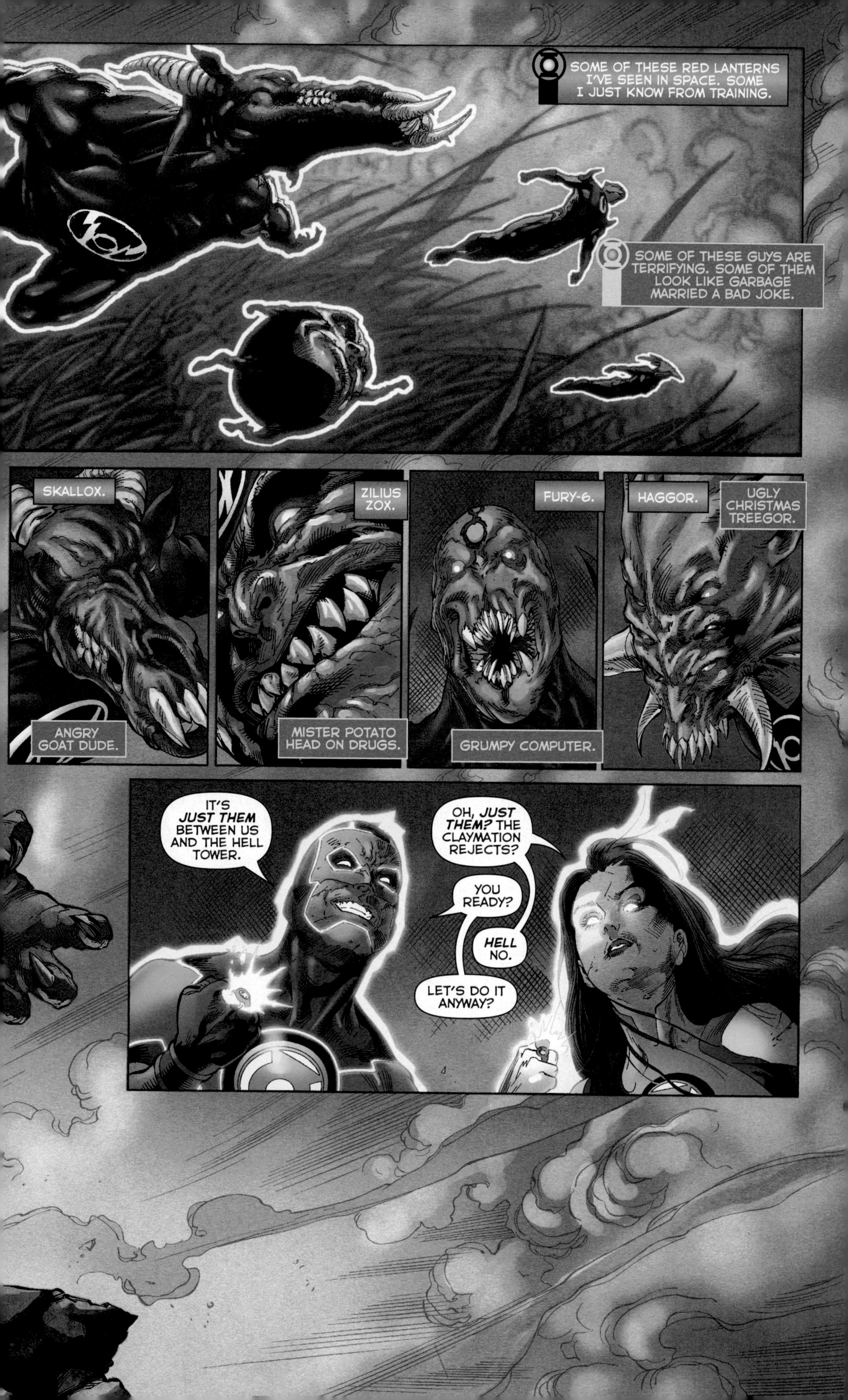
SOME OF THESE RED LANTERNS I'VE SEEN IN SPACE. SOME I JUST KNOW FROM TRAINING.
SOME OF THESE GUYS ARE TERRIFYING. SOME OF THEM LOOK LIKE GARBAGE MARRIED A BAD JOKE.
SKALLOX.
ANGRY GOAT DUDE.
ZILIUS ZOX.
MISTER POTATO HEAD ON DRUGS.
FURY-6.
GRUMPY COMPUTER.
HAGGOR.
UGLY CHRISTMAS TREEGOR.
IT'S *JUST THEM* BETWEEN US AND THE HELL TOWER.
OH, *JUST THEM?* THE CLAYMATION REJECTS?
YOU READY?
HELL NO.
LET'S DO IT ANYWAY?

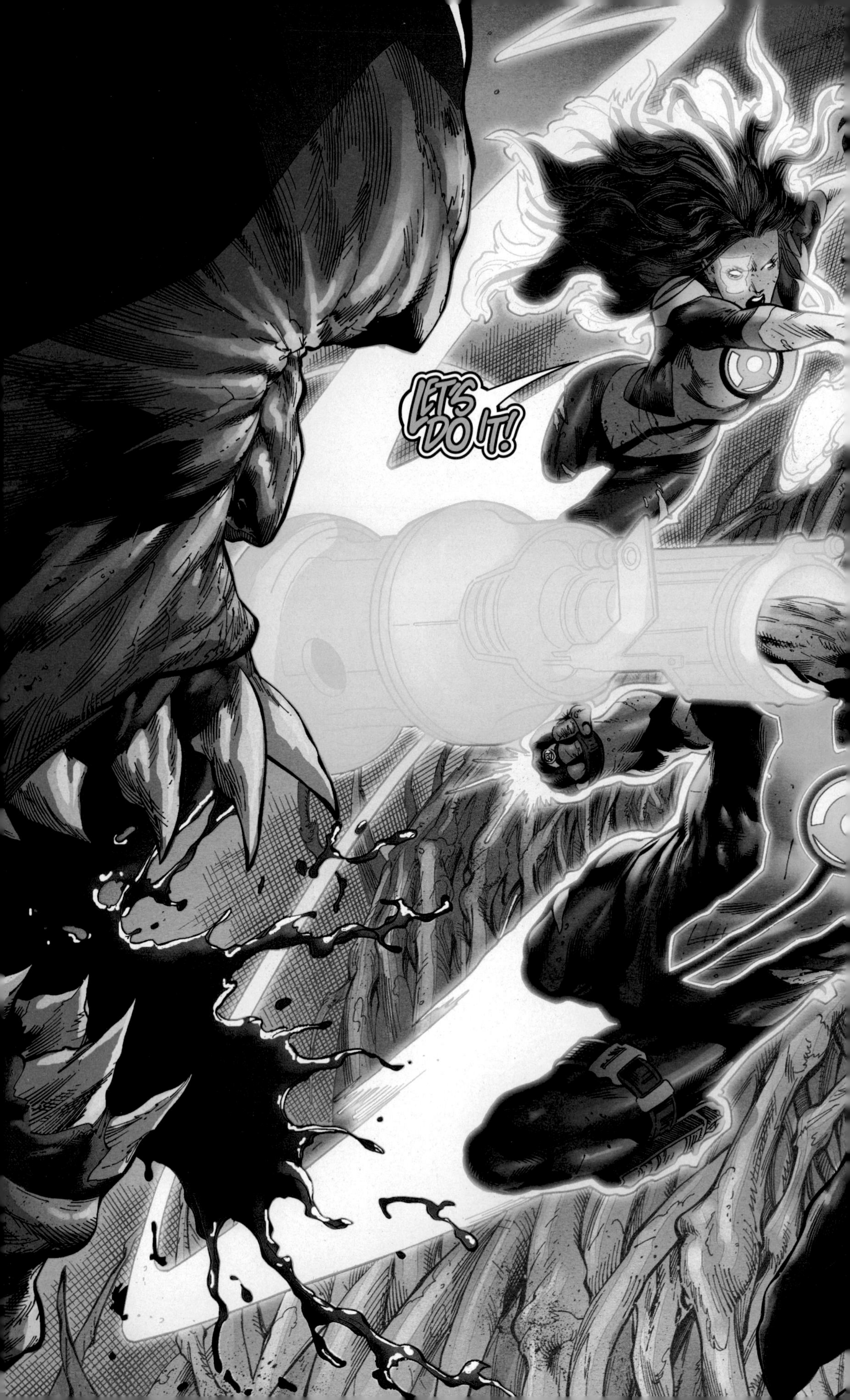
LET'S DO IT!

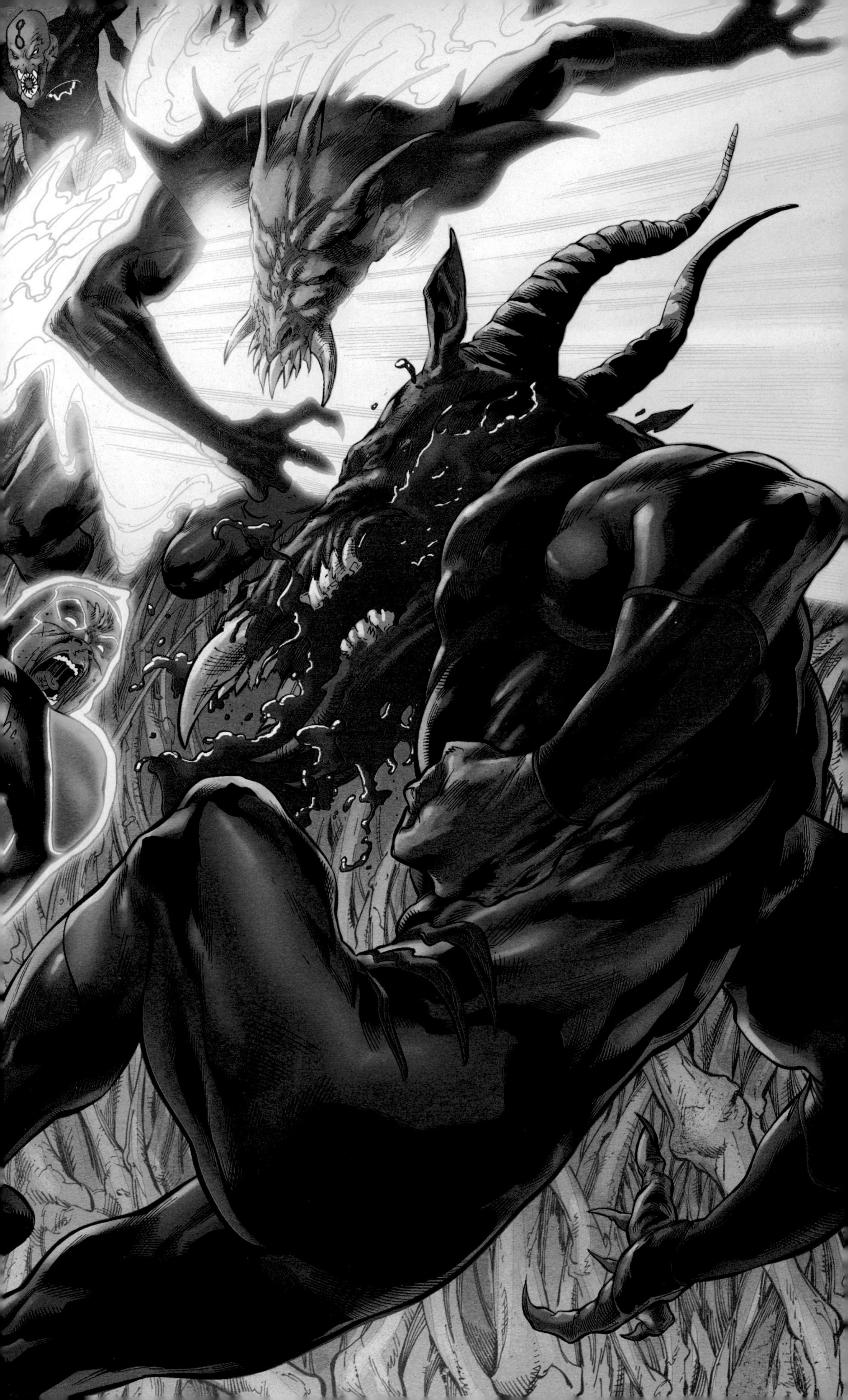

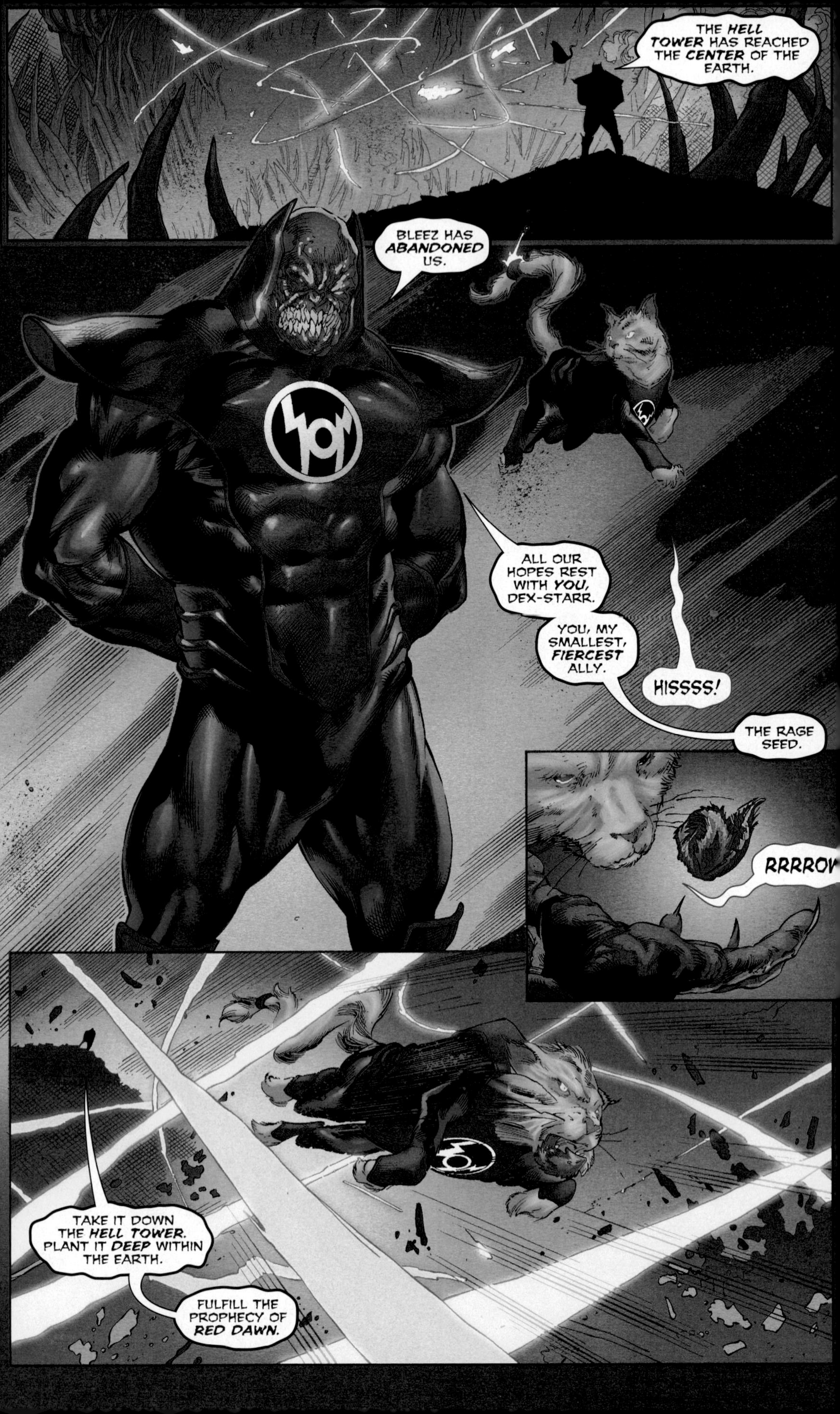

THE HELL TOWER HAS REACHED THE CENTER OF THE EARTH.
BLEEZ HAS ABANDONED US.
ALL OUR HOPES REST WITH YOU, DEX-STARR.
YOU, MY SMALLEST, FIERCEST ALLY.
HISSSS!
THE RAGE SEED.
RRRROW
TAKE IT DOWN THE HELL TOWER. PLANT IT DEEP WITHIN THE EARTH.
FULFILL THE PROPHECY OF RED DAWN.

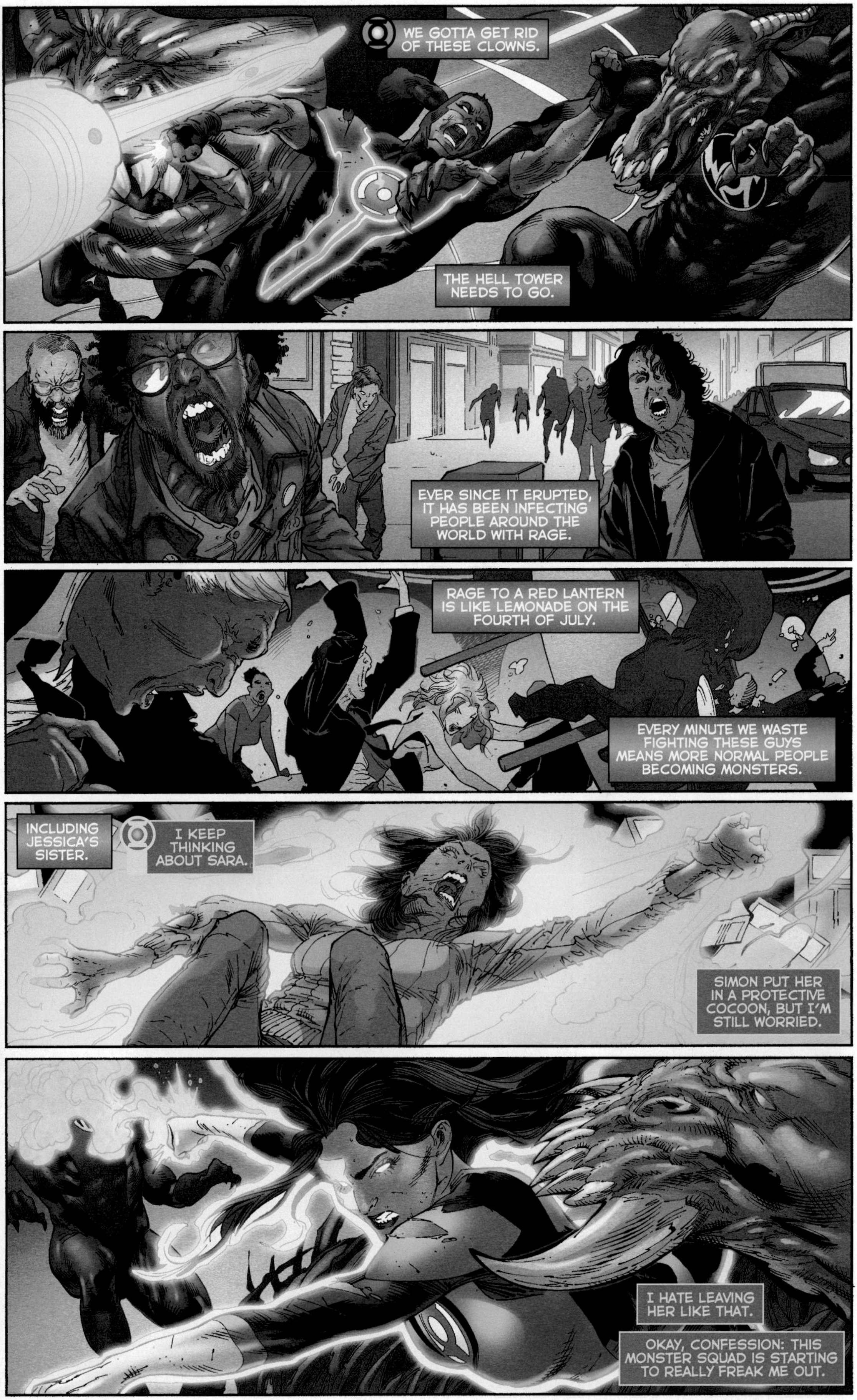
WE GOTTA GET RID OF THESE CLOWNS.
THE HELL TOWER NEEDS TO GO.
EVER SINCE IT ERUPTED, IT HAS BEEN INFECTING PEOPLE AROUND THE WORLD WITH RAGE.
RAGE TO A RED LANTERN IS LIKE LEMONADE ON THE FOURTH OF JULY.
EVERY MINUTE WE WASTE FIGHTING THESE GUYS MEANS MORE NORMAL PEOPLE BECOMING MONSTERS.
INCLUDING JESSICA'S SISTER.
I KEEP THINKING ABOUT SARA.
SIMON PUT HER IN A PROTECTIVE COCOON, BUT I'M STILL WORRIED.
I HATE LEAVING HER LIKE THAT.
OKAY, CONFESSION: THIS MONSTER SQUAD IS STARTING TO REALLY FREAK ME OUT.

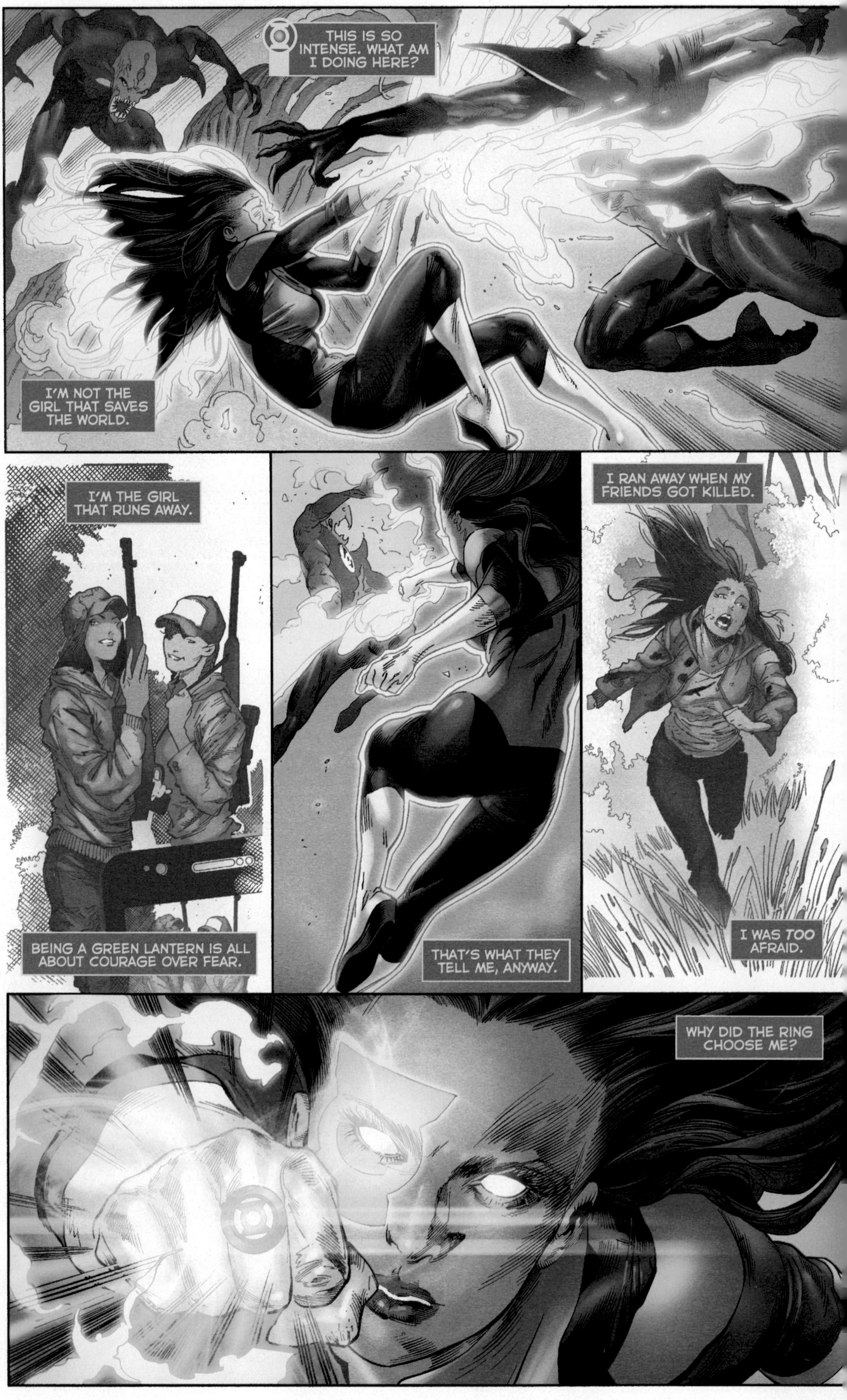

THIS IS SO INTENSE. WHAT AM I DOING HERE?
I'M NOT THE GIRL THAT SAVES THE WORLD.
I'M THE GIRL THAT RUNS AWAY.
BEING A GREEN LANTERN IS ALL ABOUT COURAGE OVER FEAR.
THAT'S WHAT THEY TELL ME, ANYWAY.
I RAN AWAY WHEN MY FRIENDS GOT KILLED.
I WAS *TOO* AFRAID.
WHY DID THE RING CHOOSE ME?

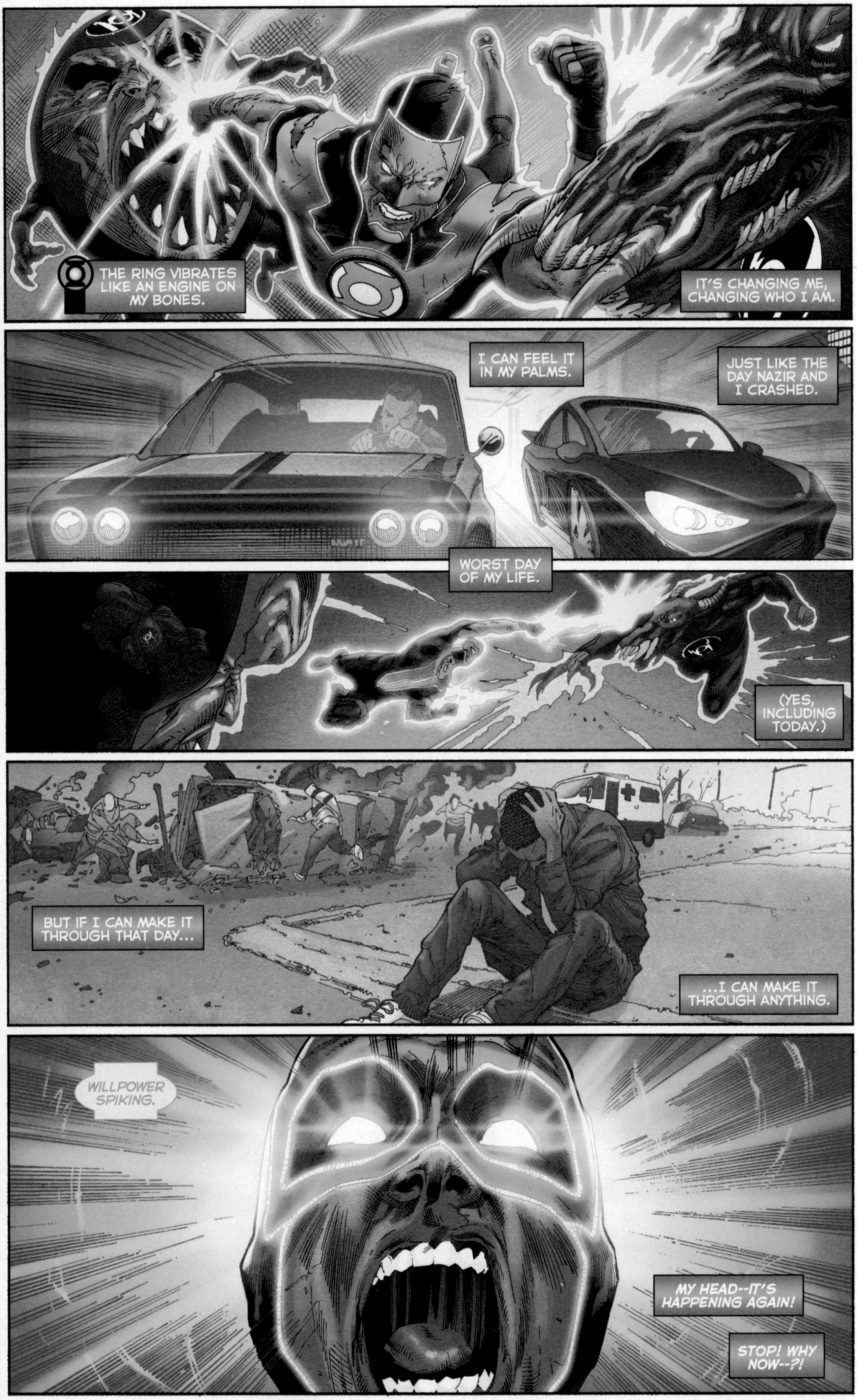
THE RING VIBRATES LIKE AN ENGINE ON MY BONES.
IT'S CHANGING ME, CHANGING WHO I AM.
I CAN FEEL IT IN MY PALMS.
JUST LIKE THE DAY NAZIR AND I CRASHED.
WORST DAY OF MY LIFE.
(YES, INCLUDING TODAY.)
BUT IF I CAN MAKE IT THROUGH THAT DAY...
...I CAN MAKE IT THROUGH ANYTHING.
WILLPOWER SPIKING.
MY HEAD--IT'S HAPPENING AGAIN!
STOP! WHY NOW--?!

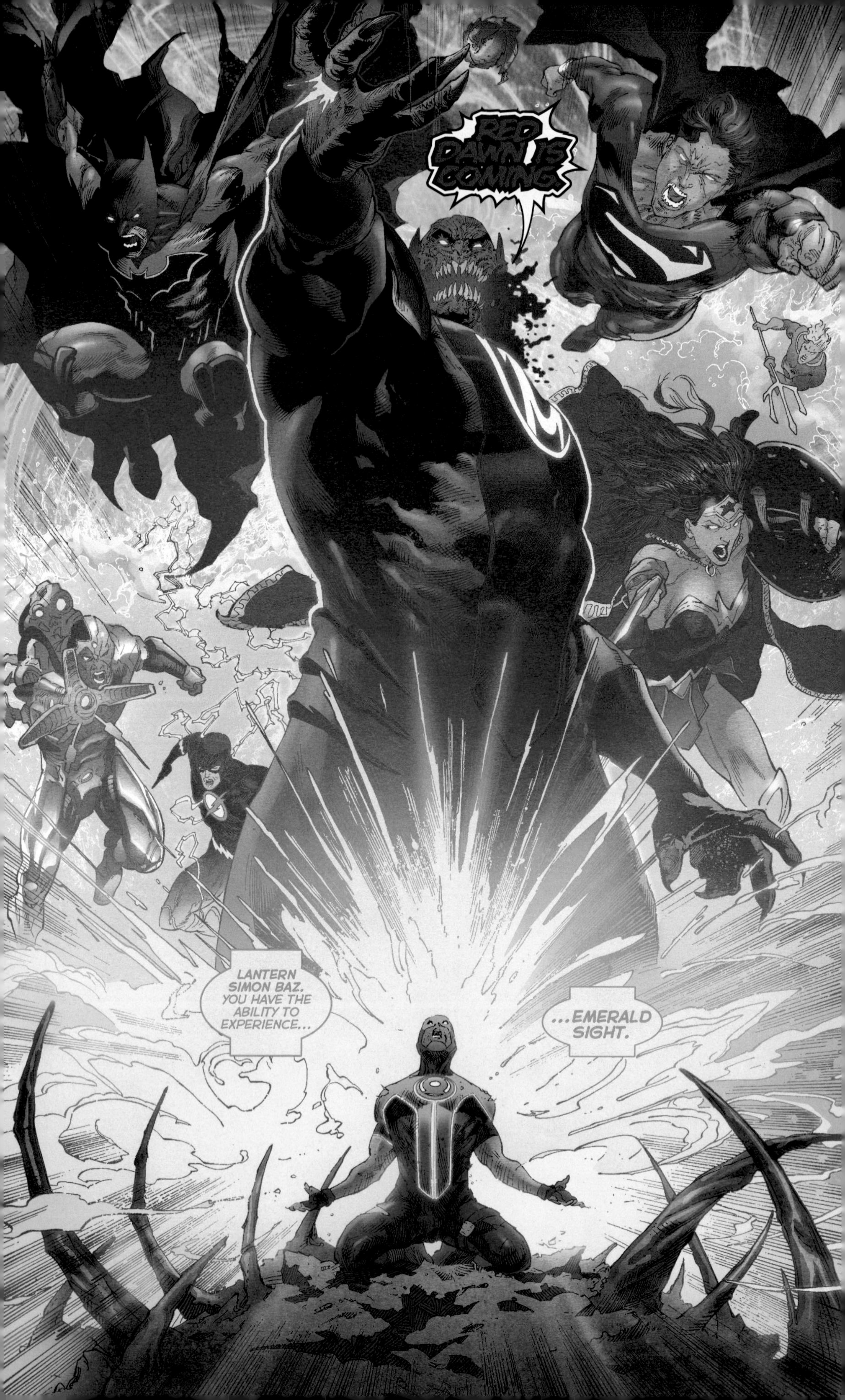
RED DAWN IS COMING.
LANTERN SIMON BAZ. YOU HAVE THE ABILITY TO EXPERIENCE...
...EMERALD SIGHT.

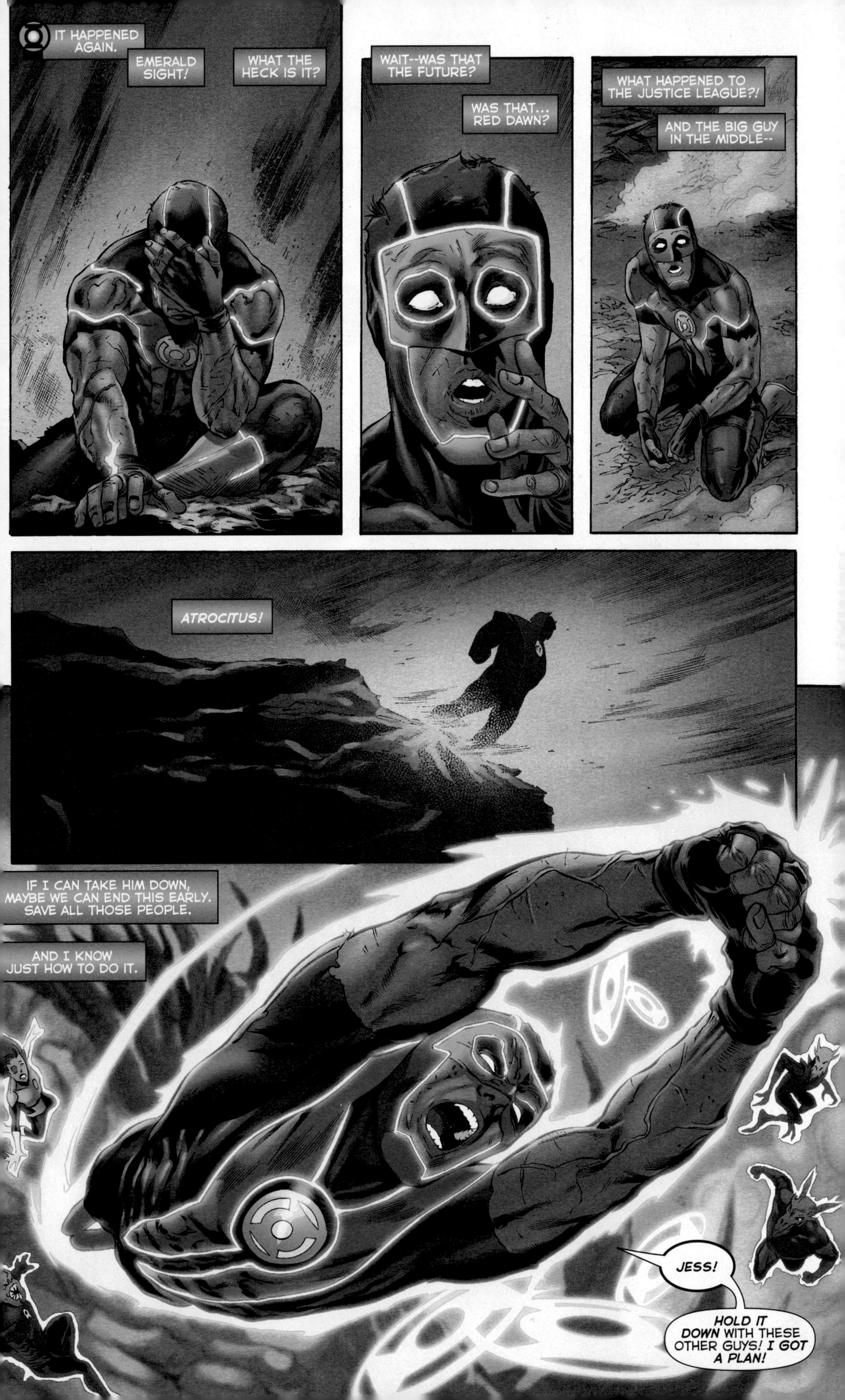
IT HAPPENED AGAIN.
EMERALD SIGHT!
WHAT THE HECK IS IT?
WAIT--WAS THAT THE FUTURE?
WAS THAT... RED DAWN?
WHAT HAPPENED TO THE JUSTICE LEAGUE?!
AND THE BIG GUY IN THE MIDDLE--
ATROCITUS!
IF I CAN TAKE HIM DOWN, MAYBE WE CAN END THIS EARLY. SAVE ALL THOSE PEOPLE.
AND I KNOW JUST HOW TO DO IT.
JESS!
HOLD IT DOWN WITH THESE OTHER GUYS! I GOT A PLAN!

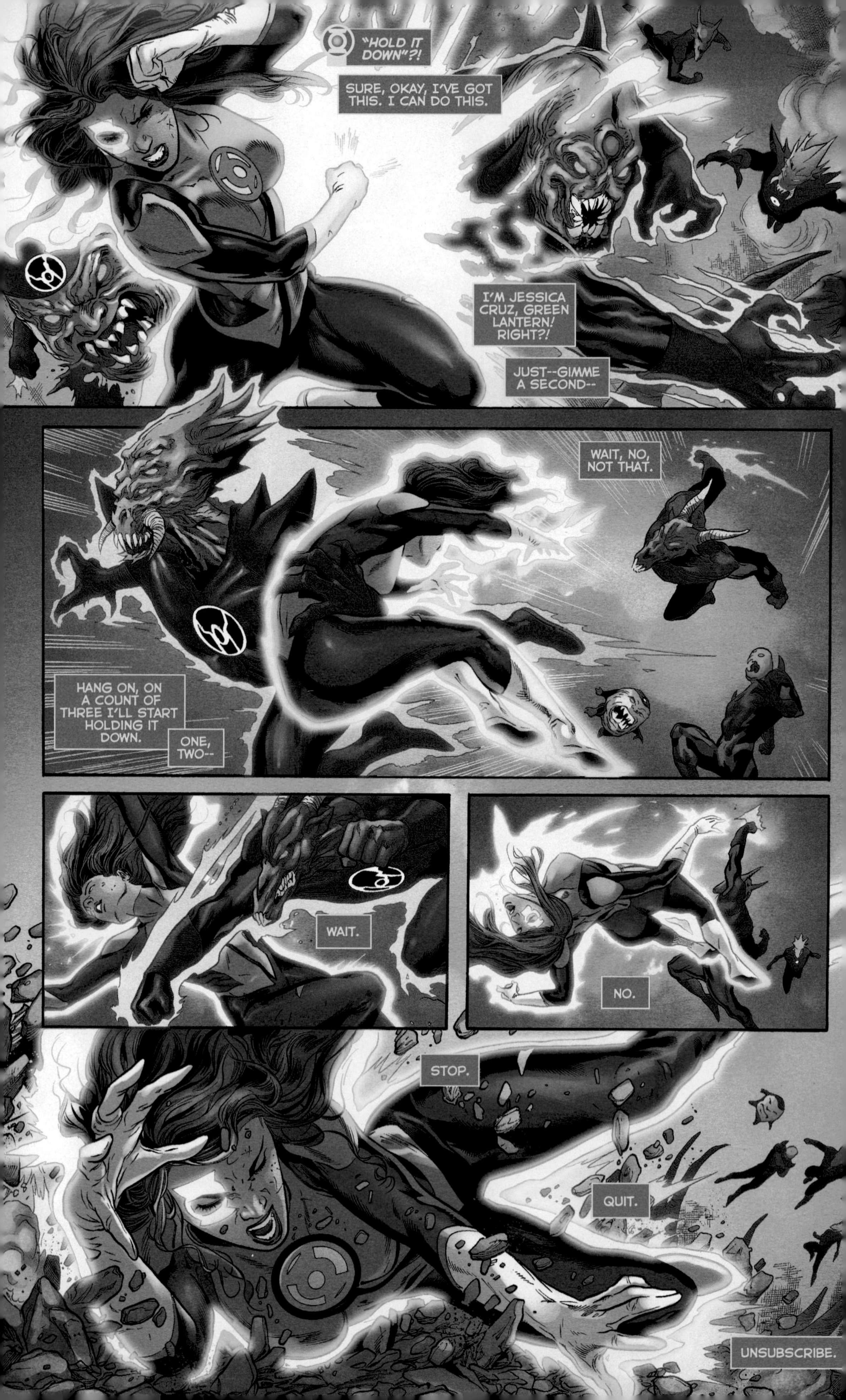
"HOLD IT DOWN"?!
SURE, OKAY, I'VE GOT THIS. I CAN DO THIS.
I'M JESSICA CRUZ, GREEN LANTERN! RIGHT?!
JUST--GIMME A SECOND--
WAIT, NO, NOT THAT.
HANG ON, ON A COUNT OF THREE I'LL START HOLDING IT DOWN.
ONE, TWO--
WAIT.
NO.
STOP.
QUIT.
UNSUBSCRIBE.

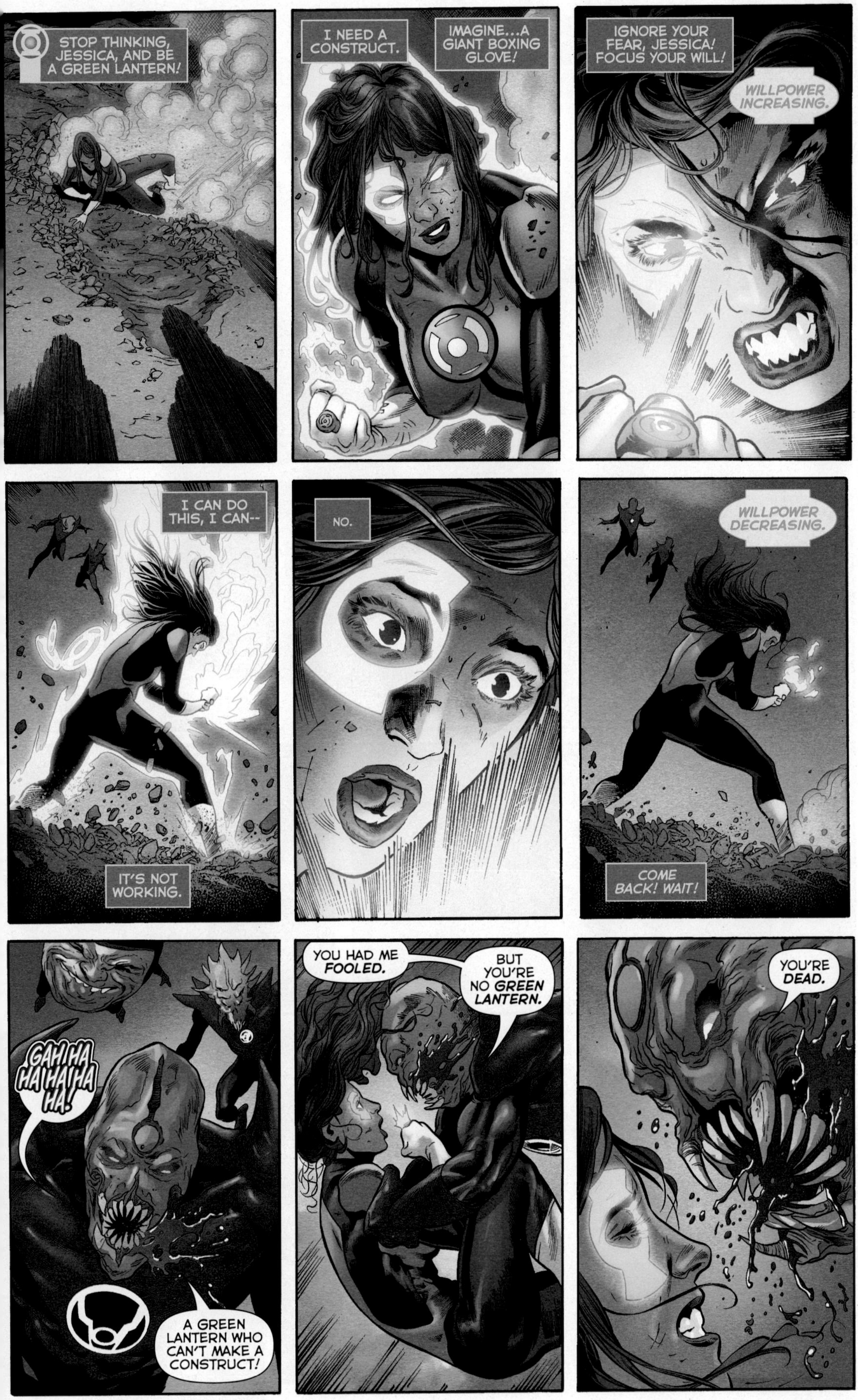
STOP THINKING, JESSICA, AND BE A GREEN LANTERN!
I NEED A CONSTRUCT.
IMAGINE...A GIANT BOXING GLOVE!
IGNORE YOUR FEAR, JESSICA! FOCUS YOUR WILL!
WILLPOWER INCREASING.
I CAN DO THIS, I CAN--
IT'S NOT WORKING.
NO.
WILLPOWER DECREASING.
COME BACK! WAIT!
GAHHA HAHAHA HA!
A GREEN LANTERN WHO CAN'T MAKE A CONSTRUCT!
YOU HAD ME FOOLED.
BUT YOU'RE NO GREEN LANTERN.
YOU'RE DEAD.

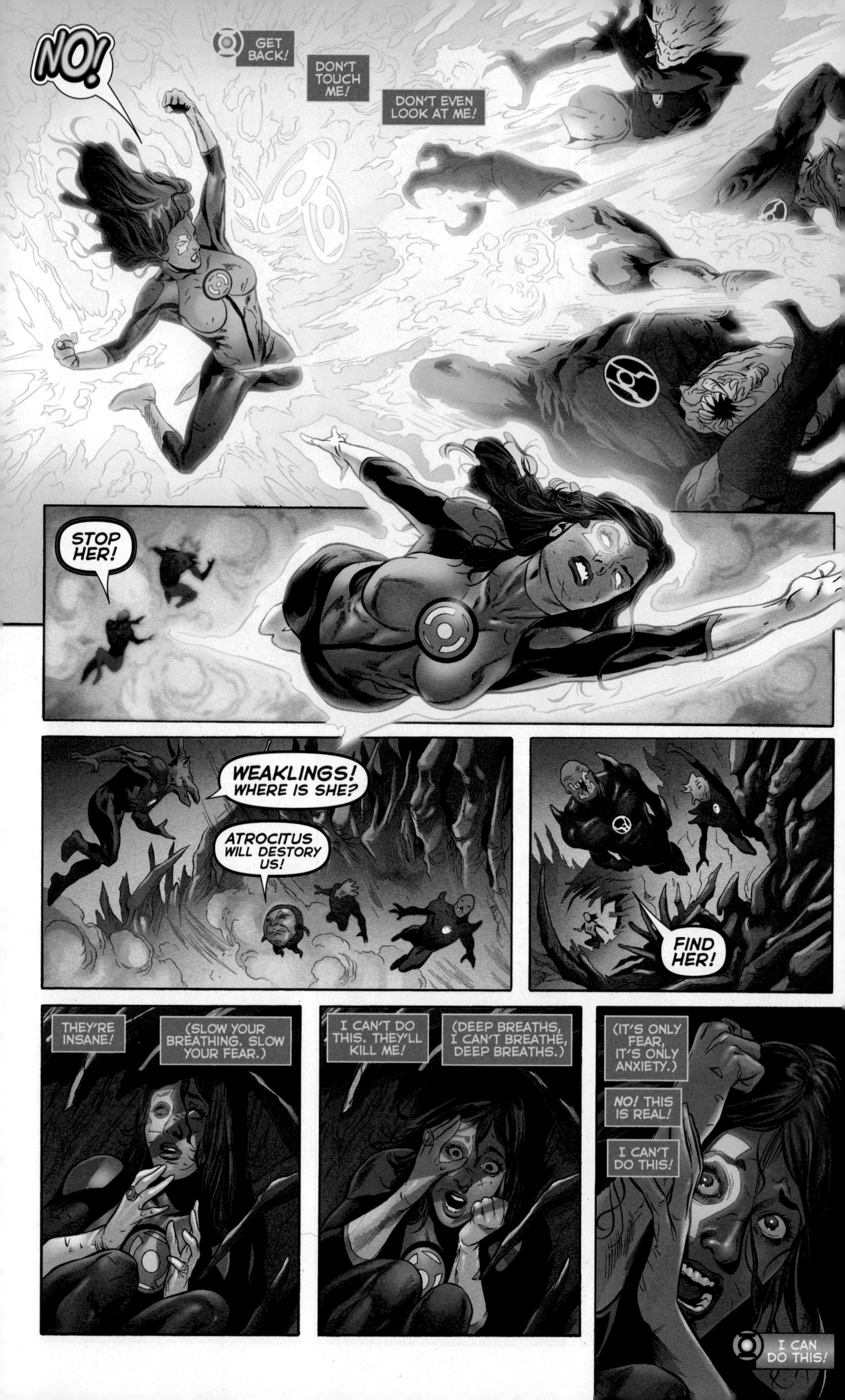
NO!
GET BACK!
DON'T TOUCH ME!
DON'T EVEN LOOK AT ME!
STOP HER!
WEAKLINGS! WHERE IS SHE?
ATROCITUS WILL DESTORY US!
FIND HER!
THEY'RE INSANE!
(SLOW YOUR BREATHING. SLOW YOUR FEAR.)
I CAN'T DO THIS. THEY'LL KILL ME!
(DEEP BREATHS, I CAN'T BREATHE, DEEP BREATHS.)
(IT'S ONLY FEAR, IT'S ONLY ANXIETY.)
NO! THIS IS REAL!
I CAN'T DO THIS!
I CAN DO THIS!

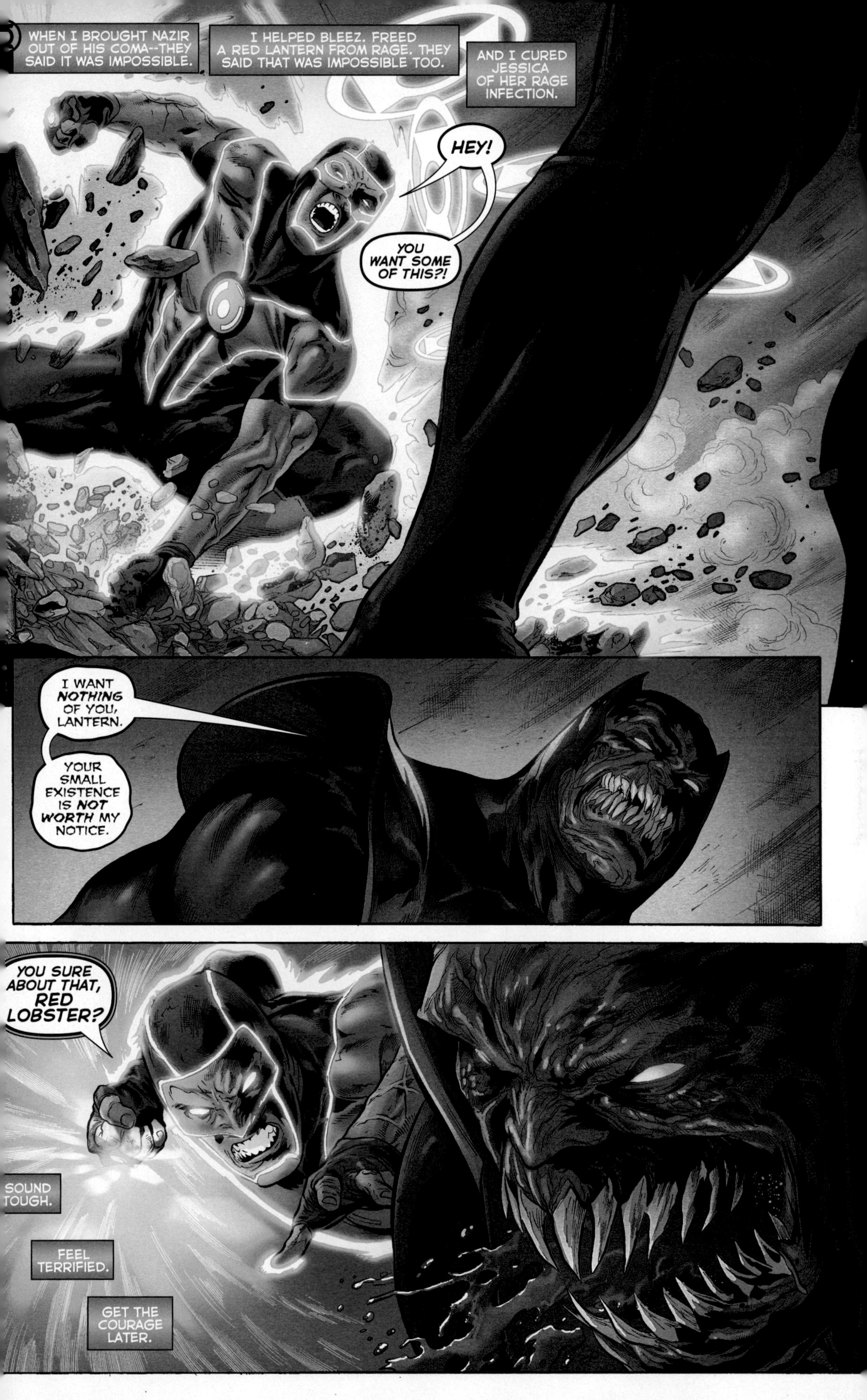
WHEN I BROUGHT NAZIR OUT OF HIS COMA--THEY SAID IT WAS IMPOSSIBLE.
I HELPED BLEEZ. FREED A RED LANTERN FROM RAGE. THEY SAID THAT WAS IMPOSSIBLE TOO.
AND I CURED JESSICA OF HER RAGE INFECTION.
HEY!
YOU WANT SOME OF THIS?!
I WANT NOTHING OF YOU, LANTERN.
YOUR SMALL EXISTENCE IS NOT WORTH MY NOTICE.
YOU SURE ABOUT THAT, RED LOBSTER?
SOUND TOUGH.
FEEL TERRIFIED.
GET THE COURAGE LATER.

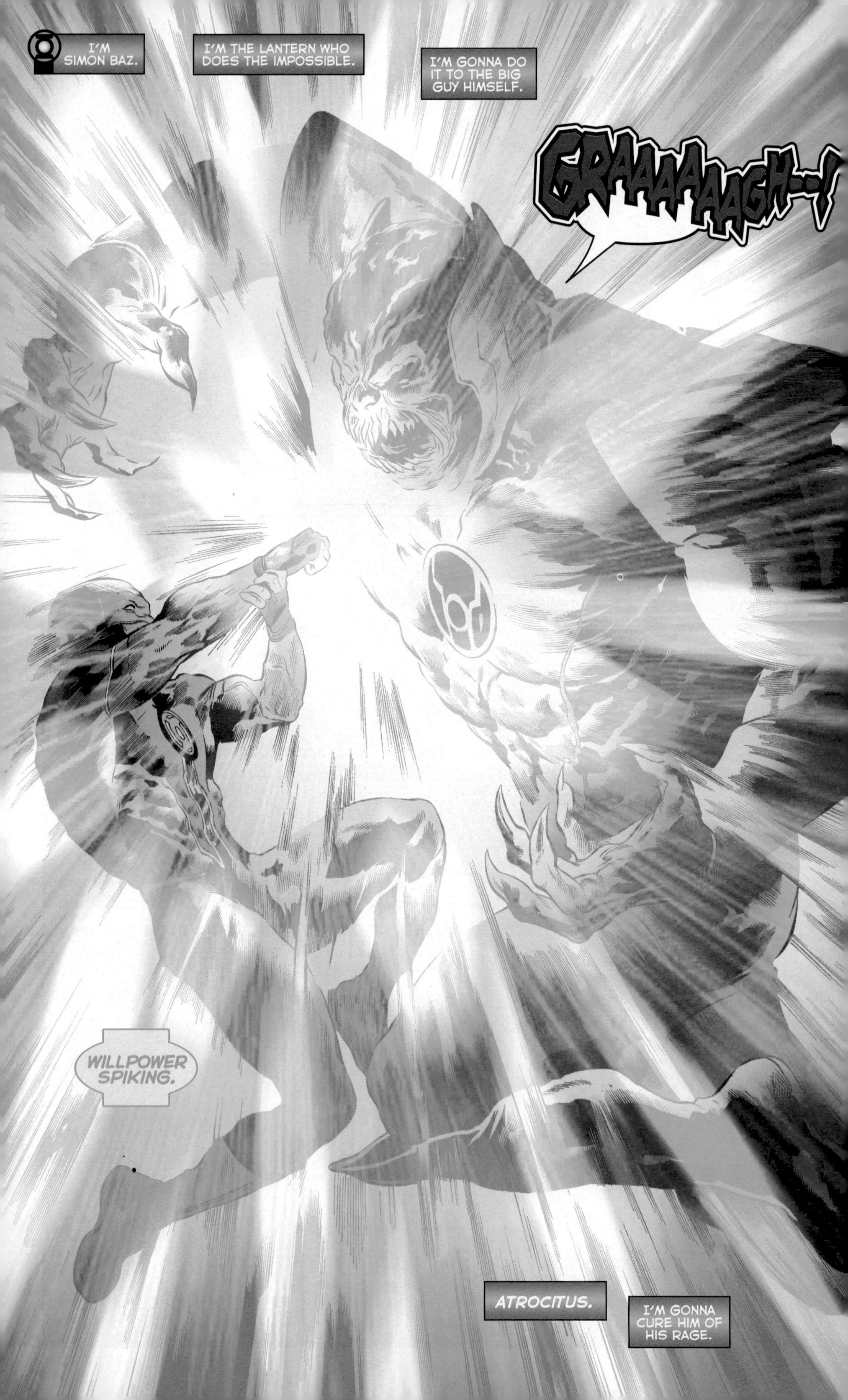
I'M SIMON BAZ.
I'M THE LANTERN WHO DOES THE IMPOSSIBLE.
I'M GONNA DO IT TO THE BIG GUY HIMSELF.
GRAAAAAAAGH--!
WILLPOWER SPIKING.
ATROCITUS.
I'M GONNA CURE HIM OF HIS RAGE.

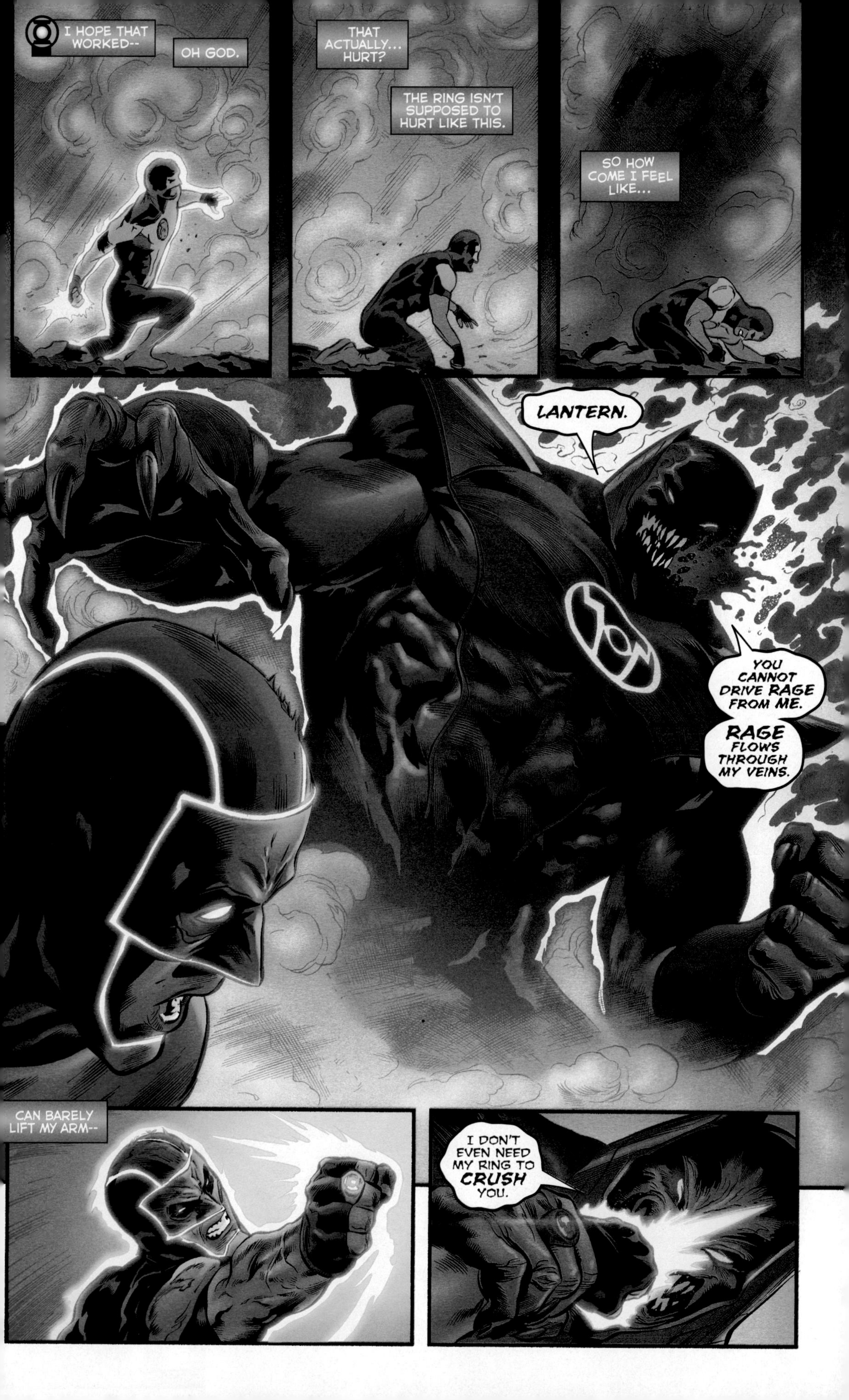
I HOPE THAT WORKED--
OH GOD.
THAT ACTUALLY... HURT?
THE RING ISN'T SUPPOSED TO HURT LIKE THIS.
SO HOW COME I FEEL LIKE...
LANTERN.
YOU CANNOT DRIVE RAGE FROM ME.
RAGE FLOWS THROUGH MY VEINS.
CAN BARELY LIFT MY ARM--
I DON'T EVEN NEED MY RING TO CRUSH YOU.

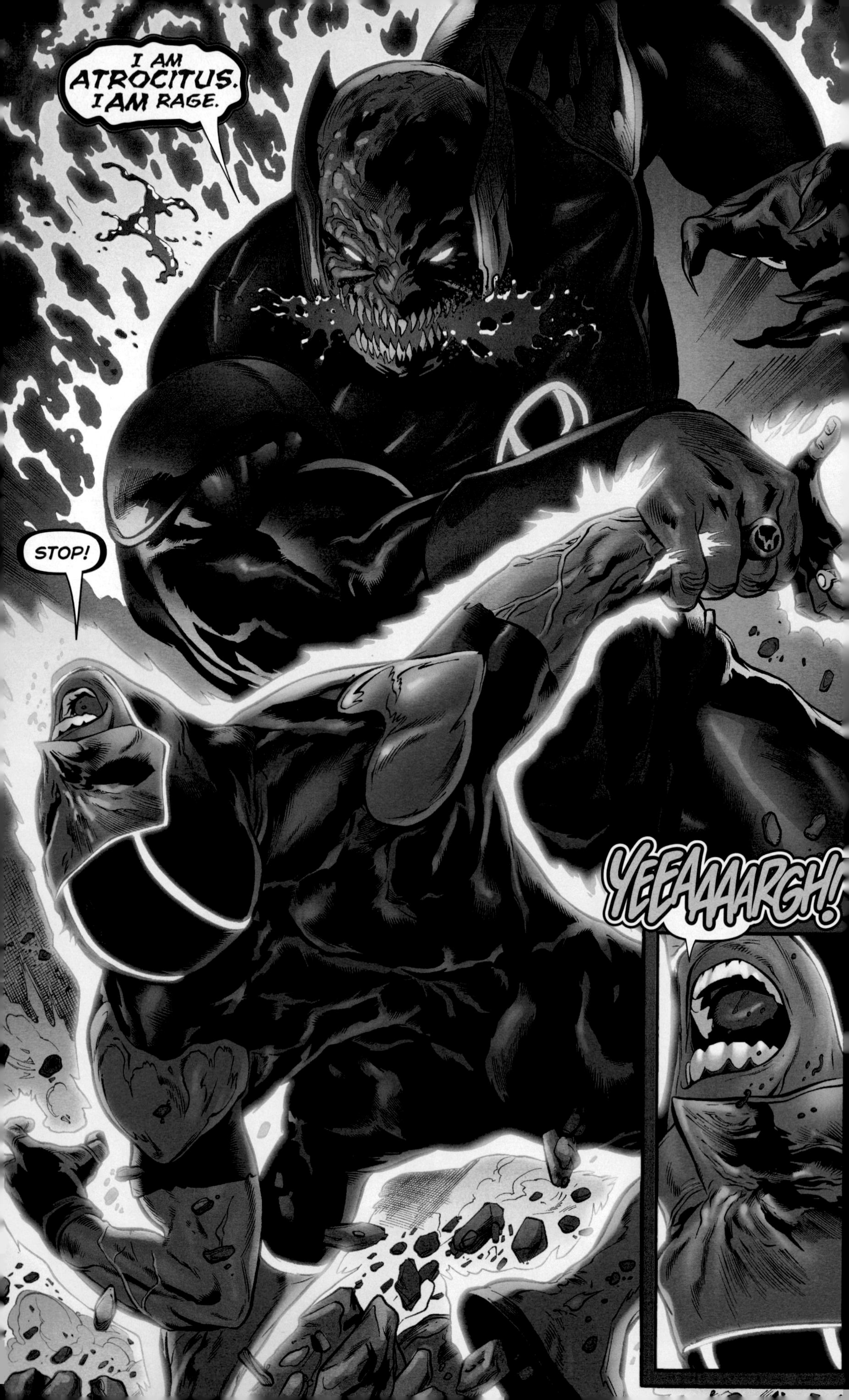
I AM ATROCITUS. I AM RAGE.
STOP!
YEEAAAARGH!

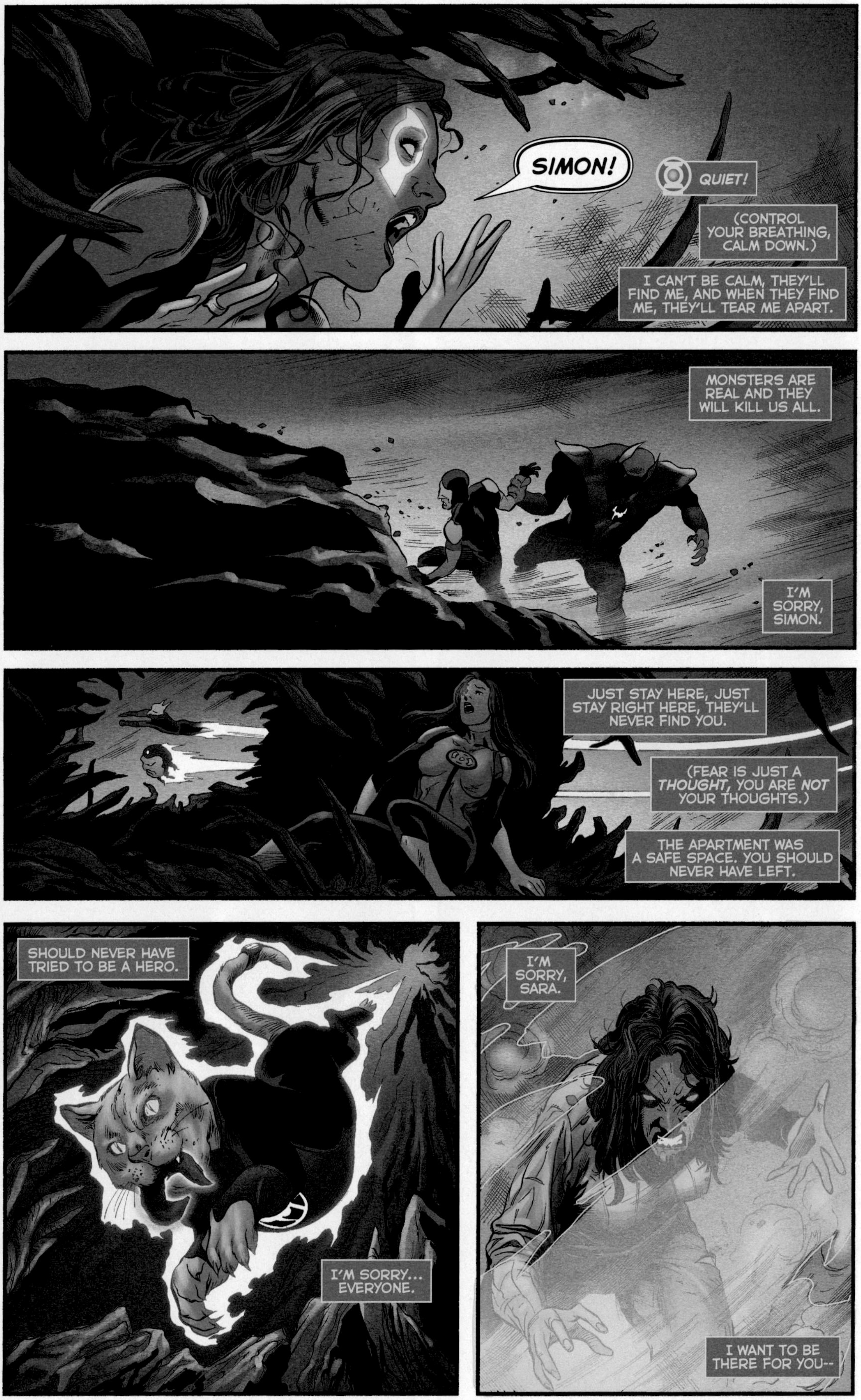
SIMON!
QUIET!
(CONTROL YOUR BREATHING, CALM DOWN.)
I CAN'T BE CALM, THEY'LL FIND ME, AND WHEN THEY FIND ME, THEY'LL TEAR ME APART.
MONSTERS ARE REAL AND THEY WILL KILL US ALL.
I'M SORRY, SIMON.
JUST STAY HERE, JUST STAY RIGHT HERE, THEY'LL NEVER FIND YOU.
(FEAR IS JUST A THOUGHT, YOU ARE NOT YOUR THOUGHTS.)
THE APARTMENT WAS A SAFE SPACE. YOU SHOULD NEVER HAVE LEFT.
SHOULD NEVER HAVE TRIED TO BE A HERO.
I'M SORRY... EVERYONE.
I'M SORRY, SARA.
I WANT TO BE THERE FOR YOU--

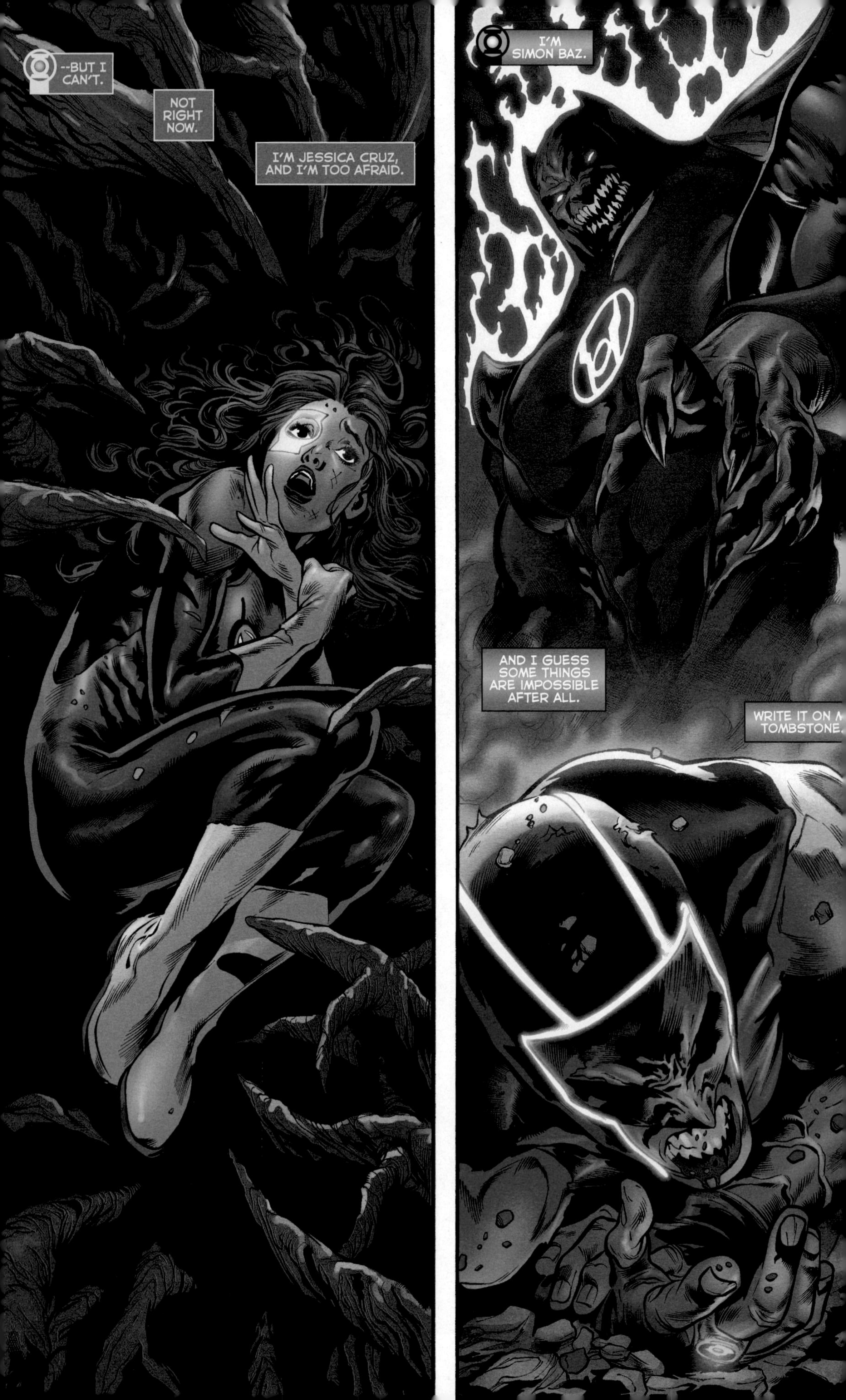
--BUT I CAN'T.
NOT RIGHT NOW.
I'M JESSICA CRUZ, AND I'M TOO AFRAID.
I'M SIMON BAZ.
AND I GUESS SOME THINGS ARE IMPOSSIBLE AFTER ALL.
WRITE IT ON M
TOMBSTONE.

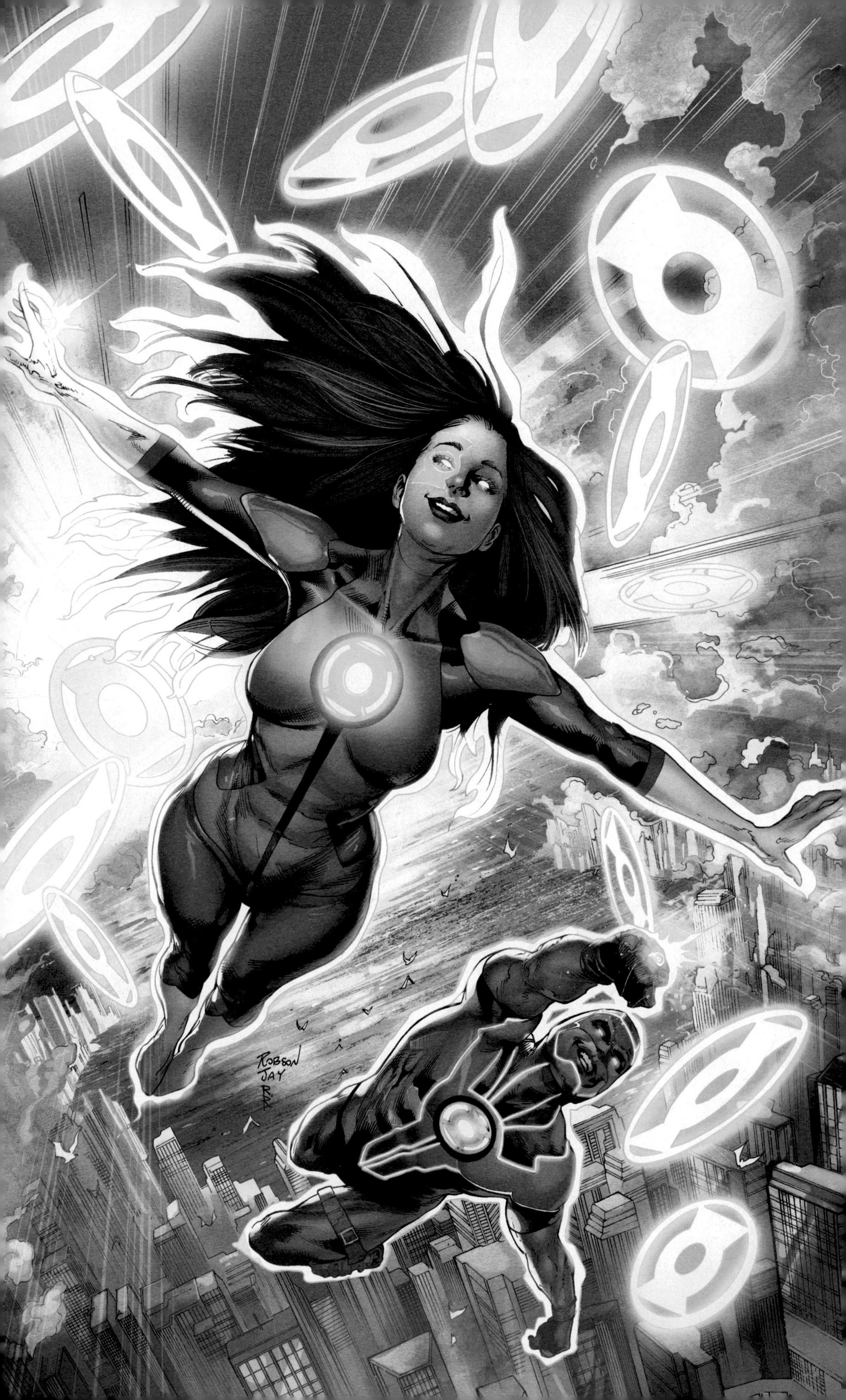
ROBSON
JAY
R.R

RAGE PLANET: PART 6

SAM HUMPHRIES writer * WILL CONRAD and JACK HERBERT artists * BLOND colorist
ROBSON ROCHA, JAY LEISTEN and ROD REIS cover artists

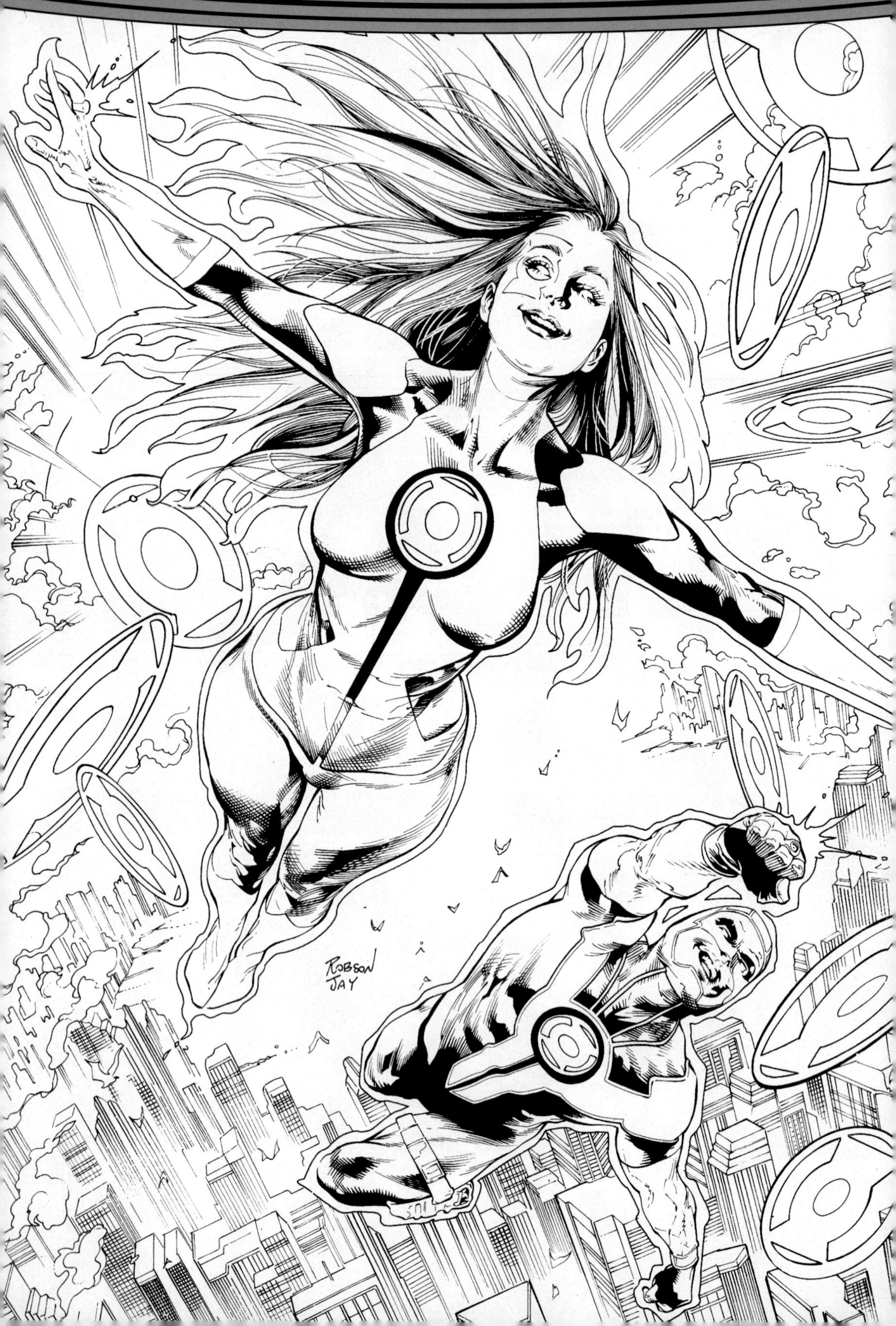
ROBSON
JAY

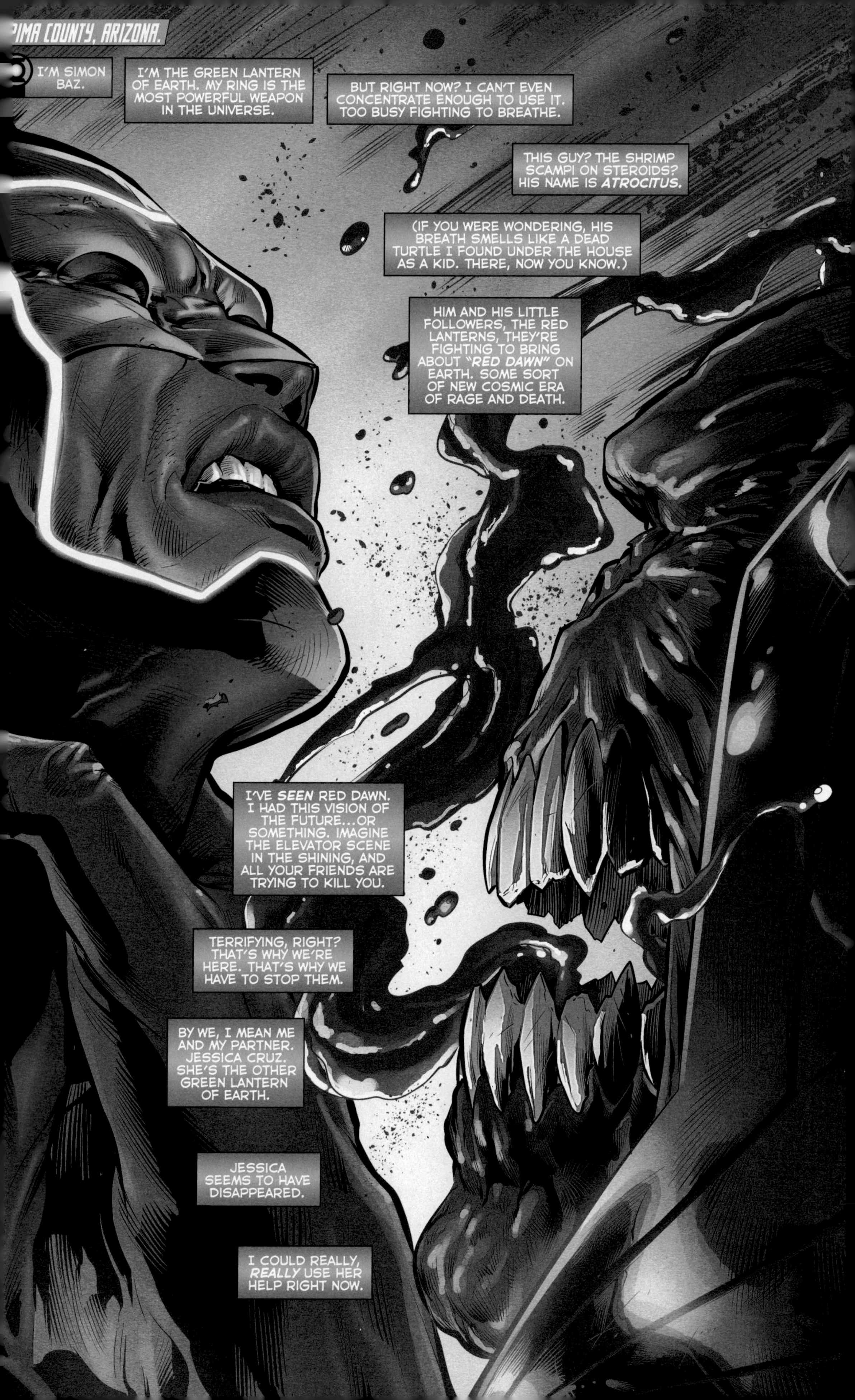
PIMA COUNTY, ARIZONA.
I'M SIMON BAZ.
I'M THE GREEN LANTERN OF EARTH. MY RING IS THE MOST POWERFUL WEAPON IN THE UNIVERSE.
BUT RIGHT NOW? I CAN'T EVEN CONCENTRATE ENOUGH TO USE IT. TOO BUSY FIGHTING TO BREATHE.
THIS GUY? THE SHRIMP SCAMPI ON STEROIDS? HIS NAME IS *ATROCITUS*.
(IF YOU WERE WONDERING, HIS BREATH SMELLS LIKE A DEAD TURTLE I FOUND UNDER THE HOUSE AS A KID. THERE, NOW YOU KNOW.)
HIM AND HIS LITTLE FOLLOWERS, THE RED LANTERNS, THEY'RE FIGHTING TO BRING ABOUT *"RED DAWN"* ON EARTH. SOME SORT OF NEW COSMIC ERA OF RAGE AND DEATH.
I'VE *SEEN* RED DAWN. I HAD THIS VISION OF THE FUTURE...OR SOMETHING. IMAGINE THE ELEVATOR SCENE IN THE SHINING, AND ALL YOUR FRIENDS ARE TRYING TO KILL YOU.
TERRIFYING, RIGHT? THAT'S WHY WE'RE HERE. THAT'S WHY WE HAVE TO STOP THEM.
BY WE, I MEAN ME AND MY PARTNER. JESSICA CRUZ. SHE'S THE OTHER GREEN LANTERN OF EARTH.
JESSICA SEEMS TO HAVE DISAPPEARED.
I COULD REALLY, *REALLY* USE HER HELP RIGHT NOW.

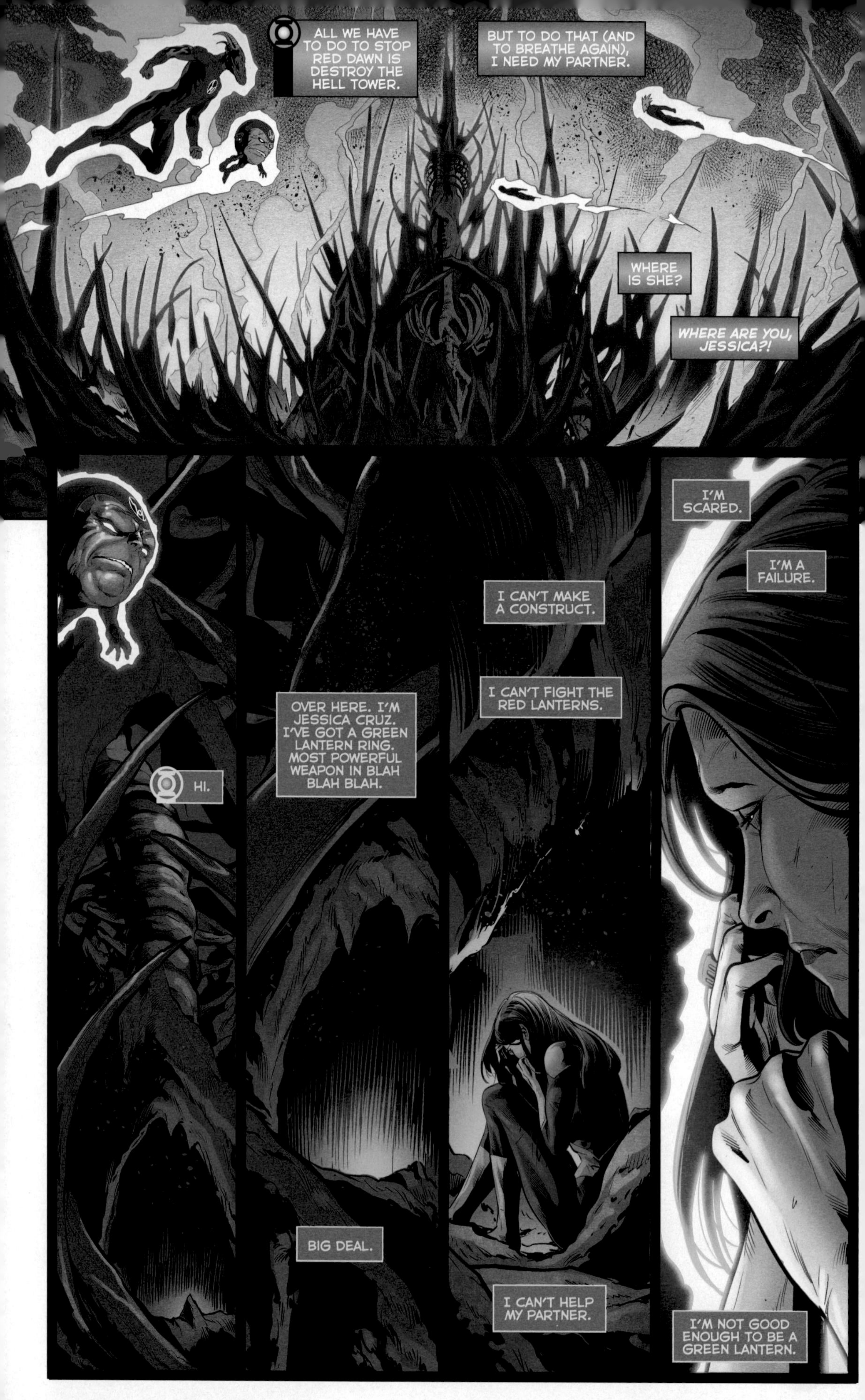
ALL WE HAVE TO DO TO STOP RED DAWN IS DESTROY THE HELL TOWER.
BUT TO DO THAT (AND TO BREATHE AGAIN), I NEED MY PARTNER.
WHERE IS SHE?
WHERE ARE YOU, JESSICA?!
HI.
OVER HERE. I'M JESSICA CRUZ. I'VE GOT A GREEN LANTERN RING. MOST POWERFUL WEAPON IN BLAH BLAH BLAH.
BIG DEAL.
I CAN'T MAKE A CONSTRUCT.
I CAN'T FIGHT THE RED LANTERNS.
I CAN'T HELP MY PARTNER.
I'M SCARED.
I'M A FAILURE.
I'M NOT GOOD ENOUGH TO BE A GREEN LANTERN.

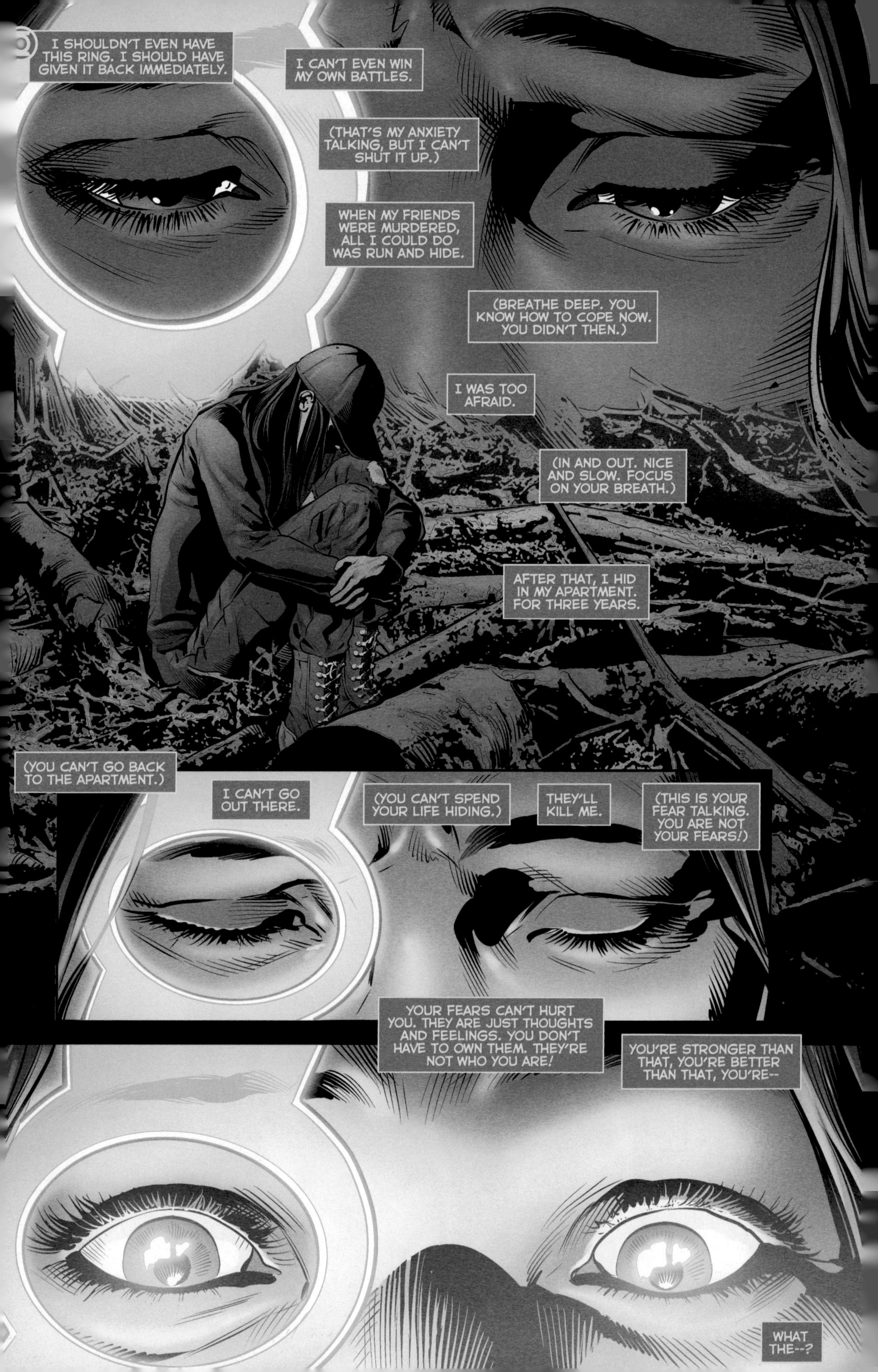
I SHOULDN'T EVEN HAVE THIS RING. I SHOULD HAVE GIVEN IT BACK IMMEDIATELY.
I CAN'T EVEN WIN MY OWN BATTLES.
(THAT'S MY ANXIETY TALKING, BUT I CAN'T SHUT IT UP.)
WHEN MY FRIENDS WERE MURDERED, ALL I COULD DO WAS RUN AND HIDE.
(BREATHE DEEP. YOU KNOW HOW TO COPE NOW. YOU DIDN'T THEN.)
I WAS TOO AFRAID.
(IN AND OUT. NICE AND SLOW. FOCUS ON YOUR BREATH.)
AFTER THAT, I HID IN MY APARTMENT. FOR THREE YEARS.
(YOU CAN'T GO BACK TO THE APARTMENT.)
I CAN'T GO OUT THERE.
(YOU CAN'T SPEND YOUR LIFE HIDING.)
THEY'LL KILL ME.
(THIS IS YOUR FEAR TALKING. YOU ARE NOT YOUR FEARS!)
YOUR FEARS CAN'T HURT YOU. THEY ARE JUST THOUGHTS AND FEELINGS. YOU DON'T HAVE TO OWN THEM. THEY'RE NOT WHO YOU ARE!
YOU'RE STRONGER THAN THAT, YOU'RE BETTER THAN THAT, YOU'RE--
WHAT THE--?

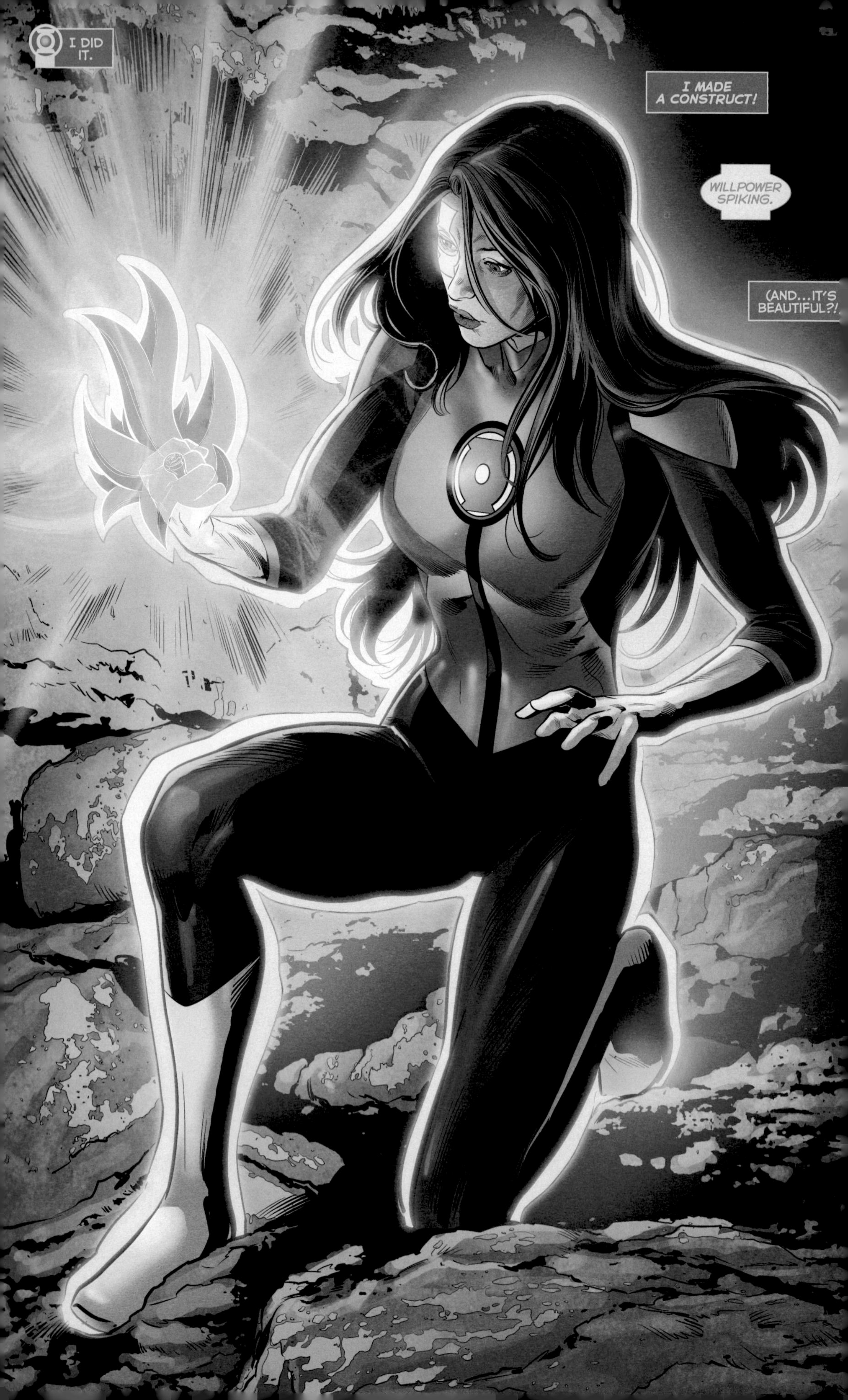
I DID IT.
I MADE A CONSTRUCT!
WILLPOWER SPIKING.
(AND...IT'S BEAUTIFUL?!)

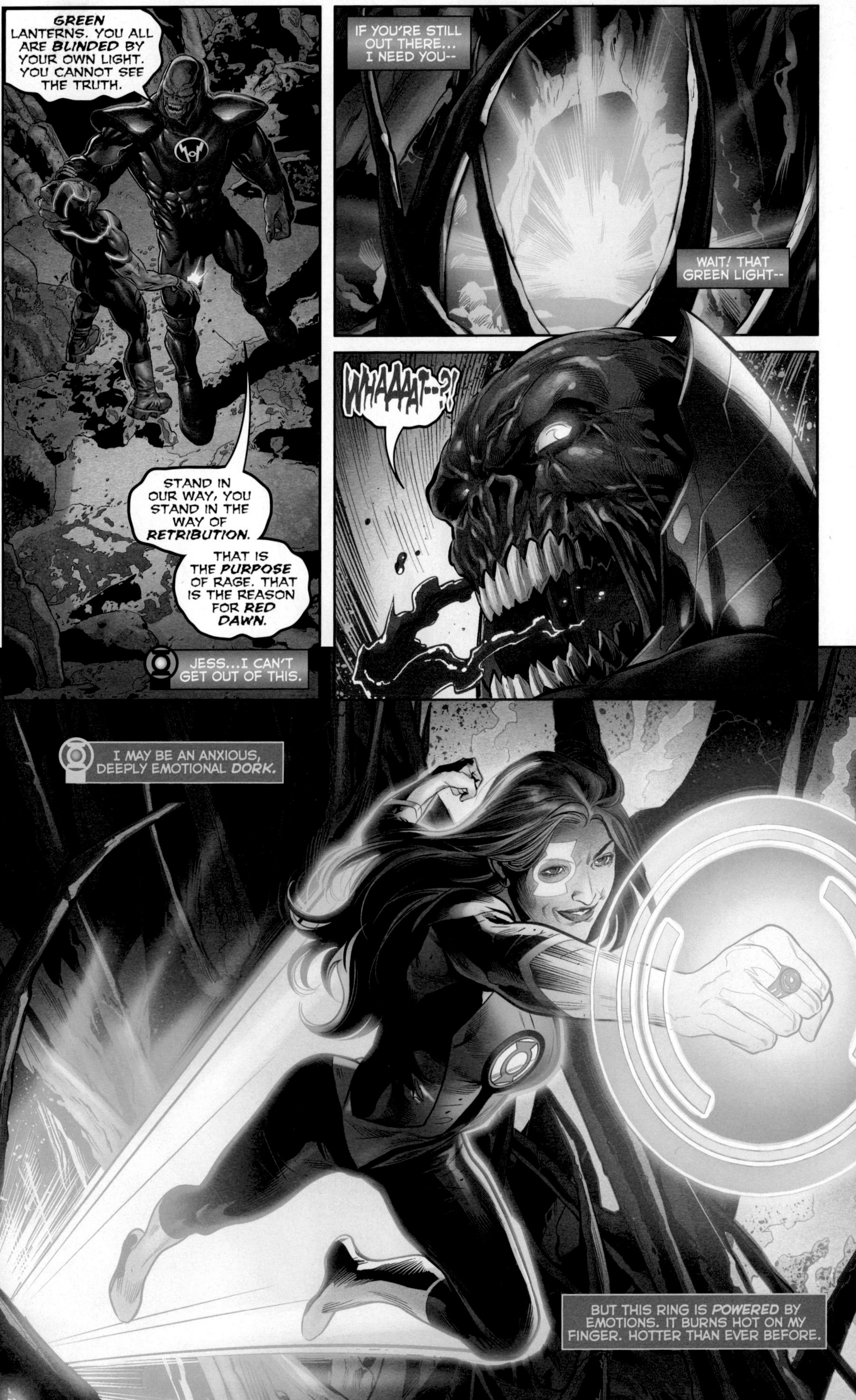
GREEN LANTERNS. YOU ALL ARE BLINDED BY YOUR OWN LIGHT. YOU CANNOT SEE THE TRUTH.
STAND IN OUR WAY, YOU STAND IN THE WAY OF RETRIBUTION.
THAT IS THE PURPOSE OF RAGE. THAT IS THE REASON FOR RED DAWN.
JESS...I CAN'T GET OUT OF THIS.
IF YOU'RE STILL OUT THERE... I NEED YOU--
WAIT! THAT GREEN LIGHT--
WHAAAAT--?!
I MAY BE AN ANXIOUS, DEEPLY EMOTIONAL DORK.
BUT THIS RING IS POWERED BY EMOTIONS. IT BURNS HOT ON MY FINGER. HOTTER THAN EVER BEFORE.

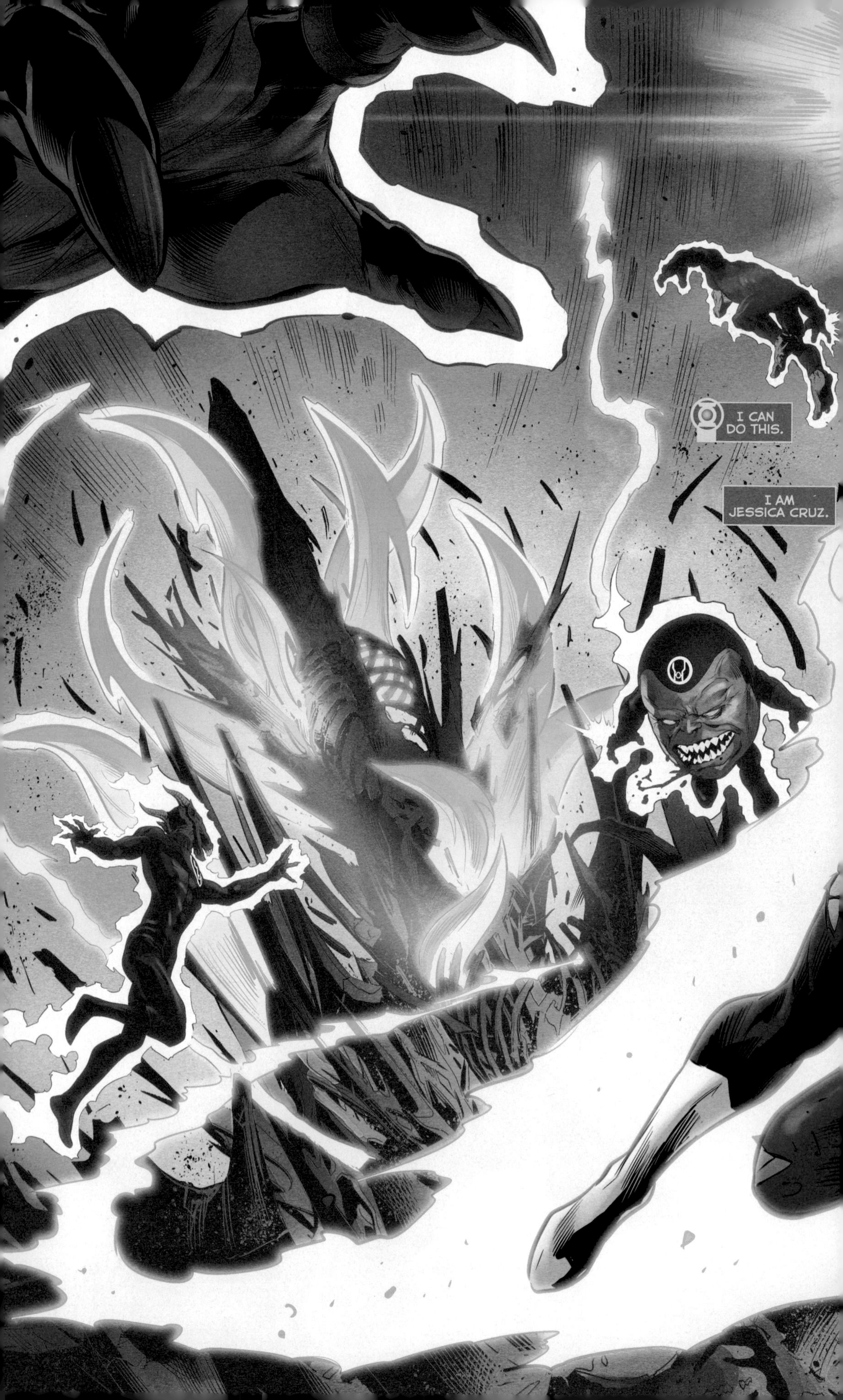
I CAN DO THIS.
I AM JESSICA CRUZ.

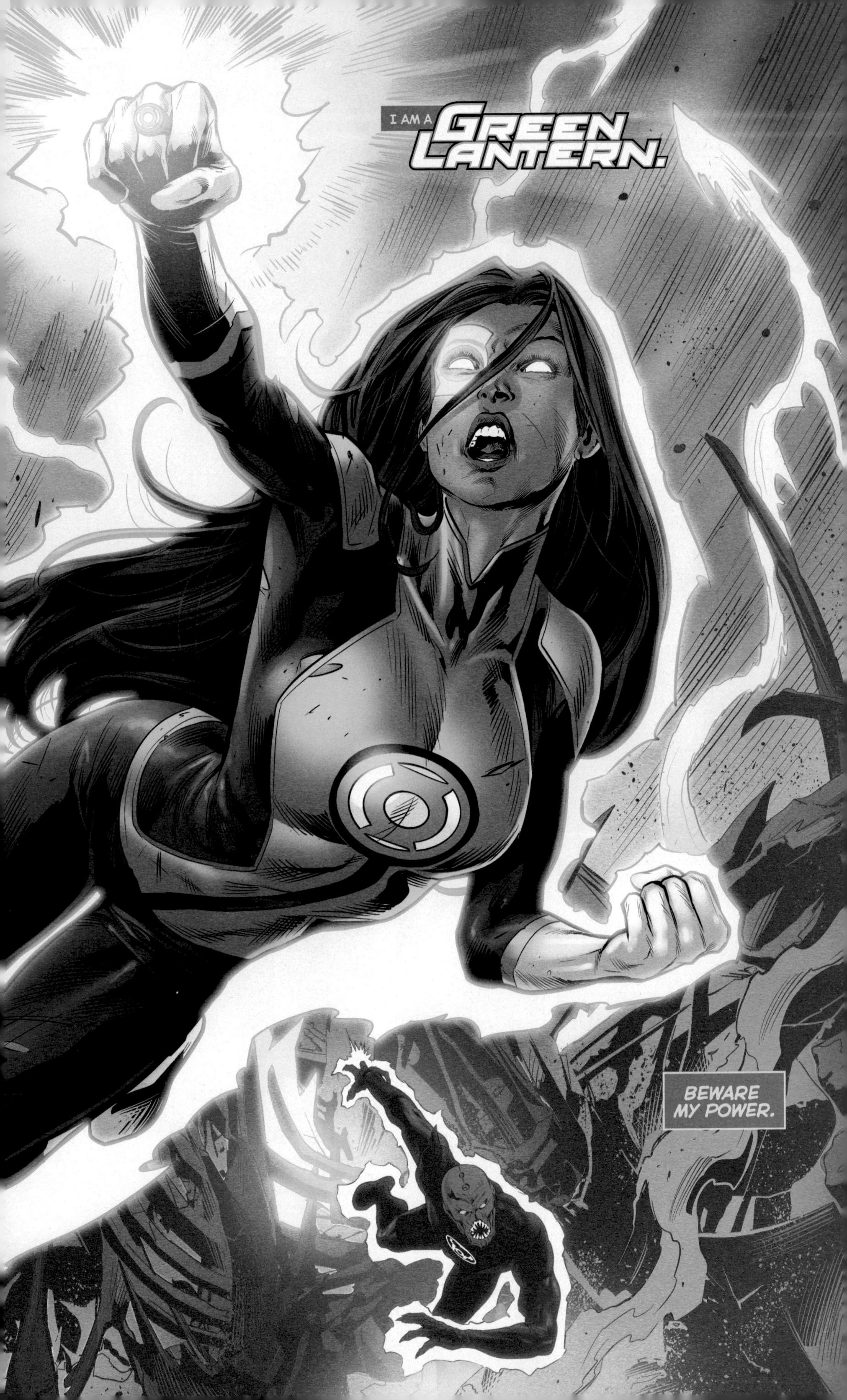
I AM A GREEN LANTERN.
BEWARE MY POWER.

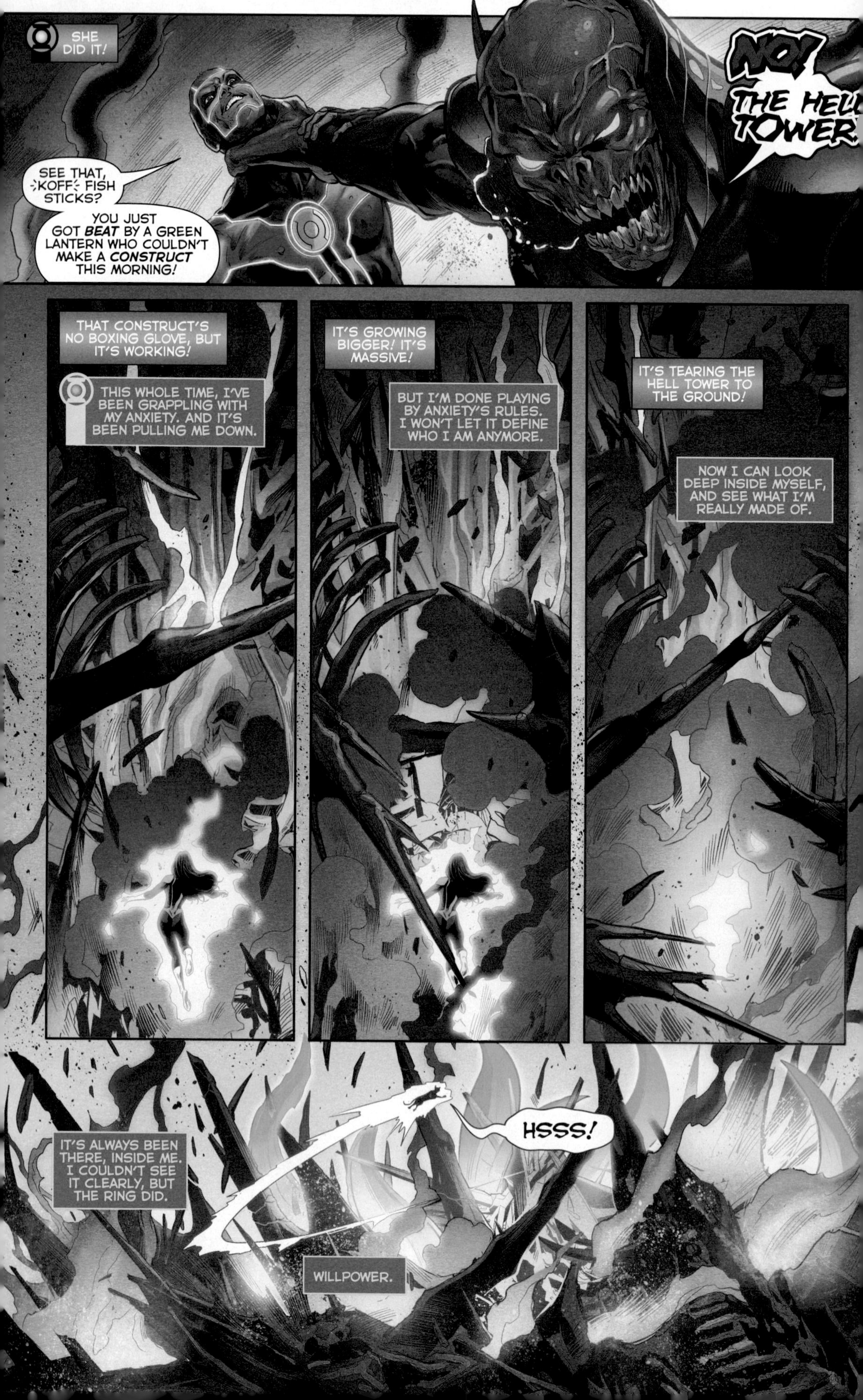
SHE DID IT!
NO! THE HELL TOWER!
SEE THAT, *KOFF* FISH STICKS?
YOU JUST GOT BEAT BY A GREEN LANTERN WHO COULDN'T MAKE A CONSTRUCT THIS MORNING!
THAT CONSTRUCT'S NO BOXING GLOVE, BUT IT'S WORKING!
THIS WHOLE TIME, I'VE BEEN GRAPPLING WITH MY ANXIETY. AND IT'S BEEN PULLING ME DOWN.
IT'S GROWING BIGGER! IT'S MASSIVE!
BUT I'M DONE PLAYING BY ANXIETY'S RULES. I WON'T LET IT DEFINE WHO I AM ANYMORE.
IT'S TEARING THE HELL TOWER TO THE GROUND!
NOW I CAN LOOK DEEP INSIDE MYSELF, AND SEE WHAT I'M REALLY MADE OF.
HSSS!
IT'S ALWAYS BEEN THERE, INSIDE ME. I COULDN'T SEE IT CLEARLY, BUT THE RING DID.
WILLPOWER.

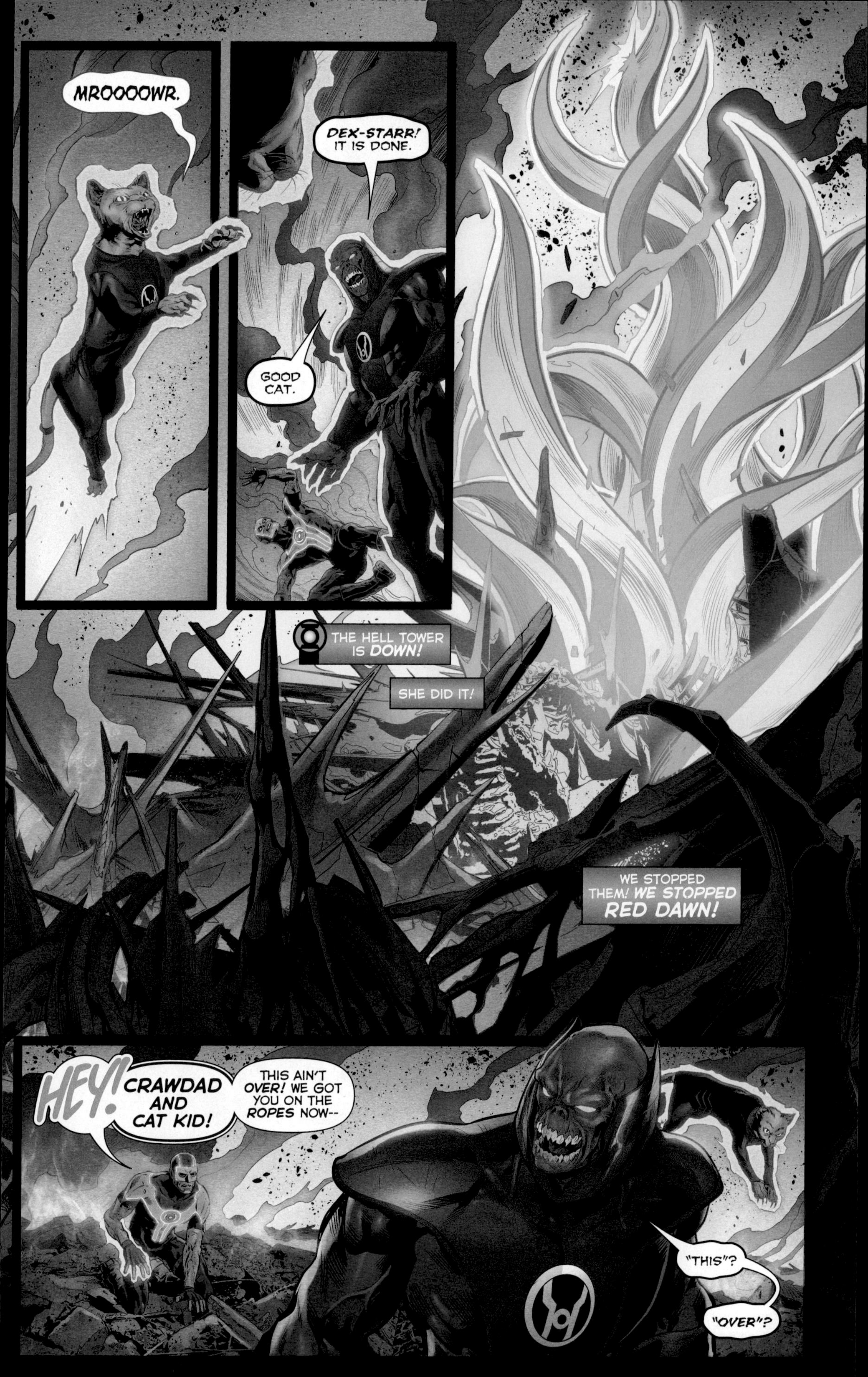
MROOOOWR.
DEX-STARR! IT IS DONE.
GOOD CAT.
THE HELL TOWER IS DOWN!
SHE DID IT!
WE STOPPED THEM! WE STOPPED RED DAWN!
HEY! CRAWDAD AND CAT KID!
THIS AIN'T OVER! WE GOT YOU ON THE ROPES NOW--
"THIS"?
"OVER"?

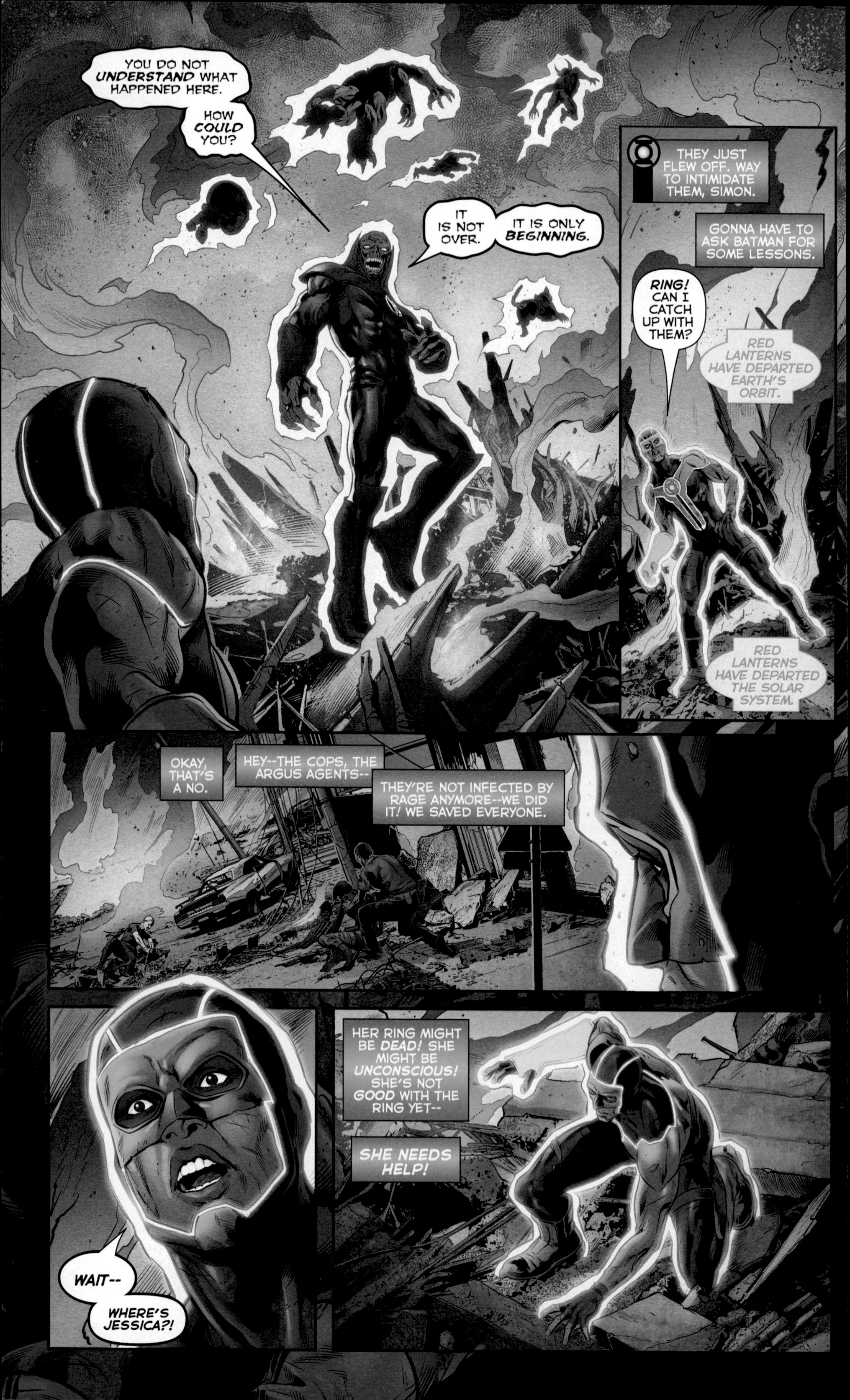
YOU DO NOT UNDERSTAND WHAT HAPPENED HERE.
HOW COULD YOU?
IT IS NOT OVER.
IT IS ONLY BEGINNING.
THEY JUST FLEW OFF. WAY TO INTIMIDATE THEM, SIMON.
GONNA HAVE TO ASK BATMAN FOR SOME LESSONS.
RING! CAN I CATCH UP WITH THEM?
RED LANTERNS HAVE DEPARTED EARTH'S ORBIT.
RED LANTERNS HAVE DEPARTED THE SOLAR SYSTEM.
OKAY, THAT'S A NO.
HEY--THE COPS, THE ARGUS AGENTS--
THEY'RE NOT INFECTED BY RAGE ANYMORE--WE DID IT! WE SAVED EVERYONE.
WAIT--
WHERE'S JESSICA?!
HER RING MIGHT BE DEAD! SHE MIGHT BE UNCONSCIOUS! SHE'S NOT GOOD WITH THE RING YET--
SHE NEEDS HELP!

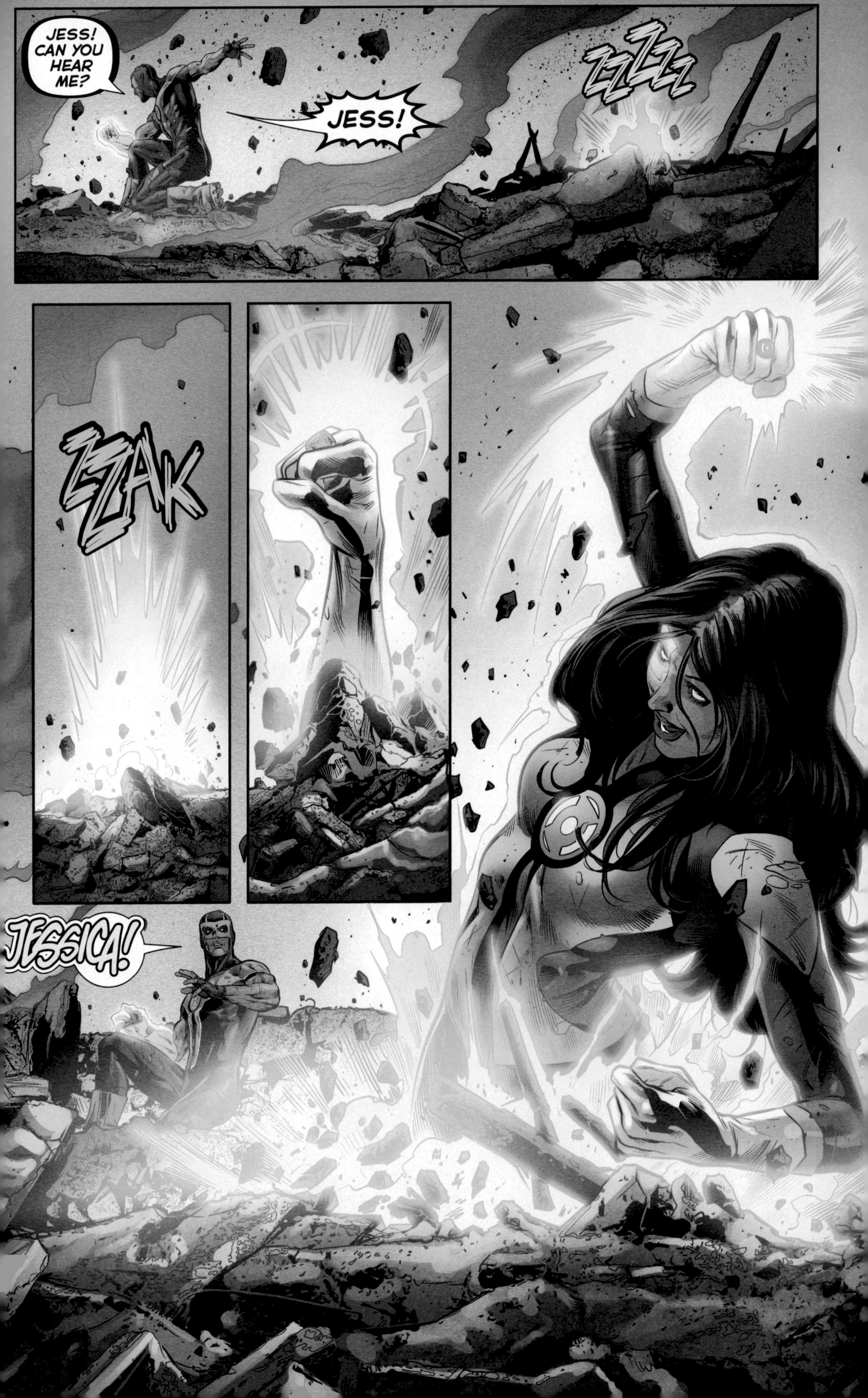
JESS! CAN YOU HEAR ME?
JESS!
ZZZZZ
ZZAK
JESSICA!

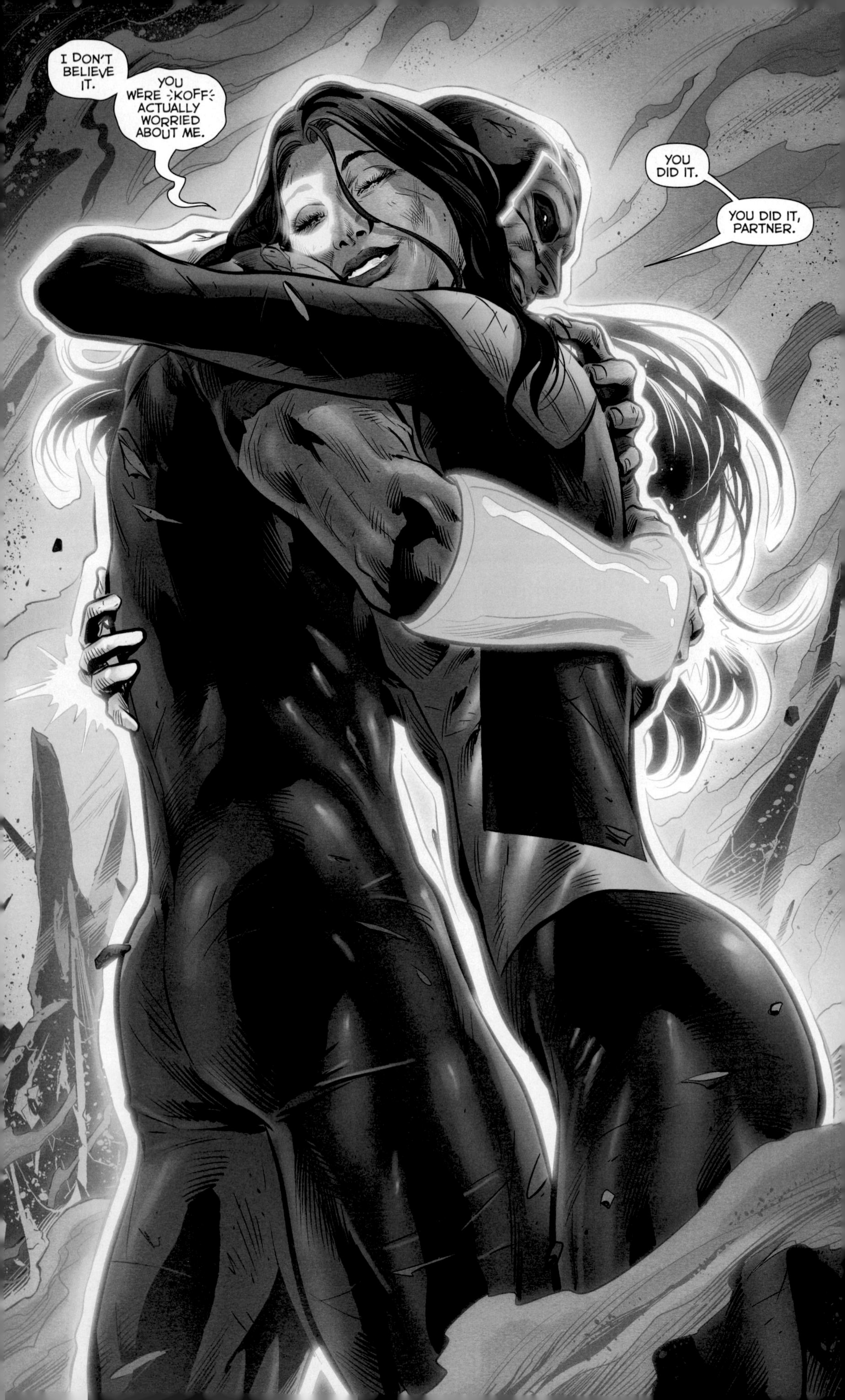
I DON'T BELIEVE IT.
YOU WERE *KOFF* ACTUALLY WORRIED ABOUT ME.
YOU DID IT.
YOU DID IT, PARTNER.

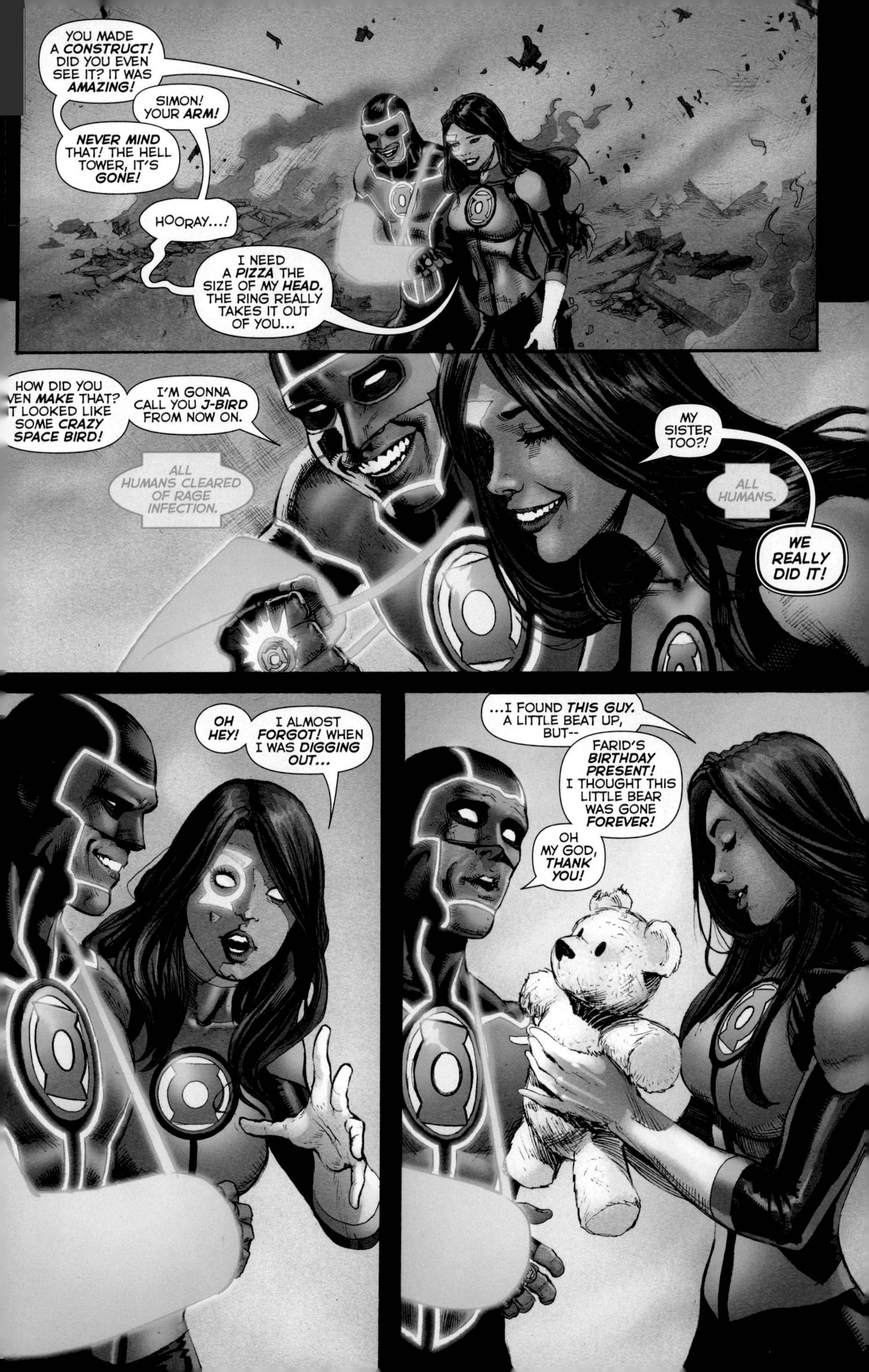
YOU MADE A CONSTRUCT! DID YOU EVEN SEE IT? IT WAS AMAZING!
SIMON! YOUR ARM!
NEVER MIND THAT! THE HELL TOWER, IT'S GONE!
HOORAY...!
I NEED A PIZZA THE SIZE OF MY HEAD. THE RING REALLY TAKES IT OUT OF YOU...
HOW DID YOU EVEN MAKE THAT? IT LOOKED LIKE SOME CRAZY SPACE BIRD!
I'M GONNA CALL YOU J-BIRD FROM NOW ON.
ALL HUMANS CLEARED OF RAGE INFECTION.
MY SISTER TOO?!
ALL HUMANS.
WE REALLY DID IT!
OH HEY!
I ALMOST FORGOT! WHEN I WAS DIGGING OUT...
...I FOUND THIS GUY. A LITTLE BEAT UP, BUT--
FARID'S BIRTHDAY PRESENT! I THOUGHT THIS LITTLE BEAR WAS GONE FOREVER!
OH MY GOD, THANK YOU!

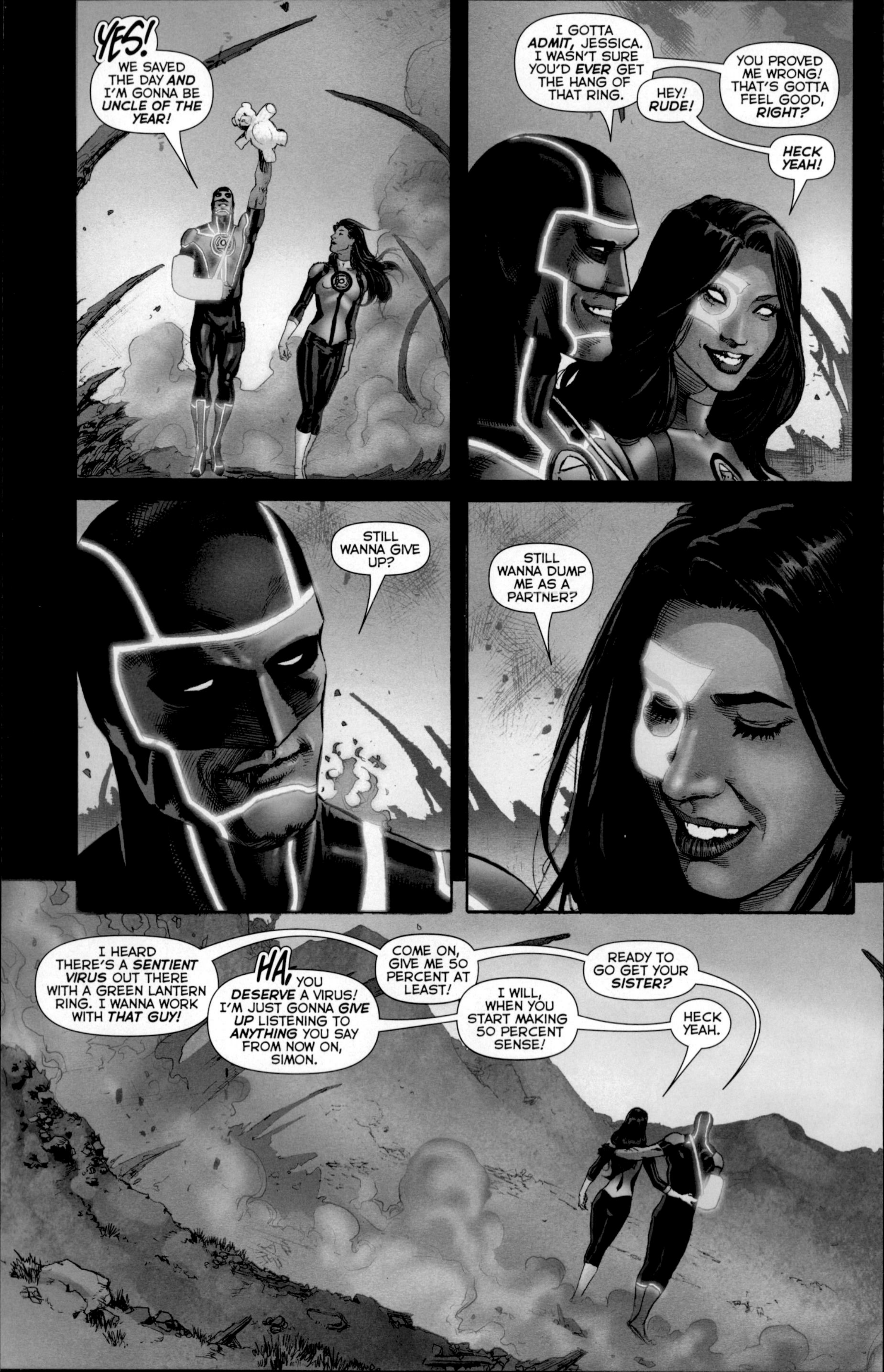
YES!
WE SAVED THE DAY AND I'M GONNA BE UNCLE OF THE YEAR!
I GOTTA ADMIT, JESSICA. I WASN'T SURE YOU'D EVER GET THE HANG OF THAT RING.
HEY! RUDE!
YOU PROVED ME WRONG! THAT'S GOTTA FEEL GOOD, RIGHT?
HECK YEAH!
STILL WANNA GIVE UP?
STILL WANNA DUMP ME AS A PARTNER?
I HEARD THERE'S A SENTIENT VIRUS OUT THERE WITH A GREEN LANTERN RING. I WANNA WORK WITH THAT GUY!
HA, YOU DESERVE A VIRUS! I'M JUST GONNA GIVE UP LISTENING TO ANYTHING YOU SAY FROM NOW ON, SIMON.
COME ON, GIVE ME 50 PERCENT AT LEAST!
I WILL, WHEN YOU START MAKING 50 PERCENT SENSE!
READY TO GO GET YOUR SISTER?
HECK YEAH.

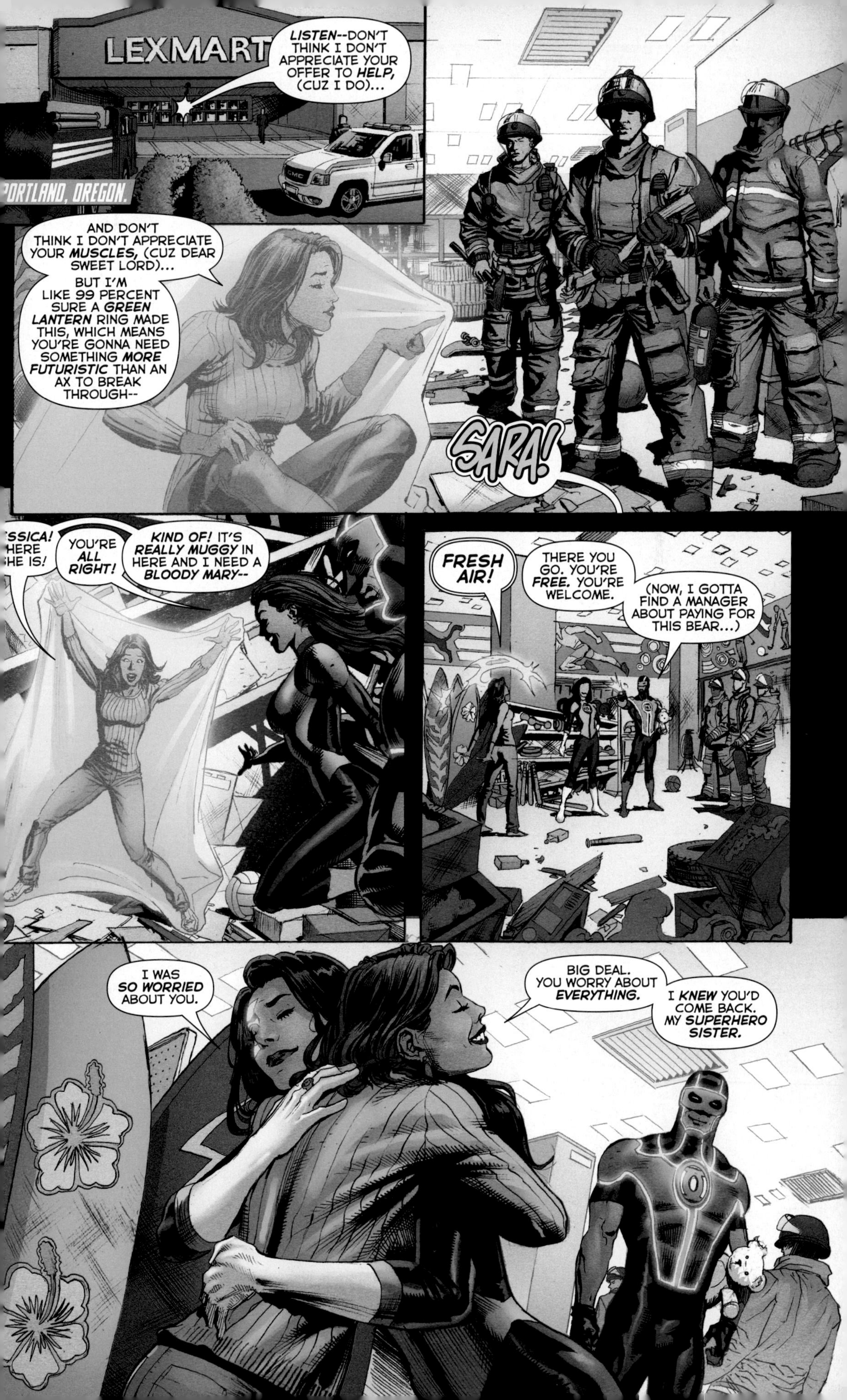
LEXMART
LISTEN--DON'T THINK I DON'T APPRECIATE YOUR OFFER TO HELP, (CUZ I DO)...
PORTLAND, OREGON.
AND DON'T THINK I DON'T APPRECIATE YOUR MUSCLES, (CUZ DEAR SWEET LORD)...
BUT I'M LIKE 99 PERCENT SURE A GREEN LANTERN RING MADE THIS, WHICH MEANS YOU'RE GONNA NEED SOMETHING MORE FUTURISTIC THAN AN AX TO BREAK THROUGH--
SARA!
YOU'RE ALL RIGHT!
KIND OF! IT'S REALLY MUGGY IN HERE AND I NEED A BLOODY MARY--
FRESH AIR!
THERE YOU GO. YOU'RE FREE. YOU'RE WELCOME.
(NOW, I GOTTA FIND A MANAGER ABOUT PAYING FOR THIS BEAR...)
I WAS SO WORRIED ABOUT YOU.
BIG DEAL. YOU WORRY ABOUT EVERYTHING.
I KNEW YOU'D COME BACK. MY SUPERHERO SISTER.

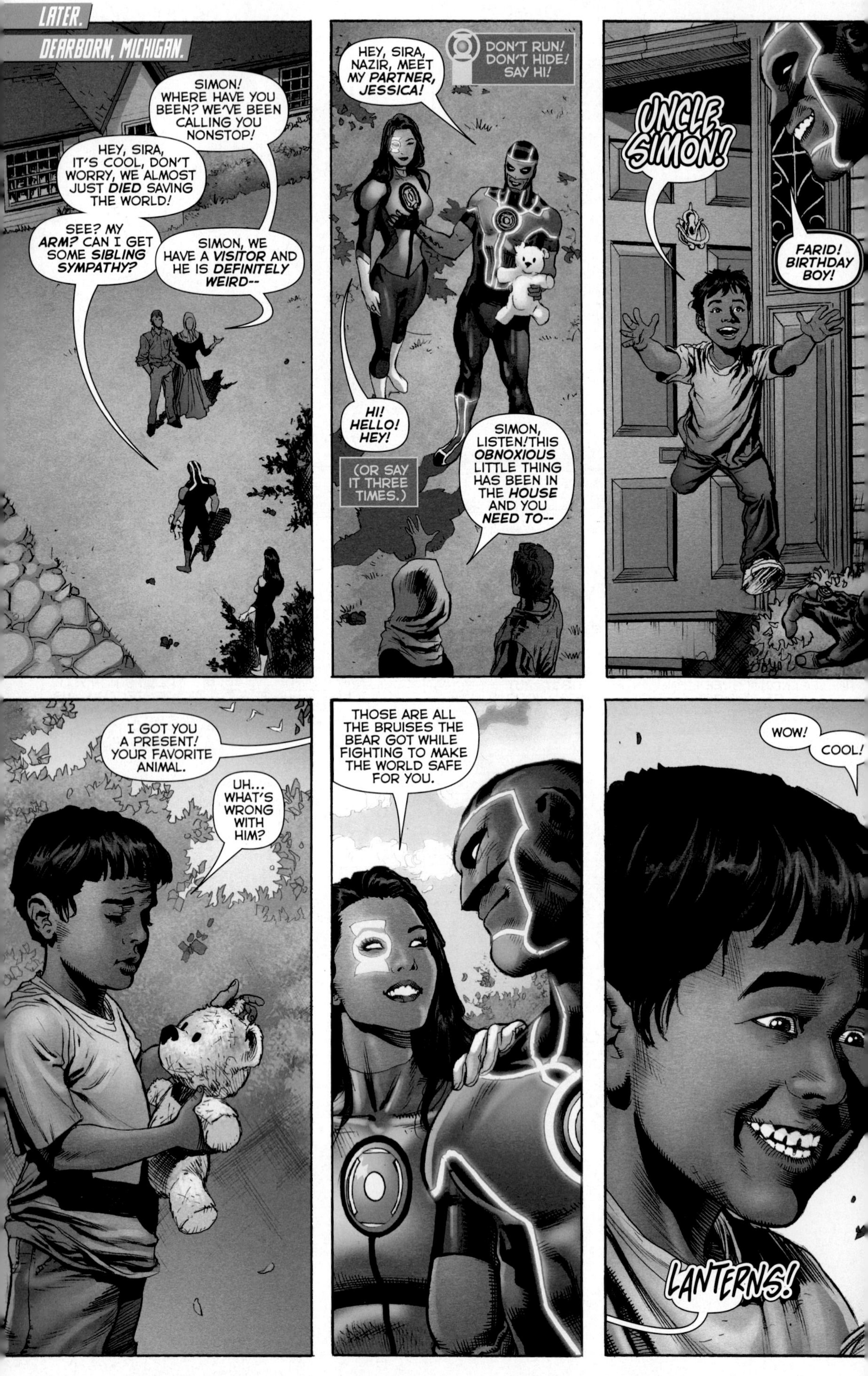
LATER.
DEARBORN, MICHIGAN.
SIMON! WHERE HAVE YOU BEEN? WE'VE BEEN CALLING YOU NONSTOP!
HEY, SIRA, IT'S COOL, DON'T WORRY, WE ALMOST JUST DIED SAVING THE WORLD!
SEE? MY ARM? CAN I GET SOME SIBLING SYMPATHY?
SIMON, WE HAVE A VISITOR AND HE IS DEFINITELY WEIRD--
HEY, SIRA, NAZIR, MEET MY PARTNER, JESSICA!
DON'T RUN! DON'T HIDE! SAY HI!
HI! HELLO! HEY!
(OR SAY IT THREE TIMES.)
SIMON, LISTEN! THIS OBNOXIOUS LITTLE THING HAS BEEN IN THE HOUSE AND YOU NEED TO--
UNCLE SIMON!
FARID! BIRTHDAY BOY!
I GOT YOU A PRESENT! YOUR FAVORITE ANIMAL.
UH... WHAT'S WRONG WITH HIM?
THOSE ARE ALL THE BRUISES THE BEAR GOT WHILE FIGHTING TO MAKE THE WORLD SAFE FOR YOU.
WOW!
COOL!
LANTERNS!

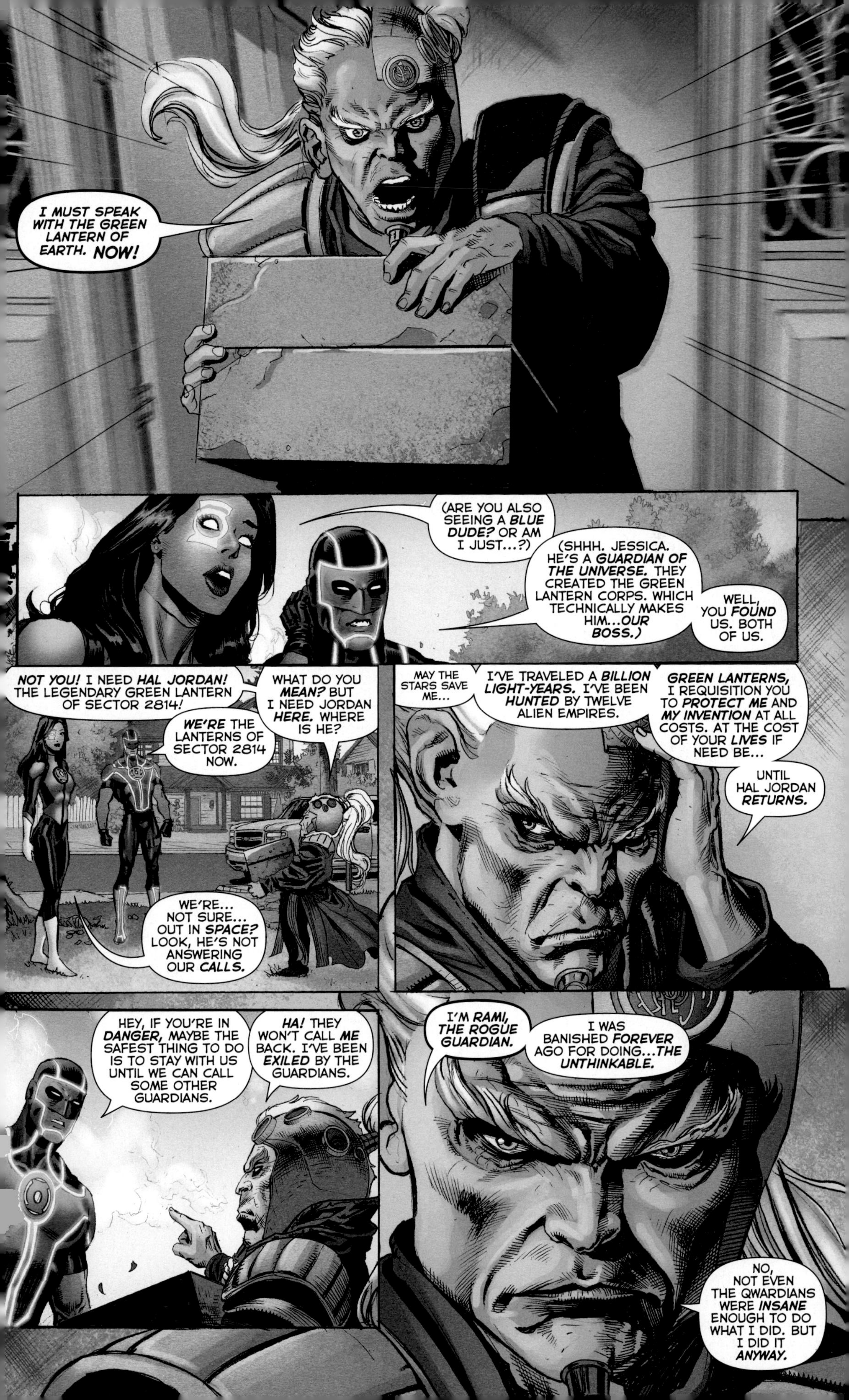
I MUST SPEAK WITH THE GREEN LANTERN OF EARTH. NOW!
(ARE YOU ALSO SEEING A BLUE DUDE? OR AM I JUST...?)
(SHHH. JESSICA. HE'S A GUARDIAN OF THE UNIVERSE. THEY CREATED THE GREEN LANTERN CORPS. WHICH TECHNICALLY MAKES HIM...OUR BOSS.)
WELL, YOU FOUND US. BOTH OF US.
NOT YOU! I NEED HAL JORDAN! THE LEGENDARY GREEN LANTERN OF SECTOR 2814!
WE'RE THE LANTERNS OF SECTOR 2814 NOW.
WHAT DO YOU MEAN? BUT I NEED JORDAN HERE. WHERE IS HE?
WE'RE... NOT SURE... OUT IN SPACE? LOOK, HE'S NOT ANSWERING OUR CALLS.
MAY THE STARS SAVE ME...
I'VE TRAVELED A BILLION LIGHT-YEARS. I'VE BEEN HUNTED BY TWELVE ALIEN EMPIRES.
GREEN LANTERNS, I REQUISITION YOU TO PROTECT ME AND MY INVENTION AT ALL COSTS. AT THE COST OF YOUR LIVES IF NEED BE...
UNTIL HAL JORDAN RETURNS.
HEY, IF YOU'RE IN DANGER, MAYBE THE SAFEST THING TO DO IS TO STAY WITH US UNTIL WE CAN CALL SOME OTHER GUARDIANS.
HA! THEY WON'T CALL ME BACK. I'VE BEEN EXILED BY THE GUARDIANS.
I'M RAMI, THE ROGUE GUARDIAN.
I WAS BANISHED FOREVER AGO FOR DOING...THE UNTHINKABLE.
NO, NOT EVEN THE QWARDIANS WERE INSANE ENOUGH TO DO WHAT I DID. BUT I DID IT ANYWAY.

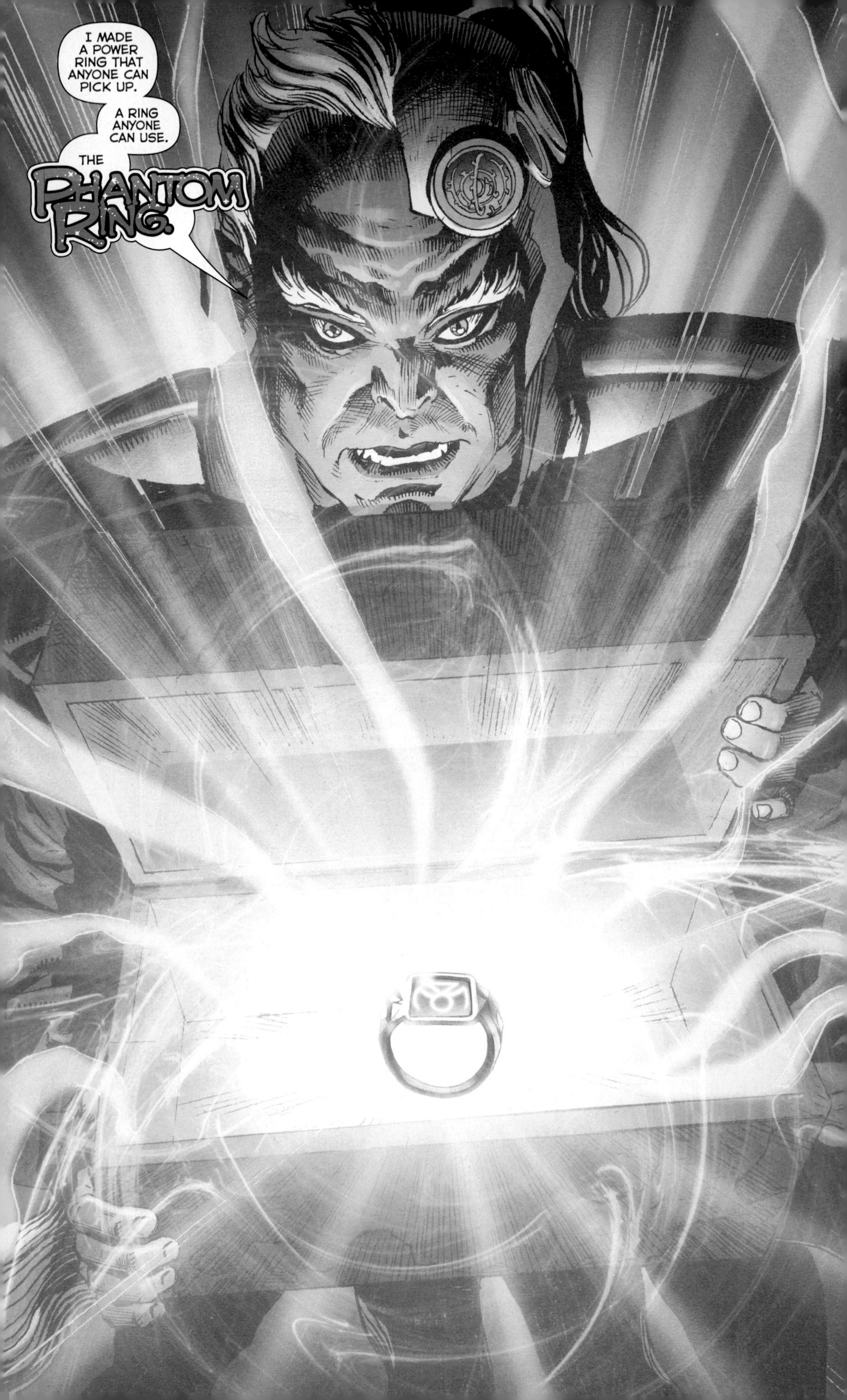
I MADE A POWER RING THAT ANYONE CAN PICK UP.
A RING ANYONE CAN USE.
THE PHANTOM RING.

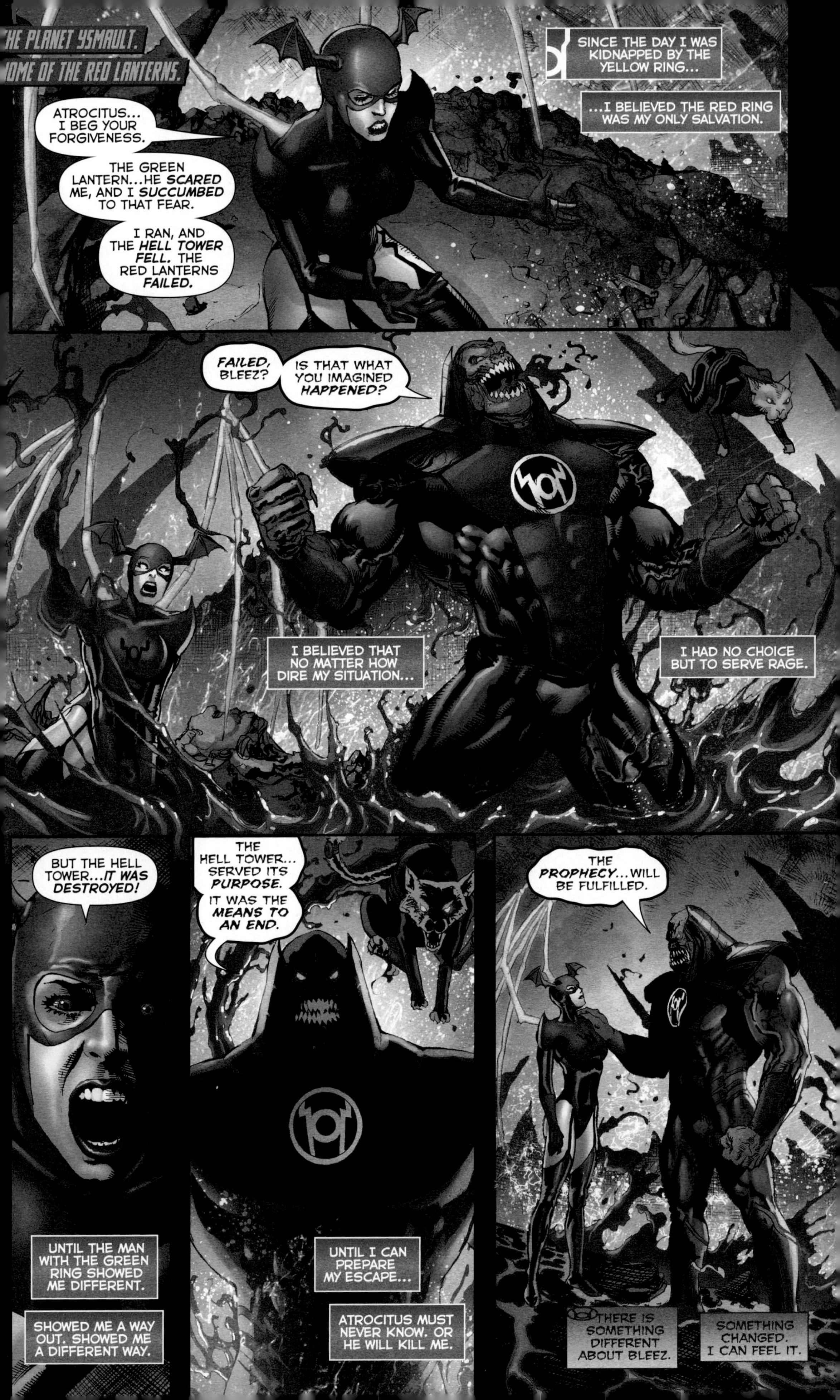

THE PLANET YSMAULT.
HOME OF THE RED LANTERNS.
SINCE THE DAY I WAS KIDNAPPED BY THE YELLOW RING...
...I BELIEVED THE RED RING WAS MY ONLY SALVATION.
ATROCITUS... I BEG YOUR FORGIVENESS.
THE GREEN LANTERN...HE SCARED ME, AND I SUCCUMBED TO THAT FEAR.
I RAN, AND THE HELL TOWER FELL. THE RED LANTERNS FAILED.
FAILED, BLEEZ?
IS THAT WHAT YOU IMAGINED HAPPENED?
I BELIEVED THAT NO MATTER HOW DIRE MY SITUATION...
I HAD NO CHOICE BUT TO SERVE RAGE.
BUT THE HELL TOWER...IT WAS DESTROYED!
UNTIL THE MAN WITH THE GREEN RING SHOWED ME DIFFERENT.
SHOWED ME A WAY OUT. SHOWED ME A DIFFERENT WAY.
THE HELL TOWER... SERVED ITS PURPOSE. IT WAS THE MEANS TO AN END.
UNTIL I CAN PREPARE MY ESCAPE...
ATROCITUS MUST NEVER KNOW. OR HE WILL KILL ME.
THE PROPHECY...WILL BE FULFILLED.
THERE IS SOMETHING DIFFERENT ABOUT BLEEZ.
SOMETHING CHANGED. I CAN FEEL IT.

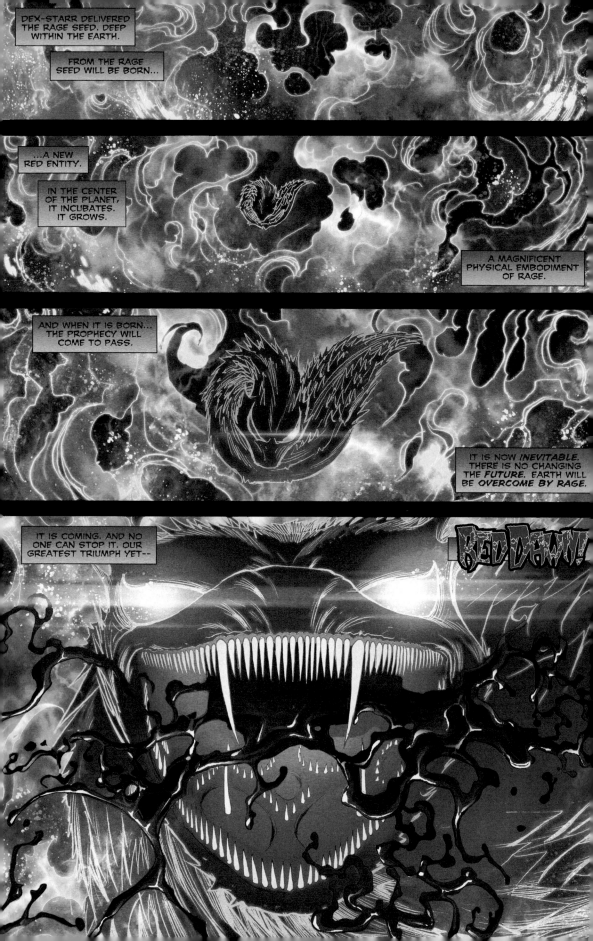

DEX-STARR DELIVERED THE RAGE SEED. DEEP WITHIN THE EARTH.

FROM THE RAGE SEED WILL BE BORN...

...A NEW RED ENTITY.

IN THE CENTER OF THE PLANET, IT INCUBATES. IT GROWS.

A MAGNIFICENT PHYSICAL EMBODIMENT OF RAGE.

AND WHEN IT IS BORN... THE PROPHECY WILL COME TO PASS.

IT IS NOW *INEVITABLE*. THERE IS NO CHANGING THE *FUTURE*. EARTH WILL BE *OVERCOME* BY RAGE.

IT IS COMING. AND NO ONE CAN STOP IT. OUR GREATEST TRIUMPH YET--

RED DAWN!

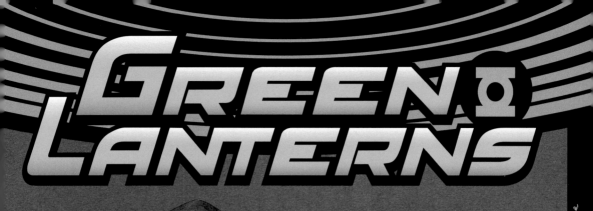

GREEN LANTERNS

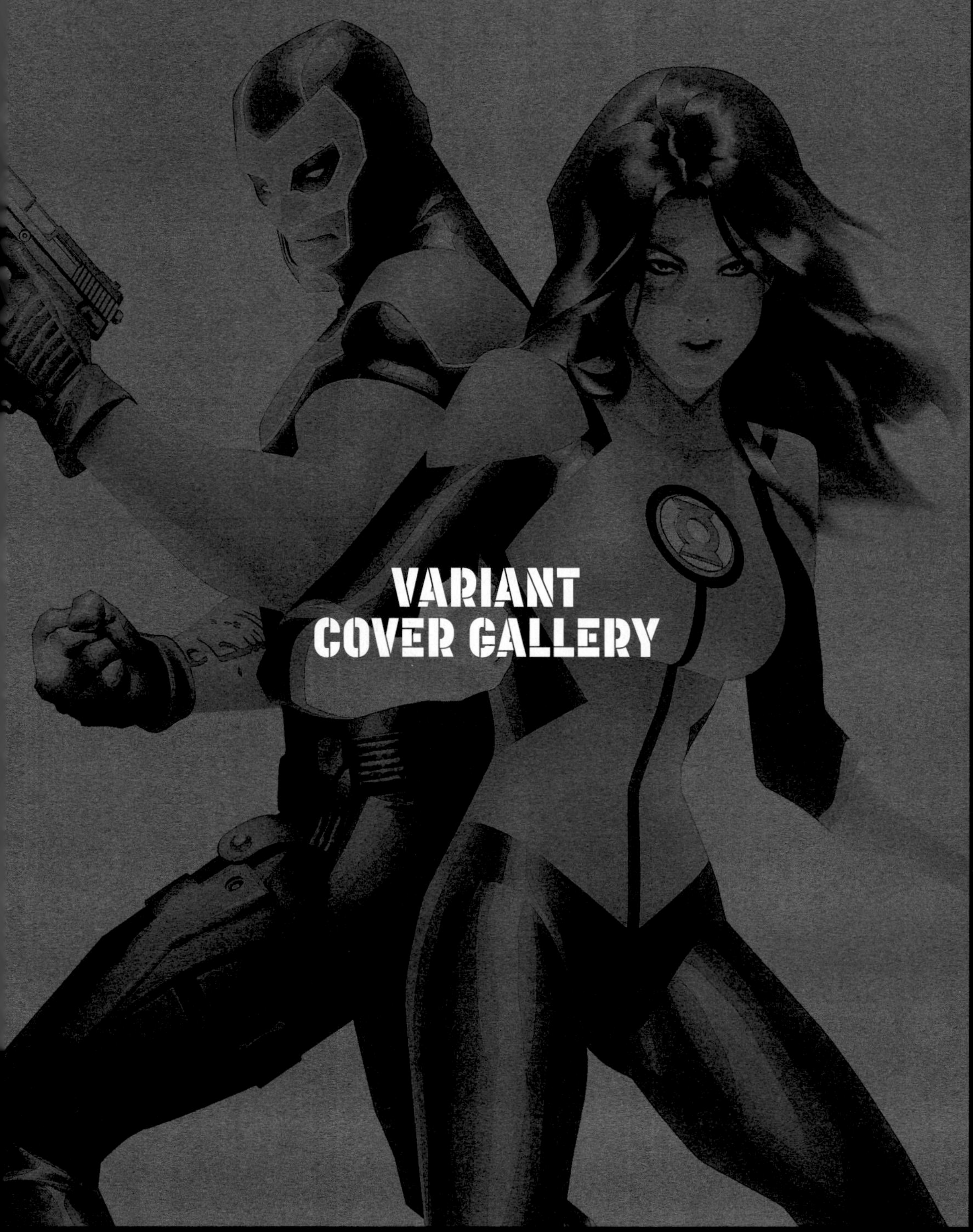

VARIANT COVER GALLERY

GREEN LANTERNS: REBIRTH #1 Variant by ALEX GARNER

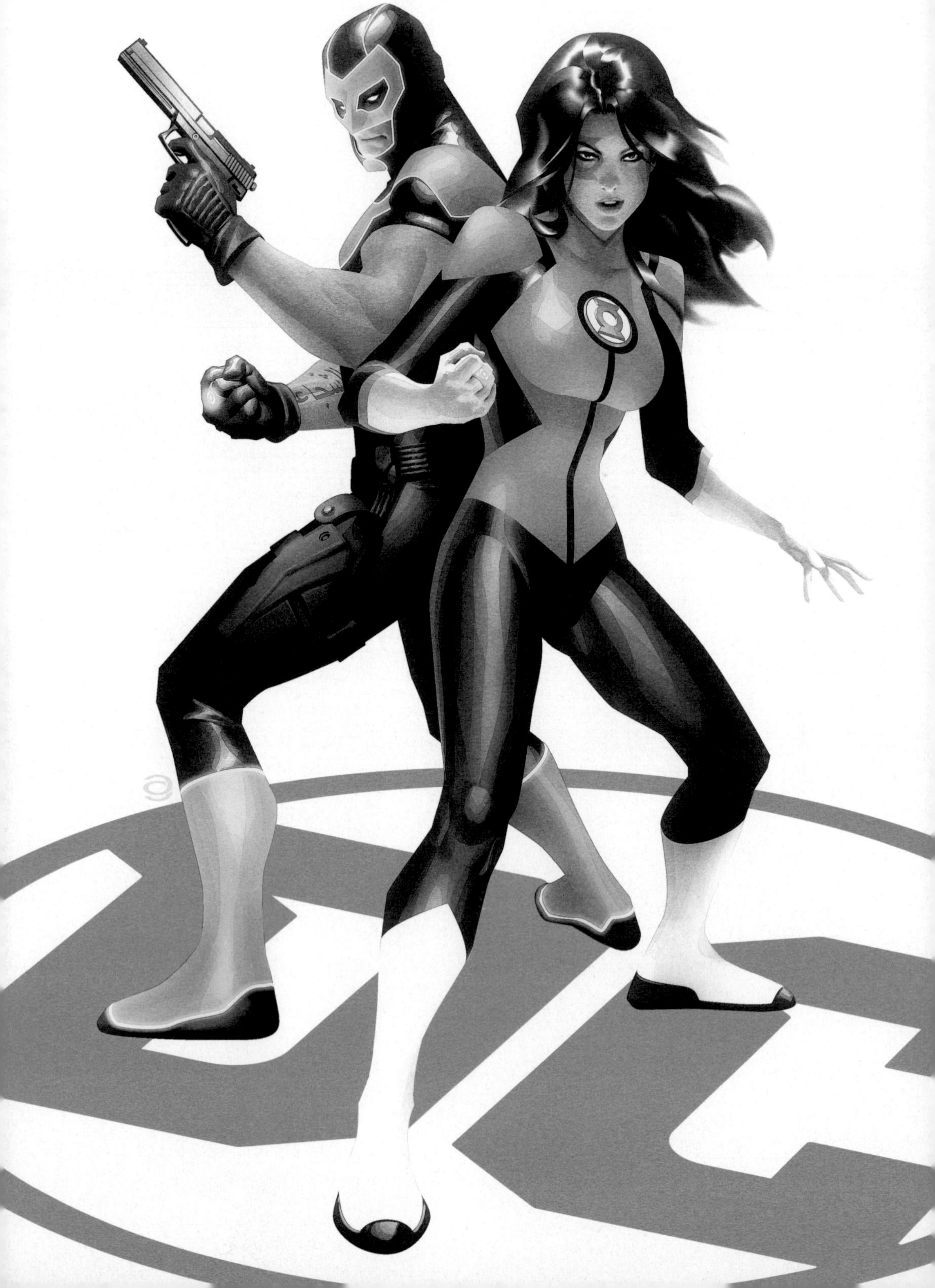

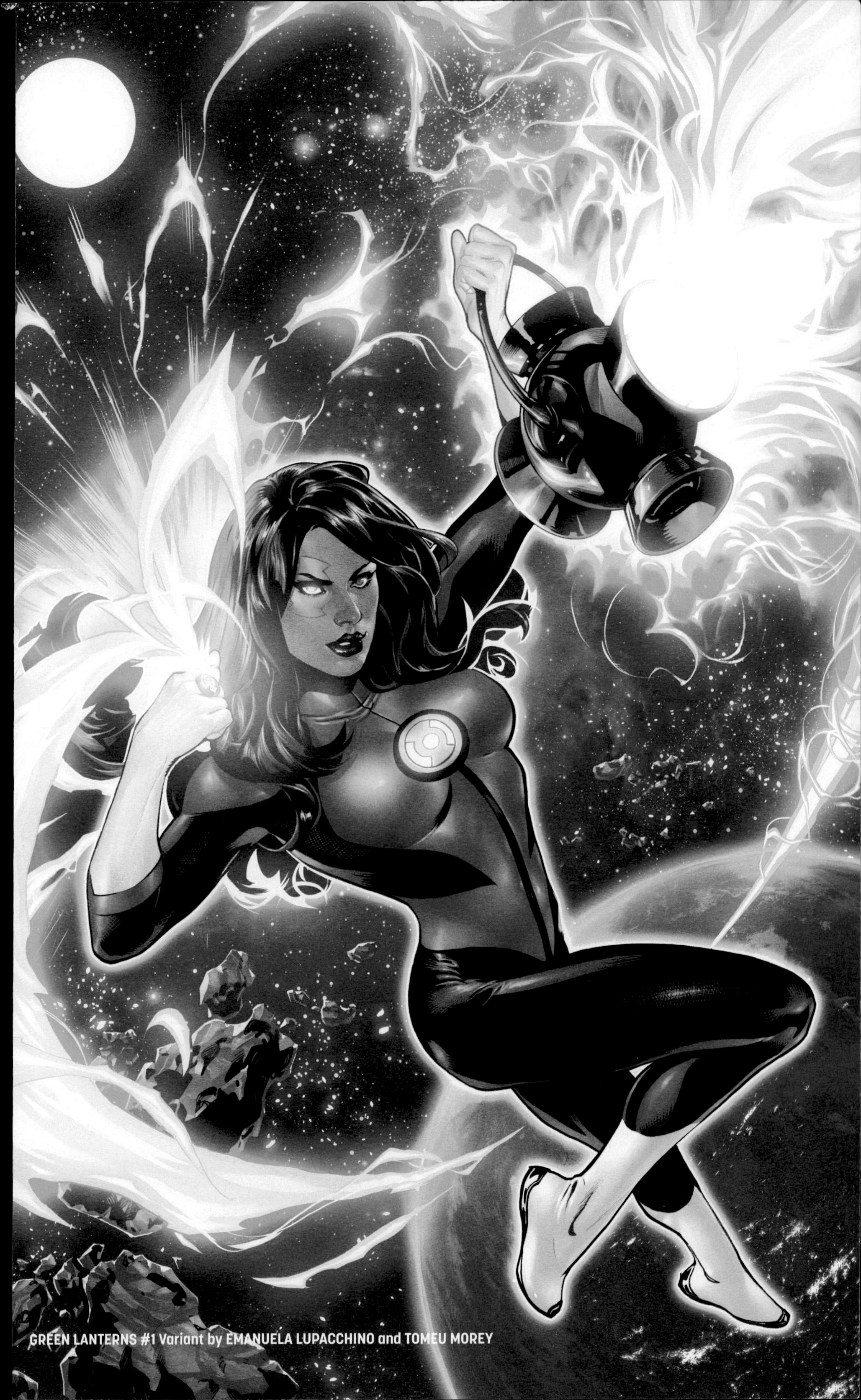

GREEN LANTERNS #1 Variant by EMANUELA LUPACCHINO and TOMEU MOREY

GREEN LANTERNS #2 Variant by EMANUELA LUPACCHINO and TOMEU MOREY

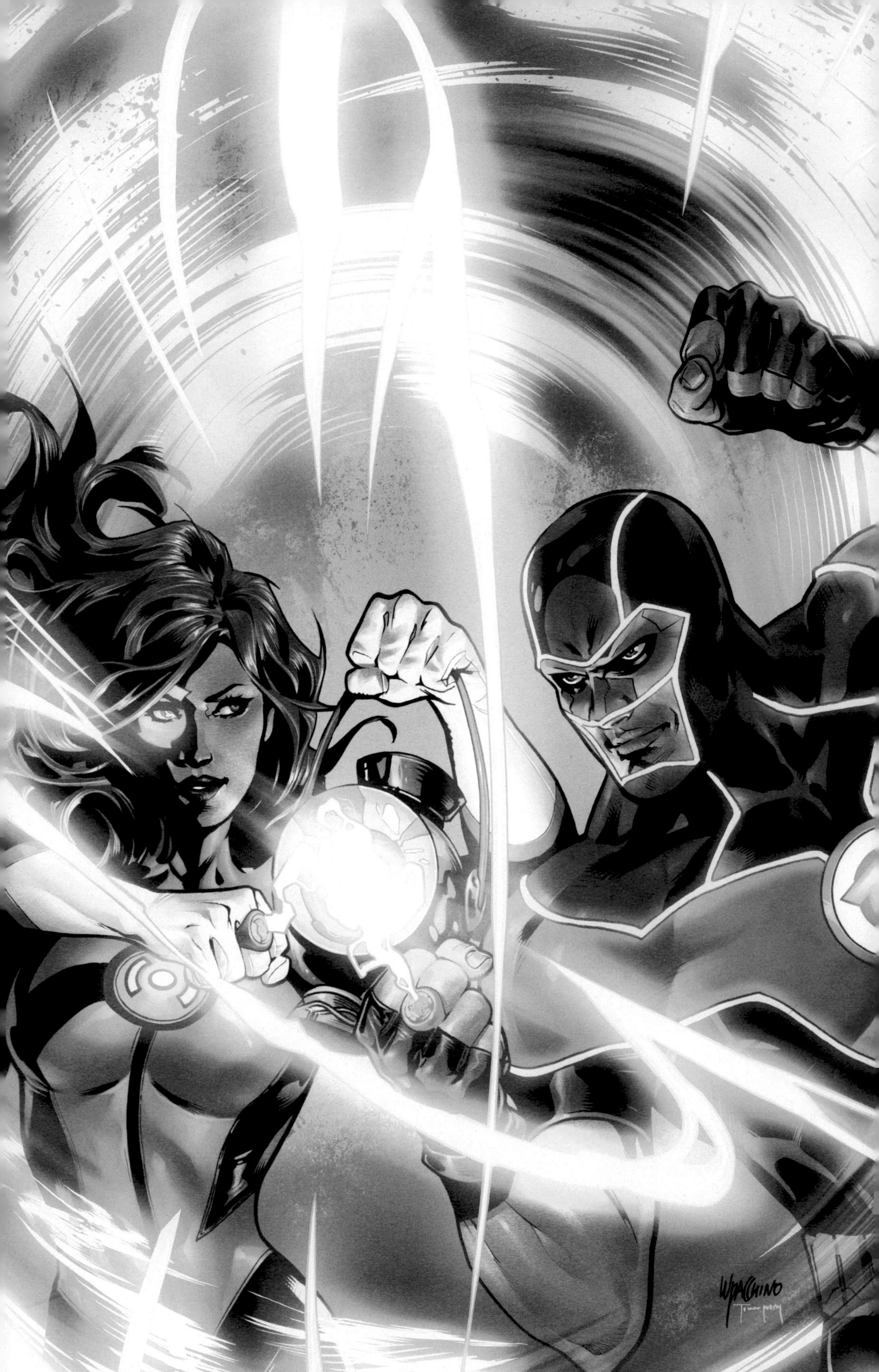

GREEN LANTERNS #3 Variant by EMANUELA LUPACCHINO and TOMEU MOREY

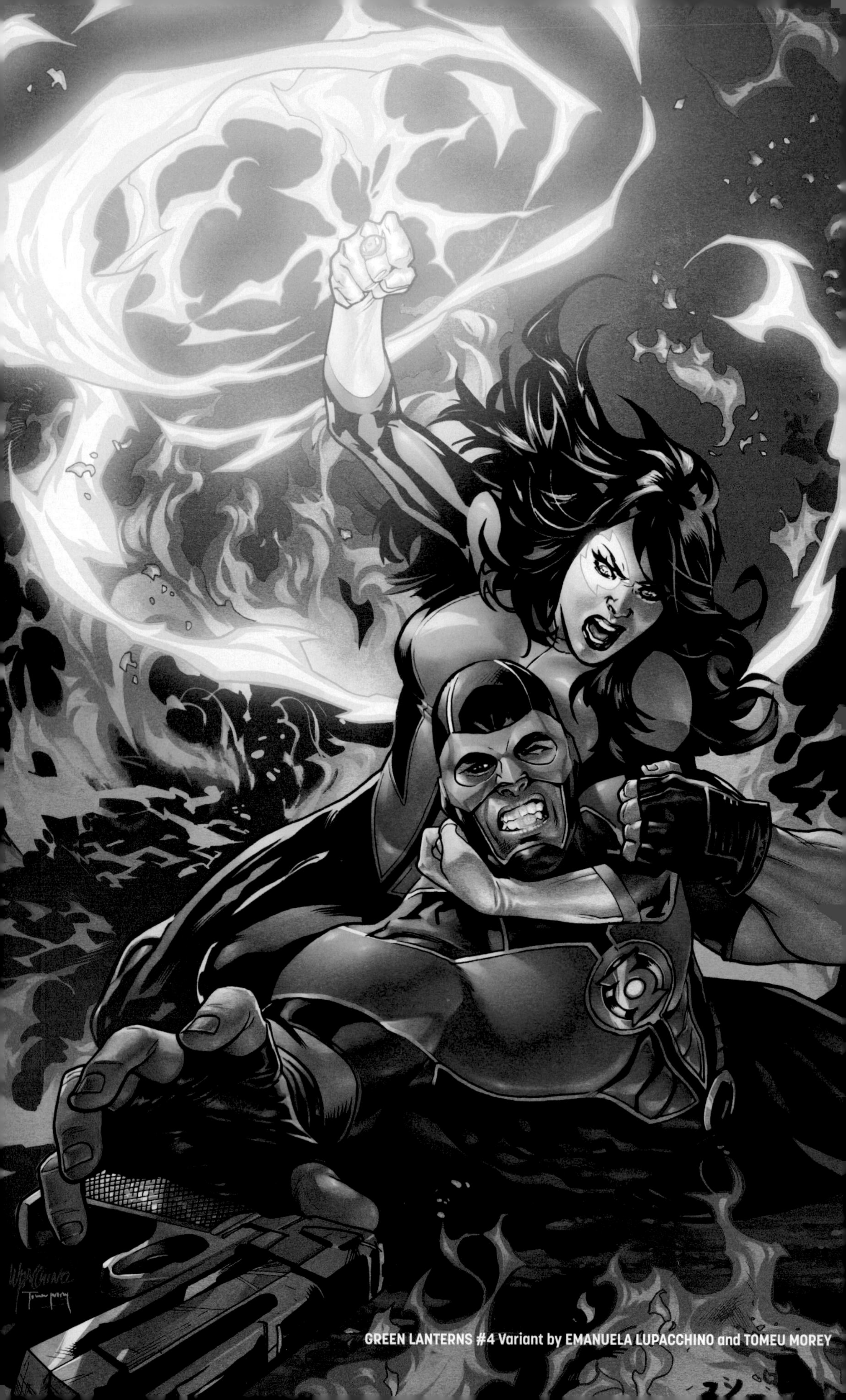

GREEN LANTERNS #4 Variant by EMANUELA LUPACCHINO and TOMEU MOREY

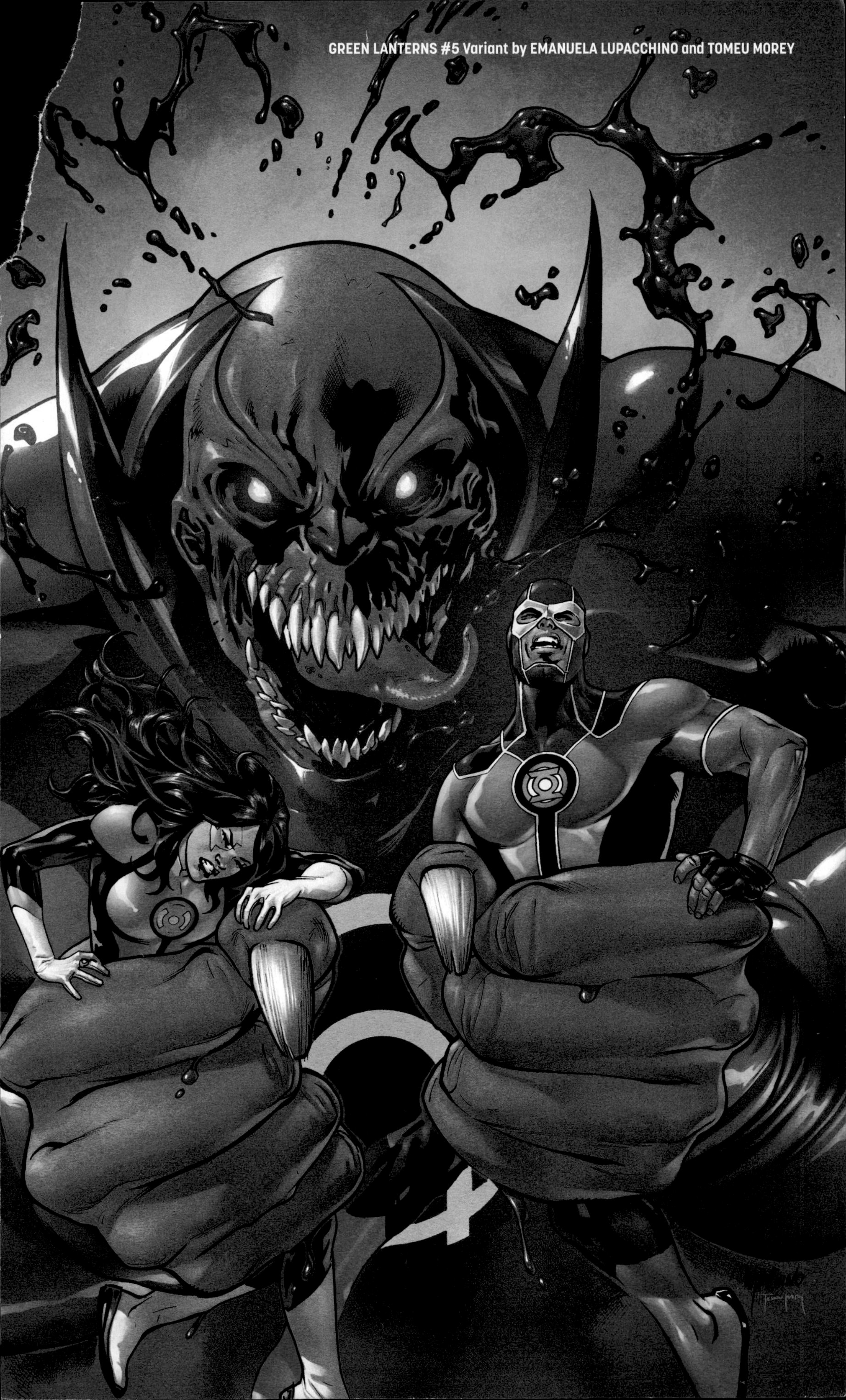

GREEN LANTERNS #5 Variant by EMANUELA LUPACCHINO and TOMEU MOREY

GREEN LANTERNS #5 Variant by EMANUELA LUPACCHINO and MICHAEL ATIYEH

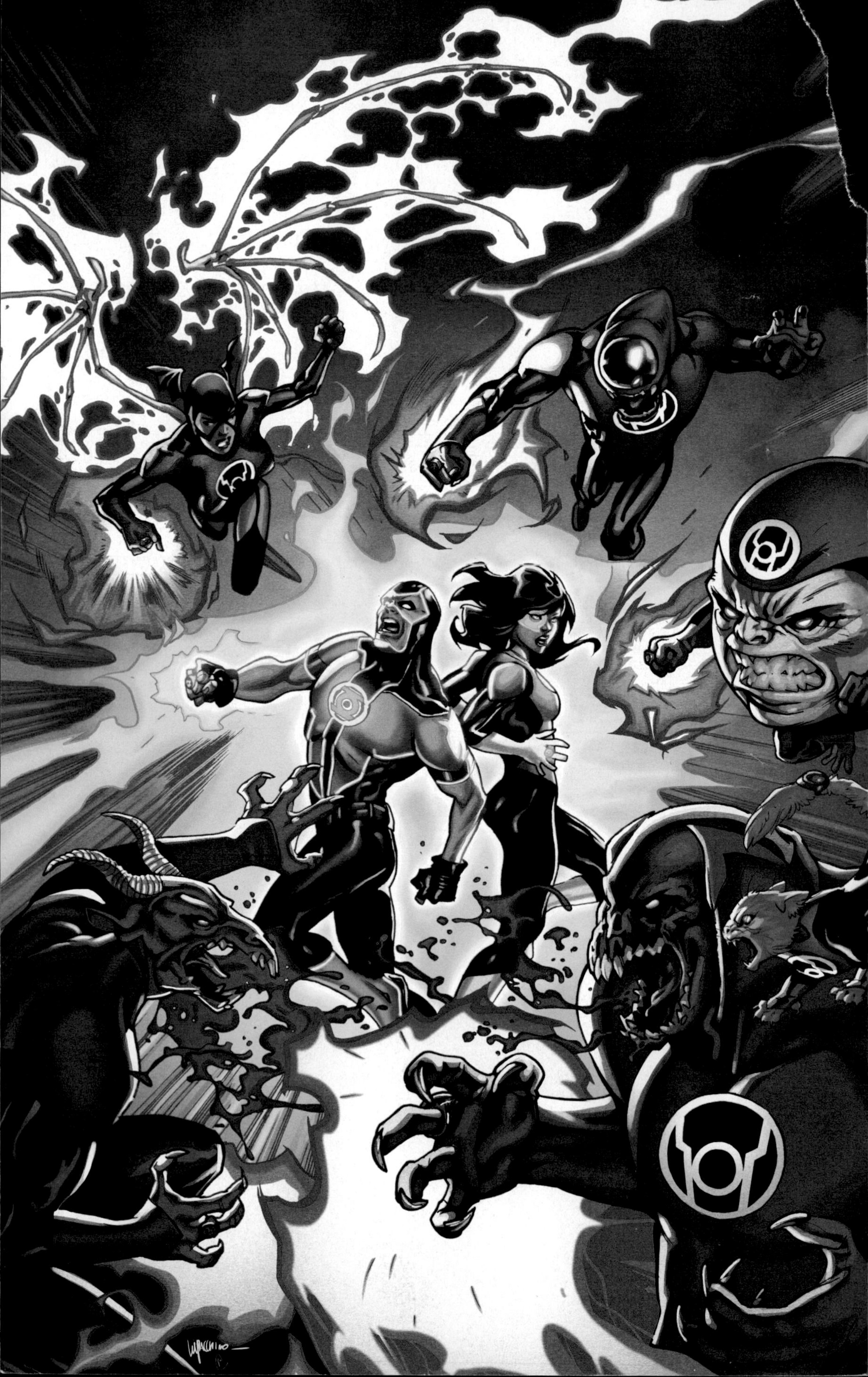

GREEN LANTERN JESSICA CRUZ

Designs by JASON FABOK

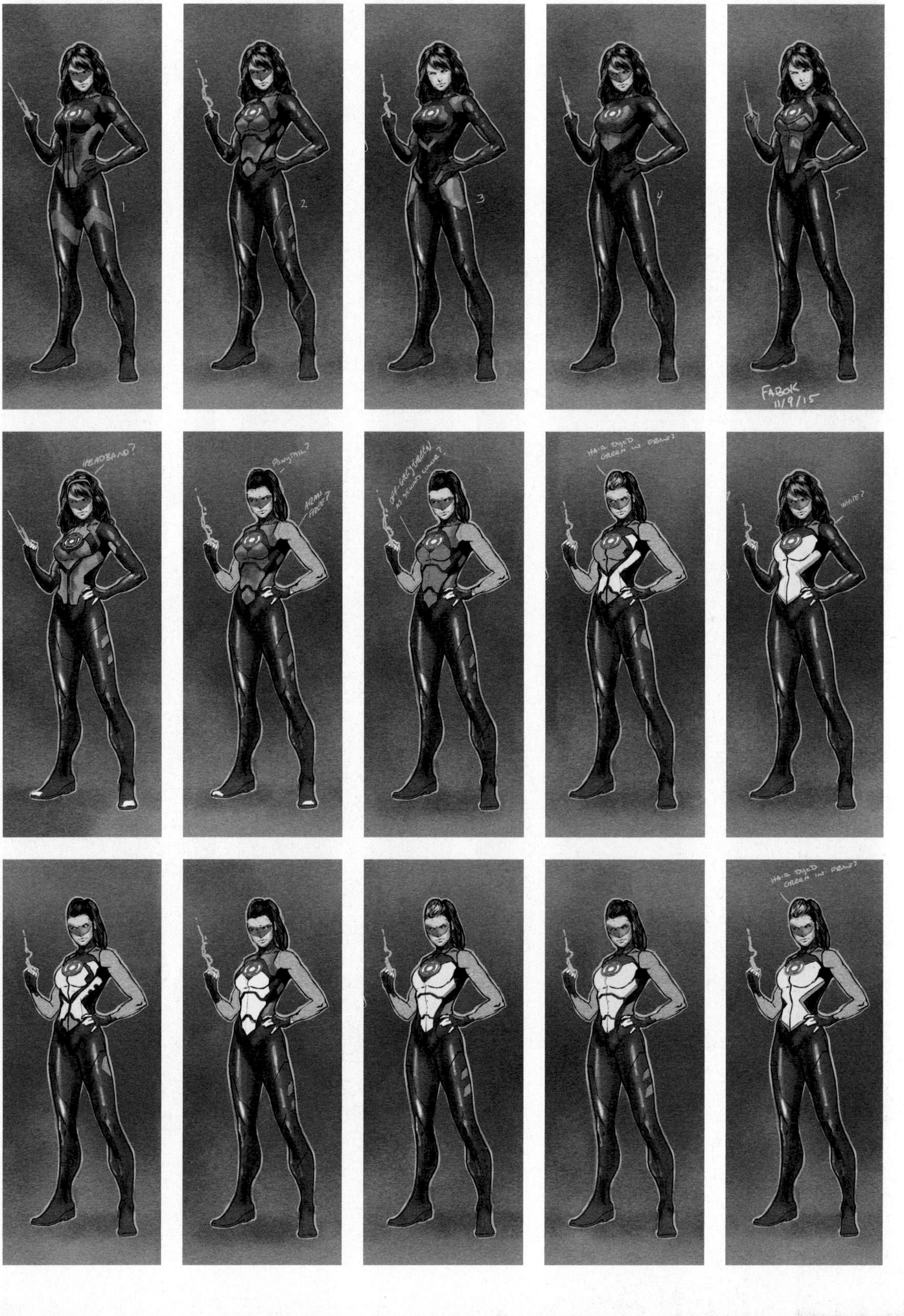
1
2
3
4
5
FABOK
11/9/15
HEADBAND?
PONYTAIL?
ARMS FREE?
OFF-GREY/GREEN AS SECOND COLOR?
HAIR DYED GREEN IN FRONT?
WHITE?
HAIR DYED GREEN IN FRONT?

FINAL DESIGN

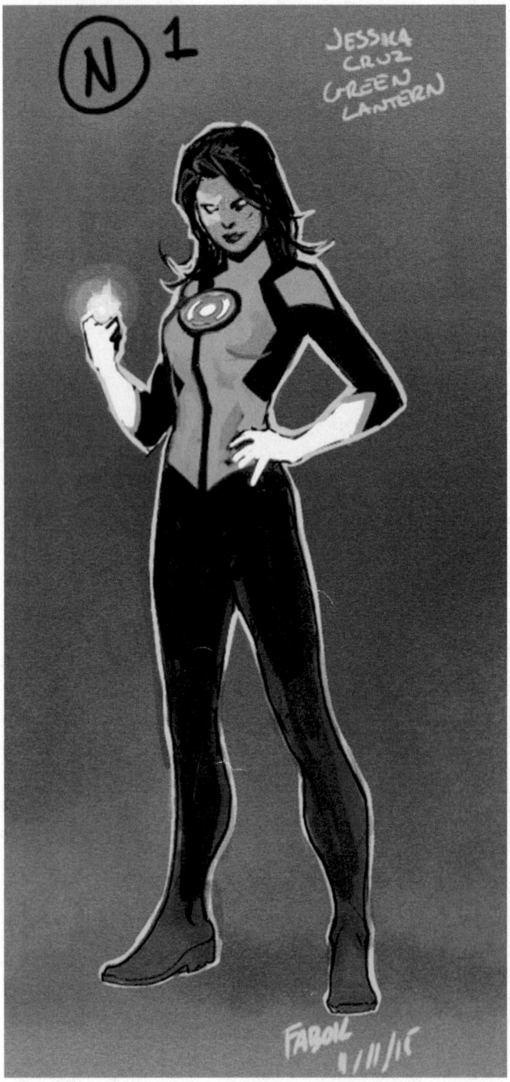
N 1
JESSICA CRUZ GREEN LANTERN
FABOK 1/11/15

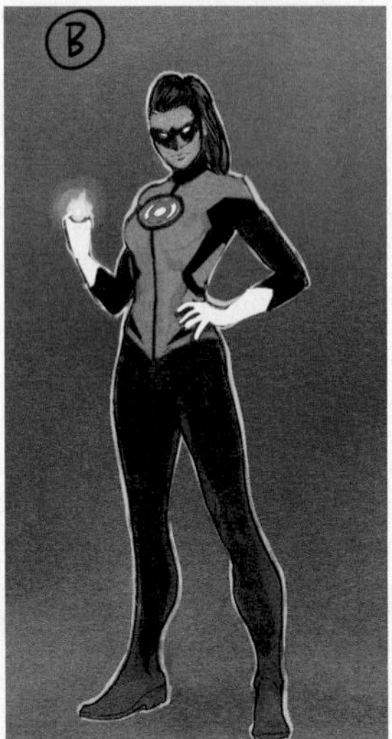
B

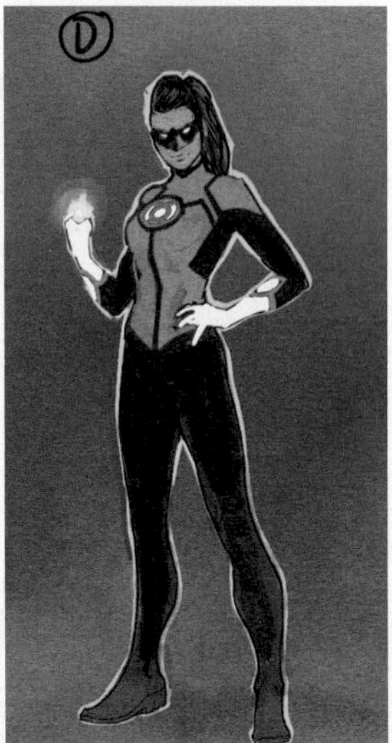
D

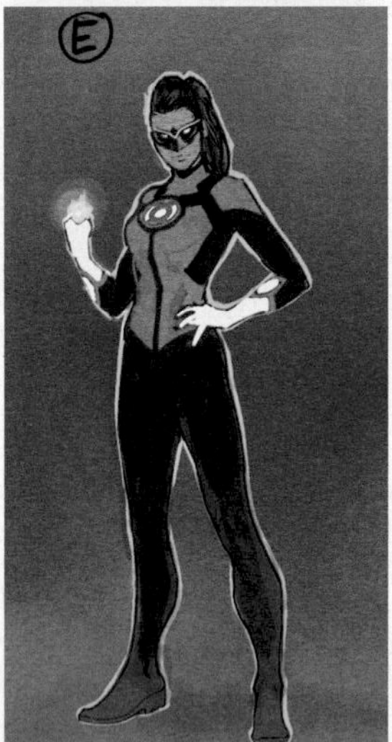
E

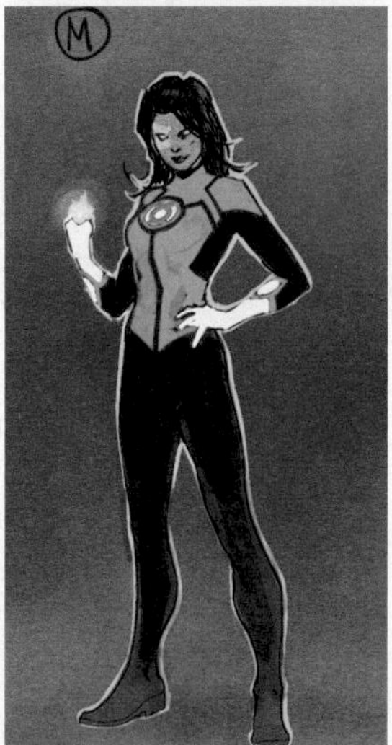
M

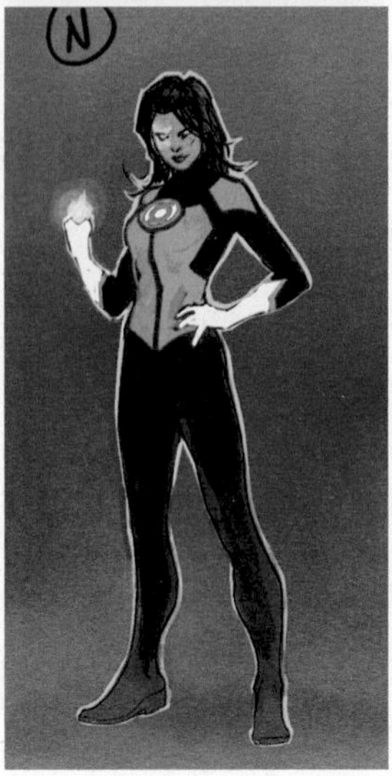
N

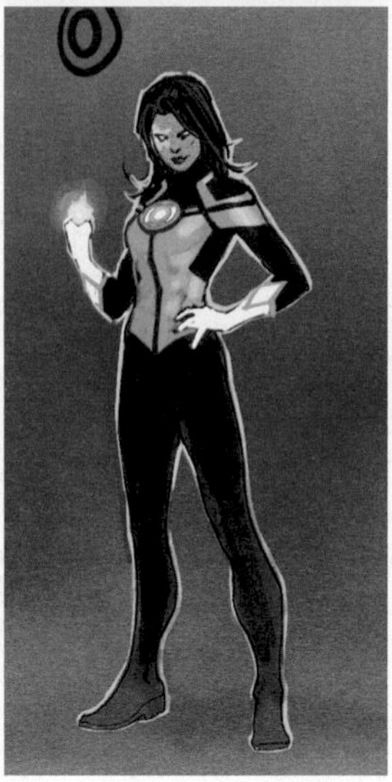
O